The Privatizatic

Challenge

WORLD BANK

REGIONAL AND

SECTORAL STUDIES

The Privatization Challenge

A Strategic, Legal, and Institutional Analysis of International Experience

PIERRE GUISLAIN

The World Bank
Washington, D.C.

The World Bank Regional and Sectoral Studies series provides an outlet for work that is relatively focused in its subject matter or geographical coverage and that contributes to the intellectual foundations of development operations and policy formulation. Some sources cited in this paper may be informal documents that are not readily available.

Pierre Guislain, a lawyer and economist by training, is Principal Private Sector Development Specialist at the World Bank's Private. Since 1984, he has advised many governments in Africa, Asia, and Eastern Europe on the design and implementation of privatization programs. In his current assignment, he promotes governments on competition and private participation in infrastructure sectors.

Cover design by Sam Ferro and Sherry Holmberg

Library of Congress Cataloging-in-Publication Data

Guislain, Pierre, 1957–
    [Privatization. English]
    The privatization challenge : a strategic, legal, and
institutional analysis of international experience/ Pierre
Guislain.
        p. cm. — (World Bank regional and sectoral studies series)
    Rev. translation of : Les privatisations.
    Includes bibliographical references and indexes.
    ISBN 0-8213-3736-X
    1. Government business enterprises—Law and legislation.
2. Government ownership—Law and legislation. 3. Privatization—Law
and legislation. 4. Government business enterprises. 5. Government
ownership. 6. Privatization. I. Title. II. Series.
    K1366.G85513   1997
    346'.067—dc20
    [342.667]   96–34223
                                                            CIP

Contents

7   Privatization of Infrastructure   203

8   Meeting the Privatization Challenge   287

Figures

Tables

Boxes

Preface

This book builds on my earlier work, in particular, *Les privatisations: un défi stratégique, juridique et institutionnel* (Brussels: De Boeck Université, 1995) and *Divestiture of State Enterprises: An Overview of the Legal Framework* (World Bank, 1992). It is primarily a reference document for professionals and policymakers who design or take part in privatization programs—government officials; staff of privatization agencies; managers of public enterprises; investors; and legal, economic, financial, and other advisers.

The privatization of public enterprises, economic sectors, or entire economies raises strategic, legal, institutional, and economic issues and challenges. This book approaches privatization from a multidisciplinary and multisectoral point of view, with an emphasis on the legal and policy dimensions of the process. It draws on the experience of countries on every continent to illustrate specific problems, issues, and solutions. The aim is neither to extract universal lessons nor to present a how-to manual for privatization. Rather, this book seeks to reveal the dynamic character of a process that is still relatively new, demonstrate the complexity of the problems that can arise during this process, and examine the efficacy of solutions that have been attempted.

I wish to thank Céline Lévesque and Michel Kerf for their invaluable contributions. Céline did much of the research that went into this book and updated the bibliography and the legislation listed in the appendix. Michel contributed extensively to the earlier French edition and provided useful comments on this updated and revised edition.

I am grateful also to the many other people who helped in the preparation of this work, especially Donna Verdier, who copyedited the final manuscript; Lucy Foit, who handled the composition; Alex Green for his translation work; and Warrick Smith for comments on chapter 7. Thanks go also to De Boeck Université for its publication and successful marketing of *Les privatisations* and to the World Bank—in particular, Magdi Iskander, Michael Klein, and the Office of the Publisher—for supporting this long-term project.

Finally, this book would not have been possible without the support and patience of my wife, Marie-France, and children, Charles and Anne-Sophie.

The views expressed in this book are my own, however, and should not be ascribed to those people whose assistance is acknowledged above or to the organizations that offered their support.

Introduction

In recent years privatization has expanded at a pace that would have been hard to predict only ten or fifteen years ago. More than 100 countries, across every continent, have privatized some of their SOEs. Argentina, Chile, Colombia, Mexico, and Peru in Latin America; Malaysia, Pakistan, and the Philippines in Asia; France, the United Kingdom, and Central and Eastern European countries in Europe; as well as Côte d'Ivoire, Morocco, Nigeria, and Togo in Africa are but a few examples.

Equally striking is the sheer volume of transactions. In 1994 and 1995 annual gross revenues from privatizations worldwide were estimated to be on the order of $80 billion.[1] Five years earlier (in 1989), the total was $25 billion. Between 1988 and 1993, over 2,600 privatization transactions with sale value exceeding $50,000 were recorded worldwide (excluding eastern Germany); these generated receipts of $271 billion, far in excess of the $150 billion that such operations brought in up to 1988. Of these 2,600 privatization transactions, close to 900 were carried out in 1993, against only about 60 in 1988. Developing and transition countries accounted for much of this tremendous growth (see Sader 1995).

To these figures must be added tens of thousands of local transactions, many of them relating to small businesses, restaurants, and workshops,[2] together with tens of thousands more enterprises transferred to private shareholders under ambitious mass privatization programs implemented in many transition countries, notably Russia and the Czech Republic. In just over two years, Russia succeeded in privatizing between 12,000 and 14,000 medium-sized and large enterprises with a total of over 14 million employees—that is, about half of Russia's industrial labor force. In the process, about 40 million

---

1. All dollar amounts are current U.S. dollars, unless otherwise specified; a billion is a thousand million.

2. Nearly 100,000 small businesses and enterprises were privatized in this way between 1991 and 1994 in Russia alone (see Lieberman and Rahuja 1995, p. 25).

Russian citizens became shareholders for the first time (see Lieberman and Nellis 1995, p. 1).

In Germany, as part of the radical economic transformation that followed the fall of the East German communist regime and reunification, over 15,000 enterprises were sold or liquidated between 1990 and 1994. An additional 91,000 transactions involved restitution of property to former owners, as well as the transfer of real estate, shops, and restaurants. New investment commitments stemming from the program implemented by the Treuhandanstalt reached about $130 billion.[3]

Privatization in one form or another has been undertaken at all times. In Thailand, for example, the prime minister issued regulations concerning the sale of SOEs or SOE shares in 1961. Chile launched a major (though not very successful) privatization program in 1974.[4] The British program launched in 1980 by Margaret Thatcher, however, is the major forerunner of the current privatization phenomenon, and it has so far raised about $100 billion.

Successive trends or waves may be observed in privatization worldwide. In the first wave, privatization focused largely on industrial, financial, and commercial ventures. Infrastructure sectors and activities followed in a second wave, starting near the end of the 1980s; a third wave, touching municipal or local services, is gaining strength. The next wave is only starting to emerge, reaching the social sectors, including health and education, and administrative activities.

The privatization phenomenon has not been confined to countries with a liberal ideology. Major privatization programs are found in countries with a long capitalist tradition and in countries in transition from a centralized to a market economy, as well as in developing countries, including some that remain under communist regimes, such as China and Cuba. The programs of the transition countries are, as would be expected, often much more ambitious. Nevertheless, some industrial countries, including New Zealand and the United Kingdom, and several developing countries, including Argentina and Mexico, have implemented privatization programs that are radical in terms of scale as well as scope.

Nor have privatization programs been homogeneous. A variety of strategies have indeed been adopted and implemented. A wide range of techniques has been used, most drawn from experience with corporate mergers

---

3. It should be noted that the overall deficit of the Treuhandanstalt, caused primarily by the high cost of physical and financial restructuring, severance payments, environmental liabilities, and other obligations of the former state-owned enterprises (SOEs), exceeded $160 billion by the time the agency closed its doors at the end of 1994.

4. The first privatization program of the Chilean military government was an economic and financial failure. Owing to the economic crisis of the early 1980s, the government had to take back many enterprises that had been privatized just a few years earlier, between 1974 and 1979. This was due in large part to the excessive concentration of shareholders within a few large conglomerates that were deeply in debt as a consequence of, in particular, the acquisitions carried out under the privatization program. These enterprises taken back by the government were later reprivatized, beginning in 1985.

and acquisitions, though some are truly new techniques designed to meet specific privatization objectives. Widespread share ownership has thus been promoted directly or indirectly through mass privatization programs in transition countries, through a capitalization program in Bolivia, and through financial incentives offered to employees and small shareholders in many countries.

Finally, privatization affects practically all economic sectors. Even activities traditionally reserved for the public sector are increasingly being entrusted to private operators.[5] As tables 1 and 2 illustrate, almost all large transactions of the past six years have occurred in "strategic" sectors that traditionally used to be publicly controlled: utilities, such as telecommunications, power, or gas; natural resources, including hydrocarbons and mines; railways; steel; and financial services, including banking and insurance.

Despite this worldwide explosion of privatization, the state sector remains strong in many countries, in particular in developing countries where SOEs drain national budgets and continue to dominate many activities. A recent study published by the World Bank found that "notwithstanding the sale of some very large firms, the state-owned enterprise share of developing market economies has remained stubbornly high since 1980, at about 11 percent of GDP [gross domestic product], even as it fell in the industrial countries from about 9 percent to less than 7 percent." Further, "The state-owned enterprise sector is larger and the problems associated with it are more severe in the world's poorest countries, where SOEs account for 14 percent of GDP," and "in sum, although the potential gains from privatization and other reforms are substantial, only a few [developing] countries have reformed their state-owned enterprises successfully" (World Bank 1995b, p. 2). Privatization has been on the agenda of many governments for over a decade now and is likely to remain a key policy instrument in many countries for decades to come.

Historical Background

The current wave of privatization follows a long period characterized by nationalization and growth of the size of the public sector in the economy. Like today's privatizations, these nationalizations took place in practically every area of economic activity and in a great majority of countries. The United States is among the few countries that was only marginally affected by this trend.

In western Europe, the surge in nationalization began in the years immediately preceding the second world war and continued after the war ended. In France, for example, the first nationalizations took place under the *Front*

---

5. The privatizations carried out in these sectors often exhibit special features, which are addressed in chapter 7.

Table 1   Large Privatizations in Industrial Countries, 1991–96

Country	Sector	Enterprise (date)	Percentage private	Amount ($ billion)
Australia (Victoria)	Electricity	Five distribution companies (1995)	100	6.2
		Two generating companies (1996)	100	3.8
Belgium	Telecom	Belgacom (1995)	49.9	2.5
Denmark	Telecom	TeleDanmark (1994)	48.3	3.3
France	Petroleum	Elf-Aquitaine (1994 and 1996)	100	8.8 for 47.7%
	Banking	BNP (1993)	100	4.8 for 72.9%
	Insurance	UAP (1994)	100	3.3 for 50.3%
	Steel	Usinor Sacilor (1995)	64	3.0
Germany	Telecom	Deutsche Telekom (1996)	26	13.3
Italy	Energy	ENI (1995–96)	31	9.8
	Insurance	INA (1994–96)	100[a]	6.1[a]
Japan	Railways	JR East (1993)	62.5	8.9
		JR West (1996)	68	4.5
	Tobacco	Japan Tobacco (1994 and 1996)	33	7.7
Netherlands	Telecom	KPN (1994–95)	55	7.8
Spain	Petroleum	Repsol (1989–96)	90	>5.0
United Kingdom	Telecom	British Telecom (1984–93)	100	22.8
	Electricity	National Power and PowerGen (1991 and 1995)	100	10.0
		Scottish Power (1991)	100	3.7
	Railways	Railtrack (1996)	100	3.2
United States	Telecom	102 PCS licenses (1995)[b]	100	7.7
		493 PCS licenses (1996)[b]	100	10.2

a. Includes a $2.1 convertible bond issue representing the remaining 34.4 percent state shareholding (June 1996).

b. Through federal auctions for personal communications system licenses (see chapter 7).

Sources: Public documents.

Table 2   Large Privatizations in Developing and Transition Countries, 1991–96

Country	Sector	Enterprise	Percentage private	Amount ($ billion)
Argentina	Telecom	Telecom Argentina (1990–92)	100	1.8
		Telefónica de Argentina (1990–91)	100	1.5
	Electricity	SEGBA, Hidronor, AEE (1992–96)	51–100	> 3.5
	Gas	Gas del Estado: split into ten enterprises (1992–95)	70–100	> 2.9
	Petroleum	YPF (1993)	61	3.0 for 45.3%
Brazil	Electricity	Light Servicos de Electricidade (1996)	51	2.2
	Steel	Usiminas (1991–94)	90	2.0
		CSN (1993)	81.9	1.5
Cuba	Telecom	Ectesa (1994)	49	1.4
Czech Republic	Telecom	SPT (1995)	27	1.5
Germany[a]	Mines	Mibrag (1993)	100	1.9
		Laubag (1994)	100	1.4
	Electricity	VEAG (1994)	100	5.2
	Tourism	InterHotel Group (1992)	100	1.3
Hungary	Electricity	Two power generation and six distribution companies (1995)	34–49	1.3
	Telecom	MATAV (1993–95)	75	1.7 for 67%
Indonesia	Telecom	Indosat (1994)	32	1.0
		PT Telkom (1995)	19	1.7
Malaysia	Electricity	Tenaga Nasional Berhad (1992)	23	1.2
Mexico	Banking	Banamex (1991)	70.7	3.2
		Bancomer (1991)	62.6	2.5
	Telecom	Telmex (1990–94)	100	7.5 for 51%
	Railways	Northeast Line (1996)	80	1.4
Peru	Telecom	CPT and Entelperú (1994–96)	95	3.1 for 59%
Singapore	Telecom	Singapore Telecom (1993)	11	2.7
Taiwan	Steel	China Steel (1989–95)	52.5	3.0
Venezuela	Telecom	CANTV (1991 and 1996)	100	2.9

a. Former German Democratic Republic.
Sources: Public documents.

Populaire governments of 1936–37 (armaments, aviation, railways); the movement resumed immediately after liberation with the nationalization of coal mining, air transport, electricity, gas, banks, and insurance companies. In Italy, too, state control of the economy tightened before the outbreak of the second world war: in 1933 the government created the Istituto per la Ricostruzione Industriale (IRI), a public holding company which by 1939 had absorbed the biggest banks and held large shareholdings in the iron and steel industry, among others. In the 1930s nationalization was directly linked in many countries to the rise in nationalism.

In central and eastern Europe, nationalizations were imposed under Soviet influence after the second world war. During the same period many Latin American countries also decided to base their development strategy on state-owned enterprises. In Argentina, for example, the government nationalized the telephone company in 1946 and at about the same time acquired six railway companies owned by British, French, and Argentine investors. The power sector was nationalized later.

Similarly, the decolonization movement in Asia and later in Africa fostered growing nationalization as the new states sought to regain control of their productive assets from foreign enterprises. In the 1960s and 1970s, on the morrow of their independence, most African countries, including many with socialist or Marxist-Leninist regimes (such as Angola, Benin, Congo, and Tanzania), undertook large nationalization programs.

Over the past twenty years, however, we have witnessed a sharp reversal of the nationalization trend, spurred by a new international economic and political environment and by other factors described below. The average number of annual nationalization operations, which peaked in the first half of the 1970s, has fallen steadily since then and is now extremely small. Over the same period, the volume of privatization operations has accelerated, surpassing the volume of nationalizations around 1980 and growing exponentially in the past few years.

Explanatory Factors

The reasons for the decline of nationalization activity vary, of course, from country to country and even from one enterprise to another. One reason, however, stands out: SOEs have generally posted disappointing performances (see World Bank 1995b; Muir and Saba 1995; Shirley and Nellis 1991; see also chapter 1 in this volume). Although some of them function well, many others are notoriously inefficient. They manage to survive through tariff protection against competing imports, preferences in public procurement, exclusive rights, preferential access to credit (often at state-owned banks), government guarantees, tax exemptions, and public subsidies. Created to alleviate the shortcomings of the private sector and spearhead the development of the national economy, many SOEs in fact helped stifle the local private sector and fostered economic stagnation. They often serve political objectives or purposes and consequently suffer frequent interference by government and bureaucrats. In some countries they have also contributed to income redistribution in favor of the relatively well-off over the poor, who generally lack access to both the jobs the SOEs provide and their products. Almost everywhere, the burden SOEs impose on state finances has become untenable.

Was privatization the only way to redress this state of affairs? Several empirical studies have compared the performance of public and private enterprises, but the results vary. Some conclude that an enterprise's efficiency is determined not so much by its public or private character as by the regulatory structure and the degree of competition under which it operates.[6] Others find that private ownership leads to greater productivity.[7]

Some reforms designed to give SOEs greater autonomy and expose them to stiffer competition, without privatizing their ownership, have produced encouraging results. In most cases, however, such reforms have proved impossible to sustain, and after initial improvements the situation of the SOEs consequently deteriorated further (see, for example, Kikeri, Nellis, and Shirley 1994, pp. 246–47). The challenge is to bring about sustainable improvements in enterprise performance, and many governments today regard privatization as the only means available to accomplish that.

Another important reason for the move to privatization is that most governments find themselves facing deep budget deficits and public finance crises. The state no longer has the financial resources either to offset the losses of SOEs or to provide the capital increases necessary for their development. Privatization can be the answer, as illustrated by the United Kingdom, where in 1981 SOEs that have since been privatized cost the treasury £50 million a week; these same companies now contribute £55 million a week in taxes (see *Euromoney*, February 1996, p. 5). A radical reform of public finances, involving an overhaul of the public sector, may also be needed to satisfy international obligations or aspirations. This applies in particular to member states of the European Union (EU), who are constrained by EU rules

6. See, for example, Borcherding, Pommerehne, and Schneider 1982; De Alessi 1982. For a survey of the litterature on the effects on economic performance of privatization, deregulation, and competition, see Kwoka 1996. The importance of competition and of an overall environment conducive to economic efficiency and development of the private sector is further discussed in chapters 3 and 7.

7. A study on productivity growth and firm ownership in the airline sector looked at 23 airlines with varying levels of private and public ownership over the period 1973–83. The authors indicate that their "empirical analysis shows, indeed, that a switch from state to private ownership unambiguously raises the rates of productivity growth, or cost decline, whereas its effect on the levels of productivity and unit cost may be ambiguous in the short run. It further indicates that partial privatization of fully state-owned enterprises would produce a substantially smaller marginal improvement in productivity growth than complete privatization would. The estimates show that a full switch from state to private ownership may increase the rate of cost decline by as much as 1.7 percent per year" (Ehrlich and others 1994, pp. 1007–08). See also note 91 in chapter 7.

in their ability to subsidize state enterprises and must comply with strict fiscal requirements imposed by the Maastricht treaty to qualify for membership in the monetary union. It also applies to countries that have committed to structural adjustment programs with the World Bank or the International Monetary Fund.

Rapid changes in the international economy have also helped hasten the decline of the typical SOE. Globalization of the economy, accelerated technological innovation, and growing integration of markets compel businesses to adopt highly flexible strategies and continuously adjust them to changing circumstances. That may, among other things, require the formation of alliances with foreign partners in the area of technology, procurement, or trade, or even through cross-shareholdings or integration in international groups. SOEs are notoriously ill-placed to function so flexibly and to forge such alliances.

Furthermore, the ideological debate on economic management and privatization has evolved substantially in response to the growing globalization of the economy and to the end of the cold war and confrontation between socialist and capitalist models of development. This narrowing of ideological schisms has produced a more pragmatic approach to economic reform, of which privatization forms part. This trend has been strengthened by the positive experience with privatization, as described in box 1.

Finally, in some economic sectors the reasons evoked to justify state intervention no longer exist. In infrastructure sectors (telecommunications and electricity generation, for example), technological and other developments have made it possible to introduce competition into activities formerly thought to be natural monopolies, thus obviating the justification for the survival of large public monopolies (see chapter 7). In other sectors, such as air transport, the rules of the game have simply changed and SOEs have been unable to adjust.[8]

The foregoing explanations for the surge in privatizations all relate to the supply side. To these must be added demand-related factors, namely, growing investor interest. Detailed analysis of this emerging demand is beyond the scope of this study, but it is clear that it stems, first, from the globalization of the economy and the sharp growth in foreign investment flows, especially toward developing and transition countries, and, second, from the advent of new types of investors. These include in particular large infrastructure companies, which until recently were almost all national

---

8. The European airline industry offers a telling example of the burden SOEs place on governments and taxpayers; it also illustrates the relative inefficiency of SOEs and their handicap in operating competitively. An article in the *Wall Street Journal* ranked the ten largest European airlines by level of state ownership and profitability. The five (southern European) airlines with majority state shareholding all posted losses in 1994, while the five privately run airlines all posted profits. Meanwhile, state subsidies to state-owned airlines have been staggering: "In the past four years, Air France, Olympic, TAP, Iberia and Sabena of Belgium received subsidies totaling $9.2 billion" ("Among European Airlines, the Privatized Soar to the Top. Government-Owned Carriers Milk State Subsidies but Still Struggle," *Wall Street Journal*, 19 July 1995).

Box 1 Positive Results of Privatization

In a study published in June 1994, Galal, Jones, Tandon, and Vogelsang performed an in-depth analysis (about 600 pages) of the effects of twelve privatization operations carried out in Chile, Malaysia, Mexico, and the United Kingdom. They studied four airlines (Aeroméxico, British Airways, Malaysian Airline Systems, and Mexicana de Aviación); three telecommunications companies (British Telecom, Compañía de Teléfonos de Chile, and Teléfonos de México); two power companies (Chilgener and Enersis); a carrier (National Freight); the container port of Kelang; and a lottery (Sports Toto Malaysia).

The purpose of the research was to compare circumstances before and after privatization by factoring in a hypothetical model representing what would probably have happened without privatization. The authors sought to distinguish the gains and losses due to privatization from those attributable to other factors. They calculated the impact on the selling country; on the buyers (domestic and foreign); on workers, users, and consumers (domestic and foreign); and on the competitors of the privatized SOE. In eleven of the twelve cases examined, the net effects of privatization were positive for the enterprise, as well as for the national economy and the world economy.

The exception was the privatization of the airline Mexicana, where the negative effects on buyers and users outweighed the benefits to the government; the net effect on the employees of the company was zero. This operation negatively affected the entire economy and foreign buyers and users (see also note 28 in chapter 3).

In none of these twelve cases did the workers as a whole find themselves worse off upon completion of the process. The study also stresses the major benefits of the economic liberalization measures that accompanied these privatizations and those of the regulatory framework set up for the privatization of the infrastructure companies.

Yet one cannot extrapolate to conclude that privatization will always have a positive effect. The situation of the four countries in question (one industrial country and three of the most prosperous developing countries) may, for example, differ greatly from that of a poor country or one in economic transition.

In another study published in 1994, Megginson, Nash, and Van Randenborgh compared the pre- and post-privatization performance of 61 enterprises in 18 different countries, which were privatized between 1961 and 1990 by public offering. The authors conclude that these enterprises, as a whole, posted substantial performance gains (increases in sales, investment, productivity, profits and dividends, and reduction in debt) following their divestiture. These gains were accompanied by an increased number of jobs.

---

monopolies or quasi monopolies that invested little if at all abroad but today aggressively invest outside their countries of origin. They also include private investment funds and institutional investors who allocate part, or even the entirety, of their resources to acquiring holdings in privatized companies (see box 6.2 on mutual funds that invest in privatized companies).

Growing privatization offerings by governments around the world and growing private investor interest and experience are clearly reinforcing each other.

Definition of Privatization

The term "privatization" can have different meanings. At one level it refers to the privatization of a public enterprise, whether through divestiture or other techniques. In a narrow sense, privatization implies permanent transfer of control, whether as a consequence of a transfer of ownership right from a public agency to one or more private parties or, for example, of a capital increase to which the public-sector shareholder has waived its right to subscribe.[9]

A broader definition of enterprise-level privatization includes any measure that results in temporary transfer to the private sector of activities exercised until then by a public agency. Such definition therefore also covers:

- Subcontracting, whereby the public agency that previously conducted the activity now subcontracts its execution to a private party; this subcontracting can cover an entire public service, such as trash collection, or only part of the activity, such as water or electricity meter reading and billing
- Management contracts, which may or may not be performance-based; in these cases there is a temporary transfer of management responsibility without transfer of ownership or real transfer of control (see, for example, World Bank 1995b)
- Lease of state-owned enterprises, equipment or assets, including lease-and-operate or *affermage* contracts in the infrastructure sectors; if the lease includes an option to buy, however, the operation could be regarded as a divestiture
- Concessions (see chapter 7), as well as build, operate, and transfer (BOT) contracts (see Augenblick and Custer 1990), often used for the privatization of infrastructure sectors with monopolistic characteristics.

At another level is privatization of a sector. Sector privatization is predicated on the introduction of private entry, often by abolishing public monopolies or other barriers to entry. It often includes, but does not have to, privatization at the enterprise level. The award of a cellular telecommunications license or of airline routes to a private firm may not be accompanied by

9. It matters little whether the assignment or transfer takes place by payment (sale) or some other means (free distribution of shares, for example). Nor does it matter whether the public agency is the state, the government, a ministry, a government department, a local authority, an enterprise effectively owned or controlled by the public sector, or any other public entity. The term divestiture is sometimes used restrictively to refer to a transfer of securities (SOE shares) or assets from the public sector to the private sector; a capital increase by an SOE may thus qualify as a privatization though not as a divestiture.

the divestiture of all or part of the incumbent operator, for instance. Similarly, independent power producers may be invited to build and operate power stations without any change in the ownership of the state utility.[10] This opening up is often, but not always, accompanied by the introduction of real competition among operators in the market (see the section in chapter 1 on the characteristics of a sector and chapter 7).

At a third level, the term privatization can have an even wider connotation, to include the privatization not just of enterprises and sectors but of an entire economy. The degree of privatization of a given economy will depend on the extent of prior state ownership and control and the scope of the reform program undertaken. Transition countries have by necessity embarked on the broadest programs of this kind, of which enterprise and sector privatizations form an integral part (see the section in chapter 1 on general country characteristics, and chapter 3). But other countries have also undertaken farreaching reforms to transform their economies. In New Zealand, for example, the government program addressed the liberalization of foreign trade, financial markets and labor as much as it did the reform of the telecommunications and air transport sectors and the restructuring and privatization of many public enterprises and activities (see Duncan and Bollard 1992).

Although each is separate and distinct, these three tiers of privatization are by no means sealed off from one another. On the contrary, there is close interaction among them. First of all, the strategy adopted for the upper levels will largely determine that applied at the lower levels. A privatization strategy for an SOE must be consistent with the country's sectoral and macroeconomic strategies. Often, the privatization of an enterprise will make sense only as a component of a sectoral or macroeconomic program. Privatization is thus an instrument of these more comprehensive approaches rather than an end in itself. Furthermore, a dialectic movement is at play: specific divestiture experiences contribute to the development or fine tuning of sectoral and general strategies, which cannot be defined unalterably at the start of a reform program.

These privatization techniques can also be classified according to the level of investment responsibility and the degree of risk transferred to the private sector, and to the relative irreversibility of the privatization transaction. These factors are in turn directly and positively linked to the magnitude of the financial commitment made by the private operator and, where relevant, to the duration of the transfer of responsibility to the latter. Figure 1 illustrates the gradation of different techniques for private sector participation, ranging from subcontracting, which requires very little

---

10. BOO (build, own, and operate) contracts may also be an instrument of sector privatization. BOO contracts are usually based on a license to build an infrastructure and to supply the related services. Unlike BOT contracts, ownership of the plant remains in private hands. When BOO (or BOT) contracts are accompanied by an exclusive purchase contract awarded by the local public service enterprise, they are more a form of subcontracting.

Figure 1   Range of Privatization Techniques

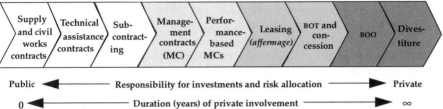

Public ◄──────────── Responsibility for investments and risk allocation ──────────► Private

0 ◄──────────────── Duration (years) of private involvement ────────────────► ∞

investment, involves little risk and can easily be terminated, all the way to total divestiture, in which the activity and its assets are permanently transferred to the private sector.[11]

To the various forms of privatization depicted in this figure must be added joint-venture companies, which can be cocontractors in any privatization arrangement; the private shareholding in these companies may range from under 1 percent to over 99 percent. Other techniques of sector privatization exist as well, such as the promotion of new entry through licenses, permits, or authorizations of varying duration granted to private operators.

Finally, it should be noted that what we call privatization goes by other names in some countries, often because privatization was deemed to be politically too delicate a term. Thus, for example, one speaks of capitalization in Bolivia (see box 5.1), peopleization in Sri Lanka, and equitization in Viet Nam. The terms "commercialization" of Canadian National (the railway company) and "strategic consolidation" of Belgacom (the Belgian telecommunications company) were used to refer to the recent privatization of these companies. In the Netherlands, on the other hand, the term privatization has been used not only to designate what is classified here as such but also to describe the process of corporatizing an SOE that continues, however, to be owned by the state (see chapter 4 for a discussion of corporatization of SOEs).

Structure of the Study

The sequencing of the chapters of this book follow the sequence of steps in preparing a privatization program. First described is the backdrop to privatization, followed by a discussion of the broad principles of design of a privatization strategy. Next examined is the constitutional, legal, and regu-

---

11. It should be noted that this work does not emphasize actual sale techniques or transactional issues. That is not, of course, to detract from the importance of the transaction aspect of privatization. On the contrary, selecting and implementing the appropriate techniques is extremely important. A good strategic, legal, and institutional framework will serve little purpose if the actual transactions are handled unskillfully by inexperienced or inadequately qualified officials. That said, the innumerable problems that can arise when structuring a privatization operation and during the ensuing negotiations are, by and large, similar to those encountered in the course of corporate mergers and acquisitions.

latory framework: what was it before privatization began, and how much must it be altered to allow or to facilitate privatization operations? Following this in-depth diagnosis is an analysis of the key provisions that authorize and regulate the privatization process and a description of the institutions and actors involved. A discussion of the privatization of infrastructure sectors, a very topical subject, precedes the concluding chapter. The main themes and issues of the book are presented as follows.

Chapter 1. Every strategy must start by clearly stating the objectives that are being pursued, because these determine the approach taken and choices made. The political setting and the specificities of the concerned country, sector, and enterprises similarly have a decisive impact on the nature of the program.

Chapter 2. A country's constitution and the treaties to which it is a party can limit the privatization options available to it. They cannot be ignored.

Chapter 3. If it is to succeed, privatization must place the divested enterprise in a stimulating economic environment. Clear rules are needed to govern the functioning of a market economy. This often means amending existing rules or even creating them from scratch. Examples are the basic rules recognizing private ownership, protecting competition, permitting the establishment and winding up of commercial companies, and regulating financial markets. Some of these rules, such as the provisions governing public offerings, also have a direct bearing on the privatization process itself.

Chapter 4. Privatization deals with transferring to the private sector SOEs or activities hitherto carried out by the public sector. The rules governing the conduct of these activities by the public sector hence also must be examined. This applies in particular to legislation concerning public property, SOEs, and public finances, which often also determines the steps the government needs to take to prepare the SOE for privatization. This chapter completes the overview of the environment that exists before privatization yet still directly affects efforts to privatize.

Chapter 5. The decision to privatize having been taken, it is important to ensure that the process is duly authorized and regulated. In many countries this is done by enacting a privatization law. This law may be either general or specific and may contain numerous provisions relating, in particular, to the topics discussed in the preceding chapters. Chapter 5 is devoted to the basic enabling provisions of privatization legislation, that is, those authorizing and regulating the process and defining its scope.

Chapter 6. The institutional framework for privatization, usually prescribed in the privatization legislation, is studied in chapter 5. An entire chapter is devoted to this subject in view of its importance and the great diversity of approaches taken. Even the best privatization legislation is worthless without a suitably designed institutional framework for implementation. In addition to national privatization agencies and committees, chapter 6 deals with privatization funds, which play a major role in mass privatization programs. The final section is devoted to privatization consultants, including legal and financial advisers.

Chapter 7. Some sectors have features that affect the way in which they can be privatized. Chapter 7 explores the special case of the privatization of infrastructure sectors, with special emphasis on telecommunications. Since the specificity of these sectors is (or was) due mainly to their monopolistic features, the analysis focuses on the strategic and economic issues that must be considered before addressing legislative and legal questions.

Chapter 8. In this concluding chapter the many facets of the privatization process are reviewed. The main challenge facing policymakers and government officials is not so much to sell an enterprise at a good price as to use this opportunity to achieve broader objectives such as a more competitive national economy.

The main body of the text is followed by detailed references to privatization laws and regulations enacted in over 100 different countries (appendix); a glossary of legal and other terms used in this book; a four-part bibliography (by author, by country or region, specialized journals, and internet resources); a subject index; a geographic index; and an index of enterprises, agencies, and other organizations.

1

Defining a Privatization Strategy

Developing a strategy is often regarded as the first step in a privatization program. In fact, since most privatization programs are an integral part of more comprehensive economic reform, the first step should be to define the key objectives driving the government's overall economic program. The privatization strategy then becomes a substrategy geared to the objectives of the broader reform program. Most former centrally planned economies, as well as, for example, Argentina, Chile, Mexico, New Zealand, Peru (see box 1.1), and the United Kingdom, opted for radical economic reform with privatization as one of its main pillars.[1]

Moreover, the sale of SOEs should rarely be an end in itself, but rather one instrument of economic policy among others. Some authors argue that privatization can be an objective in itself for transition countries on the road from a command economy to a free market economy, particularly the ex-Comecon countries. If privatization is understood in its broadest sense as the privatization of the economy, then this would indeed be right. If, however, it is understood as simply the sale of SOEs, then it should be seen as a necessary component of a broader program aimed at establishing a market economy. In transition countries, the sale of SOEs is essential for the formation of a market economy, whereas in many other countries governments may feel that they have other options available to achieve their policy objectives.

Developing a privatization strategy involves identifying government objectives, analyzing the existing constraints on execution of the program, and deciding on an approach to achieve the objectives while taking the constraints into account. The next section of this chapter is devoted to defining the objectives of a privatization program. The section that follows deals with political constraints, and others address the constraints specific to the concerned country,

1. See the geographic listing in the bibliography for further reading on each of these countries. On central and eastern Europe and the former Soviet Union, see, in particular, World Bank 1996b.

Box 1.1   Privatization and Economic Reform in Peru

In "Peru Opens Up Economy with Deluge of Laws," the *Financial Times* wrote
that a "10-day deluge of 126 laws, more than half of them intended to stimulate
private investment, has brought about the most radical reorientation in the
Peruvian state for more than 20 years. . . . State monopolies have been eliminated, private individuals and companies may now compete directly with the
state in such varied areas as telecommunications, the generation and transmission of electricity, and the provision of postal and railway services. They may
apply for concessions to administer state-owned hospitals, airports and even
schools. There is what ministers call an aggressive plan to sell off public companies, which have drained the Peruvian exchequer of up to $2.5bn annually."
The article also quoted then-prime minister Alfonso de los Heros on the importance of these reforms relative to Peru's terrorism problem: "Much more important is an adequate legal framework. If these decrees survive, then investment,
both national and foreign, will come" (*Financial Times*, 20 November 1991, p. 8).
The reforms have indeed survived: many SOEs, including the telecommunications and power companies, have been privatized, raising over $4 billion and
generating investment commitments or plans of equal magnitude; SOE subsidies have been cut from their astronomical prereform levels ($4.2 billion in fis-
cal 1989–90); interest rates and exchange rates have been liberalized; the quotation of Peruvian debt on secondary markets has risen from 5 percent to
60 percent and more of face value; the securities exchange index has soared;
inflation has been brought under control, dropping from over 7,000 percent in
1990 to about 11 percent in 1995; foreig investment has risen substantially, and
real GDP rose by an average of more than 8 percent a year from 1993 to 1995.
These impressive results, however, have been achieved at the cost of severe
restriction of political freedoms: in April 1992 parliament was dissolved, half
the members of the Supreme Court were dismissed, and strict control was instituted over television programs, all in the name of the fight against terrorism. It
is said, also, that income distribution worsened over this period.

   Sources: The Economist, 11 December 1993, pp. 90–91; *Financial Times*, 20 November
1991, 19 February 1994, and 7 March 1996.

---

sector, and enterprise. The final section briefly describes regional trends and
discusses issues concerned with implementation of a privatization strategy.

Objectives of Privatization

Defining privatization objectives is an important exercise that should be undertaken as early as possible. Many privatization programs have foundered when
clear objectives were lacking or where conflicting objectives were simultaneously pursued. The definition of objectives is not an easy task, however, and
it is made no easier by the multiplicity of possible objectives and actors with
different, often conflicting, interests. A list of the objectives most commonly
pursued, explicitly or implicitly, by privatizing governments is given in box 1.2.

As mentioned in the introduction, the current wave of privatizations is largely a response to the financial crisis facing many governments. Consequently, budgetary matters and short-term revenue maximization tend to be high on the list of governmental objectives. These may, however, lead to suboptimal policies and privatization techniques. A recent editorial stated that "privatization carried out just to raise money—not based on a broad vision of how the economy should work—is a recipe for failure" (*Euromoney*, February 1996, p. 5).

Privatization is also a response to the unsatisfactory performance of SOEs and to an increasingly competitive international environment. Raising enterprise and economy-wide efficiency should hence rank high among the objectives of a privatization program, and priority should be given to methods that maximize such efficiency. Opening the economy to domestic and international competition, removing barriers to entry, and breaking up outdated monopolies are important measures in this respect.

Governments should select the techniques and approaches that are best suited to their objectives. Where efficiency and maximization of privatization revenue are sought, a call for bids is generally preferable to direct negotiations with a single investor. As for privatization techniques, free vouchers or discounted employee shares may not be appropriate instruments if the main objective is to maximize revenue, but they may well serve the political objectives of the program. Similarly, a public flotation may be the right technique to promote widespread share ownership and stimulate financial markets, but that course involves the risk of diluting share ownership and thus control of the enterprise, and it will not necessarily generate optimal technology transfers. Mass transfers of shares to all citizens may achieve the objectives of widespread share ownership and, where appropriate, speed, but not promote those of efficiency, revenue maximization, foreign investment promotion, or technology transfer.

The chosen objectives will have significant implications not only for the choice and structuring of legal instruments and techniques but also for the need for measures preceding privatization.[2] Maximizing economic efficiency will often call for preprivatization reforms that, for example, break up the SOE to foster competition, eliminate monopolies and other barriers to entry in the sector, and, in cases of privatization of monopolistic sectors, establish a regulatory framework.

Although maximizing economic efficiency will normally be one of the main objectives of a privatization program, in practice other considerations of a political, social, or financial nature also influence the choices of the authorities. The debates aroused by the U.K. privatization program illus-

---

2. The choice of objectives is not the only determining factor. So too are the time frame adopted for implementation of the privatization process, the scope of the privatization program (number of enterprises, aggregate value of the program, and size relative to that of the private sector in the economy), the specific target levels for each of these objectives, and a series of other factors discussed later in this book.

Box 1.2   Objectives of Privatization

Efficiency and Development of the Economy

- Create a market economy—the key objective in economies in transition
- Encourage private enterprise and expansion of the private sector in general
- Promote macroeconomic or sectoral efficiency and competitiveness
- Foster economic flexibility and eliminate rigidities
- Promote competition, particularly by abolishing monopolies
- Establish or develop efficient capital markets, allowing better capture and mobilization of domestic savings
- Improve access to foreign markets for domestic products
- Promote domestic investment
- Promote foreign investment
- Promote integration of the domestic economy into the world economy
- Maintain or create employment

Efficiency and Development of the Enterprise

- Foster the enterprise's efficiency and its domestic and international competitiveness
- Introduce new technologies and promote innovation
- Upgrade plant and equipment
- Increase productivity, including utilization of industrial plant
- Improve the quality of the goods and services produced
- Introduce new management methods and teams
- Allow the enterprise to enter into domestic and international alliances essential to its survival

Budgetary and Financial Improvements

- Maximize net privatization receipts in order to fund government expenditures, reduce taxation, trim the public sector deficit, or pay off public debt
- Reduce the financial drain of the SOEs on the state (in the form of subsidies, unpaid taxes, loan arrears, guarantees given, and so on)
- Mobilize private sources to finance investments that can no longer be funded from public finances
- Generate new sources of tax revenue
- Limit the future risk of demands on the budget inherent in state ownership of businesses, including the need to provide capital for their expansion or to rescue them if they are in financial trouble
- Reduce capital flight abroad and repatriate capital already transferred

Income Distribution or Redistribution

- Foster broader capital ownership and promote popular or mass capitalism
- Develop a national middle class
- Foster the economic development of a particular group (ethnic or other) in society
- Encourage employee ownership (also important for efficiency reasons)

- Restore full rights to former owners of property expropriated by previous regimes
- Enrich those managing or implementing privatization projects (rarely an admitted objective)

Political Considerations

- Reduce the size and scope of the public sector or its share in economic activity
- Redefine the field of activity of the public sector, abandoning production tasks and focusing on the core of governmental functions, including the creation of an environment favorable to private economic activity
- Reduce or eliminate the ability of a future government to reverse the measures taken by the incumbent government to alter the role of the state in the economy
- Reduce the opportunities for corruption and misuse of public property by government officials and SOE managers
- Reduce the grip of a particular party or group (communist party, *nomenklatura*, or labor unions, for example) on the economy
- Raise the government's popularity and its likelihood of being returned to power in the next elections.

trate rather well the tension between conflicting goals. Many of the larger companies that were privatized were sold as monopolies or near-monopolies (especially British Telecom and British Gas) or with a dominant position in their market (British Airways). Reasons commonly given for this approach include the desire to proceed quickly, to secure the cooperation of SOE managers who otherwise might try to obstruct privatization, to attract large numbers of small shareholders, and to maximize sales revenue. Many commentators think that the U.K. government should have created greater competition in the concerned sectors before privatization, even at the price of a longer preparation period or lower sales proceeds. Later privatizations, such as those of the electricity and water companies, were preceded by breakup of the sector in order to create a more competitive environment.[3] Similarly, postprivatization intervention by U.K. regulators reduced the scope and duration of the monopolistic privileges originally granted to the privatized enterprises.

Privatization objectives need to be consistent not only among themselves but also with other objectives of the government. For example, some countries

3. The competition in question is yardstick competition rather than true market competition, because the water and electric power distribution enterprises were granted a monopoly. Competition in the market was established in power generation, however. On this topic, see chapter 7. See also Yarrow 1986, Graham and Prosser 1991, pp. 89 ff.

discriminate against foreign investors by barring or restricting their participation in the privatization program, and they simultaneously adopt new legislation to promote foreign investment and send cabinet members or other dignitaries around the world in quest of fresh foreign capital. Such discrimination in the privatization process may even be contrary to the provisions of the country's own foreign investment law.

The multiplicity and sometimes mutually incompatible nature of the objectives make it essential to rank them. Setting objectives, however, is not a purely abstract exercise. It is primarily a political matter, requiring specific tradeoffs. Social or political concerns may, for example, dictate second-best solutions, which are still worth pursuing when the first best approach, from an economic point of view, is not an acceptable one politically. Nonetheless, privatization is often not the best or most efficient policy instrument to pursue social or political objectives.[4]

A privatization strategy has to be assessed in light of the objectives pursued. Most privatization methods and techniques are not inherently good or bad, but merely more or less well suited to the pursuit of one or more specific objectives. The more objectives there are, the more complex the entire privatization process. Flexibility must be built into the system, especially at the implementation level, when multiple objectives exist. This calls for transparent procedures and accountability of decisionmakers.

General Country Characteristics

Privatization strategies need to be pragmatic and tailored to the specific circumstances and characteristics of the country concerned. The political, economic, social, and institutional setting and the risks associated with the interaction of all of these must be carefully analyzed. The great variance in the privatization experience of transition countries illustrates this rather well (see also chapter 3).

Political Setting

As privatization is above all a political process that can radically disrupt the situation of various stakeholders, one should anticipate possible or likely obstacles to the program. Indeed, reluctance or resistance both within and outside the government and the privatization agencies can often hinder the privatization process or limit its scope. Such opposition can stem from a variety of concerns, including: (a) the preservation of national sovereignty or independence;

---

4. Yarrow observed ten years ago that "privatization is also advanced as a weapon for reducing trade union power, encouraging wider share ownership, redistributing wealth and improving the public finances. However, there are other policy instruments better suited to achieving these objectives" (Yarrow 1986, p. 323).

(b) the desire to retain national control over certain activities or interests perceived to be strategic; (c) the sense that state ownership is needed to safeguard the "public interest"; (d) the fear that wealth might become concentrated in the hands of a few private parties; (e) a distrust of the private sector or certain segments of it; and (f) the protection of bureaucratic or other vested interests. Since new laws tend to reflect existing political forces, most of these considerations will be addressed in privatization legislation, as the following chapters show.

An in-depth study of these political arguments would exceed the scope of this book. It must be stressed, however, that minimizing political constraints and building a consensus are crucial to the success of privatization operations. That success depends above all on a firm commitment on the part of the country's leaders. Many commentators have made the point, for example, that Argentina's ambitious privatization program could not have been carried out with such success had President Menem and his government not espoused it so clearly and supported it so vigorously (see, for example, Alexander and Corti 1993, p. 3). Similarly, the roles of Margaret Thatcher in the United Kingdom and presidents Fujimori in Peru and Salinas de Gortari in Mexico were critical to the success of ambitious liberalization and privatization programs in their countries.

Economic and Social Setting

Many countries consider the privatization route to be a way to extricate themselves from an often prolonged recession or from a severe public finance crisis, characterized by large budget deficits and a growing public debt. Not surprisingly, these countries resort to privatization mainly for budgetary reasons and tend to choose approaches that maximize revenues in the short run, sometimes to the detriment of more efficient and competitive solutions. The urgency of financial needs also explains the lack of medium- and long-term economic analysis in many privatization strategies.

As for the social context, here again short-term constraints tend to dominate. The potential social impact of privatization is often calculated in terms of layoffs or lost jobs, yet the problem of excess labor, which is often caused by poor public management, would have to be remedied even in the absence of a privatization program. Moreover, the social factors usually taken into consideration focus more on short-term job losses resulting from necessary restructuring than on longer-term job creation generated by a more flexible and dynamic economy. Even so, the potential short-term social impact of a major economic reform and privatization program, as well as its political consequences, should not be underestimated. Governments will often have to prepare and adopt support measures to dampen the restructuring shock and help workers manage the transition to other jobs. Involving workers in the privatization process by seeking their inputs and giving them incentives to support the program has also proven useful (see chapters 3 and 5).

Institutional Setting

A country's institutional setting is determined by its administrative, commercial, and legal traditions and practices; the competence of its public administration; and the degree of corruption in the system, among other things. The preparation, implementation, and follow-up of privatization programs may be quite taxing on a country's institutions and civil service. Privatization is primarily a public transaction or process initiated by a government and conducted by politicians, civil servants, and SOE managers, all of whom have little or no relevant experience and many of whom may not have the right incentives to carry out the program. Institutional and human factors, absorptive capacity, and the way in which a government attempts to overcome its inexperience in these matters all play a decisive role in the success or failure of a privatization program (see chapter 6).

Country Risk

In a country with a weak or otherwise unattractive political, economic, social, and institutional environment, the government, in the role of seller, will have to develop a long-term strategy to reduce the risks run by investors. The level of risk that investors face determines their interest in the privatization program. The higher the perceived risk, the more difficult it will be to implement the program. In the short run, measures may have to be adopted to encourage venture-capital investment at the cost of lower privatization revenue because such investment can help rekindle the economy and establish a track record. The longer-run objectives of the strategy will be to reduce uncertainty and risk levels, eliminate the main obstacles to the development of a market economy, and create an environment conducive to private sector investment. The government's credibility is vital to the success of such a strategy, and that credibility must be earned. Each successful transaction contributes to a positive image.

Although some countries, such as Argentina, Colombia, or the Philippines, seem to have succeeded in moving up this ladder, others have been less successful. Indeed, some former Soviet republics and a few central and eastern European countries, as well as several African countries, have suffered fickle policies, internal unrest, programs called into question or canceled, and a certain distrust of the private sector in general and of foreign investors in particular. This has greatly reduced their credibility and complicated and slowed the implementation of their privatization programs.

More technical, or at least less political, country risks should also be noted. In a country whose accounting rules and practices do not conform to international standards, for example, buyers will be less willing to take over the liabilities of an SOE, and the government may have no choice but to privatize the SOE by selling off its assets and liquidating the remaining shell. Similarly, the absence of organized capital markets or weak financial institutions may make it more difficult to privatize by way of a public flotation or even to rely on domestic savings. In countries with nonconvertible currencies, an SOE with foreign exchange earnings will be easier to sell than one with only local currency revenue.

Characteristics of a Sector

Privatization techniques are influenced by market structure, as well as by other sector-specific characteristics. Most sectors or activities currently managed by the state or other public entities can be privatized.

Sector Structure

The structure of a market or sector may be determined mainly by economic or by legal variables, as the case may be. Legal variables dominate, for example, in the presence of legally sanctioned monopolies; in this case, the law forbids anyone except the holder of the monopoly franchise to engage in specified activities. The economic side dominates in cases of natural monopoly, where only one company could survive. The two do not necessarily overlap, however. In some countries natural monopolies are not legally protected, whereas elsewhere activities that are not natural monopolies are shielded by the protective barrier of a monopoly franchise.

If increased efficiency is a primary objective of privatization, then the options for restructuring a monopolistic SOE should be examined first. One way might be to divide the SOE into several competing entities. When legal or regulatory provisions are responsible for the monopoly position and prevent or seriously restrict entry by new businesses into the protected sector, these should be repealed or relaxed. Where it is not practical or desirable to eliminate the monopoly before privatization, it will often be necessary to enact provisions regulating the conduct of the enterprise after it has been privatized. These laws may take the form of general rules of conduct prohibiting uncompetitive behavior (as was the case in New Zealand, where ordinary competition law limits the power of all enterprises, including infrastructure companies, to abuse their dominant position) or of sector-specific regulations governing pricing and other critical aspects of the monopolistic activities (see also chapter 7, particularly the section dealing with market structure, competition, and divestiture).

Other Sector Features

Until recently, in every part of the world the telecommunications sector was dominated by national or regional monopolies. As a result, most countries lacked domestic investors with relevant sector experience. Countries such as the United Kingdom, which had a national company that inspired investor confidence and operated in a relatively mature market, have opted for a public flotation. Other countries have generally sought a strategic investor with the required experience and have therefore had to focus on foreign companies. For their part, these foreign companies were often limited in the scope of their activities and investments by their own regulatory framework. The likelihood of finding private investors with experience in running a telephone company in a country other than their own, particularly in a developing country, was rather slim until the early 1990s. The situation is

different today, however, because of the recent worldwide trend to deregulate and privatize telecommunications (see chapter 7, including box 7.2).

In many infrastructure sectors, such as toll roads or water distribution, for
example, operating receipts are mainly, or even solely, in local currency. That
situation could constrain financing options for a privatization operation.

In many service activities, including software or data processing, professional services, the media, and some skilled repair and maintenance activities, for example, fixed assets are of secondary importance. Instead, the staff,
trademark, and license to exercise the activity represent the core of a company's value. In these cases a privatization operation cannot be implemented successfully without the support of the employees, the principal
asset of the enterprise.

Privatization of state-owned banks also raises a host of specific legal
issues that are often settled by special legislation, as was the case in Belgium
and Italy, for example. Specific approvals must be sought from the national
banking regulatory agency and, if foreign subsidiaries are involved, from
foreign regulators as well. These few examples show how the SOE's sector of
activity may influence the privatization process.

Can All Sectors or Activities Be Privatized?

Different terms are used to refer to sectors or activities that are deemed to be
ineligible for privatization. In some countries, reference is made to strategic
or vital economic sectors or activities. In others, the view is that natural
monopolies should not be privatized. The magic word, in particular in Latin
countries, may be public services, a concept that may embrace the large
infrastructure sectors discussed in chapter 7, as well as commercial services
like the postal service and such functions as education, health, social security, justice, and national defense.

The term "public service" itself is ambiguous, to say the least; it has never
been precisely defined and it is often used subjectively.[5] To some, privatizing
a public service is tantamount to selling off the family jewels or abandoning
a key role of the state. Confusion very quickly surrounds the distinction

---

5. The term public service has been used to describe, among other things, services provided by
public-sector entities (for example, public administrations and SOEs); services provided under
the control, regulation, or jurisdiction of the government or a public agency; services paid for,
financed, or guaranteed by the government or a public agency; and services provided to the
public or in the public interest. The debate on the evolving nature of public services is particularly heated in France, where case law of the Conseil d'Etat often determines the attributes of
public services. "Depending on the meaning given to it, the concept of public service is more or
less extensive" (Jean Rivero, *Droit administratif*, 11th ed., sec. 448, Paris, Dalloz). A report submitted in February 1996 by a special task force on the specificity of French-style public services set
up by Prime Minister Juppé concluded that France should not hide behind doctrinal quarrels on
the notion of public service; instead, more competition is needed in these services and France
must undertake reforms matching Europe's overall liberalization trend. See *Financial Times*,
28 February 1996.

between the concept of services rendered to the public and accessible on a nondiscriminatory basis, and that of services provided by the government or a public enterprise. This semantic drift, this merging of two different concepts, unnecessarily complicates the debate about how certain services should be provided to the public. This is particularly the case in countries with an administrative tradition influenced by the French and in formerly socialist countries.[6]

In addition, what is subsumed under such terms changes over time, even within the same country. In Peru, for example, President Fujimori and his privatization minister have argued that privatization of utilities and natural resource companies would not endanger national security or strategic interests, as had been previously argued, but that on the contrary those interests were threatened most of all by the huge losses and liabilities built up by SOEs (see *Financial Times*, 17 March 1996).

Setting aside terminology and its political or emotional overtones, one can venture that all activities that can be adequately described in contractual terms and whose performance can be measured can also be privatized. This includes a priori all production of goods and services, even structurally money-losing activities, provided the required subsidies can be channeled to the private provider.

A few examples may illustrate the far reaches of privatization. Consider postal services, organized in most countries as a core governmental monopoly. The Netherlands has already privatized KPN, a holding company that includes the postal service as well as the telecommunications company. Argentina, Germany, Lebanon, the Philippines, the United Kingdom, and other countries are also working on the privatization of their postal systems; and, on March 1, 1994, Sweden abolished its postal monopoly and opened the sector, including basic letter delivery, to competition; five private companies have since been registered and entered the market to compete with the incumbent SOE.[7]

6. The economic literature is more precise and useful in the definition of the concept of public good, which applies to only a few public services. To qualify as a public good, an asset or service must possess certain features. For example, it must be impossible (at least in practice) to exclude specific people from using it (nonexcludability), and there must be nonrivalry in consumption, which implies that its consumption by one person in no way prevents its consumption by others (no crowding-out effect). Few infrastructure activities can be regarded as public goods: examples include traffic signaling, street lighting, and traffic control (see Kessides 1993). However, the fact that a service is indeed a public good in no way implies that it should be provided by a public agency. See the example of Trinity House, a private corporation with public duties established in Britain in 1566 to build and operate lighthouses (or franchise private parties to do so), with light tolls or fees being collected at the ports by customs officials (Samuel Brittan, "Symbolism of Lighthouses," in *Financial Times*, 6 November 1995).

7. Sweden Post remains an SOE, corporatized in 1994. See also the rulings of the European Court of Justice and the decisions of the European Commission limiting the area reserved to national monopolies by excluding express shipping services, among others, and also the Commission's green paper on partial deregulation of postal services (COM 91 476 final). There has also been much talk about privatizing the postal service in the United States, where mail delivery became a government monopoly following the enactment in 1845 of the Private Express Statutes.

Administration of justice would seem to be the perfect example of a pure state function, but even here private provision is a viable and often-used option, as evidenced by, for example, the frequent recourse to private arbitration and other alternative dispute resolution mechanisms. In France, the United Kingdom, the United States, and other countries, privatization has spread also to the management of prisons, and private security compar.ies are growing at a rapid pace all over the world, often substituting for or complementing the state's police force. Publication of a country's official gazette is another example of an activity that can be privatized.

Social security (see chapter 3), air traffic control (see the section in chapter 7 on the transport sector), or regulatory activities (see the section of chapter 7 on regulation) provide other illustrations, as does tax or customs administration. Customs administration was privatized in Indonesia and Latvia. Customs warehouses are managed by private operators in an increasing number of countries. In Mexico "banks are entrusted with being the sole receivers of tax payments and with putting all the information from the returns on tape. Moreover, the private sector was authorized to print and distribute tax returns, registration and notice forms" against a fixed fee schedule (Jenkins 1994, p. 78). Withholding of income taxes by employers or of taxes on interest or dividends by financial institutions are other examples of partial privatization of the tax function. Even tax collection can be privatized in some cases, with public authorities selling their tax claims to private collectors (see Byrne 1995).

Saying that something can be privatized does not mean that it should be privatized, however. In each instance, one should analyze the costs and benefits of public versus private provision of a given service, including the associated transaction costs, as well as economic, financial, political, social, and other aspects.

Characteristics of the Enterprise

Characteristics specific to an enterprise can also dictate, up to a point, the measures that need to be taken to prepare for and implement privatization of an SOE. Some of these characteristics, such as the nature of government ownership, the financial situation of the enterprise, and any applicable environmental or labor obligations and constraints, are developed in the following chapters. This section deals with the legal status and size of SOEs.

Legal Status of the Enterprise

The legal status of SOEs to be privatized varies greatly and affects the choice of privatization techniques. Box 1.3 distinguishes between three types of SOEs and state holdings, going from entities with limited autonomy from the government to companies in which the government is an ordinary, noncontrolling shareholder. Entities organized under public law range from minis-

---

Box 1.3　Legal Status of Public Enterprises or Shareholdings

Public-Law Entities

- Government departments or ministries, and divisions thereof, without distinct juridical personality
- Autonomous entities with their own budget but without separate juridical personality
- Public agencies with juridical personality
- Statutory corporations, public establishments and national corporations, which may be subject in part to private-sector laws

SOEs Organized under Private Company Law

- Joint-stock companies wholly owned by the public sector (state and/or public agencies)
- Joint-venture companies whose shareholders include public entities and private partners (local and/or foreign)
- SOE subsidiaries organized under private law

Minority Shareholdings

- Private enterprises in which the state or other public entities have a minority or noncontrolling stake.

---

tries without distinct juridical personality to public-law companies with juridical personality; state-owned enterprises organized under private law include joint-stock companies and subsidiaries of other SOEs;[8] and companies in which the state or public sector is a shareholder, though not a controlling one, are usually not included under the heading of SOE.[9]

This classification does not necessarily imply, however, that public-law bodies are subject to public law in every aspect of their organization or operations, nor that private-law SOEs are totally outside the jurisdiction of public law. The main question this classification raises is whether ownership of the enterprise to be privatized can be transferred without its prior transformation into a new legal entity. Public-law bodies are usually set up as such by law. They may have to be made subject to company law (that is, private law) before they can be transferred to the private sector as legal

---

8. Some legal systems allow public-law enterprises to establish subsidiaries organized under private law. In France and countries with legal systems based on the French system, *établissements publics* (public establishments) are often authorized to set up such subsidiaries. This allows them to circumvent restrictions imposed on public-law entities.

9. The name given to a particular form of SOE varies from one legal system or country to another. What matters is not what the class of enterprise is called but what its intrinsic characteristics are. In this book, public enterprise and SOE are synonymous unless otherwise specified.

entities.[10] Another available option is to sell the assets of the SOE to private buyers without transferring the SOE itself.

There are many other types of SOEs that may be governed by special rules. These include (a) municipal enterprises, which may be organized under public or private law; (b) party-owned enterprises, which raise special problems, especially in one-party states with a certain degree of confusion between party and state, particularly with respect to ownership rights; (c) socialist cooperatives, which may be deemed to be public or private; and (d) armed forces enterprises, which often have a privileged and sometimes secretive status.

The legal status of an SOE may have a bearing on the applicability of many other laws, particularly in the areas of labor, social security, and taxation, which can themselves affect the course of the privatization process. This matter is considered further in the chapters that follow.

Size of the Enterprise

Finally, and rather obviously, the size of the SOE to be privatized is critical, too. The issues involved in privatizing, say, a small restaurant or grocery store are far different from those that arise when a national telephone company or a major cement works undergoes privatization. Many transition countries have adopted a two-stage method of privatization, focusing first on small privatizations before moving on to larger operations (see World Bank and CEUPP 1994; Earle and others 1994). Czechoslovakia, Ukraine, and other countries have even enacted separate laws providing for different privatization techniques for each group (see the list of privatization laws in the appendix).

Defining an Approach

Once the objectives and constraints have been identified, the next step is to ascertain what reforms need to be undertaken to achieve the government's objectives. In every country a multitude of measures could be adopted to improve the environment for economic activity in general and the implementation of privatization projects in particular, but not all reforms can be implemented at once. Measures essential to the success of the privatization process have to be given priority. Pursuit of the ideal environment can only lead to endless delays and gridlock.

---

10. The law organizing such public bodies or the specific law governing the public-law SOE to be privatized usually precludes transfer of ownership to the private sector. In that case the law in question will have to be amended or abrogated to allow the SOE to be privatized as a legal entity. See the sections of chapter 4 dealing with the exercise of ownership rights and the restructuring of public enterprises.

Regional Trends

Broadly speaking, countries in different regions of the world have adopted different approaches. Former socialist countries have had to privatize their entire economy. A market economy had to be created almost from scratch. The need to create a shareholding class and the political imperatives of the reform process, together with the difficulty of arousing investor interest in turbulent times, has led some countries in central and eastern Europe and in the former Soviet Union to adopt a completely novel approach to privatization. First, private ownership had to be authorized and encouraged. To facilitate large-scale and speedy transfer of productive assets from the public to the private sector, the traditional privatization techniques had to be supplemented by new techniques, such as transfer of SOE shares to the entire population under mass privatization programs (see chapter 6).

The French and British privatization programs also aimed at widespread share ownership. Both countries, however, could rely on established capital markets and securities exchange mechanisms. Thanks to the substantial financial and human resources at its disposal, the United Kingdom was able to undertake from 1980 onward a particularly innovative privatization program affecting nearly all sectors, including the most strategic ones (see chapter 7). In the United Kingdom, privatization was part of an ambitious economic reform program, whereas the French program was more self-contained and limited in scope: utilities and transport sectors were not included, for instance. Other European countries, including Italy, Portugal, and Spain, have also relied heavily on public flotations.

In Latin America the existence of major bottlenecks caused by the inadequacy and poor state of public infrastructure has led some countries, such as Argentina, Chile, and Peru, to set up major programs of deregulation and privatization of so-called strategic sectors, such as telecommunications, electric power, banking, and natural resources. These three countries and Mexico have also integrated their privatization programs into much more comprehensive economic reform packages.

In Asia the divestiture trend has not been as pronounced. Few countries there have adopted or implemented large divestiture programs,[11] although some, including the Asian "tigers," a few traditionally socialist countries such as India, and countries still under communist systems, such as China and Viet Nam, have adopted broader privatization approaches. These have included

---

11. The Philippines is among the leading Asian countries in terms of number and volume of divestiture. Since its inception in 1987, the privatization program has brought in about $6.5 billion through transactions covering hundreds of enterprises and nonperforming assets. The biggest divestiture so far is the sale in 1994 of the oil company Petron for a total of close to $1 billion, including about $575 million for 40 percent of the shares sold to Aramco and about $270 million from a public flotation of 20 percent of the shares that followed the Aramco deal. See *Financial Times*, 12 September 1994 and 30 November 1995. See also the section on recruitment of staff of privatization bodies in chapter 6.

macroeconomic liberalization and opening of certain sectors (including infra-structure) to private investment through BOO, BOT, or concession contracts.

In Africa, where most SOEs were in a state of virtual bankruptcy and lacked financial statements worthy of the name, privatization has often had to be effected through liquidation, thereby allowing buyers to acquire SOE assets without incurring the risks of large, uncertain, or contingent liabili-ties. Leaving aside the Middle East, which has lagged even further behind in this respect, Africa is the continent where, on average, the least progress has been achieved in privatization.[12]

Sequencing Reforms

When the privatization strategy has been adopted, the timetable for the nec-essary reforms needs to be drawn up. The sequencing and pace of the priva-tization program will have to be thought through from the outset. Interac-tion with macroeconomic, sectoral, and SOE-level reforms, synchronization with any necessary support measures, congruence with adopted objectives and priorities, and compatibility with the absorptive capacity of institutions as well as markets all need to be considered. The nature of accompanying reforms and support measures may determine how well the main stake-holders and the public at large accept the privatization program.

Some reforms may be prerequisites for the use of given privatization techniques. Where, for example, the government intends to sell an SOE as such, it may first need to corporatize the enterprise. If a public flotation is proposed, it may be necessary to strengthen the country's capital markets (these and other reforms that may be necessary are described in detail in subsequent chapters).

On the other hand, some situations may accommodate privatization without the need for any other reform. In particular, the privatization of a limited number of industrial or commercial enterprises in market econo-mies, where shares can easily be sold on the securities exchange or through other well-established mechanisms, may fall into this category.

Communication and Public Relations

Having a good reform program may be a necessary condition for successful privatization, but it is not a sufficient one. One should also be able to sell the program to the major stakeholders. When preparing for privatization, the government and its advisers should try to involve the parties most directly

---

12. According to UNCTAD, Sub-Saharan Africa accounted for only slightly more than 1 percent of the $113 billion volume of privatization transactions carried out in developing countries between 1988 and 1994. Notable privatizations include the successful flotation in 1994 on the London and Accra stock exchanges of over half of the government of Ghana's shareholding in Ashanti Goldfields, which raised over $300 million, and the two-stage privatization of Kenya Airways: the Dutch carrier KLM acquired a 26 percent stake in 1995, followed by a flotation on the local stock exchange in early 1996 (see *Oxford Analytica*, 12 July 1996; see also the introduction.)

affected as much as possible. It will take a substantial effort to convince political parties, SOE managers, unions and workers,[13] civil servants, businessmen, potential purchasers, and the population at large of the benefits of the program. Although achieving a broad consensus will not always be possible, informing and educating the public and stakeholders about the privatization program and its effects is often a condition of success.

A sustained effort on the part of government to explain the expected benefits of the privatization program and the reasons for choosing specific approaches and techniques can help greatly to build a relatively wide consensus. This public relations operation, whose importance is unfortunately not always recognized by governments and bureaucrats, should be systematically integrated into the reform strategy. On this point, recent studies have shown that privatization frequently benefits the majority of the parties affected, even those often described a priori as victims or losers (see box 1). That having been said, there will often be losers, especially when economies, sectors, or enterprises in need of radical restructuring are privatized.[14] In these cases not even the best information campaign will succeed in persuading those that will be most adversely affected. The government can, however, hope to reduce their opposition by incorporating the necessary support measures into the privatization program and publicizing such measures.

As the following chapters explain, a number of measures can be taken to address the concerns or dampen some of the most common objections of opponents of the transfer of SOEs to the private sector. To take only one example, transparent and competitive sale procedures should reassure people who fear that public assets are being transferred to private operators at prices well below their true value (see chapter 5). Such measures can effectively assuage these fears, however, only if their adoption is preceded by adequate publicity and discussion.

Conclusion

The wide diversity of possible objectives under privatization programs and the mutual incompatibility of some of them compel governments to make

13. Unions and workers are often opposed to privatization. However, this is not always the case. In Romania, unions were in favor of privatization and felt that the government was dragging its feet. The two main unions even organized a nationwide strike at the end of February 1994 to protest governmental delays in implementing the privatization program and reforming the social security system. The president of one of these two unions stated in an interview that he "very, very strongly support[s] privatisatio—the faster, the better" (*Financial Times*, 3 May 1994). Trade union leaders in other transition countries have often supported privatization, whereas in industrial and developing countries opposition seems to be more common.

14. The program of restructuring and privatization of the East German economy was attended by large-scale layoffs. Of the 4.1 million jobs in the enterprises in the Treuhandanstalt's portfolio in 1990, only 1.5 million remained four years later. See *New York Times*, 12 August 1994.

choices and define priorities. In the absence of explicit ranking of objectives, the default setting should be to give priority to economic efficiency. To that end, transfers of ownership from the public to the private sector should be accompanied as much as possible by action to open these sectors to domestic and international competition.

After objectives have been defined, the constraints that could hinder the process must be assessed. Each country will have a distinct set of constraints, and it is important to tailor the privatization program to its specific environment. As experience has proved, even governments with identical objectives cannot pursue them with the same instruments in every case.

Once adopted, the strategy needs to be operationalized. This calls for good sequencing and coordination of the various reforms and activities. Finally, the quality, timeliness, and presentation of the government's public relations effort will often be decisive to the success of the operation. Privatization is, after all, as much a political as a commercial undertaking.

The privatization challenge is first and foremost a strategic challenge. Indeed, the significance of privatization cannot be limited to the transfer of assets from a public sector owner to a new private one, nor to the revenues generated in the process. The real challenge of privatization is not so much to sell off an SOE, but to seize this opportunity to introduce much-needed economic reforms, whether of a macroeconomic or a sectoral nature, and to redefine the role of the government.

This strategic approach can help change perceptions about privatization. Instead of a static process or a zero-sum game in which some win and others lose with no net benefit for the nation as a whole, privatization should be seen in a dynamic perspective in which the objective is precisely to increase overall social welfare.

The emphasis in this chapter has been on the formulation of a strategy rather than on the actual contents of one. The substance of privatization strategies is discussed in more detail in the following chapters.

2

Privatization and Basic Legal Norms

The success of a privatization program is often a function of the soundness of its foundation, especially its legal foundation. The objectives of the program must be compatible with the constitutional provisions that underpin the legal framework for business activity in general and privatization in particular. They must also be compatible with the general principles of law and other norms establishing the rule of law and with certain provisions of international law, which may be binding on the legislator. If these basic legal norms hinder achievement of program objectives, the government must determine whether they can and should be amended. If they cannot be amended, the government may have to reconsider the program objectives or the choice of specific privatization techniques in order to accommodate these higher-order constraints.

Box 2.1 summarizes basic principles common to most legal systems, which guarantee the rule of law. These principles form the basis of relationships between private economic agents and between them and the state or any part of the public sector. They are the pillars of what is often referred to as the rule of law (*l'état de droit* in French) and contribute to a legal environment conducive to private investment and hence to privatization.

This chapter examines how a country's constitution and certain provisions of international law may affect the privatization choices available to a government or legislator.

Constitutional Requirements

A country's constitution or fundamental law, where such a document exists, may contain provisions that affect privatization operations either directly or indirectly. In the absence of a written constitution, provisions of a constitutional nature may well have the same effect.[1] Provisions of this kind may

---

1. See the section in this chapter on limits on the discretion of the government. See also Prosser 1990 and Graham and Prosser 1991 for an in-depth examination of the constitutional requirements regarding privatization in the United Kingdom, which has no written constitution, and in France.

Box 2.1   Principles Guaranteeing the Rule of Law

- Publicity of laws enables all parties concerned to be aware of the laws with which they are expected to comply
- A clear and unambiguous legal framework allows the parties to know which laws apply to their situation and what their specific meaning is
- Predictability in applying laws reduces the risks associated with changes in their interpretation, implementation, or enforcement
- Nondiscrimination in the application of laws implies that all parties that are in the same objective situation will have the same substantive rules of law applied to them
- Means of legal redress and respect for due process ensure access to independent appeal and dispute settlement procedures
- Stability of the legal, political, and decisionmaking systems assures investors that the state or government will not unilaterally and unfavorably alter the basic conditions on which these investors based their investment decisions.

---

limit the scope of the privatization program, determine to whom decision-making authority belongs, or impose certain controls on privatization authorities, or address all three.

Limits on the Scope of Privatization

The constitutions of many socialist countries provided that all productive assets (including enterprises) were the property of the state or "of all the people," and granted the state (or public sector) special protection and privileges as further described in box 2.2 (see also the section of chapter 3 dealing with ownership rights). These provisions were generally based on the 1936 constitution of the former Soviet Union, particularly article 4, and had to be repealed to enable privatization.

Portugal's 1976 constitution even declared irreversible the nationalizations that followed the April 1974 revolution. It had to be amended twice, in 1982 and 1989, to authorize the privatization of these SOES. The constitution of Bangladesh also had to be amended, by a decree issued in 1977 under martial law, to authorize privatization. Similar sweeping amendments had to be made in most transition countries, but also in other countries moving away from strong state control of the economy.

Some constitutions continue to prohibit all private-sector activity in what are deemed to be strategic sectors. Until recently, article 177 of the Brazilian constitution gave the state a monopoly on prospecting for petroleum, natural gas, and other hydrocarbons; petroleum refining; import and export of petroleum products; sea transportation of domestic crude oil; and pipeline transportation of crude oil and natural gas regardless of origin. This monopoly was repealed in November 1995, but the constitutional amendment required implementation legislation which, eight months later, had not yet been enacted. Article 27

Box 2.2   Ownership Provisions of Socialist Constitutions

Soviet Union. Article 4 of the 1936 constitution proclaimed: "The economic foundation of the USSR is the socialist economic system and socialist ownership of the instruments and means of production, firmly established as a result of the liquidation of the capitalist economic system, the abolition of private ownership of the instruments and means of production, and the elimination of the exploitation of man by man."

Bulgaria. Until its revision in April 1990, article 13 of the constitution stated: "The economic system of the People's Republic of Bulgaria is socialist. It is based on the public ownership of the means of production."

Angola. Article 9 of the 1975 constitution stated: "The foundation of economic and social development is socialist ownership, consubstantiated in state ownership and cooperative ownership. The state shall adopt measures permitting continuous broadening and consolidation of socialist relations of production."

Guinea-Bissau. The 1984 constitution described the country as "a sovereign, democratic, secular, unitary, anti-colonialist and anti-imperialist republic" (article 1); the latter two adjectives have since been deleted. Its article 12, which has since been amended, declared the following to be state-owned assets: "the soil, subsoil, water resources, mineral resources, main energy sources, forests, basic means for industrial production, mass media, banks, insurance, roads and essential means of transportation."

Mozambique. Until it was revised in November 1990, the constitution, adopted in 1975, stated: "In the People's Republic of Mozambique the State economic sector is the leading and driving factor in the national economy. State property is given special protection [and] its development and expansion is incumbent upon all state agencies, social organizations and citizens" (article 10).

---

of the Mexican constitution contains similar restrictive provisions for hydrocarbons. The Mexican constitution also originally contained a provision, amended in May 1990, prohibiting privatization of public commercial banks. Such constitutional provisions covering the energy, water, and telecommunications sectors, as well as transport infrastructure, are reviewed in chapter 7.

Elsewhere, certain types of activities are reserved to the state, though participation by private entrepreneurs is permitted through joint-venture companies or under concession, lease, or management contracts (see also chapter 7). This is common in the hydrocarbons sector, as for example in Bolivia, where the constitution provides that petroleum deposits are the property of the state, which may nevertheless entrust exploration and production to private operators under concession contracts.[2] Article 33 of the Indonesian constitution of

---

2. See article 139 of the Bolivian constitution. Other examples are cited in chapter 7. Even though it does not have the same legal force, the preamble to the French constitution of 1946 also might be mentioned here; it states that "all assets, all enterprises whose operation has or acquires the characteristics of a national public service or of a de facto monopoly must become collective property." The preamble to the 1958 constitution explicitly refers to and confirms the principles set forth in the preamble of the 1946 constitution.

1945 (reinstated by a 1959 decree) declares that "branches of production which are important to the State and which affect the life of most people shall be controlled by the State"; needless to say, such ambiguity regarding the covered sectors or activities, as well as the meaning of state control, has created problems.[3]

Finally, some constitutions may include other restrictions, such as limitations on foreign investment in specific activities (see also the section of chapter 5 dealing with restrictions on foreign participation). These could clearly also hinder privatization programs. Until its repeal by constitutional amendment of August 15, 1995, article 178 of the Brazilian constitution reserved coastal and internal shipping to national vessels, meaning vessels whose carriers, ship owners, captains, and at least two-thirds of the crew are Brazilian. Similarly, article 176, which restricted mining (exploration and production) to Brazilian-controlled firms, was modified on the same day and now requires only that the firm be established under Brazilian law and have its headquarters and management in the country; subsidiaries of foreign companies qualify under these new standards. More generally, the same amendment also eliminated the constitutional discrimination in favor of "Brazilian firms of national capital," hence removing the basis for preferential treatment of Brazilian-controlled companies in public procurement and other matters. Specific legislation had to be enacted to implement these amendments; provisional measures (that is, executive decisions to be later confirmed by parliament) for implementation were expressly disallowed.

Parliamentary Approval

The constitution or constitutional traditions of a country may provide that privatization must be approved by parliament. This is the case with article 34 of the French constitution of 1958, which states that the rules governing nationalization of enterprises and transfer of ownership of public-sector enterprises to the private sector shall be set by law. The constitutions of Benin, Morocco, Senegal, Togo, and other countries with a French legal tradition similarly require that the transfer of majority state-owned enterprises to the private sector be authorized in advance by parliament, by means of a law.[4]

---

3. This constitutional clause was used in 1980 to question the legality of a 1967 agreement between the government and ITT, which gave the local subsidiary Indosat a twenty-year exclusive operating license for international telecommunications, and to justify the takeover of Indosat by the Indonesian government. See Wells and Gleason 1995, p. 48.

4. *Benin*: Article 98 of the constitution provides that the rules pertaining to nationalizations and transfers of enterprises from the public to the private sector are a matter of law.

Morocco: Article 45 of the 1972 constitution (preserved in the 1992 constitution) declares that "the nationalization of enterprises and the transfer of enterprises from the public to the private sector" are matters of law.

Senegal: Article 56 of the constitution of March 7, 1963, states: "The National Assembly shall hold the legislative power. It alone shall vote the laws. The rules concerning . . . nationalization of enterprises and transfer of enterprise ownership from the public to the private sector shall be established by law." As mandated by the constitution, Law no. 87-23 of August 18, 1987, permits privatization of the SOEs listed in a schedule annexed to the law.

In some countries the role assigned to parliament is defined more precisely. Not only must a law be enacted but it must also contain certain specific provisions. The Paraguayan constitution, for example, requires that the law spell out the procedures for granting the preferential right to shares in the privatized enterprise to which its employees are entitled.[5]

The constitutions of other civil-law countries are silent on the subject. The principle of parallelism of forms, which requires that the same instrument be used to undo something as was used to create it, would imply, however, that a law is needed to liquidate, and possibly also to privatize, an SOE that had been established by law (see also the section of chapter 1 on the legal status of enterprises).

A country's constitution, legislation, or legal traditions may allow the government or other public agencies to privatize without intervention by the legislature. In that case, no enabling legislation is legally required. This is the situation in most of the common-law countries, such as Australia, Malaysia, New Zealand, and the United Kingdom.[6] In such systems it is generally considered that, in the absence of explicit prohibition, the government possesses inherent power to privatize public assets and enterprises without the need for special legislative authorization.[7]

It must be stressed, however, that enactment of a law may be necessary even when it is not required by the constitution. As the following chapters suggest, a law may be essential in order to amend certain legislative provisions in force.

Togo: Privatizations had been carried out without any special enabling legislation. The 1979 constitution did not list privatization among the matters that are within the exclusive jurisdiction of parliament. This situation changed, however, with the constitutional revision of October 14, 1992. The constitution's new article 84 provided that "the rules concerning . . . nationalization of enterprises and transfer of ownership of public-sector enterprises to the private sector" shall be set by law. The government prepared a draft law to that effect in 1994. In the end, a privatization ordinance "executed as a law of the state" was adopted on June 10, 1994.

5. Article 111 of the 1992 constitution stipulates: "When the State decides to transfer public enterprises or its shareholdings therein to the private sector, it shall confer a preferential right on the employees and other operators directly connected with those enterprises. The manner in which this preemptive right is granted shall be regulated by law."

6. "In New Zealand, unless there is specific legislation to the contrary, the Government and individual Ministers of the Government are regarded as having power to sell Government assets. A notable exception is section 11 of the SOE Act, which prohibits the sale or other disposal of shares in companies named in a schedule to the Act (being the SOEs established by virtue of that Act). This schedule included Post Office Bank Limited and Telecom Corporation of New Zealand Limited, which have since been sold. Before their sale, the SOE Act was amended (in the case of Telecom, by the Finance Act 1990) to remove the name of those companies from the schedule to the SOE Act" (Williams and Franks, 1992, p. 67, para. 200).

7. "The natural reaction of government lawyers is to legislate to achieve the result desired by the Government. Commercial lawyers, on the other hand, do not normally have that luxury and therefore seek more commercial means of achieving their client's objective. With privatization, the Government is seeking to turn a Government Business Enterprise into a commercial enterprise operating in the market place in exactly the same way as other corporations. . . . When it comes to legislation, we should legislate to the minimum degree necessary, rather than the maximum possible" (Sly and Weigall 1991, pp. 66, 67).

Malaysia and the United Kingdom, for example, had to enact laws to corporatize SOEs organized under public law, so they might later be privatized.[8]
On the other hand, the objectives of privatization can sometimes be
achieved without a law, despite explicit constitutional language requiring
special legislation.[9]

Limits on the Discretion of the Government

Constitutional provisions may also help limit the extent of the government's
discretionary powers regarding privatization. Comparison of the French
and British examples is particularly instructive.[10]

First, the constitutional requirement that implementation of a privatization program be authorized by law subjects the French government to prior
parliamentary control. In the United Kingdom, where this obligation does
not exist, the government can sidestep such control unless a law is necessary
for some other reason, which has most often been the case (see note 8).

Valuation of the assets to be privatized also demonstrates an appreciable
difference in constraints imposed on the French and U.K. governments. In
France, the Constitutional Council, which is responsible for verifying the
constitutionality of laws before they are promulgated,[11] has ruled that the
constitutional principle of equality among all citizens and article 17 of the
Declaration of Human Rights, which mandates the payment of just compensation when property is confiscated, prohibit the transfer of public
assets to private investors at less than real value. The council judged that
enterprises to be privatized therefore had to be valued by independent

---

8. *United Kingdom*: Most privatizations have required legislation to turn the SOE into a limited
liability company whose shares could then be sold (see the appendix for a list of these laws). For
SOEs already organized under company law, this conversion was not required, and privatization could proceed without prior parliamentary authorization, as was the case for British Petroleum (see Graham and Prosser 1991, p. 83).

Malaysia: For the partial divestiture of Port Kelang Container Terminal in 1986, special legislation "was passed by Parliament to enable and facilitate the privatization exercise." The port
authority did not possess the needed powers under the Port Authorities Act of 1963 to create a
subsidiary governed by company law. The act therefore had to be amended to authorize the
establishment of KCT (Kelang Container Terminal) as a subsidiary, a preliminary step to the sale
of 51 percent of the capital of the new company to KTK, jointly owned by KN (a public enterprise,
80 percent) and POAL (an Australian private company, 20 percent). In addition, the Pensions Act
of 1980 had to be amended to allow employees of the new company to keep their pension benefits accrued while working for the port authority. See Jones and Abbas 1992, chapter 13, notes 13
and 17; see also chapter 4 concerning the corporatization of SOEs.

9. In cases where divestiture would require enabling legislation, but the government's primary concerns are speed and ease of implementation, or where it wishes to avoid seeking parliamentary approval, enabling legislation may sometimes be dispensed with by using a method of
transfer to the private sector other than divestiture, such as concessions or leases (see table 5.1).

10. This comparison draws on Prosser 1990 and Graham and Prosser 1991.

11. Article 61 of the constitution provides that a law may be submitted to the Constitutional
Council by the president of the republic, the prime minister, the president of the assembly, the
president of the senate, or a group of sixty deputies or senators.

experts and that no sale be allowed at a price below that determined by these experts. In the United Kingdom, in contrast, privatization transactions are examined only after the fact by the National Audit Office and the Public Accounts Committee.[12]

Finally, the French Constitutional Council intervened again to try to regulate use of the golden share technique by the minister of the economy (golden shares are discussed further in chapters 5 and 7). The privatization laws enacted in France in both 1986 and 1993 provide that, in any company to be privatized, the government may be granted a golden share that would enable the minister of the economy to reject any sales allowing a shareholder to amass more than a given percentage of the company's capital (see box 5.3). The council accepted the constitutionality of these provisions, but only on the condition that the minister justify each use of this right of veto and the judiciary be empowered to overrule the minister's decisions. In the United Kingdom, where privatization conditions and procedures need not be authorized by law, the rules governing the use of golden shares are contained in the articles of association of the enterprise concerned. This contractual arrangement limits the basis for judicial intervention. Some articles of association also contain provisions ruling out appeals of any kind (see section 40.12 of the British Gas articles cited in Prosser 1990) and explicitly stating that no justification need be given if the government exercises the powers conferred on it by such golden shares (see sections 43.k and 44.m of the Rolls Royce articles cited in Prosser 1990).

Clearly then, there is no equivalent in the United Kingdom for the provisions in the French constitution that grant the parliament and Constitutional Council some control over the government's privatization activities. The benefits of the French system must, however, be weighed against the costs of procedures that could become cumbersome and lengthy.[13]

Control of Constitutionality of Privatization Legislation

In France, as illustrated in the previous section, a constitutional court may review legislation before its promulgation. In Poland, President Lech Walesa referred to the constitutional court a new privatization law that had been approved by parliament in July 1995 over his earlier veto; grounds for referral were that it violated the separation of powers between the executive

12. The distinction between the French and British procedures is narrowing, however, under the influence of European law. For example, the financial terms of privatization transactions can be examined beforehand by the European Commission, pursuant to article 93 of the Treaty of Rome concerning state assistance. Thus the British government, which had undertaken to inject £547 million into the Rover Group at the time of its buyout by British Aerospace, was compelled to limit its assistance to £294 million after intervention by the commission.

13. One may, for example, question the usefulness of the requirement found in some laws to carry out a systematic valuation of the enterprise in every privatization transaction. These issues are examined in greater detail in chapter 5.

and legislative branches by requiring specific parliamentary approval for privatization transactions in numerous "strategic" sectors (see box 5.4 and Borish and Noël 1996, pp. 69, 156). The court ruled that this new law was indeed unconstitutional.

Constitutional challenges to privatization legislation have become a regular feature in Turkey. In July 1994 Turkey's constitutional court ruled that privatization enabling Law no. 3987, which authorized the government to privatize through the issuance of statutory decrees, was illegal because this power belonged exclusively to parliament. As a result of this ruling, the statutory decrees already issued to execute this law also become null and void, and the whole privatization program came to a new halt (see *Financial Times*, 13 July 1994; *Privatisation Yearbook 1995*, p. 158). A previous privatization law had already been struck down by the constitutional court. On February 28, 1996, the constitutional court annulled parts of Law no. 4000 authorizing the sale of up to 39 percent of the shares of Türk Telekom (see *Middle East Economic Digest*, 8 March 1996).

In India, members of parliament, public interest groups, labor unions, and operators filed petitions with the supreme court contesting the government's telecommunications privatization policy and the award of specific licenses. The court ruled in February 1996 that policy matters were in the ambit of the legislative and executive branches, not of the courts. It rejected the petitions against the privatization program and upheld the validity of the bidding procedures and the government's powers to grant the disputed licenses (see *Journal of Commerce*, 18 January 1996 and 22 February 1996).

Lawsuits contesting the constitutionality of privatization legislation or specific provisions thereof, or the government's right to privatize without enabling legislation, have also been filed in other countries. In Colombia, for example, the constitutional court ordered the suspension of the privatization of financial SOEs in the absence of enabling legislation (*Privatisation International*, January 1996, p. 29).

International Law

The conduct of privatization transactions in a given country can also be affected by the international treaties and agreements to which it is a party.[14] Many countries, on all continents, have entered into regional agreements on

14. The text or overviews of international economic agreements can be found in a number of publications, including: *International Economic Law Basic Documents*, Philip Kunig, Niels Lau, and Werner Meng (Eds.), Berlin-New York, Walter de Gruyter, 1989; *Basic Documents of International Economic Law*, Stephen Zamora and Ronald A. Brand (Eds), Chicago, Commerce Clearing House, 1990; and *Accords économiques internationaux. Répertoire des accords et des institutions*, Bernard Colas (Ed.), Notes et Etudes Documentaires, La Documentation Française, Paris, Wilson & Lafleur, 1990, which is a useful guide to such treaties and includes the countries that have acceded.

trade, customs controls, or broader economic integration. Examples are the European Union (EU), Mercosur (Latin America), Caricom (Caribbean), NAFTA (North America), and ASEAN (Southeast Asia). Such regional agreements often generate supranational law or foster harmonization of legislation in their member countries.

The impact on privatization of legal obligations deriving from the EU treaty, for instance, is very significant, even though the treaty itself is neutral regarding type of ownership.[15] The abolition of customs barriers, the liberalization of formerly monopolistic markets, and the imposition of common competition rules on private as well as public enterprises all foster the entry of private operators. Privatization is one of the options most governments must consider in order to reduce public-sector debt and deficits and meet the macroeconomic criteria set by the Maastricht treaty for joining the new European currency. Similarly, the scale of investments needed to upgrade water and sanitation systems to the new European standards is such that many governments must draw in the private sector to help pay for and carry out such investments. Furthermore, many provisions of European law will apply to the implementation of a privatization program. Examples include the rules on merger controls, the prohibition of state aid to enterprises, and the prohibition of discrimination among nationals of member states of the European Union, which means, for example, that foreign nationals must be allowed to acquire holdings in the capital of privatized enterprises on the same footing as local citizens. Portugal and France were told to amend their privatization legislation to abolish limits imposed on shareholdings by investors from other EU member countries (see box 5.2).

Bilateral agreements may also raise special privatization issues. This is the case for the privatization of airlines. Bilateral agreements governing air traffic between the signatory states often require that "substantial ownership" or "effective control" of the designated companies be held by a signatory state or by nationals thereof (see Rapp and Vellas 1992, p. 51). An airline privatization that would transfer control to foreign investors could hence block the application of these agreements and result in the loss of some of the airline's main assets, that is, its routes. There are ways to limit this risk. For example, when British Airways was privatized a golden share was awarded to the government, which allowed it to oppose any foreign acquisition of shares.

In the case of KLM, particularly strict measures were taken, as indicated in box 2.3: the government holds a call option that allows it to regain a majority shareholding if needed; in addition, the bylaws of the company provide that a majority of the members of the supervisory board shall be nominated by the government. For similar reasons, the Belgian government limited the

---

15. Article 222 of the Treaty of Rome states: "This Treaty shall in no way prejudice the rules in Member States governing the system of property ownership." See also the section of chapter 7 regarding the European policy in the telecommunications sector.

Box 2.3   Impact of International Agreements on Privatization: The Case of KLM

KLM was created in 1919 on a purely private basis. It was not until 1929 that a majority of shares was transferred to the state. In March 1986, on the eve of privatization, the state held 54.9 percent of the company's capital. The privatization procedure was original: the company bought back a portion of the state's shares and undertook to resell them, together with 12 million newly issued shares, to a bank syndicate commissioned to place them. This reduced the share of the state to 38.2 percent of the capital. In addition, specific measures were taken to strengthen the government's control over the company, with the purpose, in particular, to prevent jeopardizing the bilateral air traffic agreements concluded between the Netherlands and other countries.

The Dutch government signed an agreement with KLM providing that the state would lose its majority interest in the share capital of KLM as a result of the issue of common shares by KLM and of the sale of common KLM shares by the state. A provision was included allowing the state to regain its majority interest at short notice, if that were desirable for reasons of air transport policy or to prevent an undesired accumulation of power in the general meeting of shareholders.

Under the agreement KLM granted the state the option to purchase 18,000,000 B preference shares. The State could exercise this option if necessary and reasonable, in particular when (a) "under one or more international agreements or one or more licenses granted by whatever country, limitations or aggravating conditions would be imposed on the operation by KLM of scheduled services because substantial or majority ownership of KLM would no longer be demonstrably Dutch"; or (b) it is necessary to prevent one person or company or a group of persons or companies from acquiring a stake in KLM that would result in an undesirable balance of power in the general shareholders' meeting.

In addition, the government was granted, by virtue of an amendment to the company's articles of association, a majority of the seats on the supervisory board of the company, even though it is only a minority shareholder. The new paragraph 13 of article 20 of KLM's articles of association provides that "the State of the Netherlands shall appoint the smallest possible majority of the Supervisory Board".

Source: Rapp and Vellas 1992, pp. 61–91.

---

stake of Sabena it sold to Swissair in 1995 to 49.5 percent of the capital, with an option to increase it to 62.25 percent after the year 2000, when more liberal international rules may be in place.[16] Techniques of this sort have the merit of allowing airlines to be privatized without requiring renegotiation of the many existing international agreements. The fact remains, however, that

---

16. See *Financial Times*, 28 February 1996. This takeover was approved by the European Commission in July 1995; one of the conditions was that new entry take place on the Brussels-Zurich route, where the Swissair group (including Sabena) would otherwise have had a near monopoly.

the limits they impose on shareholding by foreign investors may well reduce the benefits, in terms of revenue or efficiency, that such privatizations could otherwise yield.[17]

Bilateral agreements in many other fields (concerning, for example, double taxation or investment promotion) can also affect privatization transactions by, say, partly covering gaps in the legislation of a signatory country, at least for investors of the other country. Finally, an interesting, if highly unusual, international agreement is the German Unification Treaty of 1990, which pursuant to its article 25 incorporates the East German privatization law, with some amendments, into German law.

Conclusion

The norms examined in this chapter are generally considered to have precedence over ordinary law. They are by and large binding on legislators and governments and cannot be amended except through lengthy and arduous procedures. Specific constitutional provisions and certain treaties might therefore have to be amended, no matter how onerous this procedure might be, to facilitate implementation of the privatization program.

This is particularly so for countries with socialist constitutions. Moreover, constitutional provisions may prohibit the privatization of an economic sector such as natural resources or infrastructure, subject it to special rules and limitations, or restrict foreign investment. In many cases, however, suitable legal techniques are available to allow the legislator or government to circumvent obstacles that may appear to be major constraints.

Other constitutions allow privatization but make it conditional on particular safeguards. Thus the constitutions or constitutional principles in many countries prescribe that a law be enacted to authorize the privatization of SOEs (or some of them). Privatization programs may be subject to control by the courts of their constitutionality.

Nor should the importance of treaties and other international agreements be underestimated. Witness the impact of bilateral civil aviation treaties on airline privatization and of many provisions of EU law on privatization in member states.

Finally, basic legal principles, including constitutional principles, matter because they establish the framework within which all activity (economic or other) takes place. They may inspire confidence or they may promote

17. A government preparing an airline privatization would rarely have the time to renegotiate all these bilateral air transport agreements in advance or to agree on a new interpretation. In some cases governments may agree to give a relatively wide interpretation to the terms "substantial ownership" and "effective control" contained in the agreements they have signed. A lower domestic shareholding could be regarded as adequate in certain circumstances (for example, when it constitutes a minority holding sufficient to block important decisions). See Rapp and Vellas 1992, p. 57.

skepticism. A legal system that functions efficiently and guarantees respect for the rights of citizens and economic agents, especially regarding owner-ship and contracts, can only facilitate successful development of a market economy and the privatization process itself.

3

Privatization in a Market Economy

A legal environment that fosters private-sector development is essential to the success of a privatization program.[1] For example, rules defining and protecting ownership and ensuring fair competition among economic operators, commercial law provisions affecting the privatization process itself (directly or indirectly), or legislation governing the functioning of the privatized enterprises will all have a substantial impact on the implementation of the privatization program.

Because of their importance, some of the legal provisions examined in this chapter may need to be amended, suspended, or repealed to permit or facilitate privatization. For example, measures that discriminate against the private sector will have to be abolished. Many countries have radically redefined the role of the state in the economy to create and maintain a level playing field that allows private entrepreneurs to engage in economic activity free from unfair competition or interference from government agencies. In doing so, they have shifted the focus of state intervention: the public sector is no longer directly involved in productive activities; it now plays regulatory and promotional roles.[2] As mentioned in the introduction to this book, such a change is equivalent more to privatizing the entire economy than to privatizing an enterprise or a specific economic sector. It calls for major adjustments at all levels; hence, a strong political commitment is

---

1. Some countries have attempted to privatize in the absence of minimum rules governing the functioning of a market economy. That happened, for example, in Guinea immediately following the Sékou Touré era. A fairly large privatization program was implemented in 1986–87. In view of the uncertainties of the legislation in force, the privatization agreements had to be ratified by presidential ordinance, giving them force of law. Despite this legal protection, the success of the program was less than complete: many privatized enterprises ran into difficulties in restarting production and achieving financial viability. The country's generally unfavorable business climate played a considerable role in this outcome.

2. Even in core public services, the traditional role of the state has been radically revisited in many countries, with increasingly strong participation by private operators in the provision of such services. On this subject, see chapters 1 and 7.

essential not only to push through a legislative reform program that includes privatization but also to ensure its effective implementation.

Rules that govern business activity in a country need to be reviewed before the launch of the privatization program to determine whether they are compatible with the proposed measures. This analysis should clarify whether the proposed divestiture program can be implemented within the existing legal framework or whether legislation must be modified to allow or facilitate privatization. Ideally, all the laws described in the following sections would already be in place, providing a legal framework favorable to private-sector development in general and to privatization operations in particular.

In practice, however, especially in developing and transition countries, the reform effort must focus on the core part of the legal framework that must be in place if the privatization process is to succeed. Any other approach would cause endless delay. The scope of such essential legal reforms will depend on the specific characteristics of each country and each privatization program. The relative importance of the shortcomings or inadequacies identified in relation to this ideal environment must first be established.

Needed reforms should then be undertaken by directly amending the pertinent legal instruments or by incorporating amending provisions in the privatization legislation. These amendments can be either general in scope or restricted to the privatizations carried out pursuant to the law. Many of the topics examined in this chapter have been covered by special provisions of privatization laws.[3]

This overview of the overall environment for economic activity starts with property rights, followed by competition policy and law. A broad range of laws affecting business activity is then covered, including contract law, company law, accounting, and so on. A special section on social legislation covers labor issues, employee ownership, and pensions. The chapter concludes with sections on environmental legislation, dispute settlement mechanisms, and foreign legislation.

Property Rights

Property rights are the backbone of a market economy and are normally protected by a country's constitution or constitutional tradition. As discussed in chapter 2, some constitutions or legal systems, especially those of communist countries, do not recognize the right to private ownership. In such cases the constitution will have to be amended to allow privatization to take place,

---

3. Chapter 5 deals only with the basic enabling provisions of such laws, namely those that authorize and govern the actual privatization process. Specific provisions enacted in many countries to remedy the deficiencies of the existing legal framework are addressed in chapters 2 and 4 as well as this one.

as happened in recent years in central and eastern Europe (1989–90), the former Soviet republics (1991–92), and other countries, such as Viet Nam (1992) and Guinea-Bissau (1991).

In essence, privatization is the transfer of ownership over given assets from a public entity to a private one. Ownership rights are therefore vitally important.[4] They encompass a bundle of legally recognized rights, in particular the right to use and control assets (including voting rights), to draw economic benefits from ownership (return on assets, including rent, interest, or dividends), to dispose of such assets (for example, by selling, donating, or destroying them), and to transfer any of the above rights to others. These rights may be restricted by law, but not to the point where they would become meaningless. Hence, one can speak of full ownership only if the owner is able to exercise these various rights.

Earlier reforms in many transition countries carried out before privatization exacerbated problems with property rights. Under the pure communist model, all property belongs to the state, yet during the transition process various stakeholders were given increasing elements of property rights. Managers and employees of SOEs were, for instance, given control rights that elsewhere would belong to the owners. These acquired rights could not be ignored at the time of privatization. In Poland, for example, the government could not sell SOE assets without the agreement of the workers' council of the SOE. "Attempts by the government in 1990 to abolish this right of veto through changes in the enterprise law provoked strong resistance by the Councils and could not get through the parliament. This shows that the question of ownership was by no means clear and that workers reasonably expected a preferential treatment in the course of privatization" (Albrecht and Thum 1994, p. 714). As part of the corporatization policy of Poland's 1990 privatization law, the state treasury became the legal owner of enterprises while the workers' councils were dissolved.

Successful privatization depends on the ability to transfer free and clear ownership titles. In preparing a privatization program, several items must be unambiguous: how ownership rights are defined in the country concerned; how private ownership rights are recognized and protected; what restrictions, if any, are placed on the transferability of those rights; how the titling, registration, and cadastre mechanisms function (or in what ways they are deficient); what enforcement mechanisms exist to protect the rights of individuals, and, particularly, how effective the judicial system is; what restrictions may be placed on foreigners with respect to the acquisition and exercise of ownership rights for certain types of property, such as land or other real-estate assets; and so on. It is important also to ascertain whether proper procedures exist to establish mortgages and other forms of collateral and to determine how effective foreclosure procedures are.

---

4. This section addresses private ownership; issues relating to public ownership are dealt with in chapter 4.

Privatization legislation should remove any obstacles that arise when a country's property regime is unclear, ownership rights are not properly protected, or restrictions are imposed on the acquisition of property by foreigners or other groups. If that is not feasible, or if doing so would excessively delay startup of the privatization program, other methods for circumventing these obstacles might be considered, including contractual methods such as leasing (see also table 5.1).

Past Nationalizations

As noted in the introduction to this book, the current privatization wave follows a long period of nationalization of private enterprises and assets. Privatization often reverses these transactions. Ascertaining the rights of former owners whose property was confiscated, expropriated, or nationalized may require detailed investigation. Did expropriation take place legally,[5] and do the former owners (or their heirs) still possess legally protected rights over the assets to be privatized? Were they properly compensated or indemnified, or do they have outstanding financial claims against the state? Are there various categories of previous owners, and, if so, have they all been treated in the same way? Are the claims subject to a statute of limitations or some other time frame? This section focuses on the situation of former communist countries, where these have been particularly thorny issues, especially in view of the sheer scope of past nationalizations and the variety of nationalization regimes involved.[6]

Should a detailed analysis of these issues be required, and should it reveal that the previous owners still possess enforceable legal rights, a fair balance must be struck between these rights and those of other parties, such as current occupants or new owners in good faith, taking into account also the potential cost of restoring the situation that prevailed before expropriation. These matters will often have to be clarified or settled by means of law.

Some countries have opted for restitution as a way to redress expropriations that took place illegally or without proper compensation. This formula may work satisfactorily where the expropriation laws were limited in scope and were applied relatively recently. In most other situations, however, assets are likely to become the subject of conflicting claims that will need to

5. Unfortunately, laws are not always fair. In some legal systems, unfair laws may also be illegal under certain conditions. The term "legally" means in accordance with the laws of the country, whether they are fair or not. Legality and justice are two different concepts.

6. In East Germany, for example, some assets were expropriated by the Nazi regime, others between 1945 and 1949 under the Soviet military government, and still others after 1949 by the East German communist regime. Some of these expropriations were carried out pursuant to law and others by arbitrary decision of the government. Appropriate compensation was paid in some cases but not in others. Statutes of limitation may apply. Depending on the circumstances of each case, the expropriated owner (or the owner's heirs) may or may not have legally protected rights.

be resolved. In some cases, titles or other documents evidencing previous ownership and transfers will no longer exist. Moreover, the previous owners may be deceased and different heirs may claim the same piece of property. The assets may have been developed, destroyed, or even leased or resold to a private party acting in good faith.[7] In Romania, for example, no fewer than 300,000 claims were filed in the courts as a result of restitution of alternative plots of land to former owners whose original land had, since expropriation, been converted to nonagricultural use (see World Bank 1996, p. 59). To make matters worse, the judicial systems of these countries are rarely able to adjudicate the multitude of claims that restitution laws generate. To avoid overloading the courts and to ensure more uniform treatment of claims, some countries have set up commissions or other special bodies to examine claims made by previous owners.[8]

Finally, because they foster substantial uncertainty about ownership rights, restitution laws can discourage investment, particularly foreign investment.[9] It was mainly this consideration that led the German authorities to amend their system of restitution. Indeed, the German privatization law of 1990 initially made restitution the primary method of redress for owners whose property had been unjustly confiscated. This formula proved to be impossible to apply, however, because most assets were the subject of conflicting claims; the privatization process ground to a standstill. The German parliament had to enact a "law to remove the obstacles to privatization of businesses and promote investment" (law of March 22, 1991). That law added a new article 3 (a) to the 1990 law on the settlement of disputed ownership issues, authorizing fast privatization of assets essential for investment or business purposes, regardless of outstanding restitution claims. In a statement made in Washington, D.C., on November 14, 1991, Birgit Breuel, then president of the Treuhandanstalt, stressed that new investors able to preserve jobs or provide additional investment should take precedence over former owners. Special provisions authorized the Treuhandanstalt, for a specified period (to the end of 1992), to sell disputed assets while limiting the rights of the former owners to monetary compensation from the Treuhandanstalt. This amendment substantially speeded up implementation of Germany's privatization program.

7. As Vaclav Klaus, then minister of finance of Czechoslovakia, stated in a letter of June 21, 1991, to a Czech emigre, "It is not possible to ask for the surrender of property from people who have acquired it from the State in good faith, i.e. not through illegal means."

8. See, for example, Ghana's 1979 decree setting up a "Confiscated Assets (Recovery and Disposal) Committee." See also Horn 1992, p. 26, concerning East Germany: "Successful restitutions, however, amount only to 5 percent of all restitution claims [filed by] Spring 1992. More than one million of such claims have been filed, and the great majority has still to be channeled through a special bureaucracy, the offices on open questions of property."

9. See, in particular, Gelpern 1993, pp. 325–26, which refers to a joint statement made in Czechoslovakia in February 1991 by 27 economists denouncing the burden placed on foreign investments by restitution laws.

Any country that opts for restitution must set a deadline for filing claims. After that deadline, it should be possible to privatize unclaimed assets with free and clear title; the rights of previous owners would either lapse or give rise to monetary compensation by the government.[10] Such a measure would limit the spate of postprivatization suits by former owners against the new owners that occurred in Czechoslovakia and other countries, to the detriment of the privatization programs.

In practice, the choice between restitution and compensation will be based largely on political and historical considerations. In Czechoslovakia, for example, where several laws have been enacted to deal with this matter, restitution was considered necessary to mark a definite break with a communist regime which, after the Soviet invasion of 1968, had become one of the most conservative in eastern Europe.[11] The law concerning the alleviation of certain injustices regarding ownership was probably one of the most popular and least controversial restitution laws, because it aimed at restoring assets confiscated from numerous small owners under nationalizations imposed on the morrow of the Soviet intervention of 1956. In Poland, on the other hand, the lack of special legislation concerning the rights of former owners is explained in part by the power of the unions, which are traditionally opposed to restitution on grounds of equity.

Granting compensation makes it possible to indemnify former owners, who had been illegally or unjustly dispossessed, without all the drawbacks associated with restitution. This route does, however, present other problems. Budget constraints, in particular, can prevent governments from properly compensating former owners, as has been the case in Hungary, for example (see box 3.1). This explains the low popularity of this system with dispossessed owners.

Generally speaking, though, compensation is usually preferable to restitution. Paying compensation is often both more efficient and more equitable than restitution. All affected parties can be treated in the same way, regardless of the eventual disposition of the assets they once owned. By separating the assets to be privatized from the claims to which they give rise, compensation formulas allow the government to privatize previously nationalized assets unencumbered. The buyers receive clear title, and any residual claims are pursued against the state (or another public entity), not against the new owner. Where appropriate, this system can be supplemented by granting the

10. The Bulgarian privatization law of April 1992 follows this procedure: previous owners can file a restitution claim within the two months following the date of publication of the decision to privatize an enterprise. After that deadline, owners can no longer ask for restitution but only for compensation by the state.

11. Law no. 403/90 of October 2, 1990, pertaining to the alleviation of certain injustices concerning ownership (the small restitution law) dealt with property confiscated after 1955; Law no. 87/91 of February 21, 1991, known as the extrajudicial rehabilitation law, or large federal restitution law, set February 25, 1948 (the first day of the communist regime), as the relevant date for restitution purposes; and Law no. 229/91 of May 21, 1991, dealt with the adjustment of rights pertaining to land and other agricultural assets.

Box 3.1 Compensation of Former Owners in Hungary

Hungary is one of the few central and eastern European countries not using restitution. Owners of assets expropriated by the state after June 8, 1949 (that is, under the communist regime), had to be compensated under the 1991 compensation law. However, total compensation was capped at 5 million forints (about $50,000) and calculated at regressive rates, using a formula that takes account of location and size in the case of land and buildings and of number of employees in the case of businesses. Moreover, the government did not pay the compensation in cash but in the form of interest-bearing bonds negotiable on the securities exchange and usable for buying privatized public assets (including company shares).

A 1991 article in the *Washington Post*, "Hungary's Compensation Promise Proves Hollow for Many Claimants," stated: "The 'compensation bonds' are viewed skeptically because the government has not specified which companies or apartments they can be redeemed for. Many Hungarians concluded that they would be offered only the worst of the state's assets. And just getting the dubious bonds is difficult because the government is demanding stringent documentation for each claim. . . . Applicants must provide an array of documents that are difficult to obtain. Land deeds are essential, but many families lost them over the past four decades. Often the deeds were taken by the Communist authorities." Claims are examined by regional compensation offices whose decisions can be appealed to the courts.

In addition, the former owners enjoyed a preemptive right to purchase their former assets when these were put up for sale by the government or some other public agency, except in the case of rental housing, where priority for purchase was given to tenants. Moreover, part of the equity of newly transformed enterprises or of the proceeds from privatization was allocated to a compensation fund.

The choice of compensation over restitution was explained in the preamble to the Hungarian law by the need to develop a market economy, which makes it necessary to minimize uncertainty about ownership of assets. The preamble also points out that former owners are not the only people to have suffered under the old regime.

It is estimated that, as part of this program, compensation coupons with a redemption value of over 200 billion forints (over $1.5 billion) were issued to over one million Hungarians. The supply of state assets for which such coupons could be exchanged was, however, quite inadequate for some years, which severely depressed their market value. In early 1994 they were trading at about half their nominal value; brokers or other intermediaries bought them at a discount, hired people to stand in line at privatization auctions, and participated in such auctions using the compensation coupons at their face value to pay for privatized assets. On January 25, 1996, when APV RT, the state holding and privatization agency, decided to set aside for coupon holders about 8 percent of the shares in the country's six power distribution companies and smaller percentages of other major energy companies, the price of the coupons jumped from 35 to 195 forints; by February 6, they had reached 257 forints, which was still only about a quarter of their face value.

Sources: Finance East Europe, 9 February 1996, pp. 9–10; *Privatisation Yearbook 1995*, p. 53; *Euromoney*, March 1994, pp. 15–16; *Washington Post*, 26 October 1991, p. A14. For a study of the main judicial means of redress before the enactment of this law, see "Hungary: The Constitutional Politics of Compensation," *Soviet & East European Law* 2 (4), Colombia University, June 1991.

former owners a preemptive right to, for example, buy back their assets at the price offered by the highest bidder at auction.

Future Expropriations

Depending on specific country circumstances, investors may demand guarantees against renationalization before they will commit themselves financially. Acceptable legislation on the eminent domain right of the state, which spells out the government's expropriation powers, is crucial in this respect. In practice, all countries reserve the right to expropriate property, against fair compensation, if the public interest so requires (for the construction of major infrastructure projects—roads, ports, railways, airports, and so on—for example). These expropriation rights must, however, be limited in scope and subject to judicial review.

The existence of suitable expropriation legislation does not in itself guarantee that unfair or politically motivated expropriation will not take place: the legislation may be suspended or amended and the authorities may decide to ignore it. Investors will take due account in calculating their risk of any uncertainty about the powers that the authorities retain to expropriate assets or to amend this legislation.[12]

Intellectual Property

Investment decisions, whether made by foreigners or nationals, rely on the existence and effective enforcement of laws protecting intellectual property, including international agreements to which the country is a party and domestic laws concerning patents, trademarks, copyright, trade secrets, know-how, and licenses, among other things. The tax laws determine the extent to which revenue from the transfer of technology (royalties, for example) is taxed by the state. Many countries also have specific laws or provisions for the protection of intellectual property in specified sectors of the economy (pharmaceutical products, for example).

In privatization transactions, investors will seek not only reassurance concerning the overall legislative framework for protection of intellectual property but sometimes also supplementary protection, which will not necessarily be consistent with the country's competition laws. Investors may also resist attempts by the privatizing government to compel them to transfer specific technology or licenses to the privatized enterprise. It is not uncommon for countries to simultaneously pursue a privatization program and a program to strengthen protection of intellectual property. For example, in

---

12. Insurance against political and noncommercial risks can be obtained from the Multilateral Investment Guarantee Agency (MIGA) and also from national or private insurance entities. The World Bank (IBRD) also has a guarantee program covering political risks in the broader sense, including expropriation and noncompliance by a government or other public agency with its contractual obligations.

1992 Peru embarked on a major privatization program; toward the end of that same year, it also set up a new agency responsible for the protection of competition and intellectual property. All was part of an ambitious policy for economic deregulation and modernization.[13]

Protecting and Promoting Competition

Yarrow made the point a decade ago already that "in general, competition and regulation are likely to be more important determinants of economic performance than ownership. Hence, where there are deficiencies in these areas, the policy priority should normally be to increase competition and improve regulation, not to transfer productive activities to the private sector. Indeed, preoccupation with the ownership question is likely to be damaging if it distracts attention from the more fundamental issues" (Yarrow 1986, p. 364). The protection of competition and, more generally, the creation and enforcement of a level playing field in the marketplace are among the most important and complex functions of government, affecting many different areas of economic policy and law and calling for a high level of bureaucratic competence. Preprivatization reforms and restructuring measures will often be required to create the requisite competitive environment (see also the section in chapter 4 on prior restructuring of SOEs).

Nondiscrimination against the Private Sector

Absence of discrimination between the private and public sectors is an essential part of competition policy and a particularly important factor in privatization transactions. The private sector must be allowed to compete with the public sector on an equal footing. This implies, among other things, removal of subsidies, including public loan guarantees, at least in the case of SOEs operating in competitive sectors (public finance and SOE legislation); harmonization or alignment of the tax systems applied to SOEs and private enterprises (tax legislation); uniform application of environmental law, labor law, and other legislation affecting areas of economic life important to all enterprises; removal of entry barriers hampering the private sector (sector legislation); and equal access to public contracts (public procurement regulations). Establishment and maintenance of this level playing field must be protected by law. In some countries—Brazil, for example—this type of guarantee is even found in the constitution.[14]

---

13. Pressure by the U.S. government played no small part in Peru's efforts to strengthen mechanisms for the protection of intellectual property. See *Wall Street Journal*, 15 April 1994, p. A9. See also box 1.1.

14. Article 173 of the 1988 constitution provides that public corporations, joint-venture companies, and other public entities that engage in economic activity are subject to the same legal system as private companies, including labor and tax rules (paragraph 1); in addition, public corporations and joint-venture companies shall not enjoy any tax privileges that are not extended to the private sector (paragraph 2).

Abolishing preferential treatment for SOEs in public procurement is often a vital component of good competition policy. The public contracting system is important not only from the standpoint of public finances (cost control) and public ethics (fraud prevention). In most countries, the state and the public sector in general, including municipalities, SOEs, and other public entities, are by far the largest potential customers for goods and services. Retaining access to this market is of vital importance for an investor in a newly privatized company. A fair and transparent public procurement system, consistently applied, is the best guarantee for that investor.

Price Liberalization

Free and autonomous price setting by businesses—subject only to certain limits to prevent or penalize abuses—is essential to the sound functioning of a competitive market economy (see the section below on antitrust legislation). Price liberalization should normally precede privatization, especially in countries with heavy price controls (central and eastern Europe in the early 1990s and India, for example). Without freedom to set prices, few investors would be interested in acquiring SOEs. Moreover, if an SOE were sold at a relatively low price because price controls were hampering profitability, subsequent price liberalization could produce windfall profits for the investors. This outcome would inevitably reflect badly on the authorities, who would be accused of having sold off the SOE at a bargain price.

Monopolies and Antitrust Provisions

To deter attempts to restrict competition, it may be necessary to enact laws applicable to public and private enterprises that would prohibit the establishment of cartels, trusts, monopolies, and other restrictive business practices. The introduction of such legislation might block certain privatization transactions that would have otherwise proceeded. For example, the acquisition of an SOE or other state-owned asset by one of its competitors could result in excessive concentration. The privatization process should not normally lead to the simple conversion of public monopolies into private ones, or to the formation of monopolistic or oligopolistic situations where one or a few companies control the relevant market without any countervailing checks.[15] Nevertheless, the formulation and enforcement of competition rules involve a cost that sometimes outweighs the benefits they produce.

---

15. Where natural monopolies are privatized as such, they will generally need to be regulated. This topic is examined in greater detail in chapter 7, which deals with the privatization of infrastructure. Account also has to be taken of any existing tariff protection in evaluating monopolistic or oligopolistic situations (see the section below on foreign trade legislation).

The breakup of monopolistic SOEs prior to their privatization, sometimes called demonopolization (see chapter 4), ought to be considered whether or not antitrust laws exist. This route, where feasible, is generally preferable to setting up a complex system of regulation to prevent abuse of dominant positions; this is especially true in countries with less than satisfactory administrative and judicial capacities.[16]

In the presence of natural monopolies, regulation will often be indispensable to prevent the monopoly company from extracting rents by restricting supply of its services and selling them at high prices or otherwise abusing its exclusive market position. In many countries public monopolies have not been subject to regulation, precisely because they were thought (often wrongly) to serve the public interest rather than the profit motive. Privatizing these monopolies calls for the establishment of a regulatory framework for those activities that cannot be exposed to competition (see chapter 7).

Where antitrust legislation does not exist or is ineffective, specific competition rules may also be inserted in tender documents and privatization contracts. Privatization agreements therefore sometimes include provisions that prohibit or restrict the company's potential for horizontal or vertical integration through takeovers.

Finally, it is worth noting that enforcement of antitrust or antimonopoly legislation is often entrusted to a specialized competition commission or office, such as the German federal cartel office or the U.K.'s Office of Fair Trading and Mergers and Monopolies Commission. Sector-specific competition rules, on the other hand, are often subject to special regulatory bodies, as further discussed in chapter 7.

Deregulation

Many countries are burdened by a multitude of rules and institutions governing the exercise of all economic activities. If these countries wish to attract investors, they should streamline these regulations and procedures for obtaining licenses and other official permits required to conduct business. For example, a rule that required the use of products of domestic origin might prohibit an investor from using traditional suppliers (including companies controlled by the investor); the investor might therefore lose interest in participating in the privatization program.

---

16. In an article entitled *Enforcing Anti-Trust Law in Central Europe*, Michael Reynolds wrote that despite the recent enactment in Poland, Hungary, and Czechoslovakia of competition laws modeled on European Community legislation, "newly-privatized enterprises will continue to operate in the context of a heavily concentrated distribution system. It will take a long time to shake off bad habits acquired over some 40 years in a system where markets were shared out with impunity, complete sectors were dominated by a single monopoly and enterprises traded on agreed prices fixed by government. . . . The fundamental question is: how effective will the enforcement of these laws be? Many countries have competition laws on the statute book which are often quietly ignored or enforced half-heartedly." *Financial Times*, 26 September 1991, p. 14.

Since 1991 India has abolished many industrial licensing requirements in pursuit of its liberalization program. Similarly, as part of a broader economic reform program that includes privatization of most of the country's SOEs, President Menem of Argentina signed a decree in October 1991 abolishing dozens of government agencies, including some of the 36 or so agencies involved in regulating foreign trade, and eliminating the often petty controls that beset private business activity (see *Financial Times*, 1 November 1991, p. 8).

Foreign Trade Legislation

Low or moderate external protection (for example, through low tariffs and nontariff barriers) fosters competition through imports. In their negotiations with government, however, investors will often try to have foreign trade legislation either applied or amended to their advantage, something that may conflict with the objective of an efficient and competitive economy. As an example, many investors have sought special protection against competing imports. If a buyer is indeed granted exemption from the normal provisions of a country's foreign trade legislation, this should be done transparently and factored into bid appraisal. An investor will obviously be willing to offer more for a company that is protected against competition from foreign operators on the domestic market. This higher sale price, however, will normally be outweighed by the cost to the economy of granting this protection.[17] Investors will factor in more than tariffs and quotas; among other foreign trade-related issues, they will consider export subsidies, import and export technical controls, and shipping formalities, as well as bilateral, regional, and multilateral trade agreements.

Major Aspects of Business Law

Laws governing business activity determine how attractive a country is for private investment. They also affect privatization operations directly.

Contract Law

Contract law and enforcement mechanisms for private contracts are a cornerstone of the legal framework of a market economy, because they determine how ownership rights are transferred. One of the basic concepts of any legal system is described by the rule of *pacta sunt servanda*, which reflects the obligation of the parties to honor the agreements they make. The subject is

17. Guinea, Togo, and other countries have granted very generous protection in certain privatization operations—for example, in the form of high import tariffs on competing products.

too broad to be studied here. Suffice it to say that contract law is crucially important to private-sector development and to privatization operations, which are always executed by means of contracts, typically through a complex set of closely interlocking contracts.[18]

Company Law

In principle, company law sets the basic rules for establishing, managing, operating, and liquidating companies. Company law authorizes the creation of companies with different types of legal status (with and without limited liability, joint-stock companies, and so on), grants them juridical personality, sets minimum capital requirements, lays down rules governing the sale or transfer of shares, defines the principles governing the distribution of powers within the company (notably the functions and powers of the shareholders' meeting, board of directors, management, and employees), and so on. Generally speaking, company law empowers companies to depart from certain default provisions of the law and to devise their own methods of operation, provided the company's shareholders and creditors are adequately protected. The importance of a good legislative framework governing the operation of companies cannot be overestimated; this point is illustrated by the difficulties many transition countries have encountered because they lacked such a framework (see Gray and Hanson 1993).

Privatization can be facilitated in some instances by unbundling the rights deriving from SOE shares, for example, by separating dividend and other income rights from control and voting rights, or by limiting the rights attached to certain classes of shares. Such modalities may or may not be allowed, however, under existing company or securities legislation. In some countries, such as Mexico and Jamaica, different categories of shares have been issued with different rights; some of the holdings retained by the state in partially privatized companies have been stripped of voting rights while they remain in government hands. A formula of this kind is particularly useful where the government wants to transfer an SOE to private control but does not wish to divest the majority of its shares all at once, either because the capital market is insufficiently developed or because it is counting on the new private management to improve productivity and boost the value of the stock before it puts a second tranche on sale.[19] Likewise, although

18. Moreover, in some economic sectors, such as hotel management, successful privatization may depend on the possibility of concluding and enforcing special types of business contracts, such as management contracts, leasing, or franchising.

19. Some investors may also think that continued state shareholding in the privatized company gives them additional comfort by reducing the risk that the company may be affected by adverse governmental measures. No general answer can be given to the question of whether continued state participation in the capital of a privatized company has a positive or negative effect on investor confidence and therefore on share prices. That will depend largely on the degree of control the government retains and on its reputation with investors.

investors may in some instances not wish to mobilize funds sufficient to buy outright control, they may not invest at all unless they have the right to appoint the company's management team and to designate a majority of board members and are protected by other special provisions, such as a higher quorum and qualified majorities for decisions at shareholder meetings. Company law should permit the adoption of such modalities, either by allowing the creation of different classes of shares or through other mechanisms. This technique has been applied in some privatizations of large infrastructure companies.[20]

Another technique, one that is much less reassuring to private investors, is the allocation to the state of golden shares, which confer powers exceeding those that exist under ordinary company or securities law even though the state may have a minority holding of only one share (see chapters 5 and 7). Another form of unbundling of rights (found in France, for example) is that of investment certificates issued by SOEs, which can be compared to preferred shares without voting rights. The purpose of these certificates was to raise private capital by offering investors an opportunity to share in the enterprise's profits, but without granting them a corresponding share of control.

Private shareholders in a joint-venture company with the government may be entitled, under company law and the company's own articles, to approve all transfers of shares to nonshareholders if the government chooses to divest itself of its holdings. They may also have preemptive rights. Where this is the case, the government may wish to consult the other shareholders first to explore the available options for restructuring or privatization. Moreover, some privatization laws provide for express derogation from ordinary company law to deny minority shareholders the right to block privatization transactions.[21] It may be preferable to avoid provisions of this kind, however, because they amount to a unilateral amendment by the government of a commercial agreement.

Privatization can instead be an excellent opportunity to protect the rights of minority shareholders. This is particularly important where SOEs are privatized in full or in part by public flotation. Lack of proper protection of minority shareholders, especially small ones, may either deter their participation or create important political problems down the road. This is true whether the state (or public sector) remains the controlling shareholder, whether the privatization includes the transfer of a controlling block to a

20. Examples include the privatization of Telmex (Mexico), MATAV (Hungary), and CANTV (Venezuela), three telecommunications companies in which, following a competitive bidding process, a private consortium was selected to take over control of the company with a minority shareholding, with the state remaining, at least in the initial stage, the majority shareholder. See also chapter 7 on the choice of strategic partners.

21. See, for example, article 15 of Senegal's 1987 privatization law, which provides that the provisions of the Civil Code requiring prior approval by the other shareholders of all sales to nonshareholders shall not apply to share transfers carried out pursuant to the privatization law.

single shareholder or group of shareholders, or whether that controlling stake is acquired on the secondary market following the flotation.[22]

Preemptive rights can be exercised by the private as well as public shareholders in a joint-venture company. When public sector shareholders have such rights, one may encounter situations of privatization by omission. The government may decide to waive or not to exercise its right to subscribe to a capital increase in a company; where it has a majority shareholding, that omission may even allow the company to pass into private control, as occurred in the privatization of Lufthansa, for example. The share of the German state in the airline fell from a controlling 51.4 percent of the capital before the 1994 capital increase to a minority 41 percent afterward.

The rules pertaining to the creation, operation, and sale of subsidiaries, affiliates, and branches also influence the choice of privatization techniques. This issue is an important one for many reasons, among them: (a) the proliferation of SOE subsidiaries, subject in many countries to ordinary company law;[23] (b) the existence of state holding companies that are shareholders in a whole series of SOEs; and (c) the fact that private buyers of SOEs are often existing corporations, which may wish to make the acquired company a subsidiary.

On this point, it is interesting to note that the Treuhandanstalt has been involved in legal controversy concerning the extent of its liability for the debts of companies under its control. Indeed, according to German jurisprudence, a parent company is liable for the debts of its subsidiaries if it intervenes in their business affairs or fails to keep its assets clearly separate from those of the subsidiaries (see Horn 1992). The situation is more clearcut in

---

22. A case in point is the gradual divestiture between 1987 and 1993 of the Turkish government's shareholding in Çukurova Elektrik (CEAS), an integrated power utility. Shares were sold in several tranches, some through the Istanbul stock exchange, others by subscription or through block sale. The government's remaining shares were sold in early 1993 to Rumeli Holding, a Turkish family group with broad business interests. CEAS became one of the country's most active stocks. In November 1995 management of the company was placed under the control of the energy ministry following allegations of widespread irregularities, including breach of its license and violation of the rights of minority shareholders. The controlling Uzan family had used CEAS's cash flow to finance its other business interests, including the acquisition of cement factories and a mobile telephone company, while distributing little or no dividends to minority shareholders. The investigation became "a path-finder case in upholding minority shareholder rights, as well as in regulation of privatised companies" *(Financial Times, 7 November 1995).* The Turkish capital markets board appointed a new board, but following a deal struck between the government and the Uzan family, the latter regained control of CEAS in January 1996. A month later, a Turkish court suspended the new board following a claim filed by the capital markets board as part of an attempt to force Rumeli Holding to buy back the shares CEAS bought in the cement and telephone companies. See *Power Europe (Financial Times)*, 26 January 1996; *Power Asia (Financial Times)*, 19 February 1996.

23. This means that privatization of these subsidiaries may be governed solely by ordinary company law and may therefore be effected by decision of the competent organ of the SOE, without special government or legislative decision. See also the section in chapter 4 on ownership rights and the section in chapter 5 on the scope of legislation.

Italy, where the state, if it is the sole shareholder of a company organized under private law, can be held liable for the company's debts beyond the amount of its corporate capital.

Company law is often unnecessarily complicated, ambiguous, or defective. It may therefore be necessary to redraft, amend, or simplify those laws and regulations to tailor them to the needs of the privatization program. Changes will sometimes be necessary, for example, to allow a company to be set up speedily. The formalities and administrative delays involved in company incorporation and registration will have to be eliminated. More generally, changes may need to be made to provide a favorable framework for the development of enterprises and the protection of the legitimate stakeholders. In some cases the purpose of the changes will be to remedy difficulties that arose after the start of the program. For example, a Russian presidential decree which took effect in January 1994 abolished restrictions on share transfers that some managers of privatized companies had imposed to prevent external investors from assuming control; it also prescribed that employee-shareholder representatives cannot hold more than one-third of the seats on company boards (see *The Economist*, 12 March 1994).

Accounting Law

Accounting legislation sometimes raises issues for private-sector development in general that differ from those for privatization operations in particular. In the former case, accounting and auditing procedures are important mainly because they have direct impact on the tax obligations of the company and because they require truthful information of shareholders (the legislation normally sets minimum disclosure requirements). It is important also that the law protect the freedom of a company to choose its own auditors. Many investors find it unacceptable for a company to have its accounts audited by a public agency, such as a financial inspectorate attached to the ministry of finance, a tradition in a dwindling number of countries.

Potential buyers in privatization transactions are often less interested in the official accounts of an SOE than in a precise statement of assets and liabilities. They will in any event want to perform their own valuation of the company. They will want to undertake a thorough audit of the financial situation of the SOE and will usually place little faith in its official accounts for several reasons: because the country lacks adequate accounting regulations, because the potential buyers are not familiar with the accounting standards (which may vary greatly from the standards they are used to), or because the SOE's records and accounting practices are unsatisfactory (see also the section on valuation in chapter 5).

In the case of a public flotation, on the other hand, individual investors lack both the opportunity and the means to examine the company's operations and accounts personally. They have to rely on financial statements audited and certified by reputable independent auditors. Moreover, such auditing is normally a prerequisite for listing of the company's shares on a stock exchange. The example of Chinese privatizations is interesting. The Chinese authorities have opted for a number of privatization techniques, including public flotations. When a company is to be listed on the Shanghai or Shenzhen securities exchange, the accounts have to be reformulated for that purpose. For companies listed on the Hong Kong or New York exchange, the accounting and auditing rules are far stricter, with the result that the company must take much longer to prepare the accounts and must seek assistance from international accounting firms.

The existence and effective enforcement of accounting rules consistent with generally accepted international accounting principles will improve the prospects for success of the privatization program by increasing transparency and predictability, and thereby reducing the buyers' risk.[24]

Liquidation and Bankruptcy

Liquidation and bankruptcy are market-exit mechanisms through which less efficient enterprises can be wound up and resources released for more productive uses. They are also often used as privatization techniques. Though the two concepts overlap,[25] they should be looked at as distinct privatization techniques.

The term "liquidation" applies to the winding up of an enterprise when, for whatever reason, its owners have decided to dispose of it by selling its assets, paying off its debts, and sharing the proceeds among themselves pro rata to their respective shares. Through the liquidation process a government can dispose of an SOE by transferring the ownership of its assets (and liabilities) rather than the enterprise itself. In most countries, liquidation is regulated by company law.[26] In the voluntary liquidation of a company, the owner is usually liable for any debts of the company outstanding after the liquidation and dissolution procedure has been completed. Liquidation often facilitates speedy and efficient privatization by avoiding the formalities and complications of bankruptcy. For that reason it is the preferred privatization technique in many countries, including Mexico in the initial phase of its privatization program and many Sub-Saharan African

---

24. For a more detailed discussion of accounting issues in privatization, see *Identification of Accounting Problems Arising during Privatization and their Solution*, Report of the Secretary-General, United Nations Economic and Social Council, E/C.10/AC.3/1992/5, 4 February 1992.

25. The term "liquidation" is used also to describe the stage of the bankruptcy process in which the assets of an insolvent company are sold and the proceeds distributed to its creditors and, where appropriate, its shareholders.

26. In this context, investors will want to know what rules would apply if they decided to liquidate their company voluntarily. Would they, for example, encounter restrictions on sale of assets or on repatriation of sale proceeds? Restrictions of this kind, which are found in certain regulations relating to foreign investment or foreign exchange operations, can hinder the implementation of privatization operations.

countries. Liquidation also tends to be the most practical privatization technique for SOEs with poor accounts or with unknown, uncertain, or contingent liabilities.

Bankruptcy, on the other hand, is not a recommended privatization technique.[27] It has nevertheless been used in privatization operations in Mexico and other countries.[28] Bankruptcy differs from liquidation in several ways. First, the bankruptcy procedure is managed or supervised by the courts, usually with the assistance of court-appointed trustees or receivers. Second, bankruptcy usually implies that the company is insolvent. The company's managers are sometimes required by law to file for bankruptcy if the company loses the bulk of its capital or is unable to continue to make payments; failure to file for bankruptcy may give rise to prosecution and penalties. Third, the procedure can be initiated by the creditors or the courts (or the public prosecutor), even over the objections of the owner.

The use of bankruptcy proceedings as a privatization technique assumes the existence of a smoothly functioning court system, a requirement that is lacking in many developing or transition countries where incompetent, underequipped, or corrupt judicial institutions often hamstring this critical market-exit mechanism. Lengthy litigation is not uncommon in this area. In addition, many countries lack properly trained bankruptcy receivers to whom the courts can entrust the management of companies during bankruptcy proceedings. Moreover, since a company's creditors generally play the leading role in bankruptcy proceedings, choosing bankruptcy as the privatization technique can hinder the pursuit of objectives other than reve-

---

27. In Colombia, the assets of Papelcol, a major paper manufacturer that was placed under "concordato" (similar to the "concordat" system in French commercial law and the U.S. chapter 11 bankruptcy procedure), had to be taken out of bankruptcy proceedings by the owner itself, a state-owned holding company which had become Papelcol's main creditor, before they could be transferred to a private company.

28. Aeroméxico was declared bankrupt in April 1988. In September 1988 a new company, Aerovias, with capital of about $44,000, was created with the bankruptcy receiver and the pilots' union as shareholders. Aerovias took over the airline's operations and concluded new contracts with the main unions, which represented a drastically reduced work force. In the same month the receiver put Aeroméxico's assets up for sale. The winning bidder offered to buy most assets, with the exception of the aircraft, engines, and unneeded spare parts, together with 75 percent of Aerovias, leaving the other 25 percent to the pilots' union. The bid also included leasing of the necessary aircraft. The bid was accepted, and the sale contract was signed in November 1988. Adapted from Galal and others 1994 (see also box 1). Following their privatization, Mexicana and Aeroméxico embarked on a commercial battle intensified by the arrival on the market of new air carriers. Mexicana rapidly ran into financial difficulties, burdened by the heavy debt incurred for 36 Airbuses. In February 1993 Aeroméxico acquired control of Mexicana, but did not succeed in restructuring and integrating it, and in turn found itself unable to meet its payments in September 1994. The company was then taken over by a consortium of creditor banks, which put in new management. In June 1996, following government approval, the two companies were merged; the government appeared to be concerned mainly with the health of the banks, which converted about $1 billion of debt into an equity share of over 70 percent in the new company. See *New York Times*, 6 September 1994; *Wall Street Journal*, 3 October 1994 and 4 June 1996; *Journal of Commerce*, 16 February 1995.

nue maximization.[29] Finally, in many countries, including those with centrally planned economies, where the great majority of SOE creditors are other public enterprises or agencies, distribution of the assets of a defunct enterprise can be performed more effectively by the government, which is directly or indirectly the principal shareholder and creditor.

It is important to ascertain whether the rules governing commercial liquidation, bankruptcy and insolvency effectively apply to SOEs.[30] If they do apply, one should ensure that these provisions are adequate to deal with potential SOE liquidations, especially from the standpoint of protection of private SOE creditors. The government may decide to waive certain claims it may have against an SOE (for example, tax arrears), to the benefit of the SOE's private creditors, especially its secured creditors; or it may opt to remain legally liable for claims not honored by the former SOE, including claims filed after it was dissolved.

SOEs should as far as possible be subject to the same liquidation and bankruptcy laws, regulations, and practices as private enterprises. There is a danger that more lenient rules or unequal application of rules common to both types of enterprises could allow loss-making SOEs to compete unfairly against other enterprises.[31] Sudden application of commercial bankruptcy legislation to the entire SOE sector, however—unless preceded by in-depth financial restructuring of the SOEs in question (especially those with negative net worth)—could trigger a cascade of bankruptcies that threaten the survival of the government and its reform program.[32] The challenge, then, is to strike the right balance between immediate and strict application of the bankruptcy rules to all troubled enterprises, on the one hand, and a special regime that would allow technically bankrupt SOEs to survive indefinitely, on the other.

Hungary, the Czech Republic, and Poland have attempted to meet this challenge in different ways (see box 3.2). Hungary has accorded priority to

29. It should be noted also that effective bankruptcy legislation can represent a threat (or an incentive to perform well) for managers of both private and public enterprises. This threat or incentive does not, however, come into play until the company's situation has deteriorated to the point that it effectively faces the threat of bankruptcy.

30. If commercial rules do not apply, the liquidation of SOEs may be regulated by a special law. See the section in chapter 4 on SOE liquidation.

31. Creditors, particularly state-owned or state-controlled banks, may however be reluctant to initiate bankruptcy proceedings against SOEs. Similarly, SOE managers and board members often have no incentive to initiate liquidation procedures, even if required to do so by law. In many countries, if they fail to comply with these legal obligations they are unlikely to be punished, whereas they know that initiating liquidation will very probably cost them their jobs.

32. Such could be the indirect result of a large-scale program of corporatization of SOEs. The effect would not be simply to subject these enterprises to private company law; it would also bring them under other areas of business law, such as the bankruptcy laws. This fact is often overlooked, however, by advocates of across-the-board corporatization. See chapter 4 on corporatization of SOEs.

Box 3.2   Bankruptcy Law: Hungarian, Czech, and Polish Approaches

Hungary: The Judicial Route

Hungary opted to apply strict judicial bankruptcy procedures to enterprises in difficulty. The law of September 1991 on bankruptcy procedures, liquidation procedures, and settlement of accounts required managers to initiate bankruptcy proceedings as soon as an enterprise fell more than 90 days in arrears in the payment of any of its debts. The law provided for two alternative procedures: reorganization (called, deceptively, "bankruptcy") and liquidation. The reorganization procedure gave a debtor 60 days to prepare a plan for regaining solvency. This plan had to be accepted unanimously by all the creditors, failing which the liquidation procedure would automatically apply.

The number of cases submitted to the courts soared from 528 in 1991 to 14,300 in 1992, and the increase in the number of enterprises forced to close their doors was manyfold. Of these 14,300 cases, only 4,400 related to reorganization procedures; the rest were liquidation cases. Moreover, only one-third of the reorganization cases dealt with by the courts in 1992 effectively led to acceptance of the proposed plan by the creditors. Cascading enterprise closures and bankruptcies had disastrous consequences for the commercial banks. Furthermore, as a result of the enormous increase in bankruptcies filed the courts became completely swamped. The lack of qualified bankruptcy judges and receivers—eight judges were responsible for 4,000 cases in Budapest in mid-1992—led to substantial delays in handling the cases.

To address this situation, the law was relaxed through a September 1993 amendment: the bankruptcy procedure is no longer mandatory but only optional in cases of payment delays; and, for a reorganization plan to be adopted, it needs to be accepted by one-half of the creditors, provided they hold at least two-thirds of claims on the enterprise. By the end of 1994, the assets of about 500 medium or large SOEs had already been transferred to the private sector by way of insolvency procedures.

Czech Republic: Temporization

In 1991 Czechoslovakia enacted a bankruptcy law, but the law had not, practically speaking, been applied when a moratorium was imposed up to April 1993 on suits filed against state-owned enterprises (this protection was later extended several times). Several technically bankrupt enterprises were included in the mass privatization program, hence the problem was transferred to the new shareholders. The bankruptcy law, however, could not be applied

---

speedy application, by the courts, of strict bankruptcy rules. The procedure prescribed in the September 1991 law had to be relaxed in 1993, however, in an effort to reduce both the mountain of cases submitted to the courts and the number of enterprises compelled to close their doors. In the Czech Republic, the main focus has been on seeking solutions outside the courts and allowing troubled enterprises to be restructured. The risk here is that

to enterprises privatized by means of coupons in the two months following privatization. With respect to other enterprises, rather than enforcing the bankruptcy laws, the Czech authorities chose to invite investors interested in buying SOEs to propose restructuring plans. The advantage of this system is that it does not overload the courts and tribunals and does not trigger mass liquidations.

There is a clear risk, however, of either shifting the restructuring burden to investors ill-equipped to manage it (the voucher-holding public) or, for those SOEs not included in the mass privatization program, of failing to attract investors and prolonging the burden of the SOE on the state. As a result of these policies, few bankruptcy procedures were initiated and even fewer completed. Between 1991 and 1995, only 282 bankruptcy proceedings were completed in the Czech Republic and a further 2,274 cases had been initiated "in stark contrast to the situation in Hungary and Poland, where the number of insolvencies are up to 10 times higher" (*Finance East Europe*, 1 December 1995). The low Czech numbers have been attributed to lack of political will to force bankruptcies, ineffective implementation of the laws, and lack of detailed court procedures.

Poland: An Alternative Approach

The main Polish bankruptcy legislation dates back to 1934. In addition, the 1981 law on SOEs, as amended in 1991, and the 1990 privatization law provide for administrative procedures for SOE liquidation. These laws did not, however, contain provisions triggering compulsory recourse to bankruptcy proceedings. The courts have had to deal with relatively few bankruptcy cases under the 1934 law.

Significant changes were brought by the 1993 law on financial restructuring of state enterprises and banks, which gave banks the principal role in the restructuring of insolvent SOEs. Under the aegis of the banks, creditors are given four months within which to draw up a restructuring program (conciliation procedure), typically involving debt-for-equity swaps, or to recommend liquidation through conventional bankruptcy proceedings before the courts pursuant to the 1934 legislation. The creditors' decision is binding provided it is supported by creditors with more than 50 percent of outstanding claims. This scheme provides real incentives for out-of-court reorganization and allows state claims on the SOE to be included in the reorganization plan.

Among the advantages of the Polish approach are that it avoids overloading the courts, sets a deadline for formulating a restructuring program, and enables the banks to gain experience in debt valuation and recovery.

Sources: Gray 1993a; Nestor and Thomas 1995; OECD 1995a; *Finance East Europe*, 1 December 1995.

the reallocation of resources to more productive activities may prolong the survival of unhealthy or loss-making enterprises. Poland has opted for an intermediate course: banks with debtors in arrears can choose between (a) a conciliation procedure of limited duration that must culminate in a restructuring agreement and (b) application of the bankruptcy legislation by the courts.

Nestor and Thomas 1995 comment thus: "From a comparative point of view, there seems to be a tradeoff between the implementation of effective bankruptcy procedures and the adoption of mass, or 'voucher' privatisation programmes. Where mass privatisation has been chosen, as in the Czech and Slovak Republics, application of effective insolvency procedures has been left to the 'post-privatisation' stage, so as not to delay transfer of ownership. Countries which have followed a more traditional 'sales' approach to privatisation, on the other hand, have been forced to introduce insolvency procedures at an early stage, as an alternative means of enforcing discipline on companies which have not yet been moved into private hands."

In summary, worldwide experience indicates that recourse to court-led bankruptcy proceedings is not a particularly effective way to deal with insolvent SOEs. In many cases, especially where the creditors are other public sector entities, administrative liquidation is more effective and expedient. Where private creditors are involved, safeguards will be needed. Voluntary, creditor-driven reorganization plans may be the most promising approach. Indeed, liquidation of insolvent enterprises is a critical market mechanism, which, unfortunately, courts in most developing and transition countries courts are ill-equipped to administer.

Transfer of Liabilities

Most legal systems specifically regulate the transfer of debts and obligations, including contingent liabilities deriving, for example, from ongoing or potential litigation. In civil-law countries, debt transfers are normally subject to the creditors' approval, without which the original debtor continues to be liable.

Where privatization is carried out through sale of the original SOE (that is, the legal entity that incurred the debt), whether by call for bids or through transfer of shares, the privatized company continues to be the debtor and the situation of the creditors is not fundamentally altered. In some countries, such as Bulgaria, commercial law requires the seller of a company (the state in the case of privatization of an SOE) to give the company's creditors prior notice of the upcoming sale; unless the creditors agree otherwise, the seller remains liable, even after the sale, for debts of the company contracted before privatization (see article 15 of the Bulgarian Commercial Code of May 16, 1991).

If, on the other hand, the legal status of the SOE is changed—for example, through its corporatization (see chapter 4)—the creditors may not be satisfied with their new status. The conversion of the original debtor from a public company with unlimited liability, implicitly backed by the full credit of the state, to a limited liability company organized under company law may reduce the security afforded to its creditors to the amount of the new company's declared capital. Nonetheless, in Sri Lanka, Poland, and other countries, laws governing the corporatization of public enterprises expressly call for the transfer of the former SOE's liabilities to the new company.[33] On the other hand, Italian law stipulates clearly that in the case of a breakup or demerger of an SOE, for example, the state "shall be jointly and severally liable for any debts of the company involved in the demerger which have not been paid by the company liable for the debts."[34]

Since in many instances SOEs that carry their existing debts and obligations would not attract any buyers, governments often prefer to clear off these debts either before corporatization of the SOE (see, for example, article 62 of the British Telecommunications Act of 1984) or as part of the preparation or negotiation of the privatization transaction.[35]

Moreover, where the SOE's original obligation was guaranteed by the state (as in the case of a World Bank loan, for example), this guarantee remains in force even if, following privatization, the new owner is a private entity. Here again many legal systems do not allow the state to assign its guarantee obligation to a third party without the consent of the creditors.[36] If privatization takes place through the transfer of assets and liabilities and not of the company itself or shares therein, the question of debt transfer may have to be settled case by case.

Foreign Investment Legislation

Some aspects of the foreign investment regime concern all foreign investments, while others apply to privatizations in particular. It is important to determine, among other things, whether the constitution and laws of the country properly

33. *Sri Lanka*: The corporatization law of 1987 authorizes conversion of SOEs into joint-stock companies by administrative decision and provides that the liabilities of the SOE are deemed liabilities of the new company. In practice, however, net privatization proceeds in Sri Lanka were limited "because the government incurred considerable costs in settling the accumulated liabilities of PEs [public enterprises] and paid compensation to displaced workers prior to privatization" (UNCTAD 1995, p. 273).

Poland: Article 8 (2) of the 1990 privatization law provides that a company formed by conversion of a state enterprise assumes all the rights and liabilities of the enterprise so converted.

New Zealand: See box 4.2 describing the State-Owned Enterprises Act of 1986.

34. Article 10.1.e of Decree-Law no. 332 of May 31, 1994. On the extent of state liability for SOE debts, see also the section on company law, above.

35. In an address to American investors given in Washington, D.C., on November 14, 1991, Birgit Breuel, then president of the Treuhandanstalt, stated: "With respect to existing debts and environmental liabilities [of public enterprises to be privatized], we will also negotiate flexibly. The extent of our generosity will depend on the attractiveness of your proposal. . . . In and of itself, the purchase price will not be the sole decisive factor. The amount of planned investment and the number of guaranteed jobs is also important to us. . . . Since its inception [in the fall of 1990], the Treuhand has on average assumed 85% of the existing debt of businesses which have been privatized." The Treuhandanstalt was authorized by the debt relief decree of September 1990 to assume debts contracted by SOEs before July 1, 1990. See also chapter 4 on prior restructuring.

36. In the privatization of VASP, the airline of the state of São Paulo, Brazil, this difficulty was avoided by requiring the buyer to repay VASP's creditors and issue a counterguarantee backed by hard assets to indemnify the state in the event the state guarantee was called.

protect foreign investors;[37] whether the current system discriminates against foreign investors by capping their holdings in local companies (to, for example, less than 20 or 50 percent of capital), ruling out foreign ownership of land (as does article 22 of Bulgaria's 1991 constitution), or prohibiting or restricting their activity in some of the sectors to be privatized;[38] whether the system guarantees repatriation of profits and capital; whether the foreign investment regime introduces undue discrimination against domestic investors by granting foreigners tax and customs exemptions not available to domestic investors; whether the rules applicable to foreign investors are stated in clear terms or whether they are ambiguous and leave the administration wide room for discretion;[39] whether the regulations governing the relations between a parent company and its local subsidiary are likely to deter foreigners from participating in privatization; whether the benefits of the investment code (or similar legislation) apply to privatization transactions involving the transfer of ownership of existing assets or only to investments involving the creation of new productive assets; and, finally, whether the foreign investment laws and the privatization laws of the country concerned reinforce or contradict each other.

Securities Legislation

Capital market development is a common goal pursued by governments in privatization programs. When the program includes share flotations to the

37. *Brazil*: Article 5 of the 1988 constitution guarantees a vast array of social, economic, and political rights, including the right of private ownership and the right to fair prior compensation in the event of expropriation by the government, but only for Brazilians and aliens resident in Brazil. Nonresident aliens are not protected. Article 172 of the constitution provides that "the law shall regulate foreign capital investments, encourage reinvestment and regulate the repatriation of profits, all on the basis of the national interest." These constitutional provisions and various other provisions of the privatization laws and regulations that discriminate against foreigners have created difficulties for the implementation of the government's privatization program. In response to the low foreign participation and disappointing receipts of the first privatization transactions, the government relaxed the restrictions on participation by foreign investors.

Angola: Provisions like those of article 10 of the 1975 constitution are not particularly reassuring for foreign investors either. The article states: "The People's Republic of Angola shall recognize, protect and guarantee private activities and property, even those of foreigners, as long as they are useful to the country's economy and serve the interests of the Angolan people."

On constitutional restrictions, see also box 2.2, box 5.2, and table 7.3.

38. As part of the preparation of its privatization program, Morocco repealed regulations adopted pursuant to the 1973 "moroccanization" law by opening up the banking, insurance, real estate, and livestock sectors, and certain commercial and transportation activities, to foreign investment. As a result, foreign investment rose by 75 percent in 1991 and a further 30 percent in 1992. In 1993 the government decided to also liberalize the petroleum distribution sector. See World Equity and IFC 1993.

39. In an article on Hungary, the *Financial Times* reported that "government publication of a list of strategic companies in which foreign control would not be permitted may paradoxically have had a beneficial effect. Clarifying the rules has made officials less hesitant." *Financial Times*, 30 October 1991, special section on Hungary, p. VII.

public at large (or at least to a large number of investors), buyers should be able to trade their shares on a secondary market. This does not, however, necessarily call for an organized securities exchange in the conventional sense of the term (that is, one with a trading floor, and so on). All that is required for a secondary market to exist is a system that allows private parties to transfer shares freely to one another and to obtain registration or recognition of the transfer by the issuing company. This market also needs to be regulated to protect investors.[40]

Although an established and properly structured financial market can facilitate privatization, it is not essential to the success of a privatization program. The absence of such a financial market will, however, narrow the range of available privatization options. Trying to set up such a market as a financial intermediary for privatization transactions would usually mean deferring privatization longer than authorities can wait. On the other hand, it would be desirable to enact basic securities legislation on the issuance and trading of shares and also on the operations of financial intermediaries (banks, brokers, traders, and so on).

In the United Kingdom or France, where structured financial markets already existed, privatization was instrumental in further developing and deepening of these markets by boosting total market capitalization, transaction volume, and liquidity and by encouraging participation by new shareholders. France demonstrates also how special provisions might be inserted in securities legislation to facilitate the privatization process. The French securities exchange regulations have been amended to authorize the procedure known as book-building, which lets the investment bank or financial intermediary selling the state's shares obtain revocable commitments (declarations of interest) from potential investors before the actual subscription period. Preliminary approval can now be issued by the securities agency, allowing the book-building operation to begin; a second authorization is issued only when the prospectus is finalized and the selling price of the share is determined.

Reciprocally, the development of local capital markets can foster the success of privatization, especially by boosting the ability to mobilize local savings and therefore reduce dependence on foreign capital. It is important, however, not to try to go too fast by flooding a newly organized and small financial market with shares. The flotation of shares in Poland's Slaski Bank, described in box 3.3, illustrates the point. For lack of sufficient staff, registration of the shares of the Slaski Bank—a prerequisite for the sale of shares—fell far behind schedule; hundreds of thousands of shareholders found themselves prevented from selling shares when the price of

---

40. Under Czechoslovakia's mass privatization program (see chapter 6), a large number of shares had been placed on the market before January 1, 1993, the date the securities law entered into force, without any accompanying prospectus for the information of investors. Subsequently, however, companies responsible for these share issues were forced to regularize them by publishing a prospectus a posteriori (see Goldstein and Horakova 1993).

Box 3.3   The Flotation of Slaski Bank

The privatization of Slaski, a major Polish bank, was one of the largest operations in Poland's privatization program. Nearly 800,000 persons bought shares
in Slaski Bank, and these were listed on the Warsaw securities exchange on January 25, 1994. Very few investors were in a position to trade their shares that
day, however. Indeed, shares could not be sold unless they had been registered,
and the registration process had fallen far behind schedule. This delay was
caused by a shortage of qualified brokers able to perform the registration
(fewer than 40 broker licenses had been granted in Poland). The delay was
largely responsible for the substantial fluctuations that occurred in the value of
Slaski shares. Owing to the lack of tradable shares, only 0.35 percent of the total
shares changed hands on the first day, while the value of the share rose more
than thirteenfold. The price then fell, causing frustration among many shareholders who had been unable to sell.

For having floated these shares on the exchange before most of the shareholders had an opportunity to register them, Slaski Bank, which itself held a
broker's license, had its license revoked by the securities commission. The
commission gave Slaski six months to terminate its brokerage operations
and asked the remaining brokers, who were already having enormous difficulty satisfying their own clients, to continue Slaski Bank's activities in this
field.

Source: Financial Times, 7 February 1994 and 18 February 1994.

---

these shares was fluctuating widely. Problems of this kind hurt the credibility of the privatization process in general, and they may alienate private
investors.

Measures can be taken to strengthen financial markets. Several governments have decided, for example, to promote the development of large
domestic institutional investors that can participate in the privatization program as buyers. In Italy various legislative measures were enacted to allow
financial markets to play an increased role in the privatization process: private pension funds were authorized; a new Law no. 344 of August 14, 1993,
regulates the creation of mutual funds; and amendments were made to a
1936 banking law to allow banks to acquire up to 15 percent of the shares of
industrial companies. The role of pension funds in this context is discussed
further below.

More generally, reforms that increase secondary market liquidity and
remove barriers to corporate takeovers should contribute to better corporate governance. Such reforms may be particularly relevant for countries
with large mass privatization programs or employee ownership
schemes, where established management teams may have few incentives
to provide value to their atomized shareholders (see also EBRD 1995,
chap. 8).

Banking

Financial legislation dealing not only with banking but also with collateral and sureties, credit, leasing, insurance, and so on may affect the success of a privatization program. A sound commercial banking system is essential for mobilizing savings and financing economic activity. Efficient banking mechanisms make it possible, in particular, for investors to finance their operations and working capital and make speedy payments.[41]

Most privatizing governments have had to strengthen their banking legislation so that commercial banks can play their role in a market economy; stronger mechanisms for bank supervision and adherence to international standards (including key prudential standards established by the Bank for International Settlements) have often been part of such reforms. Banking legislation may also need to be amended to facilitate the implementation of the privatization program, for instance, by enabling commercial banks to act as financial intermediaries for share issues in countries where no formal securities markets exist.

Furthermore, banking laws may need to be amended to allow the privatization of commercial banks themselves. In Pakistan, for example, the banking law was amended to allow the privatization in 1991 of Muslim Commercial Bank and Allied Banks of Pakistan. On the other hand, the 1990 law that authorized bank privatization in Italy was not followed by much action to remove the Italian banking sector from overwhelming state control.

In most socialist countries, the central bank acted as a commercial bank and no private banks were allowed. New legislation typically removed the central bank's commercial banking activities and transformed state-owned banks into corporations. In Hungary, for example, banking reform was initiated in 1987 with the transformation of the lending departments of the central bank into separate new state-owned banks, which together with two preexisting large state-owned banks dominated the commercial banking sector; 1987 also saw the first foreign-owned banks established in Hungary. The new law on financial institutions enacted in November 1991 authorized the privatization of state-owned banks, while limiting ownership by any one shareholder to a maximum of 25 percent (see section 18.1 of Law no. 69 of 1991 on financial institutions).

Restructuring of the banking sector is often hindered, especially in countries where state-owned banks dominate, by huge nonperforming loans to often insolvent public enterprises and agencies. In such cases bank reform becomes closely associated with SOE reform in general. SOE rehabilitation or privatization programs usually call for hardening the SOE's soft budget constraints by ending privileged access to credit from banks controlled or guaranteed by the state and by forcing commercial banks to bear the full risks

41. An analysis of the main issues in banking-sector reform and privatization exceeds the scope of this work (but see Borish, Long, and Noël 1995; Thorne 1993; Barnes 1992).

associated with SOE lending. Restructuring and privatizing the banking sector can hence greatly facilitate the entire privatization program by limiting the ability of SOEs to incur additional debt. Meanwhile, a solution needs to be found for the banks' existing portfolios of nonperforming loans. Some countries, including Hungary, have cleaned up their banks' balance sheets by creating special-purpose companies to take over nonperforming loans, either as a self-standing restructuring measure or as a step toward subsequent bank privatization. Others, such as Slovenia, have created a bank rehabilitation agency to take over all the troubled banks, while yet others have recapitalized the existing banks.

Restructuring and privatizing banks should normally take place at the start of the reform program, for a healthy and dynamic banking sector should contribute to the development of economic activity. Doing so, however, can be complicated, politically difficult, and expensive, a fact that explains why some governments have preferred to leave the banking sector untouched in the initial stage. If not properly designed, bank privatization could cause privatized banks to become overextended, which might prompt another takeover by the state in order to avoid a major crisis in the financial sector, as happened in Chile and Mexico, for example.

Taxation

Investors and potential buyers are naturally concerned about the overall corporate tax burden and the predictability of interpretation and enforcement of the tax laws. Businesses should be able to determine what taxes apply to them and to estimate the amount of the taxes they will have to pay. Certain technical aspects can also be important. They include the rules governing transfer pricing between enterprises of a group (for example, between a local company and its parent or sister companies established abroad); the rules governing the carrying forward of tax losses, which can greatly influence the choice of privatization technique;[42] the tax treatment of loan interest and dividends; the tax implications of employee shareholding plans, leasing, franchising, and other privatization mechanisms, which in many cases will determine the chosen technique; and, finally, the rules relating to double taxation.

The tax laws should be applied uniformly to private and to public enterprises and tax advantages granted to SOEs in the competitive sectors of the economy should be abolished. Whether governments should give special tax advantages to privatization transactions—for example, in investment legislation or in express provisions of the privatization law—is a question that might arise. Although exemptions from stamp and registration duties on share transfers will not usually affect government revenues seriously or

---

42. If the new owners are eligible for such carryovers, a loss-making SOE can be quite an attractive proposition. From the government's point of view, however, the higher sale price is offset by lower tax receipts in subsequent years.

give the beneficiaries a major competitive advantage (see, for example, article 15 of France's privatization law of August 1986), the same may not be true of temporary exemptions from corporate income taxes. Such exemptions are granted, for example, in Tunisia, where article 30 of Law no. 89-9 extends very generous tax benefits to privatized enterprises, notably exemptions from corporate income and capital gains taxes (see also the section of this chapter on foreign investment). Similar provisions exist in the Philippines and other countries.[43]

Currency and Foreign Exchange

Restrictions on foreign-exchange transactions, including allocation, availability, convertibility, repatriation, or registration of foreign exchange, will generally hamper efforts to attract foreign investors. In countries that do not have a stable and convertible currency, restrictions on domestic payments in foreign exchange, particularly remuneration of expatriate staff, payments to domestic suppliers, and payments by customers may also be cause for concern.

In the specific context of privatization operations, some governments have felt the need to establish a special, less favorable exchange rate for foreign investors bidding on SOEs or their assets in order to offset what they perceived as an artificially depressed exchange rate, which would allow foreign bidders to buy assets significantly below their value. Formulas of this kind should be avoided; they tend to be easy to circumvent and difficult to administer. This is true also of multiple exchange rates of the kind applied in Russia, where the rate for foreign investments was about ten times higher than the market rate.[44]

Social Legislation

The social climate of a country, including its labor legislation, pension regime, and social safety net, and of an enterprise is among the major determining factors in any investment decision.[45] The privatization program may contribute to a healthy climate by involving employees in the preparation for privatization (see chapter 1), giving them the opportunity to become shareholders in their enterprise, and protecting workers' rights, while

43. Section 35 of the 1986 privatization law exempts the Asset Privatization Trust from all taxes and duties (including stamp and registration fees, transfer taxes, and capital gains taxes) on the transfer of assets from government institutions to the trust and from the trust to private buyers. The article also exempts such sales or transfers from all restrictions or constraints that could derive from "the existence of any liens by way of taxes, charges or other assessments in favor of the government at the time of sale or transfer: provided, that the proceeds from such sale or transfer shall be subject to a tax lien and first be applied to satisfy such obligations secured by said liens."

44. If the purpose is to give domestic investors an edge over foreign investors, this could also be achieved by assigning a margin of preference to domestic bidders.

45. See World Bank 1995a, especially part four, "How Can Policy Choices Help Workers in Periods of Major Change?"

avoiding unsustainable settlements or labor standards. Privatization can also be an opportunity to strengthen social legislation.

Labor Legislation

The labor regime applicable to SOE personnel can be more or less conducive to implementation of the privatization program.[46] First, public sector employees often enjoy special civil service benefits.[47] These will normally have to be repealed and may be replaced by other, private-law benefits granted by the new company. Pension entitlements are a case in point (see below). Similarly, it may be necessary to confirm or modify other contractual (or statutory) rights of employees, including, in particular, wage levels, seniority rights, and other benefits. In many cases the relevant legal principle will be whether or not the employment relationship continues.[48]

Privatization agreements for enterprises or activities that are not transferred as a going concern—an SOE that will be liquidated, for example—may nonetheless provide for continuation of the contracts of selected employees. Under existing labor legislation in some countries, employees could be entitled to severance pay from the SOE even if they are immediately rehired by the new company. In others, the above-mentioned principle of continuity in the employment relationship, legislation embodying that principle, or specific contractual provisions may prevent such double-dipping. Employees not rehired by the new company would continue to be formally employed by the old SOE, which continues to exist legally until it is dissolved even though it does not carry on any activity; their contractual or statutory rights are then settled as part of the liquidation process (see chapter 4).

Labor law provisions determine the flexibility the investor has to set employee salaries and benefits, to hire and lay off staff (including foreign staff),

46. In Brazil, ports were governed by 1937 legislation that led to costs among the highest in the world. In January 1992, referring to privatization of the ports, the president of BNDES (the agency responsible for coordinating Brazil's privatization program) stated that the first priority was to modernize the legislation "or we shall never find buyers." In February 1993, after two years of discussion, parliament enacted a new ports law. More than a year later, little progress had been made. Implementation of the law had been frozen pending a union appeal to the Supreme Court on the constitutionality of the law. The unions are opposed to transfer of control of the ports to the users, which would reduce the union role to the sole function of representing their members in collective bargaining. Under the previous regime (which is still being applied), the unions decide the number and identity of the dockers assigned to load or unload each vessel, and only affiliated dockers can obtain work. See *Financial Times*, 21 January 1992, p. 24; *Journal of Commerce*, 15 April 1994.

47. In France, for example, employees of the national electricity company (EDF) and of other SOEs, unlike their private sector colleagues, pay social security taxes on their base salary only and not on their many additional benefits.

48. In Morocco, for example, there is a legal presumption of continuity of the employment relationship, despite changes in the employer's status, be it as a result of succession, sale, merger, split-up, absorption, transformation, or otherwise: "all labor contracts in effect on the day of such change remain in force between the new employer and the staff of the enterprise" (article 754 of the Obligations and Contracts Code).

and, in general, to manage the enterprise's human resources. If overstaffing is severe, potential investors may well require that the government or the SOE lay off redundant employees before privatization, especially if the legislation or the social climate makes it difficult for private employers to dismiss workers.[49] The rights of laid-off workers, including severance pay and unemployment benefits, may vary significantly depending on whether they were laid off by the new private owners or by the SOE before privatization; in the latter case, there will also be a difference depending on whether these workers were governed by general labor legislation or by special public-sector legislation.

Tradeoffs may be necessary between the protection afforded by labor law to incumbent workers and the need to create new jobs. In Germany, for example, ordinary labor law restricts the acceptable grounds for dismissal; parliament has granted buyers of privatized enterprises temporary exemption from such restrictions, however, to facilitate implementation of the privatization program.[50] On the other hand, the Treuhand has inserted a binding undertaking in many privatization contracts, under which the buyer guarantees to keep or create a specified number of jobs in the privatized company, subject to penalties (with the penalty amount specified in the contract) in the event of default (see Horn 1992, p. 19).

Such a negotiated formula is generally preferable to protecting jobs by prohibiting all dismissals following privatization. In Pakistan, for example, under an agreement between government and unions, new owners were prohibited from laying off any employees in the 12 months following privatization of an SOE.[51] In Malaysia, buyers could neither modify the terms of

49. Staff reductions at the Peruvian airline Aeroperu took place before privatization: its work force of 2,300 for six aircraft in 1990 (a ratio of over 380 employees per aircraft, compared with a normal ratio of 100 or 150 to one) was reduced to 980 by the time of its privatization in January 1993. Also in Peru, the staff of the Cerro Verde mine was reduced by half before its privatization in November 1993. See *Washington Post*, 8 December 1993. The work force of the Venezuelan airline VIASA, which had no less than 450 employees per aircraft before its privatization in 1991, had been reduced to 215 per plane two years later.

50. A March 1991 law provides for temporary exemption from "section 613 (a) of the German Civil Code, which provides that the purchaser of assets constituting a business assumes, by operation of law, the employment rights and obligations existing at the time of the purchase. A change in control through an acquisition does not constitute 'cause' for the dismissal of employees. . . . The above-mentioned exemption provides that through December 31, 1992, Section 603 (a) will not apply in the case of acquisitions of insolvent eastern German businesses" (Jones Day 1991, p. 3). See also note 14 in chapter 1.

51. This prohibition, which ran through Pakistan's entire 1991–93 privatization program, stemmed from an agreement between government and unions, the terms of which were then incorporated into bidding conditions and sale contracts. Similar agreements were reached in 1995 to stem labor opposition to privatization of parts of WAPDA, the water and power SOE; for instance, the government guaranteed the jobs of all employees of the first power plant to be sold (at Kot Addu) and improved their pay and other working conditions before privatization. The situation was even more acute with the second phase of the privatization of Sui Northern Gas Pipelines, where the financial advisers complained about "substantial politically inspired recruitment" in 1995 and wrote to the privatization commission about their "inability to explain such large-scale job-creation to prospective investors" (*Oxford Analytica*, 8 November 1995).

the employment contract nor dismiss employees of the privatized enterprise for five years after privatization. Similarly, in Sri Lanka, since March 1992 new owners have been required to extend the same benefits to employees, up to retirement age, that they enjoyed before privatization.[52] Uniform requirements of this kind make the privatization process unnecessarily inflexible and expensive. Nevertheless, some governments see them as essential for gaining the labor support deemed necessary to push through privatization. But the impact of uniform requirements has to be analyzed also in terms of the sometimes unsustainable precedents set for the economy at large, including the private sector. This may be less of a problem, however, where SOE wages are low in absolute terms as well as in relation to wages paid in the private sector.

In industrial countries, labor legislation has been at the center of controversy in privatization programs. The case of France Télécom is instructive. This enterprise, a central government service before 1991 and an autonomous public-law establishment since then, is being transformed into a limited liability company as a first step toward partial privatization. The conversion of France Télécom's personnel from a civil service to a labor code regime and the fear of privatization-related layoffs have been a major stumbling block, as evidenced by the postponement of the submission of the corporatization bill to parliament, following strong union opposition supported by a strike in October 1993. The government tried again to take steps in preparation for privatization, which led to new strikes in December 1995 and April and June 1996, though each successive strike was observed by a decreasing number of employees, reflecting in part the concessions already made by the French government, including guarantee of civil service status and job security for employees and a commitment that the company will remain at least 51 percent state owned.[53]

In Italy, a similar labor issue was settled at the time of transfer of the activities of ASST (a government service) to Iritel (a private-law company) by

52. At the start of its privatization (peopleization) program, Sri Lanka opted for a voluntary resignation bonus formula. This contributed to a drop in productivity because the best workers opted for the scheme and moved on to other jobs; the scheme had to be abandoned because too many employees wanted to avail themselves of it. The number of categories of eligible employees was then reduced, an action that created social tension. The government finally decided to introduce a two-year protection against all dismissals, before extending this protection up to retirement age. See UNCTAD, *Report to the Third Meeting of the Working Committee on Privatizations*, Geneva, November 29–December 3, 1993; Prokopenko 1995.

53. France is not the only country whose telecommunications privatization program has been blocked by social action. Other countries where this has happened include Colombia, where the discussion of a bill to privatize the telecommunications company was suspended in April 1992 following major strikes by the company's employees; Germany, where the postal service unions held demonstrations and strikes to protest restructuring and privatization of postal services and telecommunications; and Greece, where union opposition and industrial action blocked the privatization of 49 percent of OTE in 1993, contributed to the failure of a subsequent attempt to sell 25 percent in 1994, but failed to block the flotation of 8 percent of OTE's stock in March 1996 (see also the section on public flotation in chapter 7).

allowing the personnel affected to choose either to join Iritel or to be reassigned within the civil service. Of the 12,600 employees, 2,600 chose to remain in the civil service, about 1,000 took early retirement, and the rest opted for transfer to Iritel (see Gioscia 1993). In Belgium, the maintenance after privatization of the special civil service status of Belgacom's existing employees, national labor laws perceived to be restrictive, strong unionization of Belgacom employees, as well as unfunded pension liabilities exceeding $3 billion, were mentioned to explain BT's decision to withdraw from the bidding, but did not prevent two other consortia, including one led by winner Ameritech, from making bids (see *Financial Times*, 12 December 1995).

Finally, the scope of the employees' rights in the company, notably union rights and representation on the board of directors or on other management organs, may also affect privatization and investment decisions. If regulations governing union representation in SOEs differ from those governing private companies, it may be necessary to negotiate transitional arrangements with the unions concerned. A major reason for initial union opposition to Mexico's rail privatization program, for example, was the government's proposal to set up separate unions for each privatized rail company. Most privatizing governments have tried to involve workers and their unions in the preparation and implementation of the privatization process.

Employee Ownership

Whereas potential layoffs have tended to create labor opposition to privatization, potential employee ownership has had the opposite effect. A recent study on privatization in Poland illustrates the link between worker support and the extent to which employee ownership is likely to yield tangible benefits. Workers' councils in poorly performing firms (with a higher likelihood of bankruptcy or liquidation) generally opposed privatization and pursued aggressive wage policies. In the better performing SOEs, however, "the promise of participation in the privatized firms reduced the incentives for workers to carry out an excessive wage strategy" (see Albrecht and Thum 1994). Employee participation led not only to support for the privatization program but also to more reasonable wage demands.

Legislation may provide tax or other incentives for the establishment of employee stock ownership plans (ESOPs) or encourage other forms of worker participation in the ownership or control of their enterprise.[54] Furthermore, many countries have earmarked a block of shares in enterprises to be privatized for subscription by their employees, and in some cases

---

54. "Typically, an ESOP is structured as a separate legal entity to which a corporation sells shares. . . . What distinguishes an ESOP from other employee ownership programs is that shares are paid for partly or fully out of future corporate earnings. . . . An ESOP is largely a set of 'rules' governing the acquisition, allocation, and management of shares held for employees" (Gates and Saghir 1995, pp. v, 1). These authors mention Jamaica, Hungary, and Pakistan among the countries that have used the ESOP technique in their privatization program. See also Smith 1994.

employees have been given incentives to take over their company. Employee participation in privatization typically figures among the key provisions of a privatization law (see chapter 5).

Pension Entitlements

Investors also need to ascertain the situation of SOE employees who contributed to public-sector pension and insurance schemes. The conversion of their accumulated rights and benefits to a private scheme may be required as part of the privatization process. This often becomes a major stumbling block, especially when the public pension system is not vested and self-financing and the government lacks the funds to transfer accumulated staff benefits to a pension fund. Some Latin American countries have dealt with this problem by issuing state bonds and handing them over to the private pension funds. In Germany, a dispute between the government and Lufthansa concerning financing of the company's retirement obligations had to be settled before the privatization of the airline could proceed.[55] And pension financing turned out to be one of the most delicate issues in the restructuring of the German post and telecommunications company (see the section on prior restructuring in chapter 7). The problem of transferring staff from a public to a private retirement system is a common one in privatization operations.[56]

Pension Fund Reform

A privatization program can also provide the impetus to transform a typically state-run, centralized pension system into a private, more decentralized one. The portability or transferability of pensions of employees moving from the public to the private sector or from one private enterprise to another may need to be facilitated. More professional and efficient management will often need to be brought in to manage these growing financial assets.[57]

---

55. Nonparticipation by the state in the increase in Lufthansa's capital would reduce its share in the company's capital from 51.4 percent to 41 percent. Once this share falls below 50 percent, the government is no longer under the obligation to contribute to the employees' retirement fund. The agreement reached provides for withdrawal by Lufthansa from the public pension fund and the creation of a new fund, to be financed by Lufthansa. The amount of the capital to be invested in Lufthansa's pension fund to enable it to meet its existing obligations was of the order of DM 4 billion (over $2.5 billion). The government agreed to provide half of this, with the other half to be borne by the company. See *Financial Times*, 5 May 1994 and 20 September 1994.

56. See, for example, the Canadian law of January 30, 1990, authorizing the divestiture of Nordion International Inc. and Theratronics International Limited; articles 9 through 11 contain transitory provisions on retirement benefits.

57. The following sources were used for this section on pensions funds: Vittas 1996; Conradt 1993; Gioscia 1993; Sharma 1992; LatinFinance 1992, p. 62; *LatinFinance* (supplement), September 1995, pp. 45–49; *Financial Times*, 30 June 1993, 17 March 1994, and 18 January 1996; *Oxford Analytica*, 11 August 1994; *The Economist*, 11 December 1993.

Chile has played a pioneer role in this field. In 1981, Chile privatized its pension system and entrusted management of social contributions to private companies (*administradoras de fondos de pensiones*, or AFPs) owned by domestic and foreign investors. Incumbent workers could opt to stay in the state pension system or switch to an AFP. In 1985, the law on pension funds was amended to allow the AFPs to invest up to 30 percent of their funds in the equity of privatized enterprises. The pension funds became by far the largest institutional purchasers of shares of SOEs privatized between 1985 and 1990, including major companies such as Chilmetro, Endesa, Schwager, and CTC. In 15 years the AFPs have come to manage accumulated assets totaling about $25 billion, which is equivalent to close to half of Chile's GDP (up from a mere 1 percent of GDP in 1981). The AFPs are "commonly credited with playing a central role in more than doubling domestic savings, from around 14 per cent at the beginning of the 1980s to 27 per cent" in 1995 and with the development of a strong domestic capital market (*Financial Times*, 18 January 1996). Chile's large social security deficit has fallen by two-thirds.

Workers can choose their AFP and freely switch their pension accounts. Competition among funds has kept commissions relatively low and has encouraged good overall performance relative to the stock market. Yet despite these impressive results, problems remain. Many employees are not current in their payments to their plans. Intense competition between funds and legal restrictions on loyalty bonuses have resulted in high turnover, with people switching from one plan to another (in Chile about a third of all accounts are switched each year). For the first time in their history the AFPs made negative real returns of 2.5 percent in 1995; pensioners who opted to take programmed monthly withdrawals from their pension fund account rather than convert their accumulated benefits into a fixed annuity from a life insurance company may therefore see a significant drop in their retirement income.

Chile's experience has encouraged other countries, including Peru, Colombia, and Argentina, to follow its example. A similar scheme was introduced in Peru in September 1993, in parallel with the country's ambitious privatization program. The director of the regulatory agency for Chile's pension funds was in direct contact with his Peruvian counterpart, and the eight AFPs competing for the contributions of Peruvian employees are all linked to companies or AFPs operating in Chile. There is an important difference, however, between the two models: workers in Chile have been required since 1981 to belong to one of the private pension funds, but Peruvian workers affiliated with the public social security system can choose between that system and the new private funds.

The Peruvian private funds experienced some initial difficulties: in the first year, some 800,000 workers—only two-thirds of the expected number—opted for the private funds. Low membership levels, delays in the issuance by government of bonds representing workers' share in the public pension scheme, an unfavorable tax regime, delays in payment by employers and government, and high start-up costs and advertising expenses fueled by competition among funds, caused the AFPs to post losses that were larger than anticipated. Some consolidation took place: two mergers reduced the number of Peruvian AFPs from eight to six, mostly backed by large international financial institutions. Moreover, the scarcity of financial instruments on the Peruvian market prevented AFPs from complying with the investment allocation quotas imposed by law. Investment in Peruvian shares was hampered by cumbersome risk-classification procedures required by law: AFPs can only invest in securities rated by newly established rating agencies, whose assessment initially had to be confirmed by the AFP investment evaluation committee. The enactment of Law no. 26504 of July 18, 1995, which abolished some AFP-specific taxes and put the AFPs on equal footing with the public sector pension system, gave the private funds a new start, however.

Finally, Bolivia, Italy, and Singapore have also taken measures to stimulate capital markets by strengthening the role of pension funds in the broader context of their privatization programs.[58]

Social Safety Net

Staff redundancies, as discussed above, are not so much a consequence of privatization as of poor SOE management leading to overstaffing. These SOEs would have had to be restructured and streamlined sooner or later, even without a change of ownership. In many countries, especially socialist ones, SOEs provided employees unemployment insurance (in the form of guaranteed jobs) and many social services and benefits, including health, education, and housing services. As part of the transition to a market economy, these services and benefits have to be shifted from the enterprises to a national social security scheme, which does not guarantee employment or provide social services but instead guarantees a minimum safety net. Citizens falling below the thresholds of the scheme are eligible for support. Such a safety net and other social measures are often an essential component of the privatization program; unfortunately, their design and implementation are not simple matters, especially when public finances are in short supply.

---

58. *Bolivia*: Article 7 of the 1994 capitalization law (see box 5.1) provides for the transfer to pension funds (to be set up for the purpose) of shares of the SOEs referred to in article 2. Article 7 further provides that these pension funds will be managed by administrators selected following international calls for bids; a tender for the selection of two private pension fund administrators (AFPs) was launched in late 1996. Following an international competitive tender, Cititrust Ltd. had previously been chosen as the fiduciary administering the pension funds pending such selection. About 3.2 million citizens will in this way indirectly become shareholders for the first time; complementary private pension plans will also be offered by the AFPs.

Italy: Decree-Law no. 124 of April 21, 1993, authorizes the establishment of private pension funds.

Singapore: The regulations governing use of the resources of the central provident fund (equivalent to a pension fund) were amended in 1986 to allow withdrawals for the purchase of listed securities approved by the CPF board.

Environmental Law

Environmental law and privatization interact at several different levels.[59] How well the enterprises to be privatized have complied with the existing environmental regulations must be ascertained first of all. They may have been exempt from this legislation or, more simply, they may have violated it. In any event, buyers will have to find out what it will cost to compensate those who may have suffered from pollution, to correct the situation, and to end ongoing violations; they will also need to establish who will have to pay for this.

Uncertainty about the extent of environmental liability was one of the main reasons for the slow start of the German privatization program. The legislation had to be amended to allow regional governments to release investors from liability for environmental damage caused by SOEs before they were privatized, and the Treuhand had to absorb the bulk of the related cost.[60] The same thing happened in Poland, where the government was surprised by the number of investors demanding the inclusion of specific indemnity clauses in SOE takeover agreements (see Greenspan-Bell and Kolaja 1993, pp. 943–44).

Potential buyers will want to ascertain the precise extent of their liability for environmental damage or violations of environmental legislation committed by the former SOE, especially in polluting industries such as chemicals, mining, or steel. Some of these liabilities may be known and quantifiable, while others may arise only after privatization.[61] Uncertainty about the extent of the environmental damage caused by the SOE to be privatized or about the buyers' present or future liability explains the lack of interest by investors in some privatization programs.[62]

---

59. See, in particular, World Bank 1994a; Goldenman 1993 and 1994; Greenspan-Bell and Kolaja 1993.

60. "A strict application of West German environmental laws would have resulted in the shutdown of a major portion of East German industry. The 'Environment Framework Act' . . . provides that purchasers of industrial plants or other commercial real property in eastern Germany may be released from liability for environmental damages caused by the operation of the plant or use of the property before July 1, 1990. Applications for such releases must be filed by March 29, 1992. A release will be granted if it is justified in light of the interest of the investor as balanced against the public interest in environmental protection. The [March 1991] privatization Amendments now provide for the release of civil law claims of private parties as well as public law claims of the government. Previously, liabilities for civil law claims could not be released in this manner. . . . In addition to liability releases, which are issuable only after approval by the relevant German state, investors can obtain indemnification from the Treuhandanstalt with respect to past environmental liabilities" (Jones Day 1991, pp. 1–2).

61. For example, the company's liability to its employees or to the local population for diseases contracted consequent upon acts of pollution committed over a long period or several years ago.

62. An example is the failure in May 1994 of the attempt to privatize Centromin, a large mining enterprise in Peru. See *Financial Times*, 17 May 1994. Two years later the company still had not been privatized.

This problem can be resolved in several ways. The first and simplest alternative is to exempt the privatized enterprise from all liability for the consequences of acts of omission or commission on the part of the SOE, while leaving this liability with the old shareholder, that is, the state. A second alternative is to privatize the enterprise with all its rights and obligations intact but place a cap on environmental liability, above which the government would compensate the buyers, or else to negotiate some other division of responsibility between government and buyer. In a third scenario, the buyers assume all the obligations of the enterprise they acquire and reflect the contingent liabilities risk by offering a lower purchase price.

Each alternative has advantages and disadvantages that need to be assessed in light of the enterprise to be privatized, the privatization technique to be used, and the sector and country concerned. The first alternative will be the obvious choice when dealing with polluting enterprises for which it is difficult to assess the extent of environmental liability. The second alternative involves some degree of negotiation and therefore does not lend itself to privatization by public flotation, for example. The third alternative is a good choice when the enterprise is not a heavy polluter or the liability can be easily quantified; it will, however, usually be shunned when the environmental liability regulations and jurisprudence are either not very clear or not well developed. Even where the law or the agreements provide that the new owners incur no liability, buyers would be well advised to ensure that the government will effectively assume its responsibilities as previous owner.

The next step is to ascertain what rules apply when an enterprise's plant is not in compliance with environmental regulations. While buyers should not normally receive special exemptions, they are often given a certain time limit within which to make the necessary investments to bring the plant into compliance. The cost of these compliance measures is normally borne by the buyer. This was the approach taken in Poland, among other countries (see Greenspan-Bell and Kolaja 1993).

Finally, potential buyers will also want to know what new environmental regulations could affect their future obligations. The greater the uncertainty on this point, the lower the price they will be ready to offer for the enterprise. Privatization can thus offer a unique opportunity to modernize a country's environmental legislation. This can be all the more desirable where a transfer of activity from the public to the private sector could otherwise lead to increased pollution (for example, as a result of increased capacity utilization of the privatized plant). If such reform takes place before privatization, the costs it entails for private operators will be reflected in the amounts of the bids received. If reform is deferred, the new owners will tend to oppose it, because it would raise their production costs.

It should also be noted that the privatization program can have a very positive environmental impact by speeding up the replacement of obsolete and polluting technologies with more recent "green" technologies. Similarly, by eliminating the direct and indirect subsidies often received by SOEs, privatizations can promote more rational utilization of resources with, once again, a beneficial impact on the environment. Moreover, privatization can foster better compliance with environmental standards; too often, SOEs were exempted from existing legislation or else got preferential treatment through lax enforcement.

The issues raised in this section will normally have to be dealt with through specific provisions in the environmental legislation, the privatization legislation, or the privatization agreements between government and buyers.

Dispute Settlement Mechanisms

The existence of fair, efficient, and credible mechanisms for settling disputes is important not only to resolve problems arising directly from the privatization itself but also to create an environment conducive to private sector activity. Indeed, litigation can be very costly and time-consuming. The smooth (or poor) functioning of a country's judicial system is a major but often overlooked feature of the overall business environment. Potential investors will take due account of the degree of competence and independence of the judiciary, the accessibility and efficiency of the courts and tribunals, and the facilities that exist for settling disputes amicably outside the judicial system.

The way a government handles disputes with investors also determines credibility. The Peruvian government, for instance, decided to settle the main outstanding disputes between Peru and foreign investors[63] in conjunction with the adoption of its economic reform program and before starting privatization operations. A fair settlement of these disputes could only contribute to the country's good image abroad, a prerequisite for attracting new investors.

Lawsuits arising out of contracts with local employees, banks, suppliers, and customers generally fall within the jurisdiction of the local courts. This may also be the case for litigation arising out of privatization transactions per se, though for important transactions involving foreign investors, international arbitration is usually the preferred forum for settling disputes between investors and government.

63. The government indemnified the American Insurance Group, which had to compensate the Belco company following nationalization of the latter in Peru. The government also arrived at an agreement with Southern Peru Copper Corporation (SPCC): SPCC undertook to proceed with new investments and the government agreed to release a company account of over $50 million, which had been frozen under previous judicial proceedings. Finally, in the case of its dispute with Occidental Petroleum, the government agreed to raise the price per barrel of petroleum. See also *Financial Times*, 20 November 1991.

Arbitration can be either domestic or international. Domestic arbitration proceedings are normally conducted under the aegis of local law and involve local arbitration institutions. International arbitration proceedings, on the other hand, are normally governed by the rules of international business and generally take place under the auspices of agencies specially set up to settle international disputes.[64] Recourse to some form of domestic arbitration is particularly important in countries that lack efficient courts, because it offers a supplemental means of settling disputes with suppliers, customers, employees, and other local parties. International arbitration is often the preferred method for relatively large contracts, particularly those to which a government is a party.

Although the law or constitution of some countries may preclude the government and other public entities from submitting to arbitration, arbitrators typically will not allow public entities that have entered into agreements calling for arbitration to avail themselves of that escape measure. But going to arbitration is not enough, of course, in itself; it must also be possible to obtain enforcement of arbitration awards. This is a matter of major concern for potential investors. If enforcement is difficult or blocked in the host country, the aggrieved party may still obtain forced execution in another country, provided the party against which the award was issued (including public entities) has assets abroad that can be seized.

A privatization is a transaction between a public entity, typically a sovereign state, and a private one; its enforcement may thus require actions against a sovereign. In some countries the state may, however, claim immunity with respect to actions brought against it. But to attract investors and enhance the likelihood of success of the privatization program, a government may decide to waive its immunities. It should also be noted that the privatization law may grant the privatization agency and its members restricted immunity for suits filed against them, as in the Philippines (see section 32 of presidential proclamation no. 50).

Privatization is often contentious and controversial and has inevitably generated many lawsuits, usually filed by political or other opponents seeking to block or annul a privatization program or operation, by would-be buyers whose offers were not selected, or by former owners.[65] Even where these suits have been dismissed, they have nonetheless slowed down the implementation of the privatization program. Significant privatization-

64. Such as the arbitration machinery established by the International Chamber of Commerce, Paris, and the International Center for Settlement of Investment Disputes (ICSID), Washington, D.C. ICSID, which is part of the World Bank Group, handles disputes between a sovereign state and an investor who is a national of another state, provided that both the host country and the investor's country of origin have adhered to the Washington convention of 1965 establishing ICSID.

65. For constitutional challenges to privatization and related litigation, see the section of chapter 2 on control of constitutionality; see also the section on past nationalizations in this chapter.

related litigation has, for instance, occurred in Turkey, Brazil, Russia, Germany, and most eastern European countries.[66]

Foreign Legislation

Privatization is often seen as a purely national process. Foreign legislation can, however, have an important and often unexpected impact on the privatization process (for a discussion of the impact of international law, see chapter 2). In Argentina, for example, the initial tender documents for the privatization of ENTEL required that the operator of each of the two privatized telephone companies own at least 10 percent of the company's equity. Meanwhile, the Argentine government had expressed a clear preference to have one of the U.S. telephone companies as operator. Under U.S. law, however, the "Baby Bells" (companies formed from the breakup of AT&T) would not have been authorized to hold more than 4.9 percent of the capital of one of the Argentine companies. Since these two requirements were obviously incompatible, the Argentine government decided to reduce the minimum operator-owned share of the capital to 4.9 percent. Problems of this kind should normally be identified and settled before the launch of the privatization transaction.

The privatization of the Hungarian telephone company MATAV affords another interesting example. A consortium of Deutsche Telekom and Ameritech acquired 30.3 percent of the company in December 1933 (see chapter 7). Six months later, the Hungarian government wanted to sell a second tranche

66. *Turkey*: The transfer to Société des Ciments Français in 1989 of five state-owned cement companies and the transfer of a majority shareholding in the company USAS (in-flight catering services) to a subsidiary of the Scandinavian company SAS were blocked by an administrative tribunal in January 1990, because a lawsuit was instituted by the opposition parties against the decision of the privatization agency. In a judgment handed down in March 1990, the court declared the two privatization agreements to be null and void on the ground that they contravened the provisions of a 1987 decree on privatization which gave priority to Turkish buyers. In July 1990 the council of state rejected the government's appeal, thereby annulling the sales of the cement companies and USAS. The government did not seek to regain control of these companies, however. "Although the annulment of the sale of state cement factories to French interests in the late 1980s had no practical effect (the council of state decisions were simply ignored), it did unsettle prospective foreign investors" (*Oxford Analytica*, 11 December 1995). Many other lawsuits have been filed in Turkey to block implementation of the privatization program, sometimes successfully. See Kjellström 1990, pp. 30–32; see also *Wall Street Journal*, 29 April 1994.

Brazil: Dozens of lawsuits have been filed to try to block the privatization program, especially the privatization of USIMINAS, the first SOE scheduled to be sold under this program (see *Financial Times*, 21 January 1992). At the end of 1992 USIMINAS had nevertheless been privatized, together with 17 other companies (see LatinFinance 1993, p. 62).

Russia: The loans-for-shares scheme (see note 49 in chapter 6) is at the origin of some of those disputes. Following Uneximbank's takeover of Norilsk Nickel, management of the company filed suit to invalidate the loans-for-shares scheme, but their claim was rejected by the Moscow arbitration court on February 27, 1996 (see *Privatisation International*, March 1996, p. 23).

through a public flotation on the Budapest stock exchange. The foreign shareholders feared that the public offering price would be lower than the price they had paid, which would have forced Ameritech to write down its investment in MATAV and post a corresponding loss on its balance sheet to conform to U.S. accounting legislation. In December 1995 the cash-strapped Hungarian government finally sold an additional 37 percent to Deutsche Telekom and Ameritech, with the understanding that they would reduce their stake later through public flotation.

Similarly, in the case of privatization of a bank with foreign subsidiaries, the government should normally consult the foreign regulatory agencies, which may have to approve the effect of the change in ownership on the subsidiaries. More generally, privatization transactions can raise problems in another country on competition grounds, even when the privatized company is not in violation of competition law in the country in which it is established.

For large privatization operations that draw on international capital, shares of the enterprise to be privatized are sometimes placed on foreign capital markets either at the same time as the domestic market flotation or in a second stage. The securities regulations of the countries concerned will then apply. Many privatization operations in the United Kingdom were accompanied by private or public placements in the United States using the American Depository Receipts (ADR) technique.[67] The same technique was used in the privatization of numerous companies, particularly telephone companies, in Argentina, Chile, New Zealand, Indonesia, Mexico, and Venezuela (see *American Depository Receipts and Privatizations*, Bank of New York, 1991). Legislative provisions have also been adopted in China to facilitate direct offering and listing of shares of Chinese public enterprises on the Hong Kong securities exchange (see Salbaing 1993 and the section above on securities legislation).

Conclusion

This chapter has illustrated how various aspects of a country's legal environment not usually directly associated with privatization can nevertheless substantially affect a privatization program. To try to privatize an enterprise in a general environment hostile to the private sector would usually be to court immediate failure. The factors discussed in this chapter that can contribute to the success of a privatization program include, among others, recognition and protection of private ownership, elimination of all forms of dis-

---

67. An ADR is a security issued by a U.S. bank in U.S. currency in exchange for shares of the foreign company deposited with it or in a foreign bank. This security circulates as a bearer document representing the shares deposited. One ADR may represent one share of the foreign company or multiple shares (for example, ten shares).

crimination against the private sector, introduction and protection of competition, a corporate law regime fostering the creation and efficient functioning of commercial companies (as well as the liquidation of insolvent ones), development of financial markets, strengthening of social security schemes, management of environmental liabilities, and settlement of disputes. For transition countries, in particular, reforms have been needed in all or almost all categories reviewed in this chapter, amounting to the privatization of the national economy as a whole.

Although some of these factors may affect the privatization process only indirectly, others will have a direct impact. Property law is a case in point, as changes in legislation may result in transfers of assets from the public back to the private sector, especially in countries that have experienced heavy nationalizations. Moreover, many privatization transactions will be governed by corporate law, in particular in the case of SOEs organized under private law. Foreign investment legislation may well determine to what extent foreigners can participate in the privatization process, whereas securities legislation will normally apply to privatization through public offerings. Similarly, labor and social legislation will often play a key role in privatization operations.

One should, however, bear in mind that it would be pointless to try to document and remedy all the shortcomings identified in all of the areas discussed in this chapter. The scope of the reform program to be undertaken will depend mainly on each country's specific situation: a country emerging from a centrally planned economic system, for instance, will have to create a whole new framework for economic activity.

The government's legal advisers will need to identify the laws, regulations, practices, and institutions that pose major obstacles to privatization. Once these problems have been identified, their elimination must be assigned high priority. This will be achieved in some cases by repealing or amending the relevant legislation, and in others by inserting specific provisions in a privatization law. Other problems will inevitably arise during implementation of the program; these can be addressed when they occur.

The resourcefulness of the government, the buyers, and their advisers will often produce contractual techniques tailored to the specific features of the country and the transaction, which can circumvent any remaining obstacles. Indeed, governments are not alone in having to reexamine the entire legal framework for business transactions: strategic investors will do the same on their side, as illustrated in box 3.4.

Finally, having assessed a country's overall business environment, investors will often demand government undertakings and guarantees to protect themselves from shortcomings or weaknesses in the legal framework. The worse the business environment, the more likely the government will have to increase the level of comfort of the investors through formal guarantees and other sweeteners.

Box 3.4   Company Valuation by Advisers to Potential Investors

Before buying a company or asset, private buyers will normally take whatever measures they deem necessary to evaluate the company's business prospects and value its assets and liabilities, taking into account any legal defects that could encumber the company or some of its assets or hinder their transferability. A typical "due diligence" evaluation of an SOE being privatized would include (a) analysis of its corporate form and review of its bylaws, charter, articles, and so on; (b) evaluation of the company's ongoing contracts (including purchase and sale agreements), their enforceability, and the possibility of renegotiating them; (c) review of the ownership status and transferability of assets, such as intellectual property rights and real estate; (d) assessment of any labor regulations and practices applicable to SOE employees and of any labor agreements or arrangements with the employees that may have special relevance to the privatization process; (e) evaluation of the company's outstanding warranty obligations and product liability risks, if any; (f) identification of any official permits, approvals, and licenses required for exercise of the company's activities, and study of the requirements for obtaining these, as well as their transferability to the purchaser under existing law; (g) assessment of the degree of compliance of the company with applicable laws (regarding competition, the environment, labor law, and so on) and of any risk of legal action resulting from noncompliance; (h) review of the company's observance of any applicable tax laws and assessment of the situation of the privatized company with respect to the applicable company tax legislation; and (i) finally, evaluation of any pending or expected litigation and assessment of how the company will deal with these disputes after it has been privatized.

Source: Chaudhri 1991.

4

Privatization and
Public-Sector Management

Privatization is a public-sector activity, a fact that is all too often overlooked. Special attention must thus be given to the laws and regulations that affect the operations of the government and the public sector. Some of these are subsumed under the country's constitution or constitutional traditions and have already been discussed in chapter 2. Others are established specifically for the privatization program; these are discussed in chapters 5 and 6. In addition, ordinary public-sector regulations and other norms, not intended primarily to regulate the transfer of enterprises or assets from the public to the private sector, may nevertheless affect the privatization process. If they hinder privatization, they may have to be repealed or amended. These norms are the subject matter of this chapter.

Provisions determining the legal owner of a public enterprise or asset to be privatized will be discussed first, followed by an analysis of the rules that govern the exercise of ownership rights over these enterprises or assets. Issues include not only the elimination of provisions that would prohibit privatization but also whether existing legislation allows SOEs to be restructured before their privatization to make them sufficiently attractive to potential investors. This may involve, for example, taking the necessary steps to free the new enterprise of certain obligations of the old SOE. Enterprises that are organized under public law may have to be transformed into companies organized under private law before privatization can proceed. Prior restructuring may even go as far as breaking up or liquidating the SOE. The way in which finance laws can affect privatization operations is discussed in the closing section of the chapter.

Identifying the Legal Owners

In order to own property it is necessary, legally speaking, to possess juridical personality, that is, to have a separate and distinct existence in law. The state, as a legal person, and provincial and local entities, which typically also possess juridical personality, may thus be the legal owners of public enterprises. On the other hand, in many countries ministries do not possess separate juridical personality and therefore cannot own enterprises per se.

SOEs may also be owned by other SOEs or public entities. SOEs or public holding companies are usually the owners of their assets and subsidiaries. This is not, however, always the case. In Bulgaria, Guinea (up to 1985), Poland (until recently), and other countries whose legal systems are or used to be modeled on the Soviet system, the SOEs do not (or did not) own their real estate (land, buildings, plant) or sometimes even their movable assets (tools, vehicles, furniture). The state financed the procurement of these assets and in return the SOE paid an annual sum representing depreciation. These assets continued to belong to the state and could not be sold by the SOE without prior authorization. This system has important implications, in particular for the allocation of debt and privatization receipts. When a sale takes place, the proceeds normally accrue to the state, which also keeps the debt.[1]

In many socialist (or formerly socialist) countries, including Hungary, Viet Nam, and the former Yugoslavia, profound confusion existed between state property and property of a particular enterprise or its employees.[2] In addition, uncertainty prevailed as to which public authority was the true owner, a situation also found in Russia, Laos, and Germany.[3] These difficulties were

1. In Bulgaria, the law was first amended in February 1991 to allow SOEs to retain 40 percent of the proceeds of such sales. See the section in chapter 5 concerning the allocation of privatization proceeds.

2. *Viet Nam*: The state receives a fixed remuneration on the capital invested in SOEs (4 to 6 percent, depending on the sector). Some deduced that when the net income of an SOE exceeded the state's fixed remuneration, the surplus belonged to the enterprise itself. This ignores the fact that the state is not a lender receiving a fixed return for a limited risk, but an owner-investor. In these circumstances the profits of the SOEs should belong to the state, as the SOEs themselves belong to it. The Vietnamese government has apparently had to clarify the situation by declaring that the state owned the entire capital of the SOEs, including the original investment as well as any subsequent profits. This clarification of ownership rights was needed to facilitate the corporatization of SOEs and the implementation of (limited) privatization.

Former Yugoslavia: Clarifying ownership rights is a particularly difficult problem in the successor states of the former Yugoslavia because of the diffuse nature of ownership of public enterprises. Article 1 of the privatization law of the Republic of Slovenia (November 11, 1992), is informative on this point: "This law regulates the ownership transformation of enterprises with social capital into enterprises with known owners."

3. Consider, for example, the case of the East German municipalities which claimed, unsuccessfully, ownership of the electricity companies established on their territory. The power contract (Stromvertrag) concluded by the two preunification German governments prescribed that only 49 percent of the capital of these companies could be held by municipalities, the majority holding of 51 percent belonging, pursuant to this agreement, to the West German electricity companies. The Treuhandanstalt accordingly completed the sale of the power distribution companies of the former East Germany in February 1994 by selling the three companies of Thuringia to Bayernwerk, West Germany's third electricity company; the sale of the East German electricity generating company VEAG to a consortium comprising Bayernwerk and Preussen Elektra was completed in September 1994. See also table 2, and *Financial Times*, 10 February 1994 and 7 September 1994.

often complicated by past nationalizations or expropriations (see chapter 3). Prior clarification of ownership rights is obviously critical for a smooth implementation of the privatization process.

Exercise of Ownership Rights

Once the legal owner is identified, the next step is to ascertain who has the power to exercise the owner's rights. Two separate questions are involved here, though the distinction between them is not always well understood: Which entity is authorized to exercise the owner's rights? And, which official(s) within that entity has such authority? Indeed, the state, public bodies, and public enterprises are able to exercise their rights only through the agency of duly authorized persons. For a privatization transaction, it must be clear to whom the power to alienate or transfer ownership has been conferred (see also chapters 5 and 6).

If no provisions in the legislation governing public enterprises or assets spell out who has legal capacity to sell SOEs, other parts of the country's legal framework might provide guidance. In New Zealand, for example, in the absence of specific legislation to the contrary, the government or specified ministers are deemed to be authorized to sell public assets (see chapter 2 and box 4.2). The same situation prevails in most common-law countries.

No matter who is authorized to sell in the name of the state, that authorization (whether express or tacit) should be unambiguous in order to preclude legal disputes on the subject.

Alienation of Public Enterprises and Shareholdings

The legislation governing SOEs sometimes explicitly authorizes their privatization by subjecting it to specific, and usually very basic, rules. The Mexican program, one of the most ambitious and successful privatization programs, is based largely on the provisions of the public enterprise law of 1986.[4] Article 32 of that law provides that when an SOE ceases to be of strategic importance, or when the public interest or the national economy so requires, the minister responsible for privatization shall, taking into account the views of the concerned sectoral ministries, propose to the government the sale of the state's holdings in the enterprise. Article 32 further provides that in the event of such a sale, the employees of the SOE shall enjoy a preemptive right. Article 68 states that the sale of shares may be carried out through the stock exchange or through financial institutions, on the basis of guidelines issued jointly by the minister

---

4. More than 80 percent of the 1,155 SOEs in the government's portfolio at the beginning of the program were liquidated or sold in this way, bringing in total receipts of over $21 billion between 1988 and 1993 (the most active period of the program). See *New York Times*, 27 October 1993.

of programming and budget and the minister of finance and public credit. These two articles form the legal basis for most Mexican privatization operations. Similar provisions are found in the SOE legislation of other countries; in some cases, they have been replaced with more specific privatization legislation.[5]

Existing legislation may also impose specific legal forms. The principle of parallelism of forms, according to which the same legal instrument that was used to establish an SOE should be used to abolish or transform it, could mandate the use of specific and sometimes different legal instruments to privatize SOEs in a given country. This principle, which is not universal, is sometimes given legal sanction. An example is found in Togo, where article 36 of Organic Law no. 82-5 of June 16, 1982, on joint-venture companies, states that "if an SOE has been established pursuant to a ministerial decree issued by the Council of Ministers, it can only be privatized or liquidated following the same procedure."

Moreover, SOE laws often contain provisions governing (a) the acquisition and transfer by the state (or other public agencies) of holdings in joint-venture companies and (b) the creation and transfer of subsidiaries of SOEs. These laws may also limit the right of SOEs to buy or sell shares of other companies. Although such restrictions can slow the privatization process, they may be essential in order to prevent abuses, to avoid creeping renationalizations, or to subject such sales to common rules and regulations. Privatization laws sometimes carry these restrictions, too (see chapter 5).

Alienation of Public Assets

The alienation of public assets is often governed by administrative law, specific legislation on public property or public finance legislation. In countries with French legal influence, such as Morocco (see box 4.1), a distinction is

---

5. In *Burundi*, for example, article 6 of Decree-Law no. 1/027 of September 1988, which sets the legal framework for public-law companies and joint-venture companies under private law, provided that state participations can be alienated only by presidential decree issued on the advice of the minister of finance and of the minister with jurisdiction over the SOE to be privatized. This general provision was replaced by Decree-Law no. 1/21 of August 12, 1991, on privatization of public enterprises, which delegates the power to privatize to the government, regulates the privatization procedures, and empowers the minister of finance to sign the deed of sale on behalf of the government

In *Guinea*, article 7 of Ordinance no. 91/025 of March 1991 on the institutional framework for public enterprises provided that "the state's shares in public enterprises are managed by a specialized department of the Ministry of Economic Affairs and Finance. This department may transfer all or part of these participations to private persons on terms to be set by a privatization agreement." Just over a year later this provision was replaced, however, by a new article 7 which provides that "the state's shares in public enterprises shall be managed by a specialized agency of the Ministry of Finance, which may transfer all or part of these participations on the terms set by law" (Ordinance no. 92/022 of May 1992). A law setting the rules governing SOE privatizations was not enacted until more than a year later (August 20, 1993).

Box 4.1 Public Domain Legislation in Morocco

The legislation governing the state's assets, in particular its public domain, has constrained the privatization of some SOEs in Morocco. Indeed, there is "a category of assets that cannot be owned privately because they are for the use of all, which are to be administered by the state on behalf of the community" (preamble of the Dahir of July 1, 1914, on the public domain). These assets, which include roads, railroads, rivers, ports, and telephone lines, among other assets, are inalienable (they cannot be sold) and imprescriptible (the state's rights cannot be lost by way of prescription or statute of limitations). Broadly speaking, all assets assigned to the provision of public services are considered to be part of the public domain in Morocco. Those parts of the public domain not deemed to be of public utility may, however, be reclassified by decree of the prime minister.

The fact that public domain assets cannot be sold does not imply that they cannot be used by private parties, however; a temporary occupation permit or a concession may allow private use, for instance. Temporary occupation is governed by a Dahir of November 30, 1918, which provides that the public domain may be used if the minister of public works so authorizes and an annual fee is paid. Such permits are not only temporary but also revocable. They can be granted for a maximum duration of ten years, which may, exceptionally, be extended to twenty years. They can at all times be withdrawn by the administration with only three months' notice and without any compensation.

Other legal techniques allow the lease or transfer of limited rights on public domain assets without transfer of ownership rights. As public domain restrictions forbid the transfer of full ownership of two existing power plants at Jorf Lasfar, the proposed privatization contract calls for a transfer of the right to operate the plants for a thirty-year period. More generally, long-term concessions (typically between 30 and 50 years) were granted in Morocco (mainly before independence in 1956), which allowed private operators to use assets belonging to the state's public domain to provide a public service. The concession mechanism has never been codified in Morocco, however, and it remains governed by (largely preindependence) case law (see also chapter 7).

Such legislation on state property is clearly antiquated and stands in the way of many potentially desirable privatization options.

---

sometimes drawn between assets forming part of the state's public domain and those belonging to the state's private domain; the latter can be alienated more easily.[6] Public domain assets cannot be alienated except by transferring them first to the state's private domain, which can only be done by virtue of a law; they can, however, be leased.

---

6. The state's public domain comprises the assets owned by a legal entity organized under public law (such as the state, a municipality, a province, or an *établissement public*) and dedicated for public or collective use and operation (such as, for example, assets assigned to a public service, rivers, river banks and beaches, and roads). The state's private domain comprises all state assets that do not belong to the public domain.

The rules governing the sale of public assets, where such rules exist, are often ill-suited to the needs of a privatization program. In Italy, for example, the rules governing the sale of state property dated back to a 1924 law that imposed very complicated administrative procedures, including review by the council of state and control by the court of accounts. To speed up the privatization process, a decree-law was enacted in 1993 that authorized the government to follow greatly simplified procedures for the alienation of state assets.[7]

As for the sale of SOE assets, SOE legislation and statutes usually empower the management bodies of an SOE to sell its assets or subsidiaries, subject to certain limits. State holding or portfolio companies are as a rule authorized to transfer subsidiaries or financial participations (this applies, for example, to CORFO in Chile and to state holding companies in Egypt).

Company or SOE legislation and statutes often define the respective powers of the general shareholders' meeting (or government), the board of directors, and the general manager—for example, by setting financial thresholds that delimit their areas of authority with respect to the alienation or transfer of assets. Other provisions may regulate the authority of company officers to commit the SOE by contract and prescribe penalties for those who overstep their powers.

Such legislation should allow an SOE sufficient flexibility to carry out its activities efficiently. That flexibility should not, however, extend so far as to allow SOE managers or directors to sell the main components of their business or to alienate its basic assets without control by the owner (the state or other public agencies). In Viet Nam, for example, a ministry of finance circular prescribes that a public enterprise must obtain the approval of its supervising ministry if its assets are to be used to establish a joint-venture company; to purchase shares in joint-stock companies or to invest in limited liability companies, the approval of the prime minister is needed.[8]

Prohibition of Alienation

In some instances a government may wish to declare a moratorium on all transfers of assets or shares of public enterprises. This may be the case where parastatal reforms are part of a comprehensive program of public-sector reform or where they arise from radical changes in the political regime, events that often are attended by instability and uncertainty concerning the

7. This instrument, Decree-Law no. 389 of September 27, 1993, had to be renewed many times by successive decree-laws pending ratification by parliament. It also prescribes privatization arrangements and procedures. See Ulissi 1994.

8. Finance Ministry Circular no. 95 TC/CN, issuing supplemental instructions concerning utilization of the capital of public enterprises (November 11, 1993).

exercise of ownership rights. Such moratoriums have been adopted in Bulgaria, Cambodia, Russia, and Ukraine, for example, to stop the proliferation of transactions—many of them fraudulent—that took place during transitions in these countries.[9] A prohibition on transfers of public enterprises or assets is usually limited in time.

As mentioned before, a country's constitution or legislation may also place constraints on privatization. Legislation governing enterprises or businesses organized under public law may rule out their outright privatization. A public enterprise law may list certain enterprises that cannot be privatized, as was the case in New Zealand, for example (see chapter 2 and box 4.2). In other cases, privatization may be prohibited by the public enterprise's own statutes or bylaws.

Prior Restructuring of Public Enterprises

Restructuring measures are often necessary to enable the privatization of an SOE. Where the purpose is to make an enterprise at least potentially viable as a going concern once it is privatized, restructuring measures will focus mainly on the management and finances of the SOE. If the SOE is governed by public law, it will probably have to be converted into a company established under private law. In other cases, more radical action may be deemed preferable, including breaking up the SOE or liquidating it completely.

These various restructuring measures may require amendment or repeal of existing legal provisions or even the enactment of new legislation. Some measures required to effect privatization may be left to the new owners; the buyer of a former SOE may, for example, have to establish a new company to take over the privatized activities. In the context of this section, the term "prior" refers to restructuring measures carried out by the public owner before the sale, not by the buyer after or as part of the privatization.

The scope and range of possible restructuring measures may be far-reaching, as illustrated, for example, by the radical restructuring of the Argentine oil company YPF over the three years leading up to its

9. See, for example, the resolution of the National Supreme Council of Cambodia of June 10, 1993, approving Directive no. 93-7 of UNTAC (the United Nations Transitional Authority in Cambodia), which placed a moratorium on the sale, transfer, and lease of public assets and prescribed that any transactions relating to such assets occurring between the dates of the decision and the establishment of a new government would be deemed to be illegal and null and void. This resolution was published as an announcement in the domestic and foreign press (see *Far Eastern Economic Review*, 5 August 1993).

privatization.[10] Similarly, privatizing a large infrastructure company generally requires several years of preparation and prior restructuring (see chapter 7). The subject of corporate restructuring exceeds the scope of this book,
however. In the next sections the emphasis will be on issues with special
import for privatization programs.

Some governments have sometimes gone beyond the legal and organizational measures discussed here to engage in physical restructuring of plant
and equipment. They have invested large sums in SOEs before privatization
in the hope of making them more attractive to investors. Such investments,
including modernization and expansion of buildings, infrastructure, and
plant, have generally turned out to be ill-advised; governments have rarely
managed to recoup such investments at sale time (see Kikeri, Nellis, and
Shirley 1992, p. 60; Lopez-de-Silanes 1996).

Decisions on prior restructuring are often complex and difficult. Those in
charge should be committed to the privatization process and have broad
powers to take the measures that may be needed. Such responsibility could
be vested with the supervising ministry, the privatization agency, the management of the enterprise itself, or a special entity set up for the purpose, such
as the Albanian public enterprises restructuring agency. SOE management
needs to be on board. When this was not the case, countries such as Argentina
and Mexico have not hesitated to replace them with new managers committed to the restructuring and privatization process. Congo has gone one step
further by removing existing management and appointing a special administrator with broad powers to prepare major SOEs for privatization.

Contractual Obligations

If the new company is the legal successor of the old SOE, it will in principle
succeed to all the latter's rights and obligations: ongoing contracts, including labor contracts and contracts with suppliers and customers; pension
obligations; contingent liabilities (for example, those arising out of acts of
pollution committed by the SOE, or suits filed against it); payment arrears
and defaults and undisclosed obligations or debts; the right to recover sums

10. The success of the privatization of YPF is attributed in large part to the effectiveness of Jose
Estenssoro, the CEO the government installed at the head of YPF in 1990 to prepare its privatization. YPF was a poorly managed giant, characterized by serious overstaffing, highly diversified
assets, and heavy losses. The new CEO reduced the company's work force from 51,000 at the end
of 1990 to 11,000 in March 1993 and under 6,000 by the end of 1994. He sold more than two-thirds
of YPF's reserves to competitors under a demonopolization program for the oil industry, liquidated noncore assets (including 23 aircraft and 27 vessels), and turned YPF into one of Latin
America's most efficient energy producers. After losing $6 billion between 1981 and 1989, YPF
posted a net profit of $706 million in 1993 despite a fall in oil prices. YPF's public flotation, com-
pleted in July 1993, was an enormous success, bringing in over $3 billion. Jose Estenssoro died in
a plane crash in May 1995. See *International Financing Review, Review of the Year 1993*, p. 168; *The
Economist*, 2 July 1994, pp. 62–63; *Wall Street Journal*, 5 May 1995.

owed to the former SOE; the benefit of state guarantees regarding obligations of the SOE; and so on.

Such universal succession could jeopardize the success of some privatization operations. Indeed, buyers may be unwilling to assume certain obligations of the former SOE, even if they are given recourse against the seller. This would be the case in particular for contingent, uncertain, or undisclosed obligations. This problem can be circumvented, however, at the corporatization or privatization stage by limiting the new company's obligations to those expressly listed in the agreements setting it up; the state would remain responsible for residual obligations.

Changes in labor regime or levels are often required as part of the prior restructuring of an SOE, whether because the SOE was overstaffed, civil service or other exceptional elements were part of the SOE personnel regime, or other reasons. As mentioned above, the managers of an SOE will occasionally have to be terminated either because they do not support the restructuring and privatization program or because they do not have the skills required to manage the process. Where layoffs have been necessary, the choice has been between dismissing redundant employees before privatization or letting the new owner eliminate the redundancies and pay the required severance compensation, in return for a lower sale price. These and other labor issues arising in the context of privatization have already been addressed in chapter 3.

Some ongoing contracts may also need to be renegotiated to allow or facilitate privatization. These may range from management or operating contracts to simple procurement contracts. As an example, one of the first steps taken by Germany's Treuhandanstalt in preparation for the privatization of Interhotel was to cancel an operating contract between that company and a hotel group from the western part of the country; the contract was worded so that the hotel group could have obtained control of Interhotel for a very modest initial investment (see *Financial Times*, 22 November 1991). To avoid such problems, some privatization agencies or holding companies require that an enterprise to be privatized submit all major contracts for prior approval.

Financial Restructuring

Public enterprises are often technically insolvent or in a state of bankruptcy. Financial restructuring may thus be needed before privatization. The problem arises especially with corporatization, when SOEs are transformed into companies organized under private, commercial law (see below in this chapter). That transformation means that the public enterprise immediately becomes subject to existing business legislation, including the provisions on maintenance of social capital and bankruptcy. As a result, neither corporatization nor privatization may be sustainable if not preceded or accompanied by in-depth financial restructuring.

Financial restructuring will typically involve cleaning up the balance sheet by removing excess debt; deciding on the treatment of state-guaranteed obligations; renegotiating ongoing agreements with banks, donors, and other creditors (particularly when these agreements contain clauses limiting the transferability of the SOE or its assets); and setting up financial systems and preparing new financial statements in accordance with generally accepted accounting principles.

In order to attract private investors, a government will sometimes have to consider writing off all or part of the SOE's debts to the state or other public entities.[11] Such debt write-offs were common, for instance, in many of the large U.K. privatizations. An empirical study of Mexican privatizations showed, however, that debt reduction programs had no impact on net privatization proceeds; in other words, the higher sale price was canceled by the cost incurred by the government in absorbing the debt (see Lopez-de-Silanes 1996). Prior debt reduction, though often neutral from a financial point of view, may be needed politically. Indeed, success is often judged by the amount of gross privatization proceeds rather than by net revenue. Also, giving buyers money to take over an SOE with negative net worth may not be politically palatable, whereas a positive cash sale after debt restructuring may not be frowned upon.

In some cases the state may also have to take over or guarantee some of the debts contracted by the SOE with third parties, or guarantee that the obligations to be borne by the privatized company will not exceed a specific ceiling.[12] The impact that Paris and London club agreements on public and commercial debt rescheduling have on such measures, as well as the consequences of such measures on the market discount of SOE and state debt, must be carefully considered.

Although creditors often prefer sovereign debt to nonguaranteed debt of an SOE, this is not always the case. This issue has created some controversy in the preprivatization restructuring of some African telecommunications companies. The question was whether debt of the former telecommunications department of the central government should continue to be treated as state debt (trading at deep discounts) or be transferred to the books of the newly established and corporatized telecommunications company. A transfer to the new company would most likely have increased the market value of the debt significantly, because claims against the telecommunications company could be enforced more easily and from abroad.

Some have suggested that in transition countries debt should be added to the balance sheet of SOEs before their privatization. This somewhat unorthodox approach may be justified in those countries where the state corporatized its enterprises without transferring the related outstanding debt to the SOEs, which meant that the balance sheet of many corporatized SOEs was not

11. Where the state continues to be a creditor of a privatized SOE, some governments have kept a certain degree of control over the management of the privatized enterprise, through a golden share or other techniques, in order to ensure repayment (see note 32 in chapter 5).

12. Such a guarantee will usually be requested when the magnitude of the SOE's liabilities is not precisely known at the time of privatization, as stressed in the section of chapter 3 on environmental law.

sufficiently leveraged.[13] This outcome should, however, lead to a higher sale price at privatization and thus would not require the addition of debt. The problem is more serious during the period leading up to privatization, when SOE managers may have too much free cash flow and few incentives to use it in the best interest of the company or shareholder(s); weak corporate governance of SOEs further compounds the problem.

In Germany, nearly all public enterprises were converted to private-law companies as of July 1, 1990 (see articles 11 and 12 of the June 1990 privatization law). The Treuhandanstalt became the sole shareholder of the former combines (the equivalent of holding companies or conglomerates) reorganized into joint-stock companies, while the component enterprises of the combines were converted into limited liability companies held by these new joint-stock companies. Under a separate 1990 law the new companies were required to draw up their opening balance sheet in deutsche marks (see Horn 1992, pp. 15–18). This involved revaluing all their assets and liabilities. If their liabilities exceeded their assets, the shareholder (the Treuhandanstalt or a joint-stock company belonging to it) had to decide whether or not to cover the shortfall. If it decided to cover the losses, the shareholder then had to replenish the new company's capital to bring it up to the minimum level required by law. Accordingly, the Treuhandanstalt had to take over a large amount of debt and inject fresh capital into many SOEs, a fact that helps explain its large borrowing requirements and a deficit exceeding 250 billion DM at the end of its term (see also note 35 in chapter 3 and the section in chapter 6 on financing the privatization process).

In New Zealand also, the privatization of many SOEs was preceded by financial restructuring carried out as part of the corporatization process. One of the purposes of this restructuring was to start off the corporatized SOEs with opening balance sheets and accounts conforming to generally accepted accounting principles and subject them to the same financial discipline as enterprises in the private sector (see Franks 1993, and box 4.2).

Abolishing Discriminatory Practices

An essential objective of prior restructuring should be to abolish all preferential treatment or exceptional rights and obligations of SOEs. The playing field should be level for these enterprises and those in the private sector (see the section in chapter 3 on protecting and promoting competition). All special privileges granted to the SOEs to be privatized will need to be abolished, including subsidies, tax and customs exemptions, state guarantees (express or implied) on their borrowings, preferential treatment in the award of public contracts, access to

13. In addition to being unorthodox, this approach may in some countries be illegal, especially if creditors are exposed to additional risk as a result of the transfer. See also the section above in this chapter dealing with socialist accounting practices, as well as the section of chapter 3 on transfer of liabilities.

reduced prices for specific inputs (utilities or petroleum, for example), exemptions from the application of competition law, special labor law provisions, and any other advantage or form of protection. This policy was followed in most privatizations carried out in New Zealand.[14] Similarly, in Belgium the state's guarantee of the public-sector financial institutions was removed and these institutions were integrated in the deposit insurance scheme covering private banks before their privatization (royal decree of March 1, 1995; see Vincent 1995, p. 12).

Obligations borne by SOEs but not by their private competitors should also be eliminated. In many countries, SOEs have traditionally performed social or noncommercial functions without adequate government compensation, such as supplying goods and services to specific regions or categories of customers at a loss; or providing health, education, housing, and other social services to employees and their families and sometimes even to an entire village (especially in the formerly communist countries). These social activities, generally performed at a loss, are often cross-subsidized by earnings from other activities. Subsidies of this kind are possible, however, only when the enterprise enjoys a monopoly or some other form of protection. Without protection, competitors of the SOE could supply goods and services at a lower price and thereby undermine the very base of the cross-subsidization system. Where such social functions are assigned to an SOE by law, these legal provisions will have to be abolished before privatization. These functions can either be assigned to other public entities or dealt with by way of service contracts between the government and private providers.[15]

Finally, in order to bring the status of the SOEs to be privatized into line with that of private-sector enterprises, it may be necessary as part of the restructuring process to limit government interference in SOE operations. General or specific SOE legislation sometimes includes provisions that limit SOE autonomy and, for example, give the government the right to appoint (in addition to the members of the board of directors representing the state as owner) a special representative with the power to suspend decisions of the board.[16]

14. In this way the New Zealand Coal Corporation ceased to be exempt from the requirement to obtain mining licenses. Similarly, New Zealand Telecom was corporatized, while the telecommunications sector was progressively deregulated and opened up to competition (see Williams and Franks 1992, p. 22).

15. The government may enter into a contract with or grant a subsidy to the newly privatized company or to another company to continue the activity. Thus the railway and urban transit services of Buenos Aires were contracted out, following calls for bids, to the private operators that asked for the lowest subsidies. As a result, the total subsidy (about $500 million a year during the 1980s) was reduced to about $100 million a year after privatization (see World Bank 1993, p. 8). The social obligations imposed on postal services throughout the world help to explain why there have been so few privatizations in this sector. Nevertheless, there is nothing to prevent privatization of postal services, given well-designed contracts that ensure maintenance of the universal postal service (if that is indeed the overriding objective).

16. Such a provision was included, for example, in Senegal's SOE legislation until 1990, when Law no. 87-19 of August 3, 1987, was repealed by Law no. 90-07 of June 26, 1990. The new law removed many types of controls over the SOEs.

Corporatization

A law may be needed to authorize the conversion of public enterprises organized under public law (including governmental businesses) into companies organized under private law.[17] This conversion, or "corporatization" as it is often called, may be required if the public enterprise is to be privatized as a going concern, with all its assets and liabilities and without interruption of activities.[18] It is always a prerequisite where privatization of a public-law enterprise is to be done by way of public flotation or other mode of share transfer (for example, voucher or coupon privatization). It is not, however, a necessary condition for the privatization of enterprises governed by public law. Indeed, this intermediate stage may be deemed to be too time-consuming, complex, or even redundant, and techniques other than sale of shares may be chosen to effect the transfer of a public-law enterprise to private parties.[19]

Corporatization laws are sometimes tailored to a given SOE and sometimes more general in scope. In the latter case they may permit more comprehensive restructuring of the parastatal sector. Typically, corporatization laws submit the SOE(s) to company law. They often include specific transition-type provisions dealing with the SOE's corporate organization, financial restructuring, ongoing contracts, labor regime, and so on. They often waive payments of transfer taxes, stamp duties, or other such costs that ordinarily would have arisen from changes in corporate structure or from the transfer of assets from one legal entity to another. They may also include exceptions to company law reflecting the specific characteristics of state-owned enterprises, such as the fact that they may have a single owner, whereas company law may require a minimum of two, three, or seven shareholders, for example.[20]

17. "Commercialization" of a company is a similar but less far-reaching operation, in that it does not involve the incorporation of the SOE (that is, its conversion into a company under private law). The aim of commercialization is to make the enterprise more profit-oriented. It can cover the following measures: instituting commercial accounting, publishing financial statements, defining commercial objectives, allowing the enterprise freedom to choose its suppliers, and setting up an autonomous board and management. The SOE would thus be managed in accordance with commercial (or private) practice. See also the section in chapter 1 concerning the legal status of public enterprises.

18. If, on the other hand, privatization of the SOE means selling specific assets and transferring clearly identified obligations, no legal transformation would be necessary, but the remaining parts of the SOE (the public-law company and all assets and obligations that have not been transferred) will have to be liquidated. See, on this topic, the sections that follow in this chapter concerning the breakup and liquidation of SOEs.

19. One example would be to let the winning bidder in a privatization establish a new company to which the assets and liabilities of the privatized SOE would be transferred. The old SOE shell would then be liquidated.

20. Section 23 of New Zealand's 1986 SOE act, for instance, allows the ministers of finance and SOEs to incorporate a company under the company law with a minimum of two instead of seven shareholders; this section provides an explicit exception to the minimum number of members set forth in the 1955 companies act.

Corporatization laws will usually not become effective until after amendment of the SOE's statutes or articles of agreement, which will typically have to be done within a time limit specified by the law. Some countries have, however, enacted broad corporatization laws with immediate effect.

Corporatization may be designed as a self-standing SOE reform, as was the case in Italy (Decree-Law no. 333 of July 1992), New Zealand (see box 4.2), Romania, and Sri Lanka, for example, though for many SOEs in these countries it turned out to be an intermediate stage preceding privatization.[21] Elsewhere, corporatization is provided for in the privatization legislation itself, as in Argentina, Czechoslovakia, Germany, Nigeria, and the United Kingdom.[22] Other countries have opted for a combination of these two formulas: in Bulgaria, for example, corporatization provisions were included in a law of January 1989 and then, after repeated amendments, embodied in the privatization law of April 1992.

Corporatization or transformation into a commercial company should not be seen simply as a legal step. It goes well beyond a change in legal status, and it usually requires a broad range of companion restructuring measures, including deregulation and financial and labor restructuring, which have already been discussed in the preceding sections. This can be a difficult, costly, and staff-intensive process, raising many complex issues. One should question whether it is an intermediate step worth taking in the context of a specific privatization.

New Zealand has been the trendsetter and reference point in SOE corporatization. It is difficult to isolate the specific effects of the New Zealand corporatization policy, however, because many SOEs were privatized soon after their corporatization and corporatization was accompanied by important other economic liberalization measures. Yet some effects are clear: corporatization has increased the accountability of SOEs, allowed better measures of their performance and comparisons with the performance of private firms, forced significant improvements in productivity, and prepared and furthered the cause

21. In Romania, article 1 of Law no. 15 of July 31,1990 provides for restructuring of the state economic units into autonomous units or private-law companies. Under article 2, the autonomous units operate in the "strategic" sectors of the economy, such as defense, energy, mining, postal services, and telecommunications. Setting up these companies is the first stage of a process leading to their partial privatization. Article 23 requires the government, within one month after the formation of these companies, to transfer 30 percent of the shares to the national privatization agency for distribution to Romanian citizens.

22. See Argentine Law no. 23696 on the reform of the state (August 18, 1989), particularly articles 6 and 15, which authorize the government to change the legal form of all SOEs within one year. See articles 11 and 12 of the large privatization law of Czechoslovakia (February 1991) and article 11 of the German privatization law (see p. 99). Article 5 of Nigerian Decree no. 25 of July 5, 1988, provides that all SOEs to be privatized that have not yet been incorporated under private law shall be so incorporated within twelve months after the effective date of that decree. The laws authorizing the privatization of large British public enterprises have generally provided for their prior transformation into limited liability companies (see Graham and Prosser 1991, p. 78).

Box 4.2   Corporatization in New Zealand

In 1984 when the Labour Party came to power, New Zealand was in the midst of a serious economic crisis characterized by very sluggish growth, high inflation, and a deteriorating balance of payments. The previous government had tried to resolve these problems through tariff barriers as well as price and exchange controls. The Labour government opted for a policy of deregulation, a major feature of which was corporatization of public enterprises as a prelude to their transfer to the private sector.

Objectives

The objectives of the SOE reform program were primarily to improve the economic performance of the SOEs and to enhance their accountability. Further objectives were

- To free SOEs of social and other noncommercial obligations
- To effect a clear separation between ownership and management of SOEs
- To empower managers to run these enterprises as commercial entities
- To level the playing field between SOEs and private enterprises.

1986 Law on SOEs

This law governs SOEs in general. It converts a number of ministerial departments into SOEs organized under private law and provides the following:

- The shares of each public enterprise are held jointly by the minister of finance and the (newly established) minister of state-owned enterprises; the ministers are expressly prohibited from selling shares in the newly corporatized enterprises
- The transfer of rights and obligations from the state to the newly incorporated SOEs is to be carried out pursuant to an agreement concluded between the state and the newly formed SOEs to purchase the existing departmental businesses at their full commercial value
- Each SOE is governed by a board of directors, whose members (mainly representatives of the private sector) are appointed by the two competent ministers
- The main purpose of each SOE is to operate as a commercial enterprise and, in particular, to do so as profitably as a private-sector firm in the same field
- Where the government wishes an SOE to provide products or services that the SOE has deemed unprofitable, the government has to enter into an explicit contract making the proposed activity profitable for the SOE
- Each SOE must submit a draft annual statement of corporate intent to the shareholding ministers specifying its business plan, the nature and scope of its activities, its financial structure and accounting policies, policy toward subsidiaries, as well as specific objectives and performance targets

(box continues on the following page)

Box 4.2   *(continued)*

(including rate of return and dividend policy); with respect to the newly incorporated SOEs, shareholding ministers may direct the board as to the content of that statement.

Contracts concluded by SOEs with employees or third parties have usually been dealt with by special legislation at the time of corporatization. These provisions determine in particular to what extent the terms and conditions of the labor contracts remain applicable and how the employees can enjoy, after corporatization of the SOE, the benefits accumulated under the old system. As for contracts concluded with third parties, legislative provisions often maintained and transferred existing contractual obligations to the corporatized SOE.

Assessing the Results of New Zealand's Corporatization Policy

By and large, the objectives of the program have been met, even exceeded, though they cannot be attributed exclusively to the corporatization policy. "Available empirical results do not generally allow to distinguish clearly between the effects of corporatisation and deregulation, since they happened at roughly the same time. And, indeed, they do not usually control for other changes, such as improvements in technology. Most studies conclude that commercial performance improved after corporatisation and deregulation for most State-owned enterprises" (OECD 1996, annex IV). Staffing levels fell, productivity improved, prices appear to have fallen in real terms while quality improved, government subsidies fell, and SOE profitability increased. Empirical evidence is lacking to determine whether the delivery of social services through contracts entered between government and SOEs has been an efficient approach to deliver such services.

A recent World Bank report confirms that the results of corporatization were impressive. "After four years sales, profits, and output per employee had increased in ten of eleven companies examined. Even so, successive governments went on to privatize a number of the companies and contemplated privatizing several others. Why, if the reformed state firms were so successful? They did so because they recognized the intense difficulty of sustaining reforms over time. In time of crisis governments admit the priority of commercial objectives, impose harder budgets, and grant managers autonomy. But as the crisis fades or a major political claim arises, commitment to managerial autonomy also fades. For example, the postal service was pressured to reopen small, rural post offices, and the electric power company was pushed to buy locally produced coal despite its higher cost. The conclusion of many in New Zealand, both in the firms and in the government, was that privatization was required, not necessarily to improve performance in the short run but to lock in the gains of earlier reforms" (World Bank 1996b, p. 50). In the end, the discipline of the capital markets tends to be stronger and more consistent than that of governments as owners.

Sources: New Zealand's State-Owned Enterprises Act of 1986; Franks 1993; see also note 6 in chapter 2.

of privatization. In light of these benefits, the compelling questions become: Why continue to use scarce public capital on state enterprises managed as if they were private? Why not go one step further and transfer these activities to the private sector altogether, and use the freed resources for more important economic or social objectives (debt reduction, for example, a major objective of privatization in New Zealand)? This next step, privatization, is only made easier by the transformation of government businesses into stock corporations governed by company law, which is what corporatization accomplishes.

Breakup of Public Enterprises

Assets or parts of an SOE may need to be spun off, or the whole SOE broken up into smaller constituent parts, to eliminate the monopolistic or dominant position of the SOE, to make the enterprise more attractive to investors, or to maximize sales revenues by separately selling nonoperational assets, such as excess land, buildings, or machinery. In Slovenia, for example, SOEs had to transfer the forests and farmlands included among their assets to the state or the municipalities before SOE incorporation (article 5 of Slovenia's 1992 privatization law).

This fragmentation of the assets or activities of an SOE can take several forms. The old SOE can continue to exist (in public or private form), though with restricted activities, or it may be liquidated. The assets and liabilities of the old SOE that are being demerged or hived off may be transferred to other public enterprises or entities, returned to the state, or sold to private operators. Where the original SOE remains, the transfer of sale proceeds may accrue to the enterprise itself or to the state.

In many transition countries, whole sectors of the economy had to be restructured by breaking up and liquidating the monopolistic conglomerates that dominated key sectors of economic activity under the central planning system. Their main assets and liabilities were transferred to several new enterprises set up under company law and scheduled to be privatized. This technique has been used elsewhere to break up national monopolies in the infrastructure sector (see chapter 7). The practice can be called demonopolization, however, only to the extent that the smaller successor companies are no longer in a monopolistic situation.

State holding companies or funds have served as the channel for restructuring operations of this kind in, among other countries, Czechoslovakia, where SOEs to be privatized were transferred together with all of their assets and liabilities to one of the three state property funds, and Bulgaria, where a bank consolidation company was set up to take over all public participations in commercial banks and to restructure the entire banking sector by means of mergers, liquidations, and divestitures.[23] These have taken over the existing

---

23. See also the section on privatization funds in chapter 6 for descriptions of mass privatization programs and funds. The funds referred to in this section are restructuring agencies, which do not necessarily have privatization functions. In the Czech Republic and Germany, however, the same agency combined both functions.

SOEs and established new companies to which assets and liabilities of the former SOEs have been selectively transferred; in exchange, the funds received shares in these new companies. In a second stage, the fund in turn transferred these shares to private investors. This two-stage procedure offers many advantages. First, it eliminates the need to draw up a detailed inventory of the assets and liabilities of the old SOE before privatization. Second, it makes it possible to divide the old SOE into smaller companies, consolidate the assets of different enterprises into one company, and sell separately any real estate not essential to the operations of the enterprise. Third, it assigns to the fund the legal responsibility for laying off redundant employees and for doubtful debts, environmental obligations, and so on. Fourth, the fund assumes responsibility for any remaining obligations, known or unknown, of the old SOE, hence obviating reliance on burdensome bankruptcy or liquidation procedures. The new companies established by the fund can then start their operations and be privatized under good conditions.

Prior Restructuring: Lessons from Mexico

In a recent empirical study of the privatization of 361 Mexican companies, Lopez-de-Silanes 1996 analyzed six areas of SOE restructuring before privatization—namely, management, labor, debt, efficiency programs, investment, and deinvestment—and their final impact on net prices. This study provides some interesting guidelines for what type of prior measures might be worth undertaking. "For instance, the results suggest that it is worthwhile to replace the CEO with a 'privatizer' whose task is to clean up the company, to reduce the waste of resources, and to get the firm on the block as quickly as possible. Labor downsizing before selling has a positive marginal effect on [net price], while debt absorption has no impact. Investing or embarking on efficiency programs before the sale actually decreases [the net price]; the government does not get its money's worth and the performance of the company remains the same. In contrast, cutting the flow of resources and postponing large investment programs, or de-investing, fares better in terms of premiums."

The author also found that "direct costs of prior restructuring policies are quite substantial, amounting to an average of 30% of the sale price. Additionally, restructuring measures such as efficiency and investment programs slow privatization. Delays in privatization come at a substantial cost, particularly when subsidies poured on SOEs can quickly add up to outweigh privatization revenues. . . . The empirical estimates in this paper point to a premium for speed and restructuring measures that expedite privatization and halt the drain of resources. The key lesson is: do not do too much, simply sell" (Lopez-de-Silanes 1996, pp. 3, 29).

Liquidation of Public Enterprises

Liquidation of an SOE is a common (and ultimate) form of SOE restructuring. It is also a widely used privatization technique. It often refers to the disposal of the shell, consisting mainly of debts and other obligations remaining after the core assets and selected liabilities of the former SOE have been transferred to one or more new companies after corporatization, breakup, or privatization.[24] It may also refer to the winding down of an entire SOE, whether or not it was still a going concern.

Different laws may apply, depending on whether the SOE was governed by private law, in which case liquidation usually takes place under company law and commercial bankruptcy law (see chapter 3), or by public law, in which case bankruptcy is not possible and liquidation is governed by other rules.

Some countries, including Senegal, Togo, and Viet Nam, have enacted specific legislation governing the liquidation and bankruptcy of SOEs.[25] Elsewhere, for example in Guinea, where liquidation has been the main privatization technique, or in Italy (see Decree-Law no. 340 of July 1992 concerning liquidation of EFIM), a law may be required to liquidate certain SOEs.[26] Finally, in other countries such as France case law is the main source of law applicable to the liquidation of various types of public establishments (see Bienvenu 1993; Conseil d'Etat 1989).

Public Finance Legislation

Budget and public finance laws may also contain provisions governing privatization. For example, the Canadian finance legislation requires that a law be enacted by parliament before an SOE can be privatized.[27] In other countries, such as Malaysia and New Zealand, the discussion and approval of the budget or annual finance law is the main vehicle for parliamentary involvement in the privatization process; the privatization strategy of the New Zealand government established after the 1990 elections thus constitutes annex 5 to the 1991 budget law submitted to parliament.

In addition, a country's public finance regulations may apply to the allocation or use of receipts of privatization. Even where the privatization laws

24. As part of the privatization of the telecommunications company, the Argentine federal government enacted Decree no. 2762/90 setting up a liquidation commission responsible for ensuring fulfillment of the government's remaining obligations after transfer of ENTEL's staff and main assets to the private sector.

25. See Senegal's Law no. 84-64 concerning the liquidation of SOEs (August 16, 1984), Togo's Law no. 82-5 on joint-venture companies (June 16, 1982), and Resolution no. 388 of Viet Nam's Council of Ministers concerning the establishment and liquidation of SOEs (November 20, 1991).

26. See Guinean Ordinance no. 306 PRG-85 of December 12, 1985, mandating the closing down and liquidation of 12 enterprises specified therein, and Ordinance no. 315 PRG-85 of December 21, 1985, mandating the liquidation of 34 rural retail stores. Under the military regime in force in Guinea at that time, an ordinance was equivalent to a law.

27. See UNCTAD, Ad Hoc Working Group on Comparative Experiences with Privatization, third session, November 29–December 3, 1993, country presentation submitted by Canada, p. 12.

specify how the proceeds shall be allocated, other finance laws may apply (see the section in chapter 5 on allocation of privatization proceeds). In many countries with budgetary systems modeled on that of France, for example, public expenditures cannot be deducted from public revenues because the law does not allow either offsetting or contraction of expenditures and receipts; all public expenditures have to be authorized by parliament and committed, disbursed, and controlled by authorized officials pursuant to public expenditure regulations.[28]

Finally, public procurement regulations may well apply to some contracts concluded by governments as part of the preparation and implementation of the privatization program. Concession contracts or contracts for the recruitment of experts to advise the government on privatization (including attorneys, auditors, investment bankers, and other consultants) are likely candidates.

Conclusion

In the area of public-sector management and public law, just as in other areas discussed in earlier chapters, the privatization process is affected, directly or indirectly, by a multitude of rules and regulations. Privatization is a public act involving a transfer of assets owned by the public sector. It is also a public process managed by public agencies and officials.

An important distinction needs to be drawn between the public agency with the right of ownership over the enterprises or assets covered by the privatization program (the state, municipality, or another agency or public entity), on the one hand, and the authorities empowered to exercise those ownership rights—in particular, the right to alienate enterprises and assets—on the other.

The legal status of an SOE, as discussed above and in chapter 1, determines in part the measures required before privatization. Thus, if an SOE is already governed by private law, prior restructuring will likely address management, staffing, and finances (including appointing a new CEO, downsizing or "right-sizing" the labor force if necessary, cutting off subsidies, and cleaning up the accounts and balance sheet). The object is to be able to privatize a viable enterprise. It may also be necessary to renegotiate certain contracts or

---

28. In its 1990 annual report, the French Cour des Comptes (equivalent to the U.K. NAO or U.S. GAO) criticized the way in which certain expenditures for public flotations and other privatization operations (mainly commissions, reimbursements of expenses to financial intermediaries, and taxes) had been deducted directly by the financial intermediaries from the gross amount they received. Only the net proceeds of privatization were ultimately paid into the treasury's special privatization account, in direct violation of "the provisions of article 18 of the organic law relating to finance laws" (Cour des Comptes 1990, pp. 24–25). The Cour des Comptes also criticized the lack of transparency in the financial aspects of debt-swap operations, particularly the losses incurred in the redemption of gold-indexed bonds.

obligations. Similar issues arise when the enterprise is governed by public law; in that case, it may also be necessary to choose whether to corporatize the enterprise or to liquidate it.

In all these cases, the old SOE may have to be broken up to some degree and some of its activities or assets separated or demerged from its main activity. Existing discrimination toward the private sector, whether to the advantage or disadvantage of the SOE, will need to be eliminated. And proper attention will have to be paid to the management of the SOEs during the transition period leading to their privatization.

The privatization process can be affected by other public-law provisions, such as public finance rules. Also in the domain of public law are constitutional aspects of privatization (chapter 2), matters concerning the immunity of the state (chapter 3), and the privatization laws themselves, which form the subject of chapters 5 and 6.

This chapter ends the broad overview of the existing legal framework that may affect the privatization process, which started with constitutional and international law (chapter 2), continued with the analysis of a broad range of laws affecting private business activity (chapter 3), and concluded with this discussion of legislation governing the public sector and its activities. A proper understanding of this preexisting legal framework and of its limitations is essential. The laws discussed heretofore often predate privatization programs and were not enacted primarily for the purpose of the privatization program. The following chapters will focus more directly on the privatization process itself.

5

The Privatization Law

Whether or not a country needs to enact a privatization law depends on its legal and political situation and the specific characteristics of the enterprises to be privatized. In some countries the government does not need any special enabling legislation to privatize, either because constitutional principles do not require a law (see chapter 2) or because SOE legislation or other laws provide the necessary legal framework (see chapter 4).[1]

Issues discussed in this chapter are germane where a special privatization law is legally required or deemed to be politically desirable.[2] Whether legally required or not, a law offers several advantages: it represents an immediate and concrete statement of explicit political support for and commitment to the privatization process, increases the accountability of the executing agency, makes it more difficult to undo the reforms being implemented, and provides an opportunity to change (and improve) the existing business environment to facilitate privatization. Disadvantages comprise often lengthy delays in securing parliamentary approval, the possibility that the law's provisions may be too restrictive or inflexible, and the risk of parliamentary micromanagement (see the section in chapter 6 on the role of parliament).

The content of privatization laws may vary substantially. The core elements of privatization legislation, namely, the enabling provisions authorizing and organizing the privatization process, are handled very differently from one law to another.

It is essential that the law define in clear terms the respective spheres of responsibility of the various authorities that play a role in the privatization process, such as parliament, the government, the privatization minister or agency, the management of the SOEs or other institutions involved. Mechanisms must be set up that make these authorities accountable for their

1. Moreover, public enterprises do not as a rule need special laws to be able to privatize their assets or subsidiaries, as noted in chapter 4.
2. Even where privatization is legally authorized under current law, a government will sometimes wish to cover itself politically by obtaining the approval of parliament.

actions and create appropriate incentives and penalties to ensure proper execution of the privatization program. These questions, which are covered by almost all privatization laws, are examined more closely in chapter 6.

Many privatization laws also contain provisions to remedy specific shortcomings in the existing legislation, of the kind discussed in chapters 3 and 4.[3] These can be described as facilitating provisions of the law, as opposed to enabling provisions.

Furthermore, constraints that may rightly be regarded as obstacles to privatization can sometimes be circumvented with a little imagination and creativity, as table 5.1 illustrates. Where the constraint was of a legal nature, it was circumvented without recourse to a law. In some of these cases, such as the one involving coupons for the Pakistani telecommunications company, the chosen shortcut turned out not to be particularly successful. The issuance of coupons, vouchers, or bonds convertible into shares of a company scheduled to be privatized later may unnecessarily complicate a privatization. Indeed, this technique, which is sometimes chosen to collect privatization revenues in advance of the actual transaction, creates new ownership rights that cannot be ignored at the time of privatization and may limit the available options.

This chapter deals with the enabling provisions most frequently found in privatization laws.[4] After a discussion of the main legal instruments to effect privatization and of the scope of privatization laws, the following topics are addressed: the valuation of SOEs to be privatized, the selection of buyers, preferential schemes, financing of share purchases, allocation of privatization proceeds, as well as transitory provisions and amendments to privatization laws.

A Law or Subordinate Instruments?

Where privatization legislation is required, it may be preferable to limit the provisions of the law to broad principles and leave the details and modalities of its application to subordinate instruments or decisions. No universal recipe exists, however, to determine which privatization provisions should be left to the discretion of the parties involved and which should be

3. In Peru, for example, article 7 (a) of Decree-Law no. 26120 of December 28, 1992, amending the privatization law of 1991 (Decree-Law no. 674), introduces an exception to ordinary labor law for SOEs to be privatized, aimed at facilitating the personnel cuts that have to be made as part of the preprivatization restructuring process, while article 7 (c) provides for the adoption of measures to allow regularization of ownership titles, permits, licenses, and so on, of SOEs. In Romania, article 73 of Law no. 58/1991 on privatization required the government to prepare a bill for the creation of a securities exchange; a law on securities and stock exchanges was enacted in August 1994. See chapters 3 and 4 for additional examples.

4. A nonexhaustive list of worldwide privatization laws, decrees, and other regulations, covering over 100 countries, is given in the appendix.

Table 5.1   How Some Countries Have Overcome Specific Obstacles to Privatization

Constraint	Solution	Country
Ownership of land cannot be transferred to a private enterprise	Established joint-venture companies whose public-sector partner held the rights to land use	Viet Nam
	Granted long leases	Socialist countries
The state's ownership titles to certain assets are imprecise or disputed, making sale of these assets to private investors more difficult	Concluded lease-sale contracts allowing assets to be transferred without immediate sale; lessee was given an option to purchase these assets at the end of the contract	Nicaragua
The exercise of certain activities cannot be transferred permanently to the private sector	Concluded a concession contract providing for the transfer of assets to the concessionaire for the duration of the concession; assets shall be returned to the contracting authority at the end of the contract	Brazil, Mexico
The legal framework for privatization is ambiguous	The president of the republic ratified the privatization agreements	Guinea
Privatization requires enactment of an enabling law, but the government does not wish to support such a law politically	Used a method other than divestiture to transfer enterprises to private management (lease or concession contracts, for example).	China, Viet Nam
Privatization of the national telecommunications company requires a long period of preparation and enactment of a law	Sold public coupons entitling the holder to shares in the future privatized company, with the understanding that the government would buy the coupons back at a specific price if the company was not privatized within two years	Pakistan
Privatization of a company is blocked by political opposition and/or by the courts	Planned to issue state bonds convertible into shares of the new company when it has been privatized	Turkey
The government wants to sell a second tranche in a company whose market price is below the original initial public offering (IPO) price	Sold a convertible bond with the conversion price set at or above the IPO	Italy

(table continues on the following page)

Table 5.1 *(continued)*

Constraint	Solution	Country
A law is required to privatize a public-law enterprise	Public-law enterprise created subsidiaries organized under private law, which can be privatized without any need to alter their legal form	France
Shares have to be granted to the employees of the privatized enterprises, but the interested buyers do not want to share control	Issued nonvoting shares for employees	Bulgaria
The law provides that a capital increase that is not fully subscribed must be deemed null and void	By firm underwriting, a bank or other financial entity undertook to acquire all the newly issued shares, organize their resale to third parties, and bear the attendant risks	Poland

included in the privatization law, in implementing decrees or regulations, in decisions of the competent authority (for example, the minister of finance or the chairman of the privatization agency), or in general guidelines. This decision will depend partly on the country's constitutional, legal, and political system and traditions and partly on current political concerns, notably the degree of confidence parliament places in the government. The choice of the legal instrument to be used will also depend on several other factors, such as the objective to be promoted; customized and flexible approaches, as opposed to standardized and uniform ones; centralization, or some degree of decentralization, of the process; and a priori controls or accountability of the executing agencies through a posteriori controls. These choices will have to be made at the start of the process, because they will largely determine the design of the legal framework for privatization.

The French legislation of 1986 affords an interesting, though very specific, illustration of how identical provisions can find a place both in a privatization law and in implementing regulations. Article 5 of the first privatization law of 1986 authorized the government to legislate by ordinance, pursuant to article 38 of the French constitution. President Mitterrand (of the socialist party) refused, however, to sign the ordinance prepared by the government of his prime minister, Jacques Chirac (of the conservative majority coalition). To circumvent this obstacle, the Chirac government submitted the text of the ordinance to the National Assembly in the form of a bill, that is, a draft law. This explains why two consecutive laws had to be enacted, one in July and the other in August 1986, to enable the privatization program to be implemented.

Furthermore, a law should not be used to substitute for a proper privatization strategy, lest it be loaded with many considerations better left to subordinate legal instruments. Some aspects of privatization, though essential from a strategic point of view—speed, timing, or the choice of a privatization technique—should normally not be regulated by law. Legislating such matters could easily become a straitjacket: a strategy can be adjusted fairly easily to tailor it to changing circumstances or to factor in the lessons drawn from new experience; a law cannot.[5]

Scope of the Legislation

As the appendix illustrates, most privatizing countries have enacted specific privatization legislation, whether or not required to do so by the constitution or by law. In the process they have had to choose between general legislation applicable to all SOEs to be privatized and a specific law for each such SOE or group of SOEs. In some cases the targeted SOEs are specifically named; in others, the law addresses one or more categories of enterprises without naming them.

The scope of some laws, and hence the privatization mandate of the government may also be limited in time.[6] Restrictions of this kind, which are usually found in laws with a positive list of privatizable enterprises, can have adverse effects. They can easily weaken the government's position in negotiations with potential buyers, especially when the legal time limit is nearing expiration.

5. The Puerto Rican Telephone Authority Act of April 10, 1990, affords a good example of a privatization law that goes into excessive detail. It included a number of highly restrictive provisions. For example, it specified the minimum net proceeds from the sale of the company, in this case $2 billion net of the total debt at the date of sale and the sale costs; prohibited any increase in basic telephone service charges within three years following privatization; prohibited the buyer from dismissing any employee as a direct result of the sale; and, as a condition for the sale, required parliament to enact laws establishing a Permanent Fund for the Development of Education, a Permanent Infrastructure Fund (see box 5.5), and the Puerto Rico Telecommunications Regulatory Commission and to adopt a resolution proposing a constitutional amendment. These requirements, particularly the minimum sale price (which amounted to about $3 billion), prevented completion of negotiations with interested bidders. Since the government lacked room for maneuver to accommodate the concerns of bidders, it had to take the company off the market. In February 1992 the Puerto Rican authorities concluded an agreement on privatization of TLD, the company providing international and long-distance services, with Telefónica of Spain, which thus became majority shareholder in TLD (79 percent of the capital).

6. See, for example, article 1 of the Moroccan privatization law of April 1990, which sets the deadline for completion of privatizations at December 31, 1995. The law was amended in January 1995 to extend the deadline to December 31, 1998, and to add two new enterprises to the list. See also article 4 of the French privatization law of July 1986, which gave March 1, 1991, as the deadline. A new privatization law was enacted in 1993 granting the government authority to privatize a new set of SOEs and modifying the 1986 legislation.

General Legislation

A law of general scope should be considered if common rules for all privatization transactions are deemed important. Such a law may confer a general mandate on the government or an agency to privatize SOEs. This happened in the Philippines, where the law provides that it is up to the president of the republic to decide which state-owned assets or enterprises shall be privatized (see article IV of Presidential Proclamation no. 50 of December 8, 1986). A law that confers broad authorization to privatize without specifying the enterprises in question will generally define its scope of application either by defining "privatization" or other terms or by prescribing inclusion or exclusion criteria.[7] The privatization mandate may thus be limited by excluding particular sectors or SOEs, as happened in the former East Germany, where the privatization law excluded, among other sectors, transportation infrastructure, the postal service, and municipal enterprises. Another possibility is to specify the sectors in which privatization is permitted without naming any particular enterprise.[8]

Law designating privatizable enterprises. A general law may list the SOEs that are to be wholly or partially privatized. The government's authority to privatize is then usually limited to these listed SOEs. Examples are found in Argentina (see the annex to Law no. 23696 of August 18, 1989), Burkina Faso (12 SOEs), France (65 SOEs in 1986 and 21 in 1993), Morocco (112 SOEs), Nigeria (110 SOEs), and Senegal (27 SOEs).[9]

Listing privatizable SOEs in the law is not necessarily a good solution, however, because such a list limits the flexibility of the government. Constantly changing domestic and world market conditions may dictate priorities other than those originally prescribed in the law. Moreover, designating specific enterprises can create uncertainty among the management and staff of the SOE. In the absence of schemes and incentives ensuring their continued motivation and of strict corporate governance or control procedures, this uncer-

---

7. When a law states that it governs the transfer of assets, enterprises, or activities from the public sector to the private sector, these terms may need to be defined. Private sector may, for example, be defined to exclude public enterprises, other public entities, or state-controlled bodies from acquiring shares in the privatized enterprises. Some definitions of public sector may lead to the inclusion or exclusion from the scope of the law of categories of public enterprises, such as municipal enterprises or subsidiaries of public enterprises, for example. See also notes 27 and 54 below and the glossary at the end of this book.

8. See, for example, Bulgaria's Council of Ministers Decree no. 36 of April 10, 1990, authorizing privatization of stores, workshops, hotels, restaurants, and other establishments in the trade, tourism, and service sectors. This decree has since been rescinded.

9. The list appended to the French law of July 2, 1986, comprised 65 enterprises, which in fact constituted 28 different public groups. Of these, 13 groups were privatized between November 1986 and January 1988. This left 15 groups to be privatized, whose number had fallen to 12 by 1993 following certain mergers. The 21 enterprises listed in the annex to the law of July 21, 1993, comprised these 12 groups plus 9 new enterprises.

tainty can lower productivity or even trigger fraudulent activities. Long delays between the designation of an SOE to be privatized (or even rumors of such designation) and the actual implementation of the transaction have indeed led to a deterioration of the condition of the SOE, and sometimes even to pilfering and misappropriation of SOE assets by workers and managers.

Some countries have issued decrees pursuant to the privatization law that list the enterprises to be privatized. In Mozambique, for example, an initial list of six SOEs was adopted by a decree of November 1991, with new SOEs added in 1993 and 1994 by decrees taken pursuant to article 14 of the August 1991 privatization law. This method offers more flexibility than the designation of SOEs in the law itself. By reducing the time between the announcement of privatization and the actual transaction, it also reduces the risk of deterioration in the SOE's situation pending privatization.

Provisions applying to certain types of privatizations. A general law may apply also to privatization operations carried out by SOEs or state holding companies, that is, to situations where the seller is not the state but a public enterprise. In this case the law may provide for derogation from ordinary SOE or company law—for example, by requiring that all or part of the proceeds of privatization operations carried out by SOEs shall accrue to the national budget (see chapter 4 and the section in this chapter on allocation of privatization proceeds) or by conferring to the government the right both to sell shares held by an SOE in other companies and to receive the proceeds of that sale (see Graham and Prosser 1991, p. 82, with respect to the U.K. oil and gas law of 1982).

A general law may also subject different types of privatization to different regulations. In France, for example, the privatization laws of July 2 and August 6, 1986, as amended by the law of July 19, 1993, authorize three different privatization procedures. The procedures set forth in these laws apply to the enterprises listed in their annexes. The other enterprises fall into two categories. First, prior legislative authorization is required to privatize majority state-owned enterprises (state ownership of 50 percent or more) and enterprises that entered the public sector pursuant to a law.[10] Second, an executive instrument suffices for enterprises in which the state directly holds less than 50 percent of the shares and for enterprises that became part of the public sector without legislative approval; an executive instrument is used also in the case of the partial sale of shares of public enterprises in which the state is the majority shareholder and remains the majority shareholder after such sale.[11]

10. With the exception, however, of enterprises that became part of the public sector pursuant to legislative provisions but are held, directly or indirectly, by enterprises included in the list appended to the law of July 19, 1993. The transfer of enterprises of this kind to the private sector must also take place in conformity with the provisions of the law of July 1993. See article 2.1 of Law no. 93-293 of July 19, 1993.

11. See Decree no. 91-332 of April 4, 1991, which lays down the conditions under which minority shareholdings in public enterprises can be sold. See also Debène 1991; Richer and Viandier 1991; Saint-Girons 1991.

Specific Legislation

Specific laws authorizing the privatization of one or more SOEs or of an entire sector have been enacted in Argentina, Belgium, Brazil, Canada, New Zealand, the United Kingdom, and several other countries.[12] Such precisely targeted privatization laws tend to be used where the scope of the privatization program is limited or an SOE or group of SOEs poses special legal problems that cannot easily be resolved in a general enabling law.[13] This would normally apply to the privatization of an entire sector, especially a highly regulated sector such as the financial, natural resources, or infrastructure sectors (see chapter 7).

In addition, some countries with a weak legal framework have turned to a very special type of privatization law. Thus in Guinea agreements for the sale of particular enterprises have been ratified by presidential ordinance in order to give them full effect, notwithstanding conflicting provisions of other legislation. This enabled Guinea to start privatizing SOEs in 1986 without having to wait for a complete overhaul of its business legislation or the enactment of a privatization law, which occurred only in 1993.

Valuation and Sale of Enterprises to be Privatized

Parliaments and governments often build safeguards into their legislation to ensure transparency of the process and reduce some of the risks typically associated with privatization.[14] The law commonly imposes basic rules to be followed by the implementing agencies, particularly regarding prior valuation of SOEs, the use of specific sale techniques, and the procedures for selecting buyers (see the following section).

12. *Argentina* combined both procedures: a general law of 1989 applying to the enterprises named therein, followed a few years later by specific laws for certain individual enterprises such as YPF (the oil company), Gas del Estado, and certain financial institutions. In *Belgium*, article 98 of the law of July 22, 1993, authorized the government to transfer the shares it held in four public financial institutions. In *Brazil*, a law was not needed, legally speaking, to privatize VASP, the São Paulo state airline, but it was decided for political reasons to seek the approval of the legislator in order to secure the São Paulo state government's cooperation, because it was feared that this operation would meet with spirited political opposition (see Law no. 6629 of December 27, 1989). See the appendix for a listing of other specific privatization laws.

13. In the case of Petro-Canada, for example, the Canadian government did not wish to privatize PCIAC, Petro-Canada's international assistance subsidiary. The specific law provided for the transfer of Petro-Canada's PCIAC shares to the government before privatization. See the Petro-Canada Public Participation Act of February 1991.

14. Uruguay's privatization law of October 1991, for example, sets forth a number of principles that must govern privatization operations: freedom of choice for consumers, abolition of monopolies, fair competition, and adequate publicity to ensure transparency of the privatization program.

Valuation

Valuing public enterprises or public assets is a delicate operation, notably because public officials wish to avoid being accused of giving away the family silver or selling off the crown jewels. Valuation affords them political protection in the event that the decision to sell at a given price is disputed ("It is the price at which the enterprise was valued by the auditors"). In practice, however, the valuations that highly skilled experts proffer are often far off the enterprise's true market value, even in industrial countries. In some cases, overvaluation of the SOE has forced the cancellation or postponement of its privatization; this happened, for example, in the cases of VSNL, the Indian international telephone company, and the Puerto Rican telecommunications company.[15]

While setting a reference price is undeniably useful, it may be preferable to obtain the right price through competitive, transparent, and open sale procedures with wide dissemination of information. A competitive procedure usually offers the government better guarantees than does an expert valuation performed before the sale.[16] Competitive bidding by several potential buyers, each of which will perform its own valuation of the enterprise, should more accurately reveal the true value of the enterprise. This procedure is also speedier and cheaper. Many countries have nevertheless enacted laws requiring prior valuation in all privatization transactions.

Some type of prior valuation may be justified, however. In the case of an auction sale, the seller may want to set a reference or reserve price below which it does not wish to sell. For an initial public offering (IPO), prior valuation is needed to set the share price; this was done in most French, Malaysian,

---

15. The public flotation of VSNL was canceled on May 3, 1994, in response to negative reaction to the high share price following market soundings. This price, which was set by the government before the fall in Indian share prices, was apparently in the range Rs 1,400–1,600, whereas the government's financial advisers thought that the market was prepared to pay only Rs 1,100. The government did not wish to lower its price for fear of being accused of selling the company at a discount to foreigners. This was a particularly sensitive issue for the government because a parliamentary committee had just accused it of selling certain holdings in 1992 and 1993 at below their true value. Five months later the flotation was relaunched; the government instructed its bankers to obtain a price of Rs 1,100–1,200, or 25 percent less than the previous price, despite a rise in the Indian stock exchange of about 25 percent since May. This second attempt also faltered. See *Wall Street Journal*, 4 May 1994; *Emerging Markets Week*, 26 September 1994; *Euroweek*, 30 September 1994. With respect to the Puerto Rican telephone privatization, see note 5 in this chapter.

16. This method was chosen, for example, for the privatizations by auction of the municipal enterprises of the city of L'viv, which marked the start of Ukraine's privatization program. The list of enterprises to be privatized was published each month in the press to ensure that investors were informed (see article 5.2 of the program of privatization of municipal enterprises of the city of L'viv for 1992, approved by resolution of the municipal council of the city of L'viv on September 18, 1992). The value of each enterprise was then determined exclusively by the highest bid made at the auction; the offering price was deliberately set relatively low (see article 6.1.3 of the above-mentioned program). See also IFC 1993.

and U.K. privatizations, for example.[17] The share price should be fixed as close as possible to the flotation date.[18] This may require that the price resulting from these valuations be adjusted in light of the results of a market sounding—for example, by means of the book-building procedure.[19]

In addition, rigorous valuation is absolutely essential when the enterprise is sold through a directly negotiated deal, and particularly when it is sold directly to its employees (employee or management buyout). Indeed, the government must arrive at a valuation without recourse to a market test. In many cases the initial valuation may be performed by the management of the enterprise itself, which has strong incentives to underestimate the value (for example by using the book value of the SOE, which is often only a fraction of its true market value). This has happened in many transition countries, including Hungary and Viet Nam.

Where a valuation is required, it should be carried out by independent and qualified experts and in conformity with generally accepted valuation principles. The cost of the valuation should not exceed the benefits it is expected to yield. Some countries have established valuation commissions or other special bodies responsible for setting minimum prices; these are further discussed in chapter 6. Their common drawback is that members of such commissions have no real stake in the success of the privatization program; they tend to be concerned only about not selling too cheaply, and they often end up setting price floors that are too high.

Valuation rules and principles established at the time of nationalization can also be helpful, at least where they were developed with due respect for the rights of expropriated owners (as in the case of the French nationalizations of 1982; see Israël 1986). It is unwise, however, to try to prescribe a gen-

17. Both in Malaysia and in the United Kingdom, shares of SOEs to be privatized appear to have been deliberately underpriced. This was done in part to guarantee the success of the flotation and enhance the popularity of the government. In *Malaysia*, one of the explicit objectives of the privatization program was to increase share ownership and redistribute wealth toward the Bumiputra majority (as opposed to the Chinese minority, which dominates business). Part of the shares had been reserved for Bumiputra investors. "On the basis of first-day share price premia, the average amount of underpricing has been over 107%," and on the basis of the share price three months after flotation the premiums still stood, on average, at 93 percent (*Oxford Analytica*, "Malaysia: Preferential Privatisation," 27 November 1995). In the *United Kingdom*, after better-than-average performance in the initial years, total returns on shares in privatized companies have roughly kept pace with overall stock market performance. In *France*, where the government's tendency has been to maximize the sale price, share prices of privatized companies have not fared as well; they are in many cases lower than at IPO and have on average underperformed the rest of the market.

18. The flotation by the Portuguese government of CIMPOR, the country's largest cement producer, was a flop largely because the issue price had been set two months earlier. Meanwhile, the Lisbon stock exchange had dropped 15 percent. See *Financial Times*, 18 April 1995.

19. The book-building procedure is commonly used by investment banks in the United States to sell shares. It was also used in the public flotations of the Argentine petroleum company YPF and in some French privatization operations, for example. See the section in chapter 3 on accounting law.

erally applicable method of valuation. On the contrary, the method adopted will have to take into account the specific characteristics of the country, the sector to which the SOE belongs, and the nature of the assets. The usefulness of a valuation performed in a country or sector where prices are not freely set by the market may, for example, seem rather dubious. Valuation methods used in privatization transactions are generally a combination of those commonly used in corporate mergers and acquisitions—for example, net present value of an estimated stream of future cash flow (discounted cash flow analysis); replacement value of the enterprise; its book value; the liquidation value of the enterprise; comparisons with prices fetched in similar transactions or with market valuation of comparable (publicly traded) companies; and so on.

To summarize, where a valuation is made, it should serve only as a guide to the selling agency. Legislation should not prevent this agency from concluding a sale at a price below the estimate if, following a competitive selection procedure, no acceptable bid has been received at or above the estimate. Prior valuation by independent professionals may, however, be useful by providing the sellers a reference price that can help them decide whether to accept the bids received. Independent valuation may also reduce the risk of collusion between the buyer and the officials in charge of privatization. It should be required if the privatization is carried out without effective competition (see also the section in chapter 6 on valuation bodies).

Authorized Techniques

All too often privatization laws and regulations prescribe the authorized privatization methods and techniques in restrictive terms. The better approach would be to investigate what techniques would be legally authorized in the absence of restrictions in the privatization legislation. Any necessary provisions authorizing other techniques or restricting the use of certain methods, as the particular case may require, can then be added to the legislation. Implementing regulations often prescribe the circumstances in which particular techniques may be used.

In practice, the legislator is usually neither familiar with privatization techniques nor in a position to predict the various circumstances that may necessitate special methods for this or the other specific operation. The privatization law should therefore be drafted in broad terms, leaving the executing authority free to choose the appropriate methods of privatization or, at the least, authorizing a range of privatization techniques to fit the specific needs of each case.

Sales of shares held by the state or other public entities should be allowed, as well as capital increases, even without divestiture of state shares. A capital increase, with or without accompanying sale of public holdings, would be called for, for instance, where the SOE to be privatized urgently requires a new cash infusion. Liquidation should not be excluded from these options, because it is sometimes the only way or the best way to privatize some SOEs (see chapter 4). Privatization through public flotation on the stock exchange, although an option in the more sophisticated countries, would not be practicable in most developing or transition countries. The use of convertible bonds may also be on the menu of available options.[20] And so on.

Where, however, the law prescribes specific techniques, the use of other techniques (not provided for in the law) should be allowed, subject to compliance with minimum conditions. One could, for instance, require the prior approval of the competent minister or even of the council of ministers if noncompetitive privatization procedures are to be followed (for example, sale by directly negotiated contract). Such provisions are found in the legislation of Argentina, Czechoslovakia, France (see note 23 below), Nigeria, Poland, and other countries.[21]

The Argentine example shows how important it is to avoid unduly restricting the range of privatization techniques that can be used. The diversity of legal status and economic characteristics of the enterprises to be privatized has compelled authorities to resort to a wide range of techniques. This point is illustrated by table 5.2, which covers only a small portion of the privatization program, namely, that relating to the ministry of national defense.

Most privatization techniques have been borrowed from private commercial practices, where mergers and acquisitions are common. Other methods, however, are specific to SOE privatization and may have to be included in the privatization law if the government intends to use them. Privatization by free distribution of shares to the population, or by issuance of privatization vouchers or coupons, are excellent examples (on this subject, see chapter 6).

---

20. Convertible bonds and state bonds with equity warrants have been issued by various governments, redeemable for shares of the following companies, among others: Telmex (see note 49 in chapter 7), Italian insurance company INA (see note a in table 1), Brazilian power company CEMIG (in January 1994), Televisa of Mexico (in February 1993), and China Textile Machinery (in November 1993). They have also been planned for the Turkish telecommunications company. In addition, partially privatized SOEs such as Telekom Malaysia (in September 1994) have also issued convertible bonds.

21. *Argentina*: Article 17 of Law no. 23696 of 1989 sets forth a nonrestrictive list of privatization methods, while article 18 prescribes the selection procedures to be followed in all cases, laying particular emphasis on competition and transparency.

Czechoslovakia: See article 10 of the law of February 26, 1991, on the conditions of transfer of public assets to third parties.

Nigeria: Article 4 (3) of the Privatization and Commercialization Decree of 1988 provides that "whenever the Technical Committee is of the view that any enterprise is not suitable for disposal by public issue of shares, the Technical Committee shall recommend to the Federal Military Government the mode of disposal of such enterprise."

Poland: Article 23 (2) of the privatization law provides that the council of ministers, acting on the recommendation of the minister of ownership transfers, may authorize privatization procedures other than those provided for in article 23, namely, sale at auction, public flotation of securities, and competitive tender. Pursuant to this article the council of ministers granted special authorization allowing the sale of two-thirds of the shares of Polam Pila, a producer of electric light bulbs, to the Dutch company Philips (see *East European Business Law*, July 1991, p. 6).

Table 5.2 Privatization of Ministry of Defense Enterprises in Argentina

Status of the SOE	Example	Sale technique
Minority state participation in the SOE's capital	Petropol, Monomeros Vinilicos, Induclor, and Polisur (all part of the Bahia Blanca petro-chemicals complex)	State's shares sold en bloc to a private investor
Majority state participation in the SOE's capital	Tandanor shipyard	Different blocks of shares sold to different investors
Enterprises forming part of the armed forces	Area Material Cordoba aviation company	Corporatization to allow later sale of state's shares
Unprofitable enterprises, heavily subsidized by the government	Hipasam (mining)	Direct sale of SOE assets to the private sector
Heavily indebted enterprises	Somisa (a large iron and steel enterprise)	Creation of a new company, to be privatized, to which some of the assets and liabilities of the former enterprise were transferred; other assets of the former SOE were sold directly, and the debts not transferred to the new entity continued to be the government's responsibility
Enterprises that do not own the land they occupy	Tamse	Use of lease contracts
Large multipurpose enterprises that do not possess juridical personality	Altos Hornos de Zapla (an iron and steel company with forest resources for production of blast furnace charcoal)	Restructuring, before privatization, into various commercial companies, each operating in a separate area of activity

Source: De Kessler 1993, p. 135.

In addition, different techniques can be combined within a given privatization operation. In France, a public offering was typically combined with a separate sale of a core shareholding to a group of strategic or institutional investors (see the next section). Many governments have tried to combine the benefits of transferring management control to experienced international investors with national participation, especially in the case of large high-profile companies. To do so, Argentina, Mexico, and other countries

have used a staged approach to privatize their telecommunications companies, first selling a controlling interest to a group of investors (including a
telecommunications operator) and following this with public offerings (see
the section in chapter 7 on special infrastructure privatization issues). For its
part, the Bolivian capitalization law of March 1994 took an original
approach: a capital increase to be subscribed by strategic investors who were
selected competitively, accompanied by a transfer of the existing state shares
to a new privately managed pension system, as further discussed in box 5.1
(see also the section in chapter 3 on pension fund reform).

Selecting Buyers

Selecting buyers is delicate, especially given the problems caused in many
countries by corruption, nepotism, and discrimination against foreigners
and certain minorities or ethnic groups. The law should lay down the broad
principles for the selection of buyers, typically by mandating a competitive
and transparent process. This involves rules on advertising the sale, eligibility requirements, disclosure of information to investors, amount of time
given investors to prepare bids, evaluation and selection, and so on.[22]

The selection of buyers may derive directly from the choice of privatization technique. If a company is privatized by way of public flotation, the
selection process will be anonymous; all investors can subscribe and be allocated shares (with some exceptions, as noted below). If mass privatization is
chosen, all eligible citizens will have the opportunity to buy or receive shares
or coupons. Still, rules are needed to govern these processes; for public flotations, they derive from the securities legislation in effect (see chapter 3); for
mass privatization, a specific legal and regulatory framework will be established (see chapter 6).

Under other privatization techniques, the government or privatization
agency may have more discretion in the choice of buyers. This is the case, in
particular, for trade sales and for the selection of strategic or core investors,
which are the preferred privatization technique for many SOEs. A tradeoff
exists in these cases between tight rules that limit the discretion of the privatizing authorities and flexible processes which allow for negotiation between

22. *Publicity:* See note 23 below on requirements in French law.

Eligibility: Article 5 of the Czechoslovak law on small privatizations provides that all persons
wishing to participate in the sale at auction of a given enterprise must, to be eligible, furnish a
deposit of at least 10 percent of the offering price. Most privatizations of large infrastructure
enterprises, for example, are subject to prequalification and other eligibility criteria prescribed
by the law or its implementing regulations (see chapter 7 and table 7.4).

Timetable: In Hungary, a tight bidding timetable leaving only 45 days for bidders to prepare
and submit proposals, combined with repeated changes to the tender documents during that
period, were said to be among the reasons for the cool response given by investors to the privatization of the electricity sector in November–December 1995 (see *Financial Times*, 4 December
1995 and 6 December 1995).

Box 5.1   The Bolivian Capitalization Law

In light of the failure of past efforts to improve the performance of monopoly SOEs with performance contracts, the Bolivian government that took office in August 1993 opted for a more radical reform. It prepared a privatization program that was given legal status by enactment of Law no. 1544 of March 21, 1994, on capitalization.

Article 2 of the law provides for the conversion of YPFB (hydrocarbons), ENTEL (telecommunications), ENDE (electric power generation and transmission), ENFE (railways), LAB (national airline), and ENAF (smelter) into companies organized under private law, in which employees may become shareholders. Article 4 provides that these new companies shall be "capitalized" by means of a capital increase subscribed by private investors (domestic and foreign). The number of new shares may in no circumstances exceed the total number of shares that existed before the capital increase; this means, in effect, that new investors cannot hold more than 50 percent of the capital of the companies privatized in this way.

The new shareholders must be selected and the amount of their contributions determined following international calls for bids (article 4). In June 1995 three of ENDE's power generation units were transferred to as many consortia, all led by U.S. power companies; ENTEL was privatized to a group led by STET (the Italian operator) in September 1995; VASP (a Brazilian airline) acquired the control of LAB in October 1995; Chilean investors took over ENFE in early 1996; and YPFB was broken up and three international consortia were selected in December 1996 to take over the transportation unit (Enron/Shell) and two oil and gas fields (Amoco, YPF), respectively.

Article 6 empowers the government to transfer the shares it holds in the above-mentioned companies to the Bolivian adult population, free of charge. Article 7 states that this transfer must be carried out to the benefit of retirement funds that have to be set up pursuant to a special law on pensions (Law no. 1732 of November 29, 1996). The same article provides for a trust arrangement to be established pending the creation of these private pension funds. Two private pension fund administrators selected on a competitive basis will manage the collective capitalization fund and the individual pension accounts (see p. 80).

Through capitalization, the government gives up any claims on privatization proceeds, but gets the private sector to subscribe to capital increases which, owing to the state of public finances, the government is no longer able to fund itself. Moreover, the creation of retirement funds should contribute to the social security needs of the citizens, help promote the development of Bolivia's financial markets, and facilitate access by enterprises to domestic financing.

Article 10 provides that the sectors covered by this law will be governed by sector-specific legislation, and that a regulatory entity will be established by law.

---

seller and buyer. Indeed, the use of an auction-type process leading to the award to the highest bidder can work only when all key aspects of the transaction can be identified and defined as part of the bidding documents. This is easily done for simple transactions in competitive sectors. The preparation of such exhaustive bidding documentation may not always be feasible or desirable in other instances, however.

If all key aspects of the transaction have not been set and shared with all bidders before they submit their offers, postaward negotiation and modification of the bidding terms will render an auction-type award meaningless. If negotiations on substantive aspects of the deal take place after the selection of the buyer, the emphasis should be on setting rules and procedures for evaluation, selection, and negotiation that are seen as fair and reasonably transparent; privatization officials should be made accountable for their decisions; and they should be advised throughout this process by legal, financial, economic, and other experts with relevant experience and qualifications. Examples of substantive aspects that are often negotiated after the award include the size of the labor force the buyer accepts to retain; investment commitments; environmental liabilities and commitments; payment terms; pricing formulas and other regulatory features (for regulated industries); and so on.

The use of *noyaux durs* in most French privatizations illustrates how the use of discretionary powers can easily become controversial. The government selected a core group of large industrial or financial shareholders (*noyau dur*) to which it sold a controlling stake in the company.[23] The remaining shares were sold through public flotation. This procedure was intended to ensure a stable group of active shareholders and to preclude excessive shareholder dispersion as well as the risk of uncontrolled takeover. The core shareholders had to pay a premium above the price at which the shares were sold to the public and they had to retain their shares for a specified period.[24] Because the same hand-picked groups turned up in many of the core shareholding groups and, consequently, cross-shareholdings were frequent, the procedure came under fire. It may be seen as a way for the government or a technocratic elite to maintain control over enterprises, even though they have been privatized, and to keep the incumbent management—typically recruited from the senior ranks of the civil service—in place (see *Le Monde*,

23. Legally speaking, this was an exception, permitted by article 4 of the law of August 6, 1986, to the general rule of public placement of shares through the financial markets. It authorized the minister of economy to choose the buyer without going through the financial markets, after consultation with the privatization commission and pursuant to a decree setting minimum publicity conditions, including notification of the proposed privatization by publication at least one month before the deadline for receipt of bids in the official gazette (*Journal Officiel*) and two financial newspapers of wide circulation (Decree no. 86-1140 of October 24, 1986). Article 4 was amended by article 5 of the law of July 19, 1993, which strengthened the role of the privatization commission by providing that, in selecting buyers without recourse to the market, the minister could henceforth act only in conformity with the advice given by the privatization commission.

24. During the first privatization wave of 1986-88, the portion of the privatized company's capital sold to core shareholders was generally in the range of 20–30 percent of the capital, and the control premium remained modest, ranging from 2.5 percent above the public offering price for Paribas to 10 percent for Matra. The premium for TF1, a television network privatized pursuant to a different law, was 73 percent (see Cour des Comptes 1990, p. 27).

8 March 1994). It shields the enterprises from the rigor of market discipline, in particular by making hostile or foreign takeovers difficult or impossible. The core shareholding procedure was not popular with fund managers and other investors, who felt the interests of core shareholders and incumbent managers would prevail over those of noncore investors. Spain followed a similar approach when it accompanied the sale of part of its remaining shareholding in Telefónica with the creation of a group of core shareholders composed of three domestic financial institutions.

The selection process also affects other aspects of the privatization transaction: a transparent, nondiscriminatory, and competitive procedure for selecting buyers should, for instance, yield a selling price in line with the current market value of the SOE and thereby obviate the cost of a prior valuation.

It is important to let the implementing agency adopt more precise regulations and tailor bid requirements to the features of each transaction.[25] Delegation of these matters must, however, be accompanied by procedures ensuring accountability of the agency and its officials, together with control and appeal procedures. Noncompliance with the rules established for the bidding process may provide grounds for annulment of the selection.

Restrictions on Buyer Selection

The privatization law should be free of unnecessary restrictions on the selection of buyers. Some restrictions, such as the exclusion of public agencies as buyers of privatized enterprises, may, however, be necessary to protect the objectives of the program. Privatization laws often grant rights to SOE employees and management, particularly reserved share allocations and preemptive rights, that may also constrain the selection process (see next section).

Restrictions on the buyer's nationality or other characteristics are found in a number of laws. They can often be circumvented by, for example, using dummy companies; restrictions on the further resale of shares of privatized enterprises tend to be difficult to enforce. Some laws, nevertheless, introduce restrictions reflecting "national interests" or other government objectives (including industrial policy objectives), usually in the form of protective measures against foreign takeover or control of privatized enterprises. Restrictions imposed on acceptable potential buyers lead to lower sale prices; they may also scuttle the whole transaction.[26]

---

25. For example, in certain recent privatization operations in Argentina, bidders were required to attach to their bid a signed copy of the contract proposed to them. The purpose of this procedure was to avoid long and difficult negotiations after announcement of the winning bidder, as happened in the privatization of ENTEL and the award of the first railway concessions. Such negotiations can substantially alter the conditions of sale and hence introduce new factors not taken into account in bidder selection. See Alexander and Corti 1993, p. 9.

26. Lopez-de-Silanes 1996 found in an empirical study of Mexican privatization that restrictions on buyers, including exclusion of foreign buyers, did indeed lower the sale price of privatized enterprises.

Restitution of nationalized enterprises. Chapters 3 and 4 explained the importance of the existence of clear ownership rights to privatization and spelled out how these rights have been affected by earlier nationalization programs. As already discussed in chapter 3, in some countries the privatization law (or a separate "restitution" law) contains provisions entitling former owners or their heirs to ask for the restitution of their assets. This is, of course, the ultimate restriction on the selection of buyers for enterprises to be privatized.

Exclusion of or limitation on public-sector participation. In order to effectively reduce the role of the public sector in the economy, many countries, including Brazil, Bulgaria, Peru, Poland, Russia, and, indirectly, Jamaica have restricted the right of public-sector entities to participate in the privatization process by buying shares of other SOEs.[27] The very object of the privatization law may also rule out the transfer of shares or assets to SOEs or other public entities. Thus, article 1 of the Moroccan privatization law of 1990 explicitly prescribes that the ownership of shares held by the state or other public agencies in the companies listed in an annex to the law shall be transferred from the public to the private sector.

Moreover, some countries have inserted more restrictive rules under this head in their privatization laws to further support the objectives and consistency of the privatization program by limiting the creation of new SOEs. The same Moroccan law discussed above prescribes that, except when effected by law, the creation of any new public enterprise, subsidiary or secondary subsidiary of a public enterprise, and any new participation by a public enterprise in the capital of a private enterprise must be authorized, under penalty of nullity, by a government decree proposed by the minister for privatization (see article 8 of the 1990 privatization law).

---

27. *Brazil*: The steering committee set up pursuant to the privatization law adopted Resolution no. 15 on August 19, 1991, setting an overall ceiling of 15 percent on the proportion of the shares of a privatized enterprise that can be acquired by SOEs.

Bulgaria: Article 5 (4) of the privatization law of April 1992 provides that public enterprises in which the state or a municipality holds more than 50 percent of the shares cannot participate in privatization operations without written authority, given on a case-by-case basis, from the privatization agency.

Peru: Article 1 of Decree-Law no. 674 of September 25, 1991, concerning the promotion of private investment in SOEs, was amended by Decree-Law no. 26120 of December 28, 1992, by the addition of a second paragraph which defines "private investment" as one that "derives from natural or juridical persons, domestic or foreign, public or private, *distinct from the Peruvian state and from the agencies that make up the national public sector and the state-owned enterprises*" (emphasis added). This wording made it possible to exclude the national public sector without excluding foreign public enterprises.

Russia: Article 9 of the privatization law provides that entities in which public shareholders hold more than 25 percent of the corporate capital cannot act as buyers of privatized enterprises.

Jamaica: The government pursued a similar goal, but indirectly: a law, abolished in 1991, limited the share that any individual investor could acquire in the capital of the National Commercial Bank, which was partially privatized in 1986, to 7.5 percent, with the object mainly, it seems, of preventing the government from regaining control of the bank in the future (see *Privatisation Yearbook 1992*, p. 167).

Exclusions of or limitations on foreign participation. It is not uncommon for legislation to include express restrictions on participation by foreigners, as illustrated by box 5.2.

These restrictions are generally detrimental to successful privatization operations. This lesson has been learned by France and Brazil, among other countries: after introducing restrictions on foreign investors in privatizations, they had to abolish them. It is worth noting that the European Commission has exerted significant pressure on France and Portugal to lift such restrictions, which are contrary to EU law.[28] The most stringent restrictions on foreign participation are found mostly in the legislation of countries whose privatization programs have not been particularly successful.

By limiting the number of eligible buyers and excluding the potential buyers who typically possess the most resources, these provisions reduce the likelihood of completing the sale on good terms. The situation is particularly paradoxical for poor or heavily indebted countries, which most need to attract foreign capital and often enact generous investment codes to appeal to those same investors (see the section in chapter 3 on foreign investment legislation).

And restrictions are not limited to foreign participation. In some countries, the government excludes certain categories of citizens from the benefits of privatization by reserving sales to indigenous populations.[29]

Special, or Golden, Shares

The "golden" share technique has been used by some countries, including France (see box 5.3), Belgium, Brazil, Malaysia, New Zealand, Spain, Turkey, and the United Kingdom, as a way to keep some degree of government control over a privatized company, mainly with respect to future transfers of shares.[30] By allowing the government to veto some corporate decisions or

---

28. According to some observers, the French law also needed to be amended in view of the absence of large private domestic institutional investors; raising foreign capital became a precondition of the success of a broad privatization program (see *Financial Times*, 30 June 1993). In Portugal, the former (social-democrat) government used the option afforded by the 1990 privatization law to put limits on foreign shareholdings for specific privatizations; legislation submitted to parliament by the new socialist government to abolish these restrictions for EU investors was, however, defeated in June 1996. The European Commission has threatened to take Portugal to the European Court of Justice on this issue.

29. In Malaysia, one of the main objectives of privatization, and more generally of the government's economic policy, is to strengthen the economic power of the indigenous Malays, the Bumiputras, and to reduce the relative weight of the local Chinese. Thus in most privatization operations only Bumiputra investors could act as buyers of shares offered for sale by the government (see Galal and others 1994; see also note 17 above).

30. In the case of British Airports Authority (BAA), for example, the sale of an airport by BAA is subject to approval by the government, which holds the special or golden share. Generally speaking, this golden share empowers the government to block takeovers or foreign shareholding. See also the examples given in the section of chapter 7 on golden shares.

Box 5.2   Restrictions on Foreign Participation in Privatization

Brazil. Article 13 of Law no. 8031 of April 1990 (and article 44 of Decree no. 724 of January 1993) limited holdings by foreigners to 40 percent of voting shares. This restriction has since been lifted, initially by a provisional measure taken on October 26, 1993, and renewed every 30 days thereafter, allowing foreigners to acquire 100 percent of the shares of privatized enterprises. Moreover, the constitutional basis for discriminating against foreign investors in certain economic sectors was abolished in August 1995. The privatization program included other restrictions on foreign investments when made by way of debt-equity swaps: funds invested through swaps had to remain in Brazil for at least 12 years and foreign investors had to hold on to the shares so acquired for at least two years, during which they were not authorized to repatriate any funds. In light of the low participation by foreigners in the initial privatizations, however, the Brazilian government reduced the 12-year period by half and abolished the restriction on transferability of shares.

Burkina Faso. Article 10 of Ordinance no. 91-0044/PRES of July 1991 empowers the minister responsible for SOE supervision to reserve in priority a share of each privatization for Burkinabe nationals.

Chad. Article 9 of Ordinance no. 017/PR/92 of August 1992 on divestiture of SOE holdings provides: "In the sale and/or transfer of state-held assets, priority shall be accorded to natural or juridical persons of Chad nationality. The regulation of the Minister of Commerce and Industrial Development issued pursuant to article 7 of this Ordinance shall set the number or proportion of shares to be offered in priority and also the period of validity of the offer. Upon expiration of that period, sale of the remaining shares shall no longer be subject to this priority."

Czechoslovakia. Article 3 of the law of October 1990 on small privatizations provides that only nationals of the Czech and Slovak Federal Republic, and companies or other legal entities whose owners or members are all nationals, may become owners of enterprises and assets privatized pursuant to this law. The law on large privatization operations does not contain such a restriction.

France. Article 10 of the law of August 1986 limited the total amount of shares transferred by the state to foreign persons, directly or indirectly, to 20 percent of the SOE's capital. This provision was first amended by article 8 of the law of July 1993, which provides that this ceiling shall not apply to European Union investors; an amendment of April 12, 1996, abolished the remaining restriction.

Senegal. Article 11 of Law no. 87-23 of August 1987 on SOE privatization provides: "For each enterprise, the minister with responsibility for the state portfolio shall set the proportion of shares that can be transferred in priority to natural or juridical persons of Senegalese nationality."

---

share transfers, for example, this technique prolongs state control beyond privatization, even though the state is now only a minority shareholder (sometimes with a single share). Golden shares are special shares created by law or by the company's articles of agreement for the specific purpose of

---

Box 5.3   Golden Shares in France

Article 10 of the French privatization law of August 6, 1986, authorized the minister of the economy to determine, for each of the 65 privatizable companies listed in the annex to Law no. 86-793 of July 2, 1986, whether protection of the national interest required that a special share be granted to the state and, if so, to establish such a share. The company's articles then had to be amended accordingly. Article 10 provided: "The special share allows the Minister of the Economy to approve shareholdings by any person or group of persons acting together exceeding 10% of the capital. The special share may be permanently converted into an ordinary share at any time by order of the Minister of the Economy. Such conversion shall normally take place automatically after five years. . . . In cases of violation of the provisions of the first paragraph hereof, the holder(s) of the shareholdings improperly acquired may not exercise their voting rights and must transfer such shares within three months." In practice, however, there was little application of these provisions in the period 1986–88 and most SOEs were privatized without recourse to this mechanism. Other legislation in effect at the time empowered the government to control, and sometimes block, undesirable takeovers (see pp. 38–39 above, and Graham and Prosser 1991, p. 154).

Article 7 of privatization law no. 93-923 of July 19, 1993, widened the scope of application of the golden share provisions by abolishing, for example, the time limitation. It also allows a referral to the ministry of the economy for approval in cases where control thresholds are exceeded by less than 10 percent; these thresholds are no longer defined in the law but are prescribed by decree on a case-by-case basis. In addition, one or two nonvoting representatives of the government can be appointed by decree to the board of directors or supervisory board of privatized enterprises. Finally, the government can exercise a veto on company decisions concerning the transfer or pledging of assets, if such decisions have the potential to be detrimental to national interests.

The allocation of a golden share to the French government under the proposed Renault-Volvo merger was one of the reasons the Volvo shareholders decided to reject the project in December 1993. On the other hand, it does not seem to have affected the success of the last privatization for which a golden share was issued, namely that of Elf in March 1994, although the presence of two nonvoting government commissioners on the board of directors was, it seems, not well received by the international investors.

---

according their holder (the state or government) special rights that go well beyond those attached to ordinary shares. In some cases, they lapse at a predetermined date. The rights attached to them must be described in the sale prospectus for the SOE.

The golden share technique has been frequently used to enable governments to control future transfers of blocks of shares of privatized airlines, so that any future changes in shareholders do not bring the enterprise under foreign control, thereby causing it to lose the right to operate certain international routes.[31] It is also very commonly used in privatizing infrastructure companies (see chapter 7). The rights conferred by golden shares are not, however, necessarily limited to controlling shareholder composition; they can extend to other decisions of the company, as they do in Senegal.[32]

Although they may be necessary in some cases (for example, airline privatizations), golden shares are by no means an essential feature of privatization laws. On the contrary, by interfering with the normal functioning of the market and blocking certain types of takeovers (their usual purpose), golden shares can diminish incentives for management performance and adversely affect the operating results of the privatized company.

Preferential Schemes

Privatization laws often allow or require the allocation of free or discounted shares in privatized companies to specific groups, including employees and small shareholders, as well as other special benefits. The reasons for such giveaways vary, but generally include the objective of winning the targeted groups over to the privatization cause. These benefits may, for instance, create worker support for privatization (or reduce their opposition) and favorably impress citizens before an election.

Preemptive Rights and Other Employee Benefits

Many laws grant preferential terms to the employees of privatized SOEs by earmarking part of the SOE shares, granting large discounts on the share price, or both, as illustrated by box 5.4.

Some privatization laws encourage employee shareholding by authorizing interest-free loans or deferred-payment plans for the purchase of shares;

31. The minimum national shareholder percentage may vary from one treaty to another. British Airways, Malaysian Air System, VIASA (Venezuela), and Air New Zealand are among the airline companies privatized with the allocation of a golden share to the government. See also the section of chapter 2 on international law and box 2.3 on the privatization of KLM.

32. Senegal's privatization law authorizes the use of a special or golden share in certain circumstances, mainly in order to protect the state's interests as creditor of privatized enterprises that have repayment or guarantee obligations to the state. Article 14 of the law provides that "the Minister in charge of state holdings may decide by ministerial order that one of the shares held by the state in an enterprise to be privatized that has previously received loans guaranteed or onlent by the state shall be converted to a special share carrying special rights. . . . The special share allows the Minister in charge of state holdings, under conditions and procedures to be prescribed by decree, to ensure that the enterprise takes all necessary measures to provide for repayment of the loans guaranteed or onlent by the state."

Box 5.4 Preferential Allocation of Shares to Employees

In *Argentina*, a proportion of the shares, often about 10 percent, has generally been earmarked for employees under privatization operations. By May 1993 about 117,000 employees had acquired shareholdings in this way in 64 privatized SOEs. Employees are allowed to pay for the shares allocated to them out of dividends. The Banco de la Nación Argentina is the depositary for these shares (see *Privatisation International*, May 1993, p. 31).

In *Bulgaria*, articles 22 and 23 of the 1992 privatization law contain such provisions with respect to the privatization of SOEs organized under company law: article 22, which applies to SOEs organized as joint-stock companies, states that the discount is 50 percent and that up to 20 percent of the shares belonging to the state can be sold in this way; it caps the total value of the discount to which each worker is entitled at an amount determined according to the worker's seniority and salary and provides that these preferential employee shares will be nonvoting shares for the first three years.

In *France*, the privatization law of August 1986 prescribed that 10 percent of the shares offered for sale had to be set aside for employees (and some former employees). It authorized discounts for employees of up to 20 percent of the share price, with payment in installments over a maximum period of three years. Employees receiving a discount of over 5 percent could not, however, transfer their shares in the first two years, while those granted payment facilities were required to retain them until they had paid for them in full. In the case of Paribas Bank, for example, 10 percent of the shares sold were earmarked for employees (and former employees); of these shares, one-third were sold at a discount of 20 percent with deferred payment (over two years) and two-thirds for cash at a 5 percent discount. In addition, free shares could be allocated to employees who retained their shares for at least one year beyond the mandatory holding period (in the case of Paribas, one free share for each share bought and held for a year following full payment) and to small shareholders who kept their shares for a specified minimum period (18 months in the case of Paribas). Cour des Comptes 1990 (p. 27) estimated the total cost of these benefits to employees and small shareholders (in revenue forgone) at just over FF 1 billion for employee discounts and just over FF 5 billion for free shares, that is, total benefits of over FF 6 billion, equal to about $1 billion. The privatization law of July 1993 retains the discounts and deferred payment facilities for employees. It provides, however, that shares cannot be transferred for two years when a discount has been given (even of less than 5 percent of the share price).

In *Poland*, article 24 of the privatization law provides that up to 20 percent of shares be reserved for workers of the company at a 50 percent discount on the sale price to the general public (Polish citizens). The aggregate value of the discounts granted to employees of a company is capped, however. A new privatization law was prepared by the government, enacted by parliament, vetoed by President Walesa, and reconfirmed by parliament overruling the veto on July 21, 1995. Feeling that the law infringed on the powers of the executive, the president asked the Polish constitutional court to review it. The court "ruled against a portion of the legislation that said the government must offer part of a company's shares to employees for free. Instead, the court said the government should sell the shares to employees for half the price offered to investors." Following this ruling the government announced that it would submit a new bill to parliament; the new privatization law was enacted in August 1996. See *Central European Business Weekly*, 1–7 December 1995; see also pp. 39–40 above.

some even allow shares to be paid for out of future dividends. Loans and installment plans have drawbacks, however, and should not be granted for the bulk of the share purchase.[33] These advantages are sometimes combined, as in Slovenia, where managers and workers enjoy a very generous preferential scheme encompassing some free shares, as well as discounts and deferred-payment facilities.[34]

Moreover, some countries have promoted the outright takeover of enterprises by their employees (see EBRD and CEEPN 1993). Russian legislation has probably been the most generous in this respect. It offered the workers' council of corporatized SOEs three choices: (a) to receive 25 percent of the shares free of charge and 10 percent at a subsidized price; (b) to buy 51 percent of the shares at a price equivalent to 1.7 times their book value (far below their true value, especially considering Russia's high inflation rate); or (c) for small enterprises only, to enter into a management contract entitling managers to obtain 20 percent of the shares at book value if they meet contractual terms and giving all employees the right to another 20 percent at a 30 percent discount to book value. This third formula was rarely chosen in practice. Since the second option was by far the one most favorable to the workers, it is no surprise that more than 70 percent of the enterprises concerned chose it, thereby allowing employees and managers to acquire 51 percent of the shares at a fraction of their normal price and protect themselves against any hostile takeover by outside investors.[35] Another 29 percent of the company's shares was typically sold in a second stage through voucher auctions.

33. The Slovak government has been criticized for selling SOEs to managers and workers and giving them ten years to pay for their acquisition; this allows them to control these enterprises with very little money down, while using the company's cash flow to pay the government installments. Where the company provides loans to its employees to buy shares, the total amount should remain small relative to the company's overall equity so that the interests of its creditors and its other shareholders are not adversely affected. In the privatization of Telmex, the labor union was able to borrow funds at a low rate (6%) from Nafinsa, a public financial institution, to finance the acquisition of 4.4% of the company's stock. See also the section on Argentina in box 5.4; the section below on financing; and the part of chapter 3 on employee ownership legislation, including ESOPs.

34. See *Financial Times*, 12 April 1994. The fact that the enterprises of the former Yugoslavia were largely self-managed by their staffs helps explain this generosity. The previous regimes had vested employees with quasi property rights that could not be ignored. Privatization through management-employee buyouts has also been common in Slovenia and Croatia.

35. See Lieberman and Rahuja 1995, pp. 13–15. A 1995 study by the London Business School, confirming the shift of control from the state to company insiders, "found that among a random sample of privatised Russian companies, workers held 48% of the shares, managers 21% and outsiders 20%. In 65% of privatised firms, workers held a dominant share" (*The Economist*, 18 November 1995). This same scenario also took place in Kyrgyzstan and other former Soviet republics that had based their privatization legislation on the Russian model (see the section below on the choice of an equitable scheme and the section in chapter 6 dealing with conflicts of interest).

In the United Kingdom, National Freight was sold to its employees in 1982. In Mexico, the trade unions were given a preemptive right in privatizations that allowed them to buy a company by matching the highest bid obtained in competitive bidding.[36] Legislation in Bulgaria and Iran also provide for employee buyout schemes.[37]

Preferential share schemes for employees may be well suited for large enterprises organized as joint-stock companies, but they are less so for small firms. Employee buyouts, on the other hand, may be put together for small firms more easily than for large ones. Furthermore, some investors may want to be sole owners or may not want employee participation in the management of the company, especially where a company requires a lot of restructuring.[38] Other investors may view employee participation in the company's capital as a contribution to a better social climate, higher productivity, and sometimes also as a safeguard against future renationalization (see Gates and Saghir 1995, p. 8). Finally, in most transition countries, preferential rights may be a reflection or confirmation of the rights workers and managers already enjoy, whether de jure or de facto, over their enterprise before its privatization (see Boycko, Shleifer, and Vishny 1995).

Advantages Granted to Other Categories of Buyers

Discounts, rebates, free share distributions, concessional financing facilities, or preemptive rights have been offered not only to employees. They have, for example, been granted to citizens as part of mass privatization programs (see chapter 6); to lessees, as in Czechoslovakia; or to tenants, as in Hungary.[39] A great many countries have granted such advantages to shareholders as well, including France, Indonesia, Italy, Spain, and the

36. Sixteen enterprises were sold to their respective employee unions under this provision during the 1989–91 period. Resale of the enterprise was prohibited to avoid possible improper practices, such as an agreement between an interested buyer and the union under which the buyer would purchase the enterprise after the union had exercised its right, thereby guaranteeing the acquisition of the enterprise without bidding and the risk of raising the auction price (see Galal and others 1994).

37. Article 31 of Bulgaria's 1992 privatization law prescribes that, where the enterprise to be privatized is not incorporated under private law, the employees of the enterprise may bid in an auction or tender sale, on the condition that at least 30 percent of the employees participate. In the event that they offer the highest price, they will be selected as buyers and will be granted a 30 percent discount on their bid price. In Iran, privatization decree no. 5283/T 109H earmarks 33 percent of the shares of enterprises privatized in the manufacturing sector for employees and grants them a right of first refusal over the remaining 67 percent.

38. To address such concerns, the Bulgarian privatization law stipulated that shares given to employees on preferential terms would be nonvoting for a three-year period (articles 22.6 and 23.2 of the 1992 law).

39. See article 16 of the Small-Scale Privatization Law of Czechoslovakia, which gives lessees a right of first refusal with respect to property they are leasing by giving them an opportunity to purchase it before it is put up for auction. The sale price is the reserve price that would have been set at auction (article 8). On Hungary, see box 3.1.

United Kingdom.[40] Article 16 of Argentina's privatization law (1989 law on state reform) lists six categories of buyers eligible for preferential treatment: in addition to employees, the law lists current shareholders, habitual users of the services of the SOE to be privatized, producers of raw materials processed by the enterprise, and individuals and companies that bring in new sales contracts to the enterprise.

Choice of an Equitable Scheme

The preferential-treatment schemes described above have implications for public finance and will therefore, as a rule, need to be authorized by or pursuant to a law. The privatization legislation should set the minimum requirements applicable to these benefits or schemes, because they involve not only a loss of revenue for the public treasury but also a transfer of resources from the state to specific groups.

If not properly designed, provisions of this kind can raise delicate problems. The granting of benefits to employees, for example, raises questions of equity (why should employees of some SOEs receive a benefit from the government that is unavailable to the employees of other SOEs, to civil servants, to farmers, or to the unemployed, to cite only a few), of efficiency (whether employee participation in the capital of a company helps boost efficiency), and of necessity (whether benefits have to be granted to gain employees' sup-

40. *France*: Buyers who held their shares for a specified period (one or two years, depending on the company) got additional shares distributed free of charge.

Indonesia: The sweetener used for the partial flotation of PT Telkom included a 2.5 percent discount for Indonesian investors and a one-for-ten bonus share redeemable after holding the stock for one year (see *Financial Times*, 12 September 1995 and 2 November 1995).

Italy: In order to encourage small shareholders to participate in the ENI privatization, after the rather poor performance of other recently privatized companies, the government offered a creative form of insurance. "If the average ENI share price in the 20 days at the end of the 12-month period following the issue is less than the issue price, the Treasury will reimburse the difference up to a tenth of the original price—provided that investors have held their shares for the whole period" (*The Economist*, 18 November 1995). Despite this enticement, investor interest turned out to be lower than the government had hoped, and after-market performance was disappointing, too.

Spain: In the 1995 flotation of Telefónica shares, incentives for small shareholders included, in addition to a 4 percent discount, one bonus share for every twenty shares held for at least one year following the flotation. Individual shareholders who subscribed to shares in Repsol, the energy company, were not only given a 4 percent rebate on the share price but also a guarantee by the state that it would reimburse such investors (up to 10 percent of the offering price) in case the share price dropped within the 12 months following the offering (see *Financial Times*, 26 January 1996).

United Kingdom: Free shares were given to shareholders who kept their shares in electricity companies for three years, for example. Most large privatizations were done through public offerings; many of these were also underpriced, which is another way to provide immediate benefits to shareholders. Largely as a result of the privatization program, the number of shareholders rose from about 2 million before the 1984 British Telecom privatization to about 11 million in 1995.

port and thereby ensure smooth execution of the privatization program). The difficulties are compounded when it comes to enacting detailed regulations.[41]

Preferential schemes and their related provisions are not essential features of privatization legislation. Nevertheless, provisions allowing these benefits to be granted are found in many privatization laws, because they reflect the policies of many governments and are often intended to enlist the support and involvement of employees, other targeted groups, or the population at large in the privatization program. In some cases short-term electoral considerations will prevail over the broader efficiency goals that should ideally be central to the program (see chapter 1). Thus many observers feel that the benefits granted in Russia to employees and managers of privatized enterprises were excessive and slowed the development of these enterprises by protecting and strengthening the position of the management teams of the former SOEs (see also the section in chapter 6 on SOE management and restructuring bodies).

Financing

The rule in privatization programs should be that buyers of shares, assets, or enterprises pay for their acquisition in cash.[42] Exceptions will normally have to be authorized by law, as they represent benefits or subsidies selectively granted by the government (see the section above on preferential schemes).

Financing Arrangements

Almost all privatization laws or programs embody special financing techniques, which can be divided into two types: deferred payment (seller financing) and credit (bank financing). If the method of financing does not involve a subsidy—that is, if it has no adverse impact on public finances—no special legislation should be necessary. When the concessional financing is available to all interested buyers, it forms part of the general terms and conditions (it becomes in fact a price factor) and no longer amounts to preferential treatment; therefore, unless the law provides otherwise, no specific authorization should be required.

Techniques have been developed to reduce some of the risks associated with partial payment for shares. Where shares are paid for in installments,

41. Which employees should be eligible for these employee shares: current employees (including those hired recently; what should be the cutoff date?); former employees (minimum number of years of service?); retired staff; temporary staff or only permanent employees; and so on. How many shares will each employee be entitled to? Will this depend on length of service, salary level, rank, or other factors? Should the transferability of these shares be restricted (for example, by authorizing their sale only to other employees, requiring that they be retained for a minimum period, requiring the holder to sell the shares on leaving the company, and so on)? Should shares allocated without charge or at a nominal price be stripped of voting rights?

42. See, for example, article 8 of the Senegalese privatization law, which provides that "save for exceptional derogation, authorized by decree, shares offered for sale shall be paid for in cash." See also article 22 of the 1994 privatization law of Congo, which states that the sale price shall be paid for in cash; the council of ministers may, however, authorize exceptions for small shareholders.

for example, the voting rights of shareholders who have not paid in full for their shares can be limited, and their shares may be held in escrow until the last installment is paid.

Debt-Equity Swaps

Public-sector debt instruments have been accepted in payment for privatization transactions, especially in heavily indebted countries, including Argentina, Brazil, Chile, Mexico, and the Philippines, but also in France and other less indebted countries.[43] The key problem is to set the value of the debt (that is, for many developing or transition countries, the discount rate that will apply to securities that can be swapped for shares). In Brazil, the discount rate for debt-equity conversions was set at 25 percent in 1990.[44] For the privatization of the Mexican steel companies, the conversion terms were set using a formula stipulated in the bidding documents. In France the privatization law stipulated that shares could be paid for by state debt securities and investment certificates previously issued by the SOEs, the swap value of which would be set by ministerial order.[45]

Each debt security accepted in payment of shares will normally have its own swap rate, reflecting its market value. The conversion or discount rate should not include any implicit subsidy in favor of the buyer. It can be set either before the privatization operation begins (for example, in the bidding

43. In addition, in the privatization of the Argentine oil company YPF a special tranche of 45 million shares of YPF was earmarked to be exchanged by Argentine pensioners for their BOCONs, special obligations that had been issued by the state at a favorable rate (15 percent above the average market value at that time). The YPF shares acquired in this way were held by a financial institution and could not be sold during the first year. As a result, pensioners have acquired 13 percent of YPF and the BOCON discount has been appreciably reduced. See *International Financing Review, Review of the Year 1993*, p. 170; World Equity and IFC 1993, p. 91.

44. Law no. 8031 of April 12, 1990, which regulates Brazil's privatization program, provides that, in addition to cash, shares in companies to be privatized may be paid for using public sector bonds or obligations as well as funds blocked in accounts at the central bank. Resolution no. 14 of the Denationalization Program Steering Committee lists the financial instruments that can be used to buy companies being privatized and sets the rules for their conversion into local currency. The acceptable instruments include blocked funds, various public-sector bonds, promissory notes, privatization certificates, and state foreign and domestic debt paper. Privatization certificates, which can be used only to pay for shares in SOEs being privatized, were created pursuant to Law no. 8018/90, which forced financial and other institutions to acquire them (Legal Letter, Pinheiro Neto Advogados, August and September 1991). On September 29, 1995, the Central Bank lifted the "compulsory 25% discount affecting seven types of foreign debt papers when used to purchase state assets"; such bonds would be accepted in payment at face value at certain privatization auctions; this "decision caused an immediate appreciation of Brazilian debt paper in the secondary market" (*Privatisation International*, November 1995, p. 7).

45. Article 5 of the law of August 6, 1986, provides that the swap value of state bonds will be determined by their average market value on the stock exchange over the preceding 20 market days. Article 6 provides that the conversion price of an investment certificate of an SOE (which was usually structured like a preferred nonvoting share) into an ordinary share of the company will take into account, on the one hand, the value of voting rights and, on the other, the value of the preferences attached to the certificates that may be lost in the conversion.

documentation) or at the payment date.[46] Both methods involve difficulties. These include fluctuations in the market discount rate or exchange rate (or both) between publication of the bidding documentation, opening of the bids, selection of the buyer, signature of the agreements, and the payment date; the effect of the privatization process on the discount rate itself; and, finally, the risks and costs incurred by the bidders who submit bids based on a debt swap, in terms of the possibility of obtaining the necessary debt instruments at the expected price, the availability and cost of risk-hedging instruments, and the risk of acquiring debt securities without knowing whether the transaction they are intended to finance will actually take place.

Debt-equity swaps may be regulated by the privatization law, public finance legislation (with respect to amortization of the public debt), a special law or regulations on debt-equity conversion (which may predate the privatization law and apply to the conversion of public-sector as well as private-sector debt), or provisions embodied in the bidding documentation for a particular privatization operation. The likelihood of carrying out these debt-equity swaps may depend on factors such as the specific terms of the original debt instruments being swapped (for example, loan agreements between the SOE in question and its lenders, state debt to foreign banks, and state bonds) and the regulatory restrictions applying to the creditors (in many countries, for example, commercial banks are not allowed to hold shares in nonfinancial enterprises). The problem is a particularly complex one when foreign banks have to waive certain rights. Such a waiver had to be obtained, for example, in order to start the tendering procedure for privatization of the two Argentine telecommunications companies that succeeded ENTEL; 60 percent of their shares were sold in November 1990 for $214 million in cash and $5 billion (face value) in public-debt securities.

Some countries have also issued special state obligations that can be either redeemed at the end of their term (as any other bond or obligation) or used as payment for shares in enterprises privatized through public offerings. This was the case with the Balladur bonds in France in 1993 and with the 1996 Moroccan privatization bonds. Balladur bonds were four-year bonds issued at a fixed rate (6 percent); they could be exchanged, with some tax advantages, into shares of the enterprises to be privatized. If trading above par value, their exchange value would be the market price, and they could be exchanged at par if their market price fell lower; bondholders were given preference in the allocation of shares. The bond was a tremendous success, raising 110 billion francs (over $20 billion).

The interesting feature of the Moroccan bonds—a first tranche of which was issued in January 1996 and a second one in May 1996—is that privatization bondholders have an absolute priority in the allocation of shares. Privatization bonds are served first in case of oversubscription. Cash subscriptions are served

---

46. The discount margin on the outstanding debt could also be included among the variables in the tendering procedure; this would unnecessarily complicate the evaluation process, however, by making the comparison of the different financial bids quite complex.

on a reduced basis to the extent that shares remain available, as happened in the public offering of 30 percent of the oil refinery SAMIR in March 1996. Privatization bonds of this type are a way to anticipate future privatization revenue, to raise funds at a lower rate than would be the case with a standard bond, and to strengthen the government's commitment to bring privatization transactions to the market. They also create a greater constituency for privatization, namely, bondholders who want to benefit from the conversion option.

Allocation of Privatization Proceeds

Many governments envision large receipts when they embark on a privatization program. The actual result is often disappointingly different. In many developing and transition countries, the net financial balance of privatization is likely to be negative; total privatization costs may well exceed the sale proceeds. In such cases the allocation of privatization receipts should not raise any controversy; all of the receipts are needed to defray the costs of the program, including, in particular, settling SOE debts, severance pay to redundant employees, and the services of advisers (see also chapter 6).

Where total receipts exceed total costs, a prudent policy—bearing in mind that these proceeds are both nonrecurring and of a capital nature—would be to allocate net revenues to the reduction of public debt or possibly to other expenditures that may reduce the public deficit, such as the capitalization of social security funds, for example. Net privatization revenues should not, however, be used to finance current expenditures or the ordinary budget.

The privatization strategy or program will usually specify how the sale proceeds are to be used. If the country's existing laws (including its public finance and public enterprise legislation) do not include such provisions, or if it is thought that they are not well suited to the needs of the privatization program, the privatization law should prescribe the allocation of proceeds.

As box 5.5 shows, the allocation of privatization proceeds is often prescribed by law and hence is subject to control by parliament. Many countries have chosen to use the revenue from privatization to finance the costs of the privatization program. Allocation of net privatization receipts to debt reduction is a sound policy pursued by some of these countries, as well as others such as Italy, where Law no. 432 of October 1993 creates a special privatization fund to be used to repay the public debt.

Provisions in Bulgaria and Puerto Rico typify the illusions entertained by some parliamentarians regarding the amount likely to be raised through privatization. Defining the allocation of proceeds in such detail is ill-advised. It can create unrealistic expectations among the various categories of potential beneficiaries. The actual amount available for allocation may very well be low, or even zero, because in many cases all or most of the sale proceeds will go to cover the costs of the privatization program. It also rigidifies the future financing priorities of the country, which can be detrimental to sound fiscal management.

Box 5.5   Allocation of Privatization Proceeds in Selected Countries

Bulgaria. Article 6 (1) of the 1992 privatization law provides that privatization proceeds shall be paid into a special account to be used to finance five separate funds: a privatization fund (to meet expenses); a mutual fund (whose shares shall be distributed to the population at large, to expropriated former owners, and to the social security funds); a social security fund; a reconstruction and development fund; and an agricultural fund.

France. Law no. 86-824 of July 11, 1986 (first amendment to the finance law for fiscal year 1986), created a special treasury account to receive all privatization proceeds. On the income side, the privatization account was to be credited with the receipts from the sale of shares, certificates, or other securities and rights concerning enterprises whose transfer to the private sector was authorized by law. This account was intended to receive only the proceeds of sale of shares or rights for enterprises covered by the privatization law, and not proceeds of sales that could be carried out without parliamentary authorization, for example. On the expenditure side, the special account could be used for (a) public debt repayments through transfers to the national debt retirement fund, the national industry fund, and the national banks fund, and (b) capital contributions to SOEs through transfers to another special account. Of the 86 billion francs brought in by the 1986–88 privatizations, two-thirds was used to retire debt and one-third for SOE capital contributions. As in the other special treasury accounts, the transactions on this account were subject to parliamentary approval as part of the budgetary process. Including a special account of this kind in the ordinary budget procedure and subjecting it to scrutiny by parliament were deemed essential to ensure transparency and compliance with the approved objectives and procedures (see Cour des Comptes 1990).

Germany. Article 5 (1) of the 1990 privatization law provides that "the Treuhandanstalt's receipts shall be used primarily for structural adjustment of the enterprises . . . and secondarily to make contributions to the State budget and meet the Treuhandanstalt's current expenditures. The receipts shall be used in agreement with the Council of Ministers." Article 25 of the August 1990 unification treaty provided that "the Treuhand's receipts may also be used, in individual cases, to alleviate the debt burden of the agricultural enterprises."

Hungary. Article 6 of the 1993 finance law, enacted on December 17, 1992, provides that part of the receipts from privatization shall be allocated to the State Property Agency to defray expenses incurred in implementing the privatization program. It further provides that a share of privatization receipts shall be paid to three different funds: the employment fund, the regional development fund, and the fund for agricultural reconstruction and conversion.

Mexico. The sale of public enterprises yielded government receipts totaling over $21 billion, which were allocated practically entirely to repayment of the public debt.

New Zealand and United Kingdom. The receipts from privatization operations are allocated to the national budget, allowing a significant reduction in the national debt of these countries.

(box continues on the following page)

Box 5.5   *(continued)*

Philippines. Article 34 of Presidential Proclamation no. 50 provides that privatization receipts, net of the expenses incurred by the Asset Privatization Trust, form part of general government revenue and must be remitted to the treasury as soon as they are received. The trust is, however, "entitled to retain, upon approval by the [Privatization] Committee, such portion of the proceeds as may be necessary to maintain a revolving fund to be utilized for the payment of fees and reimbursable expenses and meeting the costs and expenses incurred by the Trust in the conservation and disposition of the assets held by it."

Puerto Rico. The law authorizing the privatization of telecommunications provided that, out of total net receipts, at least $1 billion was to be allocated to the Permanent Fund for the Development of Education and at least $1 billion to the Permanent Infrastructure Fund, the said funds serving exclusively to finance projects in those two sectors. However, this transaction never materialized (see note 5 in this chapter).

Where special accounts or funds are established, the law or implementing regulations will prescribe how they are to be set up and the procedures for their operation and supervision. They will specify, for example, who decides on the use of these funds (parliament, the council of ministers, a minister, the administrators of the fund, the director of the privatization agency) and how funds are to be invested. They will prescribe whether the funds shall be interest bearing and, if so, to what account accrued interest shall be allocated and for what purposes it may be used. In most legal systems privatization receipts are considered to be public receipts governed by public finance legislation, not receipts that the government can use without restriction. Expenditures financed out of these proceeds should thus be subject to public expenditure and accounting rules.

The situation may be more complicated when it is an SOE itself that sells part of its assets—for example, a division, a plant, or a subsidiary—to private investors (see also the section in chapter 4 on exercise of ownership rights). Under ordinary company law (and many public enterprise laws), the receipts belong to the seller—the SOE in this instance—which could defeat the purpose of the privatization program if, for example, the objective is to downsize the public sector or replenish the government's coffers.[47] The state, as sole or majority shareholder of the SOE, should be in a position to recover the proceeds of these privatizations, of course, or at least part of them, in the form of dividends or repayment of amounts owed by the SOE. In practice, however, this

---

47. Where the sale relates to shares newly issued by the enterprise under a capital increase, the proceeds of sale will of course accrue to the enterprise. We can nonetheless speak of privatization, even if this transaction does not in itself involve any sale of shares or assets by the government. Moreover, if the privately subscribed capital increase dilutes sufficiently the public sector's shareholding, it may also result in the privatization of management control.

may never come to pass if the mechanisms for corporate governance of the SOE are inefficient, the dividend policy is not clearly defined, or the board members and management engage in fraud or collusion. In some countries, the way in which the proceeds of sales of assets are to be distributed is prescribed in the privatization rules.[48] In others, including Brazil, the issue has sparked lively controversy between the finance ministry and the SOE concerned.[49]

Transitory Provisions

In view of the complexity of privatization operations and their lengthy implementation time, interim measures may have to be taken for the management of public enterprises and assets pending privatization. These measures may include the replacement of the management team, possibly by a new manager or administrator with special powers; a transitional system to phase out special SOE privileges and obligations; limitations imposed on SOE managers' powers of alienation during the preprivatization period; modifications in the labor status of SOE employees, including layoffs before privatization; liquidation of what remains of the SOE after its corporatization or its privatization through the sale of its assets; fulfillment of obligations for which the government continues to be responsible; and allocation of revenues and liabilities of the SOE that accrue during the transition period or between the signing of the privatization contract and the effective transfer of the enterprise to its new owners, for example.[50] Such measures are often included in the legislation for a specific enterprise or sector, particularly where preprivatization restructuring is required.[51] They may deal with different phases of the interim period, from enactment of the privatization law through corporatization all the way to effective transfer of control over the enterprise to its new owners.

Two or more privatization-related laws could contain mutually contradictory provisions, and new laws could affect ongoing privatization procedures.

---

48. Bulgaria's transitional privatization legislation (article 13 of Decree no. 56, as amended on February 28, 1991) provided that, for example, 40 percent of such proceeds were to be allocated to the enterprise, 30 percent to a state debt service fund, and 30 percent to the State Investment Fund.

49. Allocation of privatization proceeds posed many problems in Brazil, where the government's privatization program focused in the initial phase on the steel, fertilizer, and petrochemical sectors. Petrobras, the majority shareholder of Petrofertil and Petroquisa (the subholding companies for the fertilizer and petrochemical sectors, respectively), thought that it, and not the treasury, should receive the sale proceeds.

50. See, for example, Philippines Presidential Proclamation no. 50 of 1986, which contains several provisions of this kind. Section 29 provides that asset management during the transitional period preceding privatization shall be performed by the government institution previously responsible for those assets, under terms and conditions agreed upon with the government.

51. The U.K. Electricity Act of 1989, for example, includes transitional provisions concerning, first, the prior restructuring of power sector assets by creating new successor companies which would then be privatized and, second, the ways in which the government may intervene in these new companies while they are still wholly owned by the Crown. See the sections in chapter 4 and chapter 7 on prior restructuring.

In Guinea, for example, a general telecommunications law enacted on June 2, 1992, authorized the government to grant concessions for "the establishment, development, operation and maintenance of the public network and the provision of all public telecommunications services" (article 5), and a new law laying down the framework for SOE privatization was enacted on August 20, 1993. The question arose of the extent to which the procedures for privatizing Sotelgui (the public operator) should conform to the rules laid down by the new privatization law. The laws were interpreted in such a way as to validate the steps already taken to initiate the privatization of Sotelgui before the new privatization law entered into effect, while subjecting all outstanding actions, including the organization of calls for bids and the conditions of sale, to the provisions of the new privatization law. Clear language in the law can avert this type of ambiguity and uncertainty by specifying to what extent earlier legislation is abrogated, amended, suspended, or otherwise declared not applicable.

Amendments

Although privatization programs are a relatively recent innovation, many countries have already amended their original privatization legislation. Already discussed, for example, are the changes made to the French legislation regarding the privileges accorded to employees of privatized enterprises (box 5.4), the role of the privatization commission in the selection of buyers without recourse to the market (note 23), the allocation of privatization proceeds (box 5.5), the limits imposed on foreign investment, and the features of golden shares (box 5.3). The French privatization law of July 19, 1993, makes further changes to the system instituted in 1986, including provisions allowing greater flexibility in privatization operations.[52] The Czechoslovak and Peruvian legislation furnish other examples of amendments to privatization laws. In the first case, the amendments imposed new limits on the privatization process.[53] In the latter, they were intended to make the process more flexible and expeditious.[54]

52. The 1993 law authorizes transfer of the capital of a given enterprise in successive tranches. It also authorizes installment payments for shares, while leaving the buyer the option to transfer such shares before fully paying for them (see Report to the Senate no. 326, pp. 32–33, 1992–93).

53. The Czechoslovak Large-Scale Privatization Law of February 26, 1991, was amended by another law dated February 18, 1992. The latter provides in particular (article 13) that, during the first year following privatization, the privatized enterprise may engage in only those activities that the SOE was authorized to carry out. Where the transaction relates to only one unit of a privatized enterprise, the law is even more stringent, prohibiting the pursuit of any activity other than that actually exercised within the SOE before its privatization.

54. In Peru, article 1 of Decree-Law no. 26120 of December 28, 1992, amends article 1 of Decree-Law no. 674 of September 25, 1991, on private investment in SOEs to expressly allow foreign SOEs to acquire shares in privatized enterprises (see note 27 above). In addition, article 4 of Decree-Law no. 26120 amends article 16 of Decree-Law no. 674 to allow COPRI (the private investment promotion commission, the executing agency for Peru's privatization program) greater freedom of choice with respect to the method of transfer to be used in the event that, in the sale at auction of an enterprise to be privatized, no bid matches the minimum price set by the government.

Indeed, amendments have been adopted to cover practically every one of the points discussed in this and preceding chapters. Amendment of legislation is inevitable, because drafting privatization laws is neither an easy task nor an exact science, circumstances change, and experience brings new lessons. Many issues and problems have to be addressed, as the previous chapters testify, and the solutions depend in each case on the specific objectives of the privatization program and the specific legal, economic, political, and other constraints with which the government must contend. Moreover, legislators are neither omniscient nor prescient, and adjustments and corrections will frequently be needed during implementation of the program. Finally, privatization is a new process for most governments and parliaments. The lessons learned in other countries are often little known or poorly interpreted; trial and error is often the only practical process, allowing approaches and methods to be fine-tuned as and when direct experience is acquired. The legislator can substantially reduce the need for later amendment of the legislation by enacting a general law setting forth the broad principles that are to guide the privatization program and avoiding going into the details of particular procedures or techniques. This calls for a degree of confidence in the government, however, that is not always present.

Conclusion

A privatization law does not have to encompass all the issues discussed in this chapter. It is, in fact, sometimes possible to privatize without any special law, either because the constitution and the legislation in force do not require such a law or because the authorities have been able to devise original solutions that do not call for changes in existing legislation.

Law and strategy are two separate concepts that must not be confused. While it can be argued that a government's privatization strategy ought to address all major aspects of a privatization program, that does not apply to privatization legislation. One needs first to analyze the legal implications of the privatization strategy and program adopted, together with the country's existing legislation, to ascertain whether a new law is required from a legal point of view.

Yet even where a law is not strictly necessary (legally speaking), political considerations may argue in favor of one. A law may be useful or necessary, for example, to protect the government politically, to establish or cement a consensus between political forces, to impart a certain degree of stability to the new policy, or to render more difficult any reversal of approach by a future government.

Because the conditions (legal, political, or other) that led to the enactment of a law differ from country to country, it is to be expected that the content of the law will differ also. There is therefore no such thing as a legal blueprint or model law that can easily be copied from one country to another.

Where a law is needed, it should normally take the form of an enabling law, conferring authority to the government or privatization agency(ies) to privatize and regulating the process without tying their hands too tightly. Other legal instruments such as decrees, implementing regulations, directives, and resolutions, but also sales agreements negotiated directly with buyers, can be important instruments in the legal arsenal of privatization.

Detailed laws may be necessary, however, in the case of complex privatization operations that call for amendment of many existing legislative provisions. Such laws address not only the restructuring and privatization of infrastructure sectors (the British electricity and water legislation, for example, which is discussed in greater detail in chapter 7) but also necessary amendments to current legislation to facilitate privatization operations (discussed in chapters 3 and 4). A given privatization law may hence include provisions dealing with many of the topics discussed in other chapters of this book.

Flexibility is important, because it is impossible to predict all the situations and problems that might arise during the implementation of a privatization program. A flexible legal framework will allow the government and the responsible agencies to adjust their methods to changing circumstances. A rigid framework, in contrast, would very probably slow the pace, impose ineffective methods, and compel the government to go back to parliament to obtain amendments to the law.

Flexibility must not be confused with ambiguity, however. The privatization law must be clearly worded, especially with respect to delegation of powers, responsibilities of the various parties involved, scope of the mandate, minimum requirements for transparency and competitiveness of selling procedures, selection criteria, benefits accorded to specific categories of buyers, resources made available to the executing agencies, allocation of privatization proceeds, and controls that will be applied to privatization officials. The law may also prescribe simpler and more decentralized procedures for small enterprises or municipal enterprises, for example.

The privatization law should eliminate the most serious legal obstacles and constraints to privatization. If, however, the law does not address these or, even worse, includes additional constraints, restrictions, or conflicting objectives, the privatization process will be more difficult and slower, with lower net benefits to government and society.

One should also guard against legislative optimism. Even if the legislator were able to predict correctly the major problems that might arise during execution of the privatization program and could therefore design the optimal legal framework, success would not be guaranteed. It would still be necessary to apply this legislation effectively, which can be done only if the appropriate institutions and resources exist or are put in place, and each operation prepared, structured, negotiated, and implemented with competence and integrity. Institutional issues are discussed further in chapter 6.

Privatization is still a relatively recent development and it is still too early to draw definitive lessons. It is also an extremely broad and diversified process embracing widely differing scenarios, concerning a huge range of enterprises operating in every sector of activity and of every possible size; moreover, it is implemented in countries with very different political, legal, economic and social systems, conditions, and objectives. This precludes a single approach applicable to all countries and all privatization operations. A privatization law must, above all, reflect in legislative terms the strategy and program adopted by the competent national authorities and respond to the specific needs of the country.

6

Institutional Framework for Privatization

Privatization operations typically last for only a relatively short period (say, between five and fifteen years) and call for expertise and resources not found in the civil service. Many governments have therefore decided to set up one or several special institutions to manage the privatization process, or to contract out part of the work to outside experts. This chapter focuses on the role of these new institutions and experts and on their interaction with the other parties involved in the preparation and implementation of a country's privatization program. The following section examines the role of parliament; the chapter then moves to the general institutional framework for implementing, coordinating, and monitoring the privatization program. Other sections deal with staffing and financing for the privatization process. Privatization funds, which play an important role in many transition countries, are taken up next. The last sections deal with government advisers in general and legal advisers in particular.

Role of Parliament

In most countries parliament has played an important role in the privatization process, as evidenced by the multitude of privatization laws enacted worldwide (see the appendix). These laws have been analyzed in chapter 5. Debates on the bills have often been lengthy and fierce, and amendments to the text proposed by the government have in many cases been accepted to satisfy various groups. Once approved, privatization laws have often had to be amended, which required a new passage through parliament. This legislative action may not only be necessary (legally speaking) to authorize privatization operations but may also be a means of obtaining or confirming parliament's adhesion to the government's privatization policy, demonstrating a solid political support for the process.

In addition to general enabling legislation, some parliaments have given themselves a role in the implementation stage, such as the adoption of annual privatization programs. This is relatively common in transition countries, where the scope of the privatization law is usually very broad (see, for example, article 2 of Poland's 1990 privatization law). Privatization may also come under parliamentary debate as part of the scrutiny of the budget law or finance act (see chapter 4), the program of a new government, parliamentary questions, and so on.

In some cases legislators have given themselves prerogatives that have sometimes led to micromanagement of the privatization process and to direct opposition with the government. Thus, in Argentina, a joint house-senate parliamentary commission representing the various political parties initially had to ratify most privatizations.[1] In the early stages, the joint commission played an active role in the privatization process, for example, by requiring that the terms of the ENTEL call for bids be modified. The commission's powers have since been curtailed: if it does not take a position within thirty days, privatization can proceed. In Taiwan, legislative debate is required for each transfer of an SOE to the private sector.[2] In Hungary, parliament first placed the new privatization agency under its own authority (Law no. 7 of January 1990). Less than a year later the law was amended to place the agency under the authority of the council of ministers and the national accounts office, following criticisms of the first privatization operations. Finally, in the Slovak Republic, successive governments have tried to cancel privatizations agreed by their predecessors. In November 1994, for instance, the new parliament enacted a law invalidating many privatization transactions concluded by the outgoing government shortly before the elections of October 1, 1994; this law was overturned, however, in May 1995 by a ruling of the constitutional court that found that parliament had acted beyond its constitutional powers.[3]

Discrete, transaction-level interventions of this kind by parliament are generally detrimental to the smooth implementation of the privatization program. Members of parliament are usually neither the best informed nor the best placed to take the speedy decisions that privatization operations entail. As the examples above show, some countries have come to realize these shortcomings and have curtailed the role of parliament during the implementation phase.

1. This commission was created by article 14 of the 1989 state reform law. It consists of six house and six senate members elected by their peers. Its task is to coordinate relations between parliament and government concerning implementation of the law.

2. According to "A Review of Privatization in the Republic of China," a paper presented at an informal OECD seminar on privatization, Buenos Aires, March 29–30, 1994. This paper also cites a resolution of the Taiwan parliament adopted on June 18, 1992, during examination of the budget of the Taiwan Machinery Manufacturing Corporation for fiscal year 1993, which translates as follows: "In order to prevent the granting of benefits and wastage of funds earned by the blood and sweat of the people, the privatization plan of the enterprise shall be submitted to parliament for debate."

3. See Borish and Noël 1996, p. 70. See also the section in chapter 2 on the control of the constitutionality of privatization legislation.

International experience with privatization shows that relations between parliament and government can be very strained at any stage of the privatization process, however. A government may legitimately wish to limit recourse to parliament to what is strictly necessary, especially when faced with a narrow window of political opportunity. Delays attributable to intervention by parliament may be exacerbated by bicameral systems (that is, where the legislature comprises an upper chamber—senate, house of lords—and a lower chamber—house of representatives, house of commons, national assembly).

In Poland, for example, the government announced a new program in June 1991 providing for the speedy privatization of about 400 SOEs through investment funds whose shares would be sold to Polish citizens. However, the lower house of parliament, dominated by the opposition, succeeded in blocking the project by sending it back for examination at the next session of parliament. The law was finally enacted on April 30, 1993, but not until late 1995 did implementation begin. Indeed, Poland had seven successive governments between 1989 and early 1996, some of which were skeptical and even hostile to the mass privatization scheme. The prime minister of the government in place between September 1993 and the 1994 election was, for instance, opposed to the important role assigned to foreign companies in the management of the privatization funds (see the section in this chapter on privatization funds and table 6.4). In the most recent episode of this saga, outgoing president Lech Walesa, in one of his last acts as president after losing the November 1995 elections to excommunist Aleksander Kwasniewski, launched a referendum on privatization that was held on February 18, 1996. The referendum included five questions on privatization concerning, among other things, the mass privatization program and the role of the national investment funds. Ambiguity in the wording of the questions and a boycott by some parties reduced voter participation to only 32 percent; a 50 percent rate would have been needed to make the outcome of the referendum binding.[4]

The best known example of tension between government and parliament was probably between the Russian federal government, on the one hand, and the national parliament and some local assemblies, on the other.[5] Russia experienced countless skirmishes between government and parliament,

---

4. There was a large majority in favor of mass privatization and against expansion of the often foreign-managed investment funds (see *Reuter European Community Report*, 18 February 1996; *Privatisation International*, March 1996).

5. In July 1993 the federal parliament canceled a presidential decree forcing SOEs to swap at least 29 percent of their shares against privatization vouchers distributed to all citizens. Parliament announced that these vouchers could be replaced by "privatization accounts" (the workings of which were not defined) opened in state-owned savings banks. This news caused the market value of the privatization coupons to fall by 20 percent. Auctions of shares against vouchers were also suspended in the regions of Chelyabinsk and Novosibirsk. See *Privatization International* May 1993, p. 8; *The Economist*, 24 July 1993.

which culminated in the overthrow of the Supreme Soviet by force and the declaration of early elections in October 1993. The shutdown of parliament actually provided some momentum for privatization by forcing the streamlining of the process. Before these events, the responsibilities for privatization had been divided between the Russian Federal Property Fund, responsible for sales and reporting to the Supreme Soviet, and the privatization ministry (GKI), responsible for policy and answering to the government. Following the overthrow, the minister assumed the responsibility for overseeing both organizations and came to be in charge of both policy and sales. Much progress was made in this period. The Duma (lower house) that followed the Supreme Soviet in December 1993 was less powerful than parliament had been, which provided more room for action on the privatization front. However, the communists' strong showing in the December 1995 parliamentary elections and the hotly contested June 1996 presidential campaign increased the tension again between government and parliament (see Boycko, Shleifer, and Vishny 1995).

Bulgaria provides another, less dramatic, example of the institutional stalemate that can result from conflicts between government and parliament, as described in box 6.1. The French privatization laws of summer 1986 also offer an interesting example of conflict, this time between parliament and government, on the one hand, and the head of state, on the other (see chapter 5).

As a rule, parliaments will want to retain more control where the law gives a lot of latitude to the government. A law clearly limiting the set of enterprises that can be privatized and the privatization techniques and arrangements that can be used is less likely to contain provisions that allow parliament to intervene during implementation of the program. But a tightly drafted law constraining the government's flexibility in implementing the program may well slow progress. A tradeoff exists, which will be particularly acute where political majorities in government and parliament differ and mutual trust is low.

Institutional Structure

Countries around the world have chosen a variety of institutional structures to implement their privatization programs. The role of the legislature and its interaction with the executive were discussed in the previous section; the roles of the judiciary and specialized regulatory agencies are reviewed elsewhere in this book.[6]

---

6. The respective competence of parliament, government, and other bodies is sometimes disputed and referred to the courts for adjudication. Such claims are often based on alleged violations of the constitution, as discussed in the section on control of constitutionality in chapter 2. The importance of setting up efficient mechanisms to resolve disputes arising during or after privatization has also already been underscored in chapter 3. In addition, specialized regulatory bodies may need to be established or strengthened in the context of a privatization program, in particular in the infrastructure sectors (see the section on regulatory institutions in chapter 7).

Box 6.1   Blocked Institutions in Bulgaria, 1990–95

From February 1990, when Bulgaria's first post-Zhivkov government took office, privatization was a priority goal of successive governments. By May 1990 a privatization bill, drafted by the ministry of economic reform, was ready. In addition, several decrees were issued in 1990 to allow the privatization process to be started without waiting for the new law to be enacted. Nevertheless, the lack of such a law and of an executing agency greatly hampered implementation of the initial phase of privatization.

To speed the process, the council of ministers set up a privatization agency by Decree no. 16 of February 8, 1991. The agency's function was ambiguous, however, and primarily of an advisory nature. A year later the agency had still taken no major initiative, the small privatization program launched by the ministry of industry and commerce in 1991 had come to a halt, and the privatization law drafted in April 1990 and submitted to the national assembly in September 1990 had not yet been enacted, even though the government had an absolute majority (over 80 percent from January to October 1991) in the national assembly.

These delays were caused largely by political rivalries and compromises that reflected the lack of confidence among the groups involved: the parliament, government, president, parties and factions, and privatization agency. The law was finally enacted by the national assembly on April 23, 1992, two years after the first draft was adopted by the council of ministers, and a new privatization agency replaced the one set up in 1991. It then took several months to appoint the director general of the agency and the members of the oversight council.

The year 1993 brought other institutional ups and downs. A new government decided to replace the members of the oversight council of the privatization agency who had been appointed by the previous government. The members filed suit against the decision. The court declared the replacement illegal because none of the causes for termination of functions (per article 12 of the 1992 privatization law) were present. The members were therefore reinstated, but then relieved of their functions once again by the government.

Not surprisingly, Bulgaria's privatization program made little headway during this period. Only two major privatizations took place between 1990 and 1993, both in the food sector: the sales of Tsarevicni Produkti to a Belgo-Anglo-American consortium for $20 million plus $18 million in Bulgarian debt paper, and of Republika to Kraft Jacobs Suchard.

Several factors contributed to this impasse, including intransigence on the part of the political authorities, precluding all compromise; conflict and mistrust between supporters and opponents of the old regime; weakness of the two post-Zhivkov nonsocialist governments, which prevented them from dismantling the old communist networks; and commercial alliances among former communist party leaders, former members of the security forces, and SOE heads (party leaders and security personnel supplied the SOEs with raw materials and other goods in exchange for their products, which they then resold at colossal profits). In brief, these and other reasons fostered the maintenance of the status quo, from which some reaped substantial profits.

(box continues on the following page)

Box 6.1   *(continued)*

The following years (1994 and 1995) were, unfortunately, not much more productive, partly because of a new requirement to have each privatization deal
cleared with the cabinet. The major deals of 1995 included two breweries sold for
about $5 million each and a cannery. Government turnover continued, leading to
a total of half a dozen governments between 1989 and 1995. In June 1994 the
privatization law was amended to add a mass privatization program. A special
agency, separate from the privatization agency, was set up to manage this voucher
program; not much happened in terms of actual privatizations, however, whether
through trade sales or mass privatization. The list of over 1,000 companies
included in the mass privatization program was approved by parliament only in
December 1995, and the sale of privatization vouchers started in January 1996.

During this period "the Bulgarian state lost much of its capacity to monitor
enterprise performance and management. Managers channeled enterprise assets
and cash flow to themselves, leaving little to the state but liabilities. Losses of Bulgarian state enterprises, which averaged more than 12 percent of GDP between
1992 and 1994, were covered by loans from an increasingly insolvent banking
system. Bulgarian observers concluded that unclear property rights [are] turning
from a legal to a major macroeconomic problem" (World Bank 1996b, p. 50).

Sources: Reason Foundation 1994; *Washington Post*, 13 May 1994; *Privatisation International*, August 1995 and February 1996.

This section deals with the way the executive branch is organized and
allocates privatization responsibilities. The range of institutional options is
illustrated with examples from Argentina and Peru (table 6.1), Malaysia and
the Philippines (table 6.2), as well as France, Germany, and Poland
(table 6.3). There is no ideal institutional framework or model. A lot will
depend on the country's endowments, its administrative traditions and
capacities, the magnitude and scope of the privatization program, and so on.
In some cases new institutions or mechanisms had to be set up, and in others
existing institutions were deemed appropriate.

Political and Implementation Bodies

Generally speaking, responsibility for privatization lies at two levels, the
political and the technical. The political level may consist of the head of state
or government, a cabinet committee, or the cabinet (government) itself.
These political authorities define the privatization program, set its priorities,
and take the major decisions. In some countries specific powers, such as
deciding on the enterprises to be privatized and approving transfer agreements, rests with the political authorities. The technical level often consists
of either an ad hoc executing agency (for example, a privatization agency),
which may enjoy a certain degree of autonomy in implementing the privatization program, a technical committee, or central government bodies,
including ministries.

The relationships between these two levels vary greatly from one country to another and depend, in particular, on the clarity of the privatization mandate. The clearer and more specific the mandate given to the implementing agency, and the greater the consensus in its favor, the more political authorities will be able and willing to delegate their powers.

These two tiers are found, for example, in Peru, Brazil, Chile, and the Philippines. In Peru, an interministerial commission (COPRI) consisting of six members of government oversees the work of special committees (CEPRIs) responsible for specific enterprises to be privatized. Most committee members are from the private sector.

In Brazil there is a privatization committee comprising four members of government and seven representatives of the private sector, whose duties include submitting to the president the names of the enterprises to be privatized and approving the main privatization techniques and the selling price. The executing agency for the privatization program is BNDES (the Bank for National Economic and Social Development) which is responsible, as administrator of the program, for managing the privatization fund, for appointing advisers and auditors, and, more generally, for executing the privatization transactions (see World Equity and IFC 1993, p. 76).

In Chile the policy and decisionmaking function has been carried out by the board of directors of CORFO, the state holding company, which is composed of the ministers of the economy (chairman), finance and planning, the vice-minister responsible for CORFO, and one other member appointed by the president of the republic. The board authorized the sales of shares and approved the sale terms and conditions. It was assisted by a committee comprising the members' direct deputies or assistants, plus a small "standardization" unit which managed the entire process, subcontracting the bulk of the work (see Hachette and Lüders 1993, pp. 61–63).

Finally, in the Philippines the privatization committee is composed of ministers and is chaired by the minister of finance. It is assisted by a privatization bureau within the ministry of finance, which is responsible for implementing the privatization program, and a nonperforming assets privatization trust, a special agency set up to manage the liquidation of state shareholdings and debt claims.

Alongside or in lieu of cabinet-level committees may be a minister in charge of privatization. Thus in France the minister of the economy takes the decision to privatize the enterprises listed in the annex to the privatization law and sets their selling price, in accordance with the advice of the privatization commission.[7] In Morocco implementation of the privatization law promulgated in April 1990 is entrusted to a "minister responsible for implementing transfers of public enterprises to the private sector," assisted by an interministerial

7. See title II of the July 1986 privatization law, as amended by the July 1993 law; see also note 23 in chapter 5.

(text continues on page 163)

Table 6.1 Institutional Framework for Privatization in Argentina and Peru

Main feature	Argentina	Peru
Major privatization agencies	Special unit within the ministry of the economy Various secretariats within the ministry of the economy (including energy, transportation, and public works) and defense Various privatization commissions set up for each SOE to be privatized	Private Investment Promotion Commission (COPRI) Various special committees (CEPRIs) set up for each SOE to be privatized
Legal basis	Government reform law of September 15, 1989	Decree-Law no. 674 of September 25, 1991, on private investment in SOEs, as amended
Internal structure and staffing	The special unit is headed by an under-secretary for privatization The various privatization commissions, each headed by a full-time director, comprise representatives of the special unit, the relevant secretariats and the SOE to be privatized, plus members of the provincial and municipal executives and auditors	COPRI is an interministerial commission composed of six members of the government appointed by the president of the republic; a small technical secretariat was created in February 1992 to assist COPRI The members of each CEPRI are appointed by supreme resolution of the executive on the proposal of COPRI; most of them come from the private sector and they may not, as a rule, be employed in the SOE to be privatized
Functions	The special unit is responsible for ensuring the use of uniform and transparent procedures The various secretariats supervise the implementation of privatization operations The privatization commissions carry out the transfer of the SOEs to the private sector	COPRI draws up the list of SOEs to be privatized, designates the members of the CEPRI responsible for carrying out the privatization operations for each SOE, and supervises the work of each CEPRI Each CEPRI prepares, for the SOE for which it is responsible, a plan for promoting private investment; this plan includes a description of the privatization techniques to be used, an assessment of the SOE's value, and a timetable for implementation; once this plan is approved by COPRI, the CEPRI is responsible for implementing it

Degree of autonomy	Initially, a joint parliamentary commission representing the various political parties had to ratify most privatization operations; the commission's powers were later reduced; and now, if it does not take a position within 30 days, privatization can proceed Each privatization commission enjoys broad autonomy regarding the privatization techniques used in the operation for which it is responsible; its director reports on its activities to the relevant secretariat	All major decisions of COPRI have to be ratified by the executive; this applies, for example, to the list of SOEs to be privatized, the appointment of the members of each CEPRI, and the approval of the plans submitted to COPRI by the CEPRIs The CEPRIs send regular reports on their activities to COPRI; each CEPRI has exclusive competence to settle disputes relating to the privatization operations it conducts
Other entities involved	The ministry of defense intervenes when SOEs under its jurisdiction are to be privatized Argentine legislation requires that a public agency value each enterprise and set a minimum sale price; most valuations have been performed by the SOE audit agency (Sindicatura General de Empresas Públicas) or the national development bank (Banco Nacional de Desarrollo, BANADE) Each privatization commission can hire lawyers and financial and sector experts to restructure the enterprises and to draw up the bidding documentation, as well as the ownership transfer contracts	Each CEPRI may use the services of consultants; COPRI can also do so to, for example, identify structural reforms in a given economic sector that will be needed before privatization (it hired such consultants to determine how the oil monopoly Petroperu should be divided prior to privatization)

Sources: World Bank 1993; Noya, Ossio, and Amado 1992, pp. 41–44.

Table 6.2   Institutional Framework for Privatization in Malaysia and the Philippines

Main feature	Malaysia	Philippines
Major privatization agencies	Interministerial privatization committee Privatization secretariat A technical committee for each of the following four sectors: transportation; manufacturing and trade; energy, postal services, and telecommunications; and social and other services	Committee on Privatization Privatization Office Asset Privatization Trust
Legal basis	Government decisions	Presidential Proclamation no. 50 of December 8, 1986, as amended The privatization office was created by Decree-Law no. 127-A of July 1987
Internal structure and staffing	The privatization committee is headed by the director of the economic planning unit within the office of the prime minister and includes senior civil servants from key ministries The privatization secretariat is a small team of civil servants The technical committees comprise representatives of the ministry with jurisdiction over the SOEs to be privatized and representatives of those SOEs	The privatization committee comprises the secretary of finance (chairman), the secretary of trade and industry, the secretary of economic planning, the secretary of budget and management, and the secretary of justice The Asset Privatization Trust consists of five members, a director and four associates, appointed by the president on the recommendation of the privatization committee
Functions	The privatization committee is responsible for planning, coordinating, implementing, evaluating, and monitoring the privatization program The privatization secretariat provides liaison between the various technical committees and the privatization committee; it also studies the feasibility of privatization operations and advises the privatization committee	The privatization committee is responsible for identifying the assets and enterprises to be privatized, establishing the guidelines, and designating the executing agency (for example, the Asset Privatization Trust or the parent company of the enterprise to be privatized) for each privatization The privatization office was set up to assist the minister of

	The four technical committees prepare information reports for the privatization operations and submit recommendations to the privatization committee	finance in the duties of chairman of the privatization committee
		The Asset Privatization Trust is responsible for transferring the assets entrusted to it by the privatization committee, either directly or through other agencies; it exercises the ownership rights pertaining to these assets and manages them pending their transfer to the private sector
		The list of assets and enterprises to be privatized is drawn up by the privatization committee but has to be approved by the government
		The privatization committee must submit a report on its activities to the president and the legislative assembly
		The Asset Privatization Trust has to obtain the agreement of the privatization committee on the price, the buyer, and the method of transfer before proceeding to sell assets; the Asset Privatization Trust must submit a quarterly report on its activities and financial situation to the privatization committee and an annual report to the president and the legislative assembly
Degree of autonomy	The entire process is highly centralized; every decision to proceed with the privatization of a given SOE, as well as the techniques to be used in every privatization operation, have to be approved by the government	
Other entities involved	The private sector is encouraged to take the initiative; a private investor submitting a specific privatization proposal enjoys a certain degree of exclusivity Private experts (bankers, lawyers, accountants) assisted government in drawing up the privatization master plan, which set forth the broad lines of the privatization program for 1991–95; private experts also provide advisory assistance on specific transactions	When assets that were originally entrusted to the Asset Privatization Trust but were subsequently transferred by the trust to other agencies are in imminent danger of being lost or destroyed, the Securities and Exchange Commission appoints, at the request of the trust, a temporary administrator to manage such assets; Presidential Proclamation no. 50 expressly states that the Asset Privatization Trust may use the services of domestic or foreign private experts

Sources: Nankani 1988; Hensley and White 1993.

Table 6.3　Institutional Framework for Privatization in France, Germany, and Poland

Main feature	France	Germany (until the end of 1994)	Poland
Major privatization agencies	Ministry of the economy Privatization commission	The Treuhandanstalt (THA) was the privatization and restructuring agency from 1990 to 1994; it was the sole shareholder of East German SOEs	Ministry of ownership changes National Investment Funds (see table 6.4)
Legal basis	Law no. 86-793 of July 2, 1986, and Law no. 86-912 of August 6, 1986, as amended by Law no. 93-923 of July 19, 1993	Law of June 17, 1990, on privatization and reorganization of community assets (Treuhandgesetz); see also law of August 9, 1994, on the termination of the activities of the THA	Law of July 13, 1990, creating the office of minister of ownership changes, and the privatization law of the same date
Internal structure and staffing	The direction du trésor of the ministry of finance is the administrative department in charge of implementing the privatization program The privatization commission comprises seven members appointed by decree for a term of five years, who are supported by a secretary general	THA staff reached its peak in 1992 at about 4,100; half the staff were assigned to the head office in Berlin and half to the fifteen regional offices in the five new Länder THA was headed by a supervisory council, whose members—appointed by the federal government and parliament—comprised representatives of the industrial sector and of the political class; the council oversaw the activities of THA's management board, comprising at least five members THA operations were organized on a sectoral basis; in addition, THA created affiliates responsible for privatizing real estate properties, an affiliate for monitoring and managing privatization contracts, restoring assets to their former owners, and liquidating nonviable enterprises; and an advisory bureau,	The ministry of ownership changes has had since its inception a staff ranging between 300 and 400 civil servants working in a number of departments and supervised by four or five vice-ministers

			Treuhand Osteuropa Beratungsgesellschaft (TOB), to export its expertise to the countries of central and eastern Europe (TOB was itself privatized in 1994 and bought by a German accounting firm)
Functions	The privatization commission is responsible for setting a minimum price for the shares of SOEs to be privatized The commission's powers were strengthened by the July 1993 privatization law: when the minister opts to select a buyer without pursuing competitive bids or to select a group of core shareholders for the so-called *noyaux durs*, the commission must concur	THA was a holding company, owner of the SOEs to be privatized; it was assigned the key role in privatization and was required to transfer the SOEs in its portfolio to the private sector whenever possible, restructuring them first if need be; THA had to liquidate SOEs that could not be restructured to become viable entities, and it was responsible for managing SOEs not yet liquidated or privatized	The ministry of ownership changes is responsible for organizing the privatization process, executing ownership transfers, and disseminating information on privatization and on the promotion of private initiative The ministry exercises the government's ownership rights over SOEs after their commercialization and pending their effective transfer to the private sector; it designates the executive directors and a majority of the members of the supervisory council of the SOEs
Degree of autonomy	Each transaction affecting the 21 SOEs listed in the annex to the July 1993 law is submitted to the commission by the minister of economy; the commission was set up to underscore the independence of the valuation process from the ministry of economy and to protect the latter from	THA reported on its activities to the minister of finance; completion of major sales (those relating to an SOE with more than 2,000 employees, whose value was estimated at over DM 100 million, or whose turnover exceeded DM 300 million) required the agreement not only of the minister of finance but also of the supervisory council. It was originally envisaged that the regional offices would be largely independent, but	Major decisions, such as determining which companies are deemed essential to the national economy and ineligible for privatization, have to be taken by the council of ministers as a whole Parliament defines the privatization program guidelines each year and decides on the allocation of privatization receipts

(table continues on the following page)

Table 6.3 *(continued)*

Main feature	France	Germany (until the end of 1994)	Poland
	accusations of favoring certain investors; its members are chosen for their competence and their experience in the economic, financial, and legal areas	it soon became clear that many decisions called for a high degree of coordination, and the regional offices started working in very close coordination with headquarters in Berlin	Ministry of finance authorization is required, in particular, to let the ministry of ownership changes take over the debts of SOEs to be privatized
Other entities involved	Auditing firms and investment banks are selected by the minister of economy to carry out valuation studies of SOEs to be privatized; these studies serve as the basis for the work of the privatization commission	The minister of finance, the minister of economy, and other ministers may also be involved in major policy issues arising in the context of privatization In the case of real estate sales, THA had to consult with representatives of the municipal authorities to identify the obligations to be imposed upon investors Having largely accomplished the purposes for which it was created, THA closed its doors in December 1994; its remaining tasks were taken over by the Federal Agency for Special Tasks Arising from Unification (BVS) and the Holdings Management Company Berlin, (BMGB) both under the supervision of the ministry of finance	The National Investment Funds, are described in table 6.4 The ministry of trade and industry takes part in liquidation operations and privatization negotiations for large enterprises The Industrial Development Agency cooperates with the ministry of ownership changes when enterprises have to be restructured before they can be privatized The ministry of ownership changes extensively uses the services of consultants and investment banks

Sources: Elling 1992; Dodds and Wächter 1993; Durupty 1988; French Sénat, *Rapport de la commission des finances, du contrôle budgétaire et des comptes économiques de la Nation, 1992–93*, doc. no. 326; OECD 1993.

transfers commission and a valuation commission (see the section below on valuation bodies). In Poland, although the public treasury, an agency with juridical personality placed under the ministry of finance, is legally the owner of the SOEs and the government's shareholdings, it is mainly the minister of ownership changes who is responsible for their transfer.[8] In the Czech Republic privatization was the responsibility of a ministry for administration and privatization of state property, which was in charge of the transfer of thousands of companies to the private sector; it closed its doors in July 1996, its mission having been substantially accomplished; the remaining responsibilities of the privatization ministry were devolved to a special office in the finance ministry.

Privatization Agencies and Units

As far as the technical bodies are concerned, many countries have entrusted major responsibility for implementing privatization to a new, independent agency created for that purpose. This is the case, for example, in Russia and most of the central and eastern European countries. It is also true of Germany, where the Treuhandanstalt was set up and endowed with substantial powers and large resources in order to privatize the economy of the former East Germany. In Pakistan three different bodies were created: a privatization commission responsible for the industrial and banking sectors, an electric power commission, and a telecommunications committee; the commissions are more or less permanent agencies, and the committee is an ad hoc agency without separate staff. The sectoral distribution of privatization responsibilities was abolished by a governmental decision of August 1993, which merged the three entities into a single privatization commission. This merger was intended, in particular, to extend the benefits of the experience acquired in one sector to all sectors and thereby avoid repeating the same mistakes and reinventing the wheel. Many of these privatization agencies have a management or supervisory board whose composition is usually more political and whose responsibilities often include approving all, or at least the major, privatization agreements.

While some countries have set up large technical bodies, others have opted for small units. In Mexico, for example, the government set up in 1988 a small privatization unit within the ministry of finance. This unit was responsible for managing the entire process, but it delegated the main tasks to commercial banks acting as agents of the government. This simple technique has proved to be very effective, particularly by permitting broad delegation and distribution of the work to institutions having the required skills and experience.[9]

8. See, in particular, articles 1 and 19 of the 1990 privatization law and also the 1990 law defining the mandate of the minister of ownership changes.

9. The technique was authorized by article 12 of the implementing decree of the public enterprises law (January 1990), which provides that, for each sale of shares of a public enterprise held by the federal government or other parastatal agencies, the minister of finance shall designate a financial institution with responsibility to carry out that sale.

SOE Management and Restructuring Bodies

Public holding companies or financial institutions have been given responsibility for executing privatizations in many countries, either by transferring part of their own portfolio holdings or by acting as agent of the government in SOE sales. In Colombia, for example, IFI, the public holding company responsible for industrial development, was given responsibility for privatization in the industrial sector, and Fogafin, the financial institutions guarantee fund, that for bank privatization. In Venezuela, the FIV (Venezuelan Investment Fund) is in charge of implementing the privatization program.

Conversely, privatization agencies have been given responsibility for managing SOEs before their privatization. In Poland the ministry of ownership changes exercises the government's ownership rights over commercialized SOEs. Since the government originally hoped to complete the privatization process very quickly, the ministry has tended to regard its management role as secondary to its privatization function. However, the deterioration in the economic and financial situation of enterprises under its care, beginning in 1991–92, compelled the ministry to strengthen its oversight of these companies, intervening, in particular, through the members of the supervisory boards. The German Treuhand has also been severely criticized for having put the emphasis on speedy sale of SOEs, to the detriment of prior restructuring, maintenance of industrial capabilities, and job protection. As a result, it paid more attention to managing the enterprises remaining in its portfolio toward the end of its mandate. Generally speaking, it has proved very difficult for a single institution to do justice to the twin roles of restructuring and portfolio management agency, on the one hand, and privatization agency, on the other.

In transition countries and other countries that need to radically restructure their parastatal sectors, a separate body is often designated to manage the public enterprises during the preprivatization period (see also chapter 4); Albania, Romania, and Slovenia have set up separate SOE management and restructuring agencies. Though they avoid the problem of overburdening a single agency with too many responsibilities and often conflicting goals, parallel agencies may increase the likelihood of battles over power and influence with the privatization agency, as illustrated by the pre-1995 situation in Hungary (see the section below on coordination). As is often the case, the choice between these two approaches will be dictated by country-specific circumstances, constraints, and objectives.

Valuation Bodies

Special committees have been set up to value the enterprises to be privatized or to determine the share price. The example of the French privatization commission has already been mentioned (see the section above on political and implementation bodies). The 1989 Moroccan privatization law entrusted key responsibilities to three different bodies, the privatization minister, the evaluation commission, and the transfer commission. Though the program is the most dynamic in the region, it has been significantly slowed by the power granted to the evaluation commission to fix a minimum price, below which the privatization minister cannot sell an enterprise. The members of this commission have systematically set minimum prices exceeding the maximum price range determined by independent auditors, which has led to numerous unsuccessful transactions.[10] The situation of the enterprises has generally continued to deteriorate following these failed tenders; those enterprises that were subsequently sold often did so at a lower price than could have been obtained at the first tender. The government is now considering a merger of the evaluation and transfer commissions and modification of the pricing role; instead of setting a floor, the commission would set an indicative price range, which could be overridden in specific circumstances and with established safeguards.

In Argentina, the Public Enterprises Auditing Agency and the National Development Bank are responsible for valuing each enterprise to be privatized and setting a minimum sale price. The Belgian commission for the valuation of state assets has a similar function.

Although such special commissions may provide an additional safeguard, they can also become a bottleneck. Indeed, commission members often see their role mainly as ensuring that SOEs or other state assets are not sold too cheaply, and not as fostering the success of the overall privatization program. They will be blamed for letting the family silver go at bargain basement prices, but they will not get any credit for successfully completed transactions. The inherent bias, therefore, is to establish a high, above-market minimum sale price, which leaves the implementing agency unable to dispose of SOEs or assets, as illustrated by the Moroccan experience (see also the section in chapter 5 on valuation of SOEs).

Local Governments

Municipalities and other local or regional authorities are often directly responsible for some privatization operations, typically those that affect municipal enterprises or small businesses (see also the sections on ownership in chapter 4). Even where they are the formal owners of enterprises or assets, local governments may not be able to dispose of them freely. A privatization law may impose divestiture and may even entrust all or part of its implementation to central government bodies. Proceeds from municipal divestiture may revert in all or in part to the central government (see chapter 5). Central

---

10. In the three-year period from the end of 1992 to the end of 1995, 28 (or 65 percent) of the 43 tenders for the privatization of hotels and nonfinancial enterprises failed to attract a buyer willing to pay the floor price. Of these, some have since been sold through direct negotiation at lower prices. In two cases the privatization ministry went back to the evaluation commission to ask for a lower price; in both cases they agreed to lower the price, but they still set it above the range suggested by the auditors.

privatization bodies may also be asked to assist and advise the local governments in their privatization transactions.

In Bulgaria, for example, the 1992 privatization law covered SOEs as well as municipal enterprises and provided that the municipal council was competent to decide on the privatization of municipal enterprises and to implement the transaction or delegate its implementation (article 3). Some large municipalities, such as Sofia, established their own privatization agency. Pursuant to article 6.2 of the same law, only half of the proceeds of such municipal privatizations reverted to the municipalities, and then only to a fund to be used "on a priority basis to settle the bad debts of the municipally-owned enterprises and for investment purposes"; it further stipulated that these proceeds could not be used for current expenditures. This made privatization rather unattractive for municipal governments and slowed down the process. The law was amended in 1994 to increase the municipalities' share of the proceeds to about 80 percent and to facilitate the sale of municipal enterprises to their current leaseholders.

In Russia, a special decree of President Yeltsin in February 1995 strengthened the power of the city governments in the privatization of municipal enterprises, clarifying the relationship with the national privatization program and allowing the cities to keep revenue from privatization sales. In Hungary, the telecommunications law gives local authorities the right to propose the concessioning of local telecommunications networks (see article 4.3 of the 1992 telecommunications law; see also chapter 7). In the United States, the privatization wave manifests itself mostly at the local level, where most public enterprises are located.

Central governments have also transferred state property to local governments as part of national privatization programs, as was the case in Argentina, Czechoslovakia, Germany, and Mexico, for example, leaving it up to the local authorities to decide whether to manage these as municipal enterprises or to privatize them.[11] Local governments may also have a role to play in the central government's privatization process, as in Germany where the privatization law prescribed, for example, that the Treuhandanstalt should, before selling real estate located in their jurisdiction, consult with representatives of the city and state on the type of investment the buyer would be required to make.[12]

---

11. In the Argentine transport sector, responsibility for many services, including ports, airports, railways, and roads, was shifted from the federal government to the provinces as part of the country's broader privatization program started in 1989. In Colombia, Mexico, and Venezuela the central government similarly transferred responsibility for ports to state and local governments. In the case of Mexico, however, the inexperience and lack of resources of local governments may have contributed to the slowness of port privatization. Canada also has transferred many smaller airports and ports to local authorities as part of its reform of the transport sector. See also section 1.1 of Germany's June 1990 privatization law and the Czech law of April 1991.

12. See Elling 1992, pp. 633–34. Note that municipal privatizations fell outside the scope of the June 1990 privatization law (section 1.5 of the law). See also, in chapter 4, note 3 on municipal ownership of power companies.

Other Bodies

In addition to the privatization bodies discussed above, other institutions are often asked to participate in the privatization process in one capacity or another (see tables 6.1, 6.2, and 6.3). Sector or line ministries frequently have an important role; that happened, for example, when enterprises under the jurisdiction of the Argentine defense ministry had to be privatized (see table 5.2). Ministries that control the portfolio of active SOEs in their sector tend to be hostile to privatization, fearing that it may substantially undercut their power and sometimes even the justification for their existence. This fact helps explain why special privatization agencies are set up. Sectoral reforms associated with privatization are normally, however, the responsibility of the technical ministries, though here again ministers in charge of the economy, finance, or privatization have often had to take the lead in overcoming opposition from sector ministries seeking to defend vested interests.

Similarly, some laws require consultation with labor unions or other interests as part of the privatization process. Finally, special mechanisms have been set up in some cases to facilitate public placement of the shares of privatized companies. In Pakistan, for example, a committee comprising representatives of Pakistan's three securities exchanges has been created to draw up the rules for regulating privatization by public offering on the exchanges.

Coordination of Implementation Authority

Although there is no such thing as a unique or ideal institutional structure for the agency in charge of implementing a privatization program, it is always essential to define clearly the respective roles and powers of the major authorities involved in the program: parliament, cabinet, privatization minister, finance minister, minister in charge of the enterprise concerned, privatization agency or agencies, public holding companies, privatization funds, securities exchanges, SOE management and board of directors, and so on.

The allocation of responsibilities will need to be defined in clear terms, whether in general regulations governing public sector operations, new provisions contained in a privatization law, a special law such as one creating the privatization agency (if it is different from the enabling law), or, for the sale by SOEs of their assets or subsidiaries, applicable provisions of company or SOE legislation (see chapter 4).[13]

13. The Hungarian law establishing the state property agency (January 26, 1990) and the Polish law creating the ministry of ownership changes (July 13, 1990) are examples of laws dealing specifically with the establishment of a new entity to manage the privatization program.

The legal instruments should indicate who is empowered to initiate a privatization transaction; request the initiation of a transaction (for example, any person; the employees, management or board of directors of an SOE; the sector ministry; other ministries or central government agencies; local authorities; or interested investors); prepare the transaction; organize the buyer selection process; negotiate the deal; authorize the conclusion of the operation (the law may, for example, require that privatizations negotiated by another body, as in the sale of assets by an SOE or the sale of an enterprise by a municipality, be approved by the privatization agency or the Council of Ministers); sign the pertinent agreements; ratify these agreements where appropriate; implement the privatization agreements; and ensure their correct execution by all the parties.[14] It will be necessary also to examine whether the same rules apply to the privatization of SOEs, their liquidation, and their restructuring (including the breakup of SOEs and any other forms of enterprise restructuring), and whether the same or different bodies are responsible for each one of these measures.

Implementation authority will often be shared by different bodies. Division of responsibilities is, for instance, part of the institutional framework of countries that have political decisionmaking bodies and implementing bodies (see above). Specific prior approvals may be needed to conclude transactions or make important decisions. Valuation commissions have to be consulted beforehand in some countries. In Poland, the ministry of ownership changes initially needed authorization from the minister of finance to grant payment facilities to Polish citizens buying shares in privatized enterprises and to let public-sector entities acquire shares of such enterprises. That minister still needs such approval to take over or assume SOE debts before their privatization, whereas other decisions, such as transfers of shares free of charge, require the approval of the council of ministers (article 18.2 of the privatization law).

To the extent possible, it is important to avoid allocating competitive or overlapping powers and responsibilities to different agencies, which might well adopt conflicting approaches or engage in interminable bureaucratic haggling, with a damaging impact on the credibility of the privatization program. Failure to allocate privatization responsibilities clearly and unambiguously may also cause unnecessary delays or litigation; the many lawsuits filed in Pakistan, the Philippines, Turkey, and Uganda, which seek to annul transactions on the basis that the privatization agency did not have the authority to conclude them, prove the point.

---

14. In Guinea, before the enactment of the 1993 privatization law, privatization agreements were usually signed by the minister concerned (usually the minister of industry) and the investors, then ratified by an ordinance of the president (equivalent to a law). This procedure was used particularly to guard against or eliminate any element of illegality that might have tainted the agreements or the way in which they were concluded. Their ratification by law thus exempted them from the effects of any other laws they might have infringed. See also note 1 in chapter 3.

The temptation exists to create new institutions or institutional mechanisms (such as consultative processes) to deal with a variety of issues, concerns, and stakeholders. Experience has shown, however, that institutional overdesign can kill, or at least significantly slow down, a privatization program. The institutional framework should not be overly complex.

In Tunisia, the 1987 privatization law called for the involvement of three separate bodies in the privatization process, namely, a commission for restructuring public enterprises (article 4), a ministerial committee (article 7), and a monitoring commission set up within the securities exchange (article 9). It also conferred other powers on several ministers. The law turned out to be too complicated to implement, and it was repealed and replaced by Law no. 89-9 of 1989, which provides only for the creation of an SOE rehabilitation and restructuring commission (article 24). Following the enactment of this new law, Tunisia's privatization program finally got off the ground.[15] Morocco, which also has three privatization bodies, is considering a similar streamlining, as mentioned above.

Romania, with a national agency for privatization, a state ownership fund, and five private ownership funds, provides another example of the stifling nature of an overly complicated institutional setup for privatization (see the section below on privatization funds and table 6.4). Part of the problem resided in the allocation of the government's shares among different funds: 70 percent of the shares of each SOE to be privatized was allocated to the state property fund and 30 percent was shared among five private funds. Tension ran high between the state fund and the SOE managers, on the one hand, and the private funds, on the other. This greatly delayed implementation of the privatization program, a result apparently sought by many SOE and state fund managers.[16]

In Hungary, the creation in 1990 of two separate agencies, one responsible for privatizing and the other for managing SOEs, has also created problems. In particular, their differing philosophies or special interests have generated tension when both were shareholders of the same enterprise to be privatized, as in the electric power sector. Privatization of the telecommunications company MATAV was also complicated by the lack of a clear lead agency at the national level to prepare for and negotiate the operation and to coordinate the actions of the two agencies, the telecommunications ministry,

---

15. "As of December 31, 1994, 46 companies had been privatised including 100 operations involving sales of assets, some companies having been broken down and sold in units" (*Privatization Yearbook 1995*, p. 335). Another 17 SOEs were privatized in 1995, and a few hundred remain in the state's portfolio, which still leaves Tunisia with one of the largest public sectors in the world, accounting for close to a quarter of domestic output.

16. The tension that existed between the private funds and the state fund apparently lessened following the replacement of the chairman of the state fund in early 1994. The retention of the SOEs' old management teams continues to pose a problem, however, because they have little incentive to manage their enterprises efficiently; moreover, corruption seems widespread in the SOEs. See *Financial Times*, 3 May 1994; *Journal of Commerce*, 29 September 1994. See also table 6.4 and notes 37 and 43 below.

and the company itself; the steering committee that was set up for the purpose, composed of representatives of the major agencies involved, could
hardly be called efficient. In May 1995 parliament passed a new privatization law merging the two agencies into the privatization and state holding
company (APV RT), partly to avoid the repetition of such problems and
partly to use human and technical resources more efficiently (see Law no. 39
of 1995).

Control of the Privatization Process

Privatization tends to be politically sensitive. It is also new for many governments and it raises issues of public revenues (generation and allocation) and
public expenditures. Hence the need for controls. As illustrated by
tables 6.1, 6.2, and 6.3, control mechanisms have been set up in practically
every country. Some are exercised by the judiciary (see chapters 2 and 3) or
regulatory bodies (see chapter 7), some pertain to a priori authorization of
privatization decisions by political bodies and others to prior valuation (see
above), while yet others are exercised a posteriori.

A Posteriori Controls

Ex post controls may take the form of audits performed by a national
accounting office reporting to parliament—for example, the U.K. National
Audit Office, which has prepared ex post reports on most British privatizations, or the French Cour des Comptes, which issued a comprehensive
report on the 1986-88 privatizations (see Cour des Comptes 1990)—by the
finance ministry or another government agency, or by private auditors.

In addition, privatization agencies should normally be required to abide
by public disclosure rules and to report periodically to the council of ministers, parliament, or some other body. In the Philippines, for example, the
main privatization agencies are required to transmit annual reports to the
president and the legislative assembly (see article 38 of Presidential Proclamation no. 50 of December 1986). In Russia, the Duma (the lower house of
parliament) established a special commission to investigate privatization in
what appears to be largely a political move to discredit the privatization
process.[17]

A balance may have to be struck between the requirement to transmit
information to the control agencies and the need to safeguard the confidential nature of the relevant transactions. This issue gave rise to serious

17. The commission, which was labeled "Commission for the analysis of privatization in
1992–1996 and for establishing the responsibility of officials for its negative results," does not
have the power to prosecute, however. It was planning to submit its report before the June 1996
presidential elections (see *Wall Street Journal*, 13 February 1996).

problems in Germany. The Treuhand refused to transmit its files to a parliamentary commission that was investigating the way in which the ministry of finance had exercised its supervisory power over the privatization agency. The parliamentary commission thereupon decided to file a suit with the constitutional court to obtain access to the files (see *The Economist*, 30 April 1994).

Prosecution of Fraud and Corruption

It is essential that public officials, whether SOE managers or directors, civil servants, or any other kind of official, be held accountable for their actions. The creation of a transparent and competitive privatization process should go a long way toward reducing the opportunities for fraud and illegal enrichment. In addition to these preventive rules and policies for good governance, the legislation in effect must deal with the repression of corruption, fraud, misappropriation of public funds, insider dealing, collusion, and similar misbehavior. Privatizations have been tarnished by allegations of fraud in many countries, including Germany, Hungary, India, Italy, Mexico, Pakistan, Panama, Puerto Rico, Russia, and Viet Nam.[18] Fraud and corruption are more prevalent—and documentation and prosecution of such fraud more difficult and thus rarer—in countries with less transparent procedures.

---

18. *Germany*: The regional director of the Treuhand for the Halle region, arrested in Texas, was the subject of extradition proceedings and two of the major buyers of the region were apprehended in Germany and accused of fraud and of having used forged documents. One of them had acquired 29 enterprises from the Treuhand, and the other, 10. As a consequence of this scandal, the Treuhand had to reexamine the contracts for some 800 enterprises and assets that had been privatized by the Halle office to make sure they were not tainted by fraud (see *Financial Times*, 4 May 1994).

Hungary: For an exposition of the problems of fraud encountered while attempting to privatize HungarHotels, for example, see Crane 1991, p. 88. Four years later, the problem of fraud was still on the agenda. In September 1994 the new Hungarian government dismissed eight of the ten members of the state holding agency and initiated an investigation into the actions of its managing director, who was accused of corruption (see *Financial Times*, 5 October 1994).

Italy: The beginning of Italy's privatization program dates to the creation in 1985 of the Cassese Commission, which set up a register of SOEs to be privatized. It was not until 1992 that a serious start was made on the preparatory work, and at the end of 1993 almost no SOEs had been privatized. According to an UNCTAD report, the slowness was caused by several factors, including differences of opinion concerning the valuation of the assets to be sold, lack of private capital in a period of recession, the subsidies that alone enabled the SOEs to survive, cumbersome decisionmaking mechanisms and sluggish administrative procedures (owing in particular to the involvement of three different ministries in the privatization process), as well as the corruption that prevailed in the Italian SOEs (UNCTAD 1993b, p. 89, box 8).

Pakistan: The chairman of the privatization commission and a leading businessman who bought privatized SOEs during his tenure were jailed in 1995 on fraud charges (*Privatisation International*, November 1995, p. 9).

Russia: See "Stealing the Family Silver," Euromoney, February 1996, pp. 62–66; see also, below, note 49.

(continued on the following page)

In Poland, for example, the self-appropriation of public assets by the *nomenklatura* was facilitated by the explosive growth of joint-stock and limited-liability companies. Some operations in which SOE managers participated on both sides of the transaction, as vendors on behalf of their SOEs and as buyers on behalf of their private (or joint-venture) companies, were annulled by the supreme court. Most transactions of this kind, however, were never contested.[19]

In some countries, allegations of fraud and illegality have led to the enactment of new, more stringent legislation on supervision of the privatization process. In Moldova, for example, a parliamentary decree was issued in March 1993 to try to put a stop to the numerous illegal sales of state property carried out, in particular, by public authorities and SOEs who overstepped their powers. This decree instructs the government to revoke all acts concluded in violation of the privatization law; to issue the necessary implementing regulations to enforce the leasing law; and to submit draft penal, administrative, and civil laws to parliament amending the current legislation to make it easier to prosecute the persons responsible for the illegal transfers (see article 6 of the decree of March 12, 1993, on measures to prevent illegal privatization transactions).

In transition countries, fighting abuses committed during the privatization process may pose special problems. Some acts, though unscrupulous, may not strictly speaking be illegal, owing to the absence of the usual legal framework of a market economy, especially securities regulations. Moreover, the authorities have to gauge their response extremely carefully: too lenient an attitude could give the public the impression that the reform process serves only to allow some people to enrich themselves fraudulently, while unrelenting controls could make for unwieldy administrative procedures and discourage investment. A firm attitude on the part of the government and judicial authorities toward this type of fraud, or even the appearance of fraudulent situations, is crucial to avoid doubt being cast on the entire reform process.

(continued)

Viet Nam: Allegations of corruption have multiplied since the reform process began. More than 1,000 civil servants were arraigned during the first half of 1988 alone. In 1994 the managers of Legamex, a textile enterprise in the process of being privatized, were dismissed for having allegedly used SOE assets to facilitate the business operations of family members. The sale of shares in this enterprise was suspended on that occasion. See *Viet Nam Investment Review*, 11–17 April 1994, p. 3; *The Economist*, 4 June 1994, p. 33

19. A known case is that of Igloopol, Poland's leading agroindustrial complex, which, although valued at 145 billion zlotys, was artificially liquidated and transferred for 55 billion zlotys to a joint-stock company which had the same directors and whose shareholders were organizations and leaders of the former communist party. The ministry of agriculture (whose vice-minister was the managing director of Igloopol) approved the liquidation proceedings, despite a report by the ministry of finance declaring it illegal and economically unjustified. A decree of the Mazowiecki government subsequently made it illegal for managers and employees' associations of SOEs to own shares in the capital of companies founded by their own SOE. Adapted from Nuti 1991, p. 66, n 13.

Compliance with Buyers' Obligations

The privatization process does not end when a contract is signed, as the contract imposes terms that the buyer (and the government) must fulfill. These obligations, which may extend over many years, often concern the maintenance of existing jobs or the creation of new ones, the protection of the environment, and the achievement of specific investment goals. The privatization agency needs to have the resources to monitor the contracts and to institute proceedings, if necessary, to compel buyers to honor their commitments.

In Poland, for example, the ministry of ownership changes was required to privatize many enterprises as speedily as possible, but it had only limited staff. At the beginning it did not supervise the application of environmental standards, and instead delegated the monitoring of compliance with these standards to the regional authorities. It quickly became clear, however, that oversight at the national level was necessary to ensure uniform application of the environmental legislation. As a result, a new interministerial unit was set up for that purpose in February 1993 by the ministries for ownership changes and environment (see Greenspan-Bell and Kolaja 1993).

In Germany, the Treuhand inserted clauses in many SOE transfer contracts requiring investors to maintain a minimum number of jobs or to carry out certain investments. Owing to the difficult economic situation in Germany, many entrepreneurs failed to honor their obligations, believing that they would not be required to pay the fines prescribed in the contracts. At first the Treuhand did indeed hesitate to enforce these penalty clauses. The risk was twofold: if too many newly privatized firms went bankrupt, it could, one, be accused of having disposed of the enterprises without properly restructuring them first and, two, be forced to take them back into its portfolio. To ensure better monitoring of these contracts (close to 50,000 of them in 1994), the Treuhand decided to set up a special department responsible for enforcing privatization contracts. After the Treuhand closed its doors on December 31, 1994, the management of these contracts, including collection of amounts still due by the buyers and the disposal of remaining SOEs and assets, was transferred to the Federal Agency for Special Tasks Arising from Unification (BVS), which was given until 1998 to carry out its mandate (*see Privatization Yearbook 1995*, p. 127; *Euromoney*, February 1996, pp. 14–15).

Staff of Privatization Bodies

The success of a privatization program will depend largely on the quality of the people in charge of its preparation, implementation, and oversight, and on the incentives they have to do the job well. This includes government staff, the subject of this section, as well as outside experts and advisers, whose role is further discussed below.

Recruitment

Special attention needs to be paid to the recruitment and remuneration of staff responsible for drawing up and implementing a country's privatization program. They will often have to negotiate difficult transactions with powerful and experienced partners, make proposals with far-reaching repercussions for the parties concerned, take decisions involving very large sums, and perform other duties of a commercial rather than administrative nature. Even where most of these tasks are contracted out, major policy decisions and oversight of private firms or advisers will usually still rest with civil servants. Most civil servants do not have such qualifications. It will therefore be important to attract staff with the required background and business experience and to provide them with the resources they need to achieve the objectives of the program. Similarly, where the government delegates responsibility for executing the program to other agencies, it will need to ensure that their staff possess such qualifications.

In the Philippines, for example, the privatization trust for nonperforming assets was first headed by an experienced businessman and staffed by professionals recruited from the private sector and remunerated accordingly. From 1986 to 1992, this team accomplished the sale of nearly 300 unproductive assets (financial participations, properties, accounts receivable) out of the 400 entrusted to it, bringing in a total of 32 billion pesos (about $1.2 billion). A lawyer later took over the helm, and the agency generated revenues of over $200 million in 1994 and over $150 million in 1995. As a result of its success, the agency was also asked to act as the government's adviser in large privatizations that were not part of its basic mandate (see *Institutional Investor*, March 1996, pp. 21–22; see also note 11 in chapter 1).

In Guinea, on the other hand, discretionary powers were left to the ministry of industry, trade, and crafts, whose staff lacked privatization as well as business experience. The value of the enterprises to be privatized was not always assessed, many sales were handled without a competitive call for bids, and several sales are said to have been completed at ridiculously low prices. In addition, for several transactions the government selected investors who lacked adequate technical or financial expertise (see Suzuki 1992). Moreover, in 1986 the government decided to terminate its contract with international privatization experts before it began negotiations with interested buyers; that decision did nothing to enhance the transparency and quality of the transactions.

Incentives

Whether responsibility for a task goes to the staff of the ministry or privatization agency, or to the staff of a private entity hired on contract by the government, a suitable incentive system should be introduced to encourage the staff to perform their duties in accordance with the interests of the state and the objectives set by government or parliament. The example of Germany is once again instructive, because the German government had clearly indicated that the Treuhandanstalt would cease to exist as soon as it had accomplished its task. Treuhand staff might well have been expected to delay restructuring or privatizing the enterprises in their portfolio to defer the closing date. In fact, the pace of privatization tended to quicken, so that staff could qualify for bonuses that would be awarded for achieving certain targets (see Dodds and Wächter 1993). The Treuhand closed its doors, as scheduled, at the end of December 1994.

Conflicts of Interest

Privatization laws and regulations usually contain prohibitions designed to limit the risk of conflicts of interest.[20] For example, the staff of an SOE or privatization agency who are involved directly (or indirectly) in the privatization process are often precluded from acting as buyers of enterprises or shares offered for sale.[21] It may be prudent to impose restrictions applicable after privatization, too, for example, prohibiting management staff involved in the privatization process, and particularly in buyer selection, from accepting employment with any of the bidders for a specified period following completion of the privatization operation, as is the case in Belgium.[22]

In Russia and in other former Soviet republics that followed the Russian privatization model, the choice of privatization technique was entrusted to an important category of potential buyers, namely, the management and employees of the enterprise to be privatized.[23] It is not surprising that the latter have generally opted for a privatization method that allocates the

20. Other sections, below, in this chapter discuss possible conflicts of interest affecting lawyers and investment bankers involved in privatization transactions.

21. Article 17 of Burundi's August 1991 decree-law on privatization forbids "members of the government, the other members of the inter-ministerial privatization committee, the general commissioner for public enterprises and their spouses and direct descendants from acting as buyers of shares of SOEs to be privatized. The same prohibition applies to the members of the technical valuation commission, the auditors and their spouses and direct descendants, but solely with respect to enterprises in whose valuation they have taken part."

22. The royal decree of October 8, 1992, concerning the state property valuation commission provides: "The chairman and members of the commission may not, while in office, and for a period of five years following the end of their term of office, exercise any remunerated activity in the service of a company valued by them or of the buyer of an asset sold by the State."

23. The same situation is found in the Kyrgyz Republic. In December 1992, the Kyrgyz Supreme Soviet approved the "concept of denationalization and privatization of assets belonging to the State and the communes for the year 1993." This document lists three "standard options" for distributing the shares of privatized enterprises among various categories of shareholders. No precise instructions were given, however, as to the conditions under which a particular option was to be adopted. The choice is hence often left to the discretion of the privatization commissions, which are set up on a case-by-case basis for each privatization operation. Those commissions are made up of representatives of the state assets fund and the workers' associations. See also the section in chapter 5 on benefits granted to employees by privatization laws.

majority of the shares to the workers' associations themselves. Hence in practice the privatization process excludes many citizens, contrary to an explicit objective of Russia's privatization program, which is the broad dissemination of the ownership of shares. When the remaining shares are put up for sale, the price offered is often only a fraction of the company's intrinsic value, a fact that may reflect the lack of confidence investors have in the new management structure and the difficulty, not to say near impossibility, of bringing in new management.

Financing the Privatization Process

Privatization is not a routine government task. Whatever institutional setup is chosen, the privatization agency or bodies will need adequate resources to prepare for, negotiate, and monitor privatization transactions. Some laws define in precise terms how the responsible agencies are to defray their expenses, including the costs of day-to-day operations, prior restructuring, settlement of SOE debts, environmental liabilities, labor redundancies, advisory assistance, and other costs arising out of their activities. In many cases these expenditures are covered through a special account or fund financed out of privatization receipts, general budget revenue, or borrowing (where these agencies possess borrowing power).[24]

In Peru, for example, article 29 of Decree-Law no. 674 established a privatization fund (FOPRI), which is managed by the privatization agency (COPRI); the fund is to be used to cover the expenditures incurred by the privatization process. Article 30 prescribes that FOPRI's primary source of revenue consists of 2 percent of all privatization and liquidation proceeds.[25]

In Germany, the law provided that privatization receipts would be used in particular to defray the expenses of the Treuhandanstalt. Article 25 of the August 1990 reunification treaty limited the agency's borrowing capacity to DM 25 billion (less than $17 billion), which could be raised by decision of the federal minister of finance. In fact, the agency had to borrow rather heavily to meet its expenditures and left a total debt of DM 256 billion (over $165 billion) by the time it closed down at the end of 1994.[26] The heavy net drain on Germany's budget caused by the east German privatization program was financed through a solidarity tax and borrowing.

---

24. See the section in chapter 5 on the allocation of privatization proceeds (including box 5.5) and box 6.3 below on advisory fees in privatization transactions.

25. Article 27 of Supreme Decree no. 070-92-PCM of July 16, 1992, which implements the law, further stipulates that the 2 percent is to be calculated based on gross receipts.

26. The Treuhandanstalt final report issued in June 1995 revised the amount of its total debt from DM 270 billion down to DM 256.4 billion; this downward revision was caused by lower interest costs and lower-than-expected refurbishment costs in mining and nuclear energy (see *Privatisation International*, July 1995).

In Belgium, the relatively modest role played by the privatization commission is due in part to the scanty resources at its disposal: its budget is very small, its secretariat services are provided by the public credit department of the ministry of finance, it meets only once a week, its members are not remunerated, and both its members and its secretariat have little experience with privatizations or mergers and acquisitions.[27]

Privatization programs in many countries have been hampered by inadequate resources. In Morocco, for example, this was because the privatization process relied heavily on external funding from donors. This funding dried up at the end of 1995; no other financing mechanism had been set up. Elsewhere, overoptimistic assumptions about gross privatization revenue and underestimation of the costs of the privatization process account for the shortfall.

Privatization Funds

The term "privatization fund" covers a broad spectrum of institutions which can have widely varying objectives and structures. The funds discussed in this section are portfolio holding companies set up in central and eastern European countries, either on the initiative of the government or with its support, as intermediaries between the general public and enterprises to be privatized. They are a key institutional mechanism for mass privatization programs.

This section does not deal with other types of privatization funds, such as private investment funds set up to acquire the shares of privatized enterprises outside the context of a specific mass privatization program. Box 6.2 describes some private funds of this type, namely, privatization mutual funds established by international investment banks for international investors.

This section does not cover privatization agencies that have a portfolio management function, either. The holding companies are, for instance, responsible for managing and transferring government shares (see the section above on SOE management and restructuring bodies); the German Treuhandanstalt could thus be regarded as a fund, in that it held the shares of enterprises to be privatized in its portfolio.[28] Nor does this section deal with

27. See *Le Soir*, 27 August 1993. This changed somewhat with the March 1995 appointment of an investment banker as president of the committee—the committee's fourth president since its creation in 1992—but a new president was expected to be appointed in late 1996.

28. As discussed earlier, the purpose of funds of this kind (that are also privatization agencies) is generally to restructure the enterprises and to sell the shares they hold to the private sector. They normally have a limited timespan and should be abolished when they have accomplished their mission.

Box 6.2   Privatization Mutual Funds

Private investment funds are set up by financial institutions without any government involvement, other than compliance with the securities regulations in effect. Many privatization funds on the market are closed-end funds, meaning that they accept investors only when they are first established; an investor can leave the fund only by selling his or her shares in it to another investor. Once the shares are issued, they are quoted on a securities exchange just like ordinary company shares. The share price may therefore diverge from the net asset value of the underlying securities held by the fund. Others are open-end mutual funds (or unit trusts, in British parlance), which accept new investors after start-up and directly reimburse investors (at book value, minus fees where applicable) who wish to withdraw their money; their capital fluctuates as a result of investments and redemptions made by investors. The purpose—often the sole purpose—of privatization investment funds is to invest in securities of enterprises that have been or are being privatized.

Several privatization funds have recently been set up. The Kleinwort European Privatization Investment Trust was launched in January–February 1994 by the merchant bank Kleinwort Benson to invest in privatized companies in continental Europe and the United Kingdom, including those in the industrial, financial, and public services (particularly telecommunications) sectors. Other examples are Mercury European Privatization Trust, set up at the same time to carry out similar investments, and Guinness Flight Global Privatisation Fund, set up in February 1994, which invests in privatization securities worldwide though it concentrates a large part of its activity in Europe. Alliance Capital was the adviser of the Global Privatization Fund, set up in March 1994 as a closed-end fund to invest in privatized enterprises worldwide; its shares consistently traded at a discount of about 10 percent to net asset value; this triggered a conversion mechanism that led to the absorption of that fund in October 1995 by Alliance's open-end Worldwide Privatization Fund. Finally, there are privatization funds limited to a single country, such as the Peru Privatization Fund, managed by Montagu Mining Finance, a subsidiary of Midland Bank.

By and large, the performance of these funds has turned out to be rather disappointing, reflecting the disappointing performance of recent privatization offerings. The enthusiasm for privatization issues, which prompted the creation of these funds, was fueled by the large initial returns made by investors in many U.K. privatizations. In other countries, returns on shares in privatized enterprises have been underperforming the market, however; this is the case, for example, with recent French and Italian issues. *Euromoney* reported in February 1996 that "of the 24 biggest western European privatization issues since October 1993, only nine trade today at above their issue price."

Sources: Fund prospectuses; *International Financing Review*, 31 December 1993, p. 28; *Financial Times*, 3 February 1994 and 17 March 1994; *Euromoney*, February 1996, p. 30; *The Economist*, 29 June 1996; see also note 17 in chapter 5.

warehousing funds that temporarily manage government participations.[29] Not included either are the special treasury account funds set up to collect privatization proceeds, which are only budgetary accounts and not distinct institutions (see the section in chapter 5 on allocation of privatization proceeds).

Privatization Funds in Mass Privatization Programs

Mass privatization programs designed and implemented in the 1990s were supposed to deal with the specific problems faced by former Soviet block countries that want to privatize their economies speedily.[30] The task was formidable indeed: to transfer a significant portion of public assets to a large and diverse group of new private owners as quickly as possible, in a way that would foster the creation of a sound market economy. Fundamentally, mass privatization involves the transfer of shares in a large number of enterprises rather than the sale of individual companies, though the latter method was often used in conjunction with mass privatization programs. In addition to economic goals, mass privatization programs typically also seek to meet political objectives (wide popular participation and support) as well as social ones (distribution of shares to the general public).[31]

In many countries shares have been distributed through a coupon allocation scheme. These coupons (sometimes called vouchers or checks) are typically convertible through an auction into shares in funds or specific

29. A fund may be set up as a warehousing or bridging device when transfer to the public of shares of enterprises to be privatized cannot take place immediately, because, for example, no financial market exists yet or because the amounts involved could overwhelm a small domestic market. These funds can also act as temporary trustees of shares to be transferred to the public in stages as and when the situation permits. This applies, for example, to the Zambian Privatisation Trust Fund (ZPTF), established in 1993 as part of the country's broader privatization program. Since it became operational in 1994 the ZPTF has received in trust significant government holdings in companies that had been privatized. In the case of Chilanga Cement, for instance, the U.K. CDC, which was already a minority shareholder, bought a 29.9 percent stake from the government in October 1994 to bring its holding to 50.1 percent; the government's remaining holdings were transferred to ZPTF, which floated the shares on the Lusaka stock exchange in April 1995. In October 1995, ZPTF offered its holdings in Rothmans of Pall Mall (Zambia), but was only able to sell about half the shares on offer; it may either try to sell the unsold shares again at a later date or hold on to them until ZPTF's conversion at the end of the trust period into a unit trust (mutual fund).

30. Note that several countries had already carried out free distributions of shares or privatization coupons before they were introduced in transition countries. Examples are Chile and Canada. Thus in 1979 part of the shares of British Columbia Resources Investment Corporation were distributed free of charge to the people of the Canadian province of British Columbia. This distribution took place in response to a wave of public dissatisfaction: people felt that they should not have to buy what already belonged to them, and they had the impression that the government was selling off SOEs for the benefit of the rich (see Vuylsteke 1988, vol. 1, p. 14).

31. On mass privatization, see Lieberman and others 1995; OECD 1995b; Anderson 1994; Shafik 1993; English 1991.

enterprises.[32] Private and public privatization funds have been established to act as intermediaries between the public and enterprises being privatized under mass privatization programs. States have used several methods to allocate the coupons to the population. The differences between them include whether (a) the shares of privatizable SOEs are transferred to one or more funds or directly to the public; (b) the program applies to all privatizable SOEs or only to some of them; (c) the shares or coupons are sold or are distributed free of charge; (d) the coupons are freely tradable bearer certificates (which can be sold for cash), are registered certificates (often with restrictions on resale), or are nontransferable; and (e) oversubscribed issues are reoffered at a higher price or are reduced pro rata to the bid.

Where funds are set up, the most common way for citizens to become shareholders is to exchange coupons distributed by the government for shares issued by the fund. This method was used, for example, in the Czech Republic, Kazakstan, Poland, Russia, and Ukraine.[33] In many countries, including the Czech Republic and Russia, citizens can opt to use their coupons to acquire fund shares or to acquire enterprise shares directly.[34] In Kazakstan only the funds are allowed to participate in SOE share auctions, and citizens therefore have to choose a fund to which to present their coupons. In Poland, the government allocates shares to the privatization funds and voucherholders choose to exchange their vouchers for shares in the funds of their choice. Table 6.4 highlights the main features of the Czech,

32. Mongolia was the first transition country to launch a voucher-based mass privatization program; it may be the only country that issued vouchers but did not allow intermediation by funds. Partly as a result, atomized shareholders have had little say and privatized companies have come under the control of employees and managers. See World Bank 1996b, p. 56.

33. Article 22 of the Czech and Slovak federal law on large privatizations holds: "An investment coupon . . . is a security conferring on the bearer the right to buy shares expressly declared to be saleable in exchange for coupons. Said coupon is nontransferable, and the rights attaching to it can only be transmitted to a legitimate heir." Article 23 provides that the coupons (or vouchers) shall be issued and sold by the federal minister of finance. Privatization coupon books were put on sale at a modest price. Article 24 provides that "every Czechoslovak citizen permanently resident in the Czech and Slovak Federal Republic and aged 18 or over at the date of issue of the coupons is entitled to such coupons."

34. The Czech private investment funds conducted intensive publicity campaigns during the months preceding the closing date for sales of coupons to be used for the first privatization wave, promising high dividends to investors who entrusted their coupons to them. On February 28, 1992, the final sale date for the first tranche, 8.5 million coupon booklets had been sold (against only 2 million a month earlier), and over 70 percent of the coupons issued were entrusted to the investment funds. The second wave of coupon sales closed in December 1993 with the sale of coupon booklets with a value of 1,050 koruny (about $35) to some 5.5 million Czech citizens. Investments funds again attracted the bulk (64 percent) of all vouchers, hence maintaining their central role in the mass privatization process. After these two successive waves, over 6 million Czech citizens, or about 80 percent of the eligible population, became shareholders in over 1,600 privatized enterprises by exchanging their coupons for fund shares or directly for SOE shares (see Lieberman and others 1995, p. 7; OECD 1995b, p. 48; *Wall Street Journal*, 28 November 1994; see also table 6.4).

Table 6.4 Features of Privatization Funds in Selected Countries

Characteristic	Czech Republic	Poland	Romania	Russia
Name	Privatization Investment Funds	National Investment Funds	Private Ownership Funds	Coupon-based Investment Funds
Sponsor	Private sector	Government	Government	Private sector
Number of funds	In the first wave of privatization, 264 competing funds were set up (439 for the whole of then-Czechoslovakia); 353 followed in the second wave	Fifteen funds have been created. By early 1996, fund managers had been selected, management contracts signed, and enterprise shares contributed to the funds' portfolios	Five funds (POFs) have been set up	Over 650 regional and national funds had been licensed by May 1994
Fund ownership	Shareholders of the funds are citizens; they can swap their coupons (bought at a price roughly equal to one week's average wage) either directly against shares of the enterprises put up for auction or against shares in the funds. Coupons were issued in two successive waves completed in December 1992 and December 1994	The funds are initially government owned. Each citizen aged over 18 could acquire a universal certificate for a nominal fee of 20 zlotys (about $8), which gives the right to one share of each of the 15 funds. Distribution of the universal certificates started in November 1995, to be continued for one year. By May 1996, 13 million out of the 27 million eligible Poles had purchased universal	Shareholders of the funds are citizens aged 18 or older, to whom the coupons were distributed free of charge. These coupons represent shares in the POFs. During the first five years of the privatization program the POFs were supposed to play a dual role: one, manage their portfolio for the benefit of the citizens who retain their coupons; and two, swap the shares they hold in corporatized enterprises	Shareholders of the funds are citizens, who can exchange the coupons distributed to them for shares in the funds. As of May 1994, Russian funds held approximately 45.2 million coupons, or 33 percent of all coupons distributed to the population. The distribution of coupons was announced in July 1992, and by the first quarter of 1993, 95 percent of citizens had received their coupons for a

(table continues on the following page)

Table 6.4 (continued)

Characteristic	Czech Republic	Poland	Romania	Russia
	certificates. Funds will be listed on the stock exchange after the first year of operation and an audit		against the coupons which citizens opt to remit. After completion of the exchange of coupons and certificates, the funds have to be converted into private investment companies	nominal price. The Russian mass privatization program was concluded in July 1994
Fixed or variable capital	Fixed until June 1994; closed or open-end thereafter	Fixed for the first four years, with the option then of variable capital	Fixed for the first five years and variable thereafter	Fixed
Management	Funds are administered by private fund managers. The largest funds are managed by banks and insurance companies. A fund may not hold more than 20 percent of the capital of any given enterprise. Some of them, however, play an active role in the management of the enterprises. Moreover, some banks control several funds, which together can hold a large participation in the capital of certain enterprises. These banks can thus indirectly control such enterprises	Funds are managed by experienced professionals (including reputable foreign firms) under ten-year management contracts. In addition to a fixed annual fee (about $3 million), managers are given performance-related incentives to increase the value of their portfolios. Fearful of large foreign influence, parliament added supervisory boards, soon filled by political appointees. The government has allocated 60 percent of the shares of 508 large and medium-size enterprises to these funds:	POFs are managed by nationals, but each fund receives technical assistance from foreign advisers. The first board of directors of each fund is appointed by the government and has to be approved by parliament; subsequent boards are appointed by shareholders. The government has allocated 30 percent of the shares of 6,000 enterprises to the POFs. The other 70 percent are held, at least initially, by the state property fund. The POFs should play an active role in	Funds are administered by private fund managers. These play a passive role in the management of the enterprises (initially, a fund could not hold more than 10 percent of the capital of a given enterprise; later, the figure was amended to 25 percent)

	the management of these enterprises; they appoint their representatives to the board of directors	Standard bylaws, approved by the government in 1992, which the funds are required to adopt. These bylaws prescribe, in particular, the conditions and procedures for exchange of the shares held by the funds against coupons, the procedural rules applicable to the board of directors, and the accounting requirements imposed on the POFs	Decree no. 1186 of the President of the Russian Federation of October 7, 1992, regulating the coupon-based investment funds. The decree assigns responsibility for regulating the funds to the minister of finance. The funds may not invest more than 5 percent of their capital in a given enterprise. They are also prohibited from borrowing from financial institutions
Regulation	33 percent to a lead fund and 27 percent distributed among the other funds. Provisions in bylaws ensure that the lead fund effectively controls its enterprises. Most funds have already sold some of their participations and listed some on Polish exchanges Law no. 248/92, regulating the privatization investment funds. This law includes specific disclosure requirements to shareholders and limits the remuneration of fund managers	Law of April 30, 1993, concerning the National Investment Funds	

Sources: Privatisation Yearbook 1993; Lieberman 1993; Czech Ministry 1993; Shafik 1993; Egerer 1995; Lieberman and others 1995; *Institutional Investor*, February 1996, pp. 143–46; *Financial Times*, 4 June 1996.

Polish, Romanian, and Russian privatization funds. The Russian model was followed by many other former Soviet republics.

In Slovakia, where a first wave of voucher privatization had been implemented before the separation from the Czech Republic, a new government decided in 1995 to cancel the mass privatization program launched by the previous government and to compensate the 3.5 million citizens who had already bought coupons for this second wave by exchanging them for five-year, interest-bearing state bonds backed by the assets of the National Property Fund (see *Financial Times*, 20 December 1995; Borish and Noël 1996, p. 70).

Establishment of Privatization Funds

Mass privatization funds fall into two main categories: those set up by or at the initiative of the government, to which the government directly transfers a portfolio of shares in enterprises to be privatized, as in Poland and Romania; and those set up by private entrepreneurs who compete to obtain the coupons distributed to citizens and use them to acquire enterprise shares at auction sales organized by the government.

There is usually a sponsor who puts in place a management team to establish and administer the fund proper. In Poland and Romania the sponsor is the government. Where the fund is set up at the initiative of private parties, as in the Czech Republic and Russia, the sponsors may be, for example, banks, insurance companies, or private individuals.[35] The management team will usually be set up in the form of a company and will often exercise ownership rights over the fund until its shares are distributed to coupon holders.

Where the government has directly assigned SOE shares to privatization funds, it has generally been involved in the creation of these funds, including the selection of fund managers. In Romania, for example, the first administrators of privately owned funds were selected by the government, and their appointment, for a term of five years, had to be approved by parliament (see article 8 of Law no. 58 of August 14, 1991, on the privatization of commercial companies). In Poland, managers of the 15 national investment funds have been selected by a committee, independent of the government, that is responsible for appraising bids according to criteria prescribed by the council of ministers.[36]

---

35. In Czechoslovakia, the creation of privatization funds, while encouraged by the government, was left to private initiative. The minister of finance set up a center for coupon-based privatization, which was responsible, in particular, for the technical aspects of the mass privatization process. Once they had met the registration requirements for participation in the process, the privatization funds obtained through the center the data processing equipment required to electronically transmit their orders (see Czech Ministry 1993).

36. See the invitation to bid for contracts to manage the Polish privatization funds, published in September 1993 in various national and international publications, including the *Financial Times*.

Initial schemes have had to be modified in various countries to remove constraining features. This was the case in Romania, where the poor record of the mass privatization program can be attributed to nonreliance on market mechanisms, inadequate public information on companies, refusal to let private brokerage houses intermediate, and complexity of the overall scheme.[37]

Purposes of Privatization Funds

The main function of privatization funds is to manage their portfolios and pay dividends to their own shareholders; in some countries the scheme is somewhat different, as illustrated in table 6.4. Privatization funds have three major purposes. First, they allow citizens to diversify their portfolios indirectly and thereby to lower their risks. These funds also play a vital role in promoting wide dissemination of shares among the population. Without the funds, few citizens could participate effectively in the privatization process. Small shareholders do not—particularly in transition countries—have the means to monitor the performance of individual companies or to spread their risk by dividing a small capital among a large number of holdings.

Second, privatization funds foster the development of financial markets when they promote popular participation in capital markets and contribute to the creation of financial intermediaries and institutional investors. Shareholders in the funds must be able to sell or exchange their shares, of course, to allow this deepening of financial markets.[38] The law or the agreements establishing these funds will need to specify whether a fund is to be closed-end or

37. In the first wave of mass privatization, coupons representing shares in the privatization funds (POFs) were distributed free of charge to citizens. For as long as they retained their coupons, citizens were to receive dividends paid by the fund; however, they could exchange their coupons within five years, at market conditions, for shares held by the funds in the enterprises themselves (see articles 3 and 7 of Law no. 58 of August 14, 1991). This scheme was not too successful, and a new Law no. 55 on the acceleration of privatization was enacted in June 1995. Under this law, new vouchers were given free of charge to citizens who had not converted their previously issued coupons. They were given until the end of 1995 to convert their vouchers at par into shares of an enterprise that was part of the mass privatization program or to entrust their vouchers to one of the five POFs. This deadline had to be extended to March and April 1996 for conversions into company shares and into POF shares, respectively—by mid-December only 7 percent of the nearly 18 million eligible Romanians had subscribed shares (see *Financial Times*, 20 December 1995). These deadlines had to be extended further. On average about 30 percent of an enterprise's shares were exchanged for vouchers, though this could be increased to 60 percent under certain circumstances. The remaining shares of the enterprise could be sold for cash at a predetermined price based on book value.

38. Article 19 of the Romanian privatization law of August 1991 expressly provides that shares held by citizens in privatization funds can be exchanged on the securities exchange under the conditions set forth in the law on the securities exchange. Law no. 52 of 1994 established the Romanian Securities Exchange Commission and the rules for operation of the exchange.

open-end and, where appropriate, from what date the fund must reimburse shareholders who wish to withdraw their capital.[39]

Third, the existence of privatization funds allows some concentration of voting power in privatized enterprises. Without such funds, shares would be dispersed among a multitude of small individual shareholders, who lack the cohesion to exercise their ownership rights effectively. For example, a fund can ensure that a core of professional investors is represented on the management body of the enterprise and thus minimize the adverse effects of atomized shareholding. Corporate governance is particularly important in transition countries which, after decades of central planning, have few corporate managers capable of leading enterprises efficiently in a market economy.

Regulation of Privatization Funds

The regulation of privatization funds encompasses a wide range of issues such as licensing, minimum capital requirements, prudential investment limits, fee structure of management firms, corporate governance, information and disclosure requirements, and so on. Two general models for privatization funds have emerged. One, in which funds are set up at private initiative ("bottom-up"), involves minimal regulation; the second model, in which government creates the funds ("top-down"), requires substantial regulation. Russia and the Czech Republic took the first approach; the privatization funds were established by private initiative, and only when their role as intermediaries became clearer was the regulation tightened to deal with discrete issues (the protection of shareholders against abuse on the part of fund managers, for example).

In Poland and Romania, on the other hand, the top-down approach was chosen, leading to lengthy delays. The Polish funds were the centerpiece of the government's mass privatization scheme; much attention was given to the selection of the management team for each fund and detailed regulations, including prudential rules intended to protect investors, were formulated (see Lieberman and others 1995, p. 32). To avoid the appearance of foreign control of the privatization program, the government appointed local supervisory boards for each of the 15 national investment funds (NIFs). This soon led to considerable tension between some management teams and their boards. A U.S. management group was even fired by its board. When another board threatened to fire its Japanese management team, the government stepped in and fired the board in an attempt to preempt dismissals at other NIFs (see *Financial Times*, 4 June 1996).

---

39. The shares in Czech investment funds issued in 1992 could not be redeemed before June 1994, when the funds could become open-end funds with variable capital. That restriction did not exist in the second wave. Because of deep discounts to net asset value of fund shares trading on the secondary market, voucher holders in the second wave opted predominantly for the liquidity afforded by open-end funds, though managers of these funds typically allowed redemptions only after two or three years (see Egerer 1995, p. 32).

Although direct government intervention in the launch of privatization funds has not produced laudatory results, such intervention is required to regulate fund activities. A satisfactory regulatory framework will protect fund shareholders while allowing the funds to become operational quickly and to perform their functions efficiently. It is important, for example, to encourage fund shareholders to exercise their ownership rights and monitor the performance of the fund's management. There is indeed a risk that fund administrators may take advantage of the problem that originally justified their intervention, namely, the inability of an atomized or fragmented shareholder body to supervise enterprise managers effectively. The dispersal of the share capital of each fund among a multitude of small shareholders could allow fund managers to pursue their own interests and objectives, which may not coincide with the interests of the owners (namely, the maximization of the fund's overall appreciation and return).[40]

Fund managers should report regularly to the shareholders on their activities and performance.[41] In many cases, other rules are prescribed to protect the interests of the shareholders, such as the requirement that the funds diversify their investments to limit their portfolio risk; limits may also be imposed on fund managers' fees, and their remuneration may be tied directly to the results achieved.[42] In addition, in order to eliminate the risk of conflicts of interests, the law may prohibit fund managers from holding other functions.[43]

The issue of conflict of interest is prominent in the Czech Republic, where some think that the criteria for fund creation were too flexible and that banks should not have been allowed to set up funds. It is argued that these banks tend to give the enterprises in their portfolio preferential treatment in lending decisions; moreover, they are often reluctant to institute proceedings that could bankrupt enterprises in which they hold shares. On the other hand, some argue that close links between banks and enterprises have contributed

40. Over sixty years ago, Berle and Means 1933 drew attention to the fact that wide dispersal of a company's shareholder body could lead to a decline in the performance of its managers.

41. In Russia, for example, privatization fund managers are required to publish in the press, at regular intervals, a detailed financial report audited by an independent accountant (see article 40 of supplement 2 to the decree of October 7, 1992). In Romania also, the annual report of each privatization fund must be published in the press (see article 12 of the August 1991 privatization law).

42. In Russia, privatization funds were not allowed to invest more than 5 percent of their resources in securities issued by any given enterprise (see article 25 of supplement 2 to the decree of October 7, 1992); and the total annual remuneration of privatization fund managers may not exceed 10 percent of the aggregate value of the securities held by the fund (see article 34 of supplement 2 to the decree of October 7, 1992).

43. See, for example, article 5 of Romania's August 1991 privatization law, which provides that an individual may not be a member of the board of directors for more than one privatization fund, nor simultaneously a member of the boards of a fund and an enterprise whose securities are held by that fund. This and other conflict-of-interest provisions should be part of prudential rules; they are commonly found in legislation on securities and financial institutions, which normally govern these funds (see also chapter 3).

to the strong performance of the German and Japanese economies. They maintain that a close relationship may, in transition economies, be less a conflict of interest than a way for banks to learn about firm performance in an environment where information costs are high and collateral-based lending is fraught with uncertainty. Bank-sponsored funds therefore reduce lending risks and costs through lower information and monitoring costs, the argument goes, as well as make it easier to solve problem loans (see Egerer 1995).

Some countries have introduced provisions limiting the portion of the capital of an enterprise that can be held by any one fund. The Czech law of April 1992 on investment funds sets this limit at 20 percent. In Russia, the limit was first 10 percent and later raised to 25 percent (see St. Giles and Buxton 1995). These provisions seem inspired by the legislation of some Western countries, where investment funds are not supposed to play an active role in the management of the enterprises whose shares they hold.[44] In central and eastern European countries, the usefulness of rules of this kind is more debatable. First, as stated earlier, it is important that privatization funds be able to participate actively in the management of privatized enterprises. Second, these rules are not essential either to prevent privatization funds from exercising monopoly power over specific economic sectors (competition law may be better suited to that purpose) or to ensure that they will always have diversified portfolios (a fund with substantial resources could hold a large portion of the capital of particular enterprises). However, a threshold of, say, 20 percent should normally allow the funds to build up an equity stake large enough to be represented on the board of directors. If the purpose of a ceiling is to limit the scope for manipulation or monopolization of shares of specific enterprises at government-organized auctions, then reform of the auction procedures to foster active and competitive bidding may be a better solution.

Preliminary Lessons

The institutional and regulatory framework for privatization funds shapes the results. Funds set up with heavy government involvement are exposed to the hazards of the political process and to bureaucratic inertia. This is a serious drawback when mass privatization programs are adopted for their supposed speed of implementation and when delays cause deterioration of the situation of the enterprises to be privatized. More limited government intervention in the establishment of privatization funds may prove more efficient, as it did in the Czech Republic.

To identify other factors that contribute to success with privatization funds, it may be helpful to consider the main purposes of these funds. The

---

44. In the United States, for example, the Investment Companies Act of 1940 makes it practically impossible for a mutual fund to play any role other than that of passive investor (see Gray and Hanson 1993, p. 4).

first objective is to diversify portfolios and to promote popular shareholding. Poland, unlike the Czech Republic, has emphasized risk diversification through the mandatory use of government-sponsored investment funds; in doing so it has limited citizens' choice or initiative. Because the Polish scheme has been delayed for years, no lessons can yet be drawn from its operation. In the Czech Republic, where early interest on the part of the population was low, the emergence of hundreds of market-oriented funds, extensive advertising, and promises of big returns boosted popular interest. In Russia, excessive insider ownership by managers and workers has promoted neither diversification nor meaningful popular ownership.

A second objective in fostering privatization funds is to develop financial markets through popular participation in equity markets and promotion of financial intermediaries and institutional investors. The Prague Stock Exchange was revived in April 1993 after a fifty-year hiatus and an over-the-counter trading system has been created in the Czech Republic. Mass privatization contributed to the fast development of capital markets, but important problems remain, linked to the weakness of the banking system, lack of transparency, speculation about collusion and insider trading, widespread "off-market" transactions, and other factors (see Lieberman and others 1995, p. 8). In Russia, the capital markets and the related regulatory framework have been unable to cope with the results of privatization, mainly because of the speed and sequencing of reforms.

The third objective of privatization funds is to provide an efficient corporate governance structure, which cannot be achieved under mass privatization programs without some concentration in voting power. Questions remain with respect to the role that the funds effectively play in governance and enterprise restructuring. The Polish model has the potential to supply strong corporate governance at the enterprise level, as each investment fund has a controlling share in specific enterprises ("lead fund") and has the means to initiate and carry out enterprise restructuring. The model is too new to be evaluated yet, though the early tension between the NIF supervisory boards and their management teams does not augur well. In most other transition countries, funds do not have the powers or majorities required to restructure enterprises (employee layoffs, selling of assets, and so on); in Russia and the Czech Republic, for instance, ceilings limit a fund's ownership stake in a single enterprise to 20 percent or 25 percent. Initial indications suggest, however, that at least some Czech funds, notably those that have opted to concentrate their holdings in a limited number of enterprises, play an active role on the boards of directors of privatized enterprises and seek to upgrade the performance of those companies. Measures adopted to that effect include, for example, pressing for personnel cuts and for the replacement, in rare cases, of underperforming senior management (see, for example, Anderson 1994, pp. 21–22).

Other issues of governance take the form of potential conflict of interest. In the case of the Czech Republic, the concern is with the concentration of ownership and economic power by the largest funds, dominated by the banking sector, and with cross-ownership between the funds and the banks. In Russia, a battle for corporate control is often fought between large investment funds, individual investors, and the "insider" managers. Managers were granted generous share allocations at privatization and have protected themselves through antitakeover clauses and other schemes, which have contributed to inefficient management.

In summary, privatization funds have an uneven track record. They have played a critical role in the fast transition to a shareholder-based system in the Czech Republic, for instance, yet in many other countries their role has not been significant. Funds created by or at the initiative of the government should gradually be emancipated from government involvement and become private investment funds governed by ordinary securities legislation.

Role of Advisers

All governments that have successfully carried out a major privatization program have used the services of advisers. The selection of these advisers deserves special attention. The range of external expertise needed varies widely, depending on the type of country, the scope of the privatization program, the sectors and enterprises involved, and the internal capabilities of the privatization agency or other entities responsible for preparing and implementing the program. The kinds of advisers that may be needed to perform essential tasks are, among others, economists, lawyers, financial advisers (including auditing firms and investment banks), sectoral specialists, and tax and labor experts. External advisers have assisted agencies and governments in preparing an enterprise for privatization, starting up the process, defining the techniques and procedures to be used in specific privatization operations, negotiating the transactions, and even in formulating an overall privatization strategy.

Although the need for outside expertise may be greater in developing and transition countries than in OECD countries such as France, New Zealand, or the United Kingdom, the latter have systematically had recourse to outside advisers and experts to help prepare and manage their privatization programs. Even the Treuhandanstalt, which had a staff of over 4,000 at the peak of its activity, turned to scores of lawyers, accountants, and other outside experts for advice and assistance.

Economic, Financial, and Technical Advisers

Problems arise if the right adviser is not brought in at the right time. Privatization should be driven by a strategy that focuses on increasing overall economic performance while protecting the legitimate interests of the different affected parties. This has implications for who should be asked for advice and when. Investment bankers, for example, are not particularly well suited or well placed to advise on broad economic and sector strategy. If such a strategy is supposed to drive the deal they are asked to structure and place, that should be defined up front with assistance from strategic advisers and economists. Key issues include the degree of competition and the type of market structure that will be introduced before or at privatization. Indeed, an enterprise with monopoly rents will be easier to sell, and will sell at a higher price, than one operating in a competitive environment. Governments would generally be well advised to choose medium- and long-term benefits over short-term ones. That requires the right set of advisers intervening in the proper sequence and with the right incentives (see also the sections below on advisers' conflicts of interest).

Governments are sometimes sensitive to the nationality of advisers they retain and worried by the appearance of foreign influence on policymaking. But for many privatization operations—sector privatizations and transactions for which foreign investors or foreign flotations are considered, in particular—recourse to foreign advisers is necessary. Countries do not always have the required national expertise, even for simpler transactions. A privatization program can contribute to the development of such expertise, however. In Poland, for example, most of the consulting firms and investment banks hired by the ministry of ownership changes at the beginning of the privatization process were of foreign nationality; local expertise has developed since then, and the ministry is increasingly using Polish experts.

The selection of advisers may have significant implications for the way privatization will be carried out. Indeed, advisers (whether firms or individuals) come with specific experience and baggage, which will often be their reference point during their assignment. It is, for example, not surprising that the privatization of telecommunications operators in different countries has followed a similar path, because the same U.K. investment bank advised the different governments. Likewise, the trend in many East Asian countries to privatize through initial public offerings that are largely discounted and yield a substantial first-day premium has been linked to the use of privatization advisers from the United Kingdom, where a similar approach was chosen for many privatizations (see *Oxford Analytica*, "Malaysia: Preferential Privatisation," 27 November 1995).

Advisers should, in general, be selected through a competitive process. This is often done in two stages: a general invitation asking for expressions of interest in the assignment leads to the prequalification of a short list of firms; those firms then participate in a formal tender process. Some governments or privatization agencies decentralize and speed up the process by maintaining a list or roster of prequalified advisers; the various ministries, agencies, or local governments involved in the privatization program can then proceed with the selection of advisers without issuing a general call for bids.

In most developing countries, as well as in countries in economic transition, the services of these advisers have been financed by bilateral or multilateral development agencies, such as the World Bank and the African, Asian, European, and Inter-American development banks. In many countries privatization receipts also have been used to defray the costs of this assistance (see chapter 5 on the allocation of privatization receipts and the section of this chapter on financing the privatization process). In any event, these costs will normally be amply offset by the benefits reaped from better-prepared programs and better-negotiated transactions. Box 6.3 illustrates various fee levels encountered in recent privatizations.

Legal Advisers

This section focuses particularly on the role of lawyers, for two main reasons. First, the examination of the legal issues that arise in the various stages of the privatization process constitutes much of the content of this book; the role of lawyers in that process is obviously germane. Second, the role of the lawyer is all too often poorly understood, or else reduced to that of a legal adviser brought in at the closing stage to negotiate the privatization agreements.

The role of lawyers. Three categories of lawyers are involved in privatizations: public-sector lawyers, often belonging to the privatization agency, a ministry, or an SOE; independent lawyers advising the government, the SOE, the buyers, or other parties (local or foreign lawyers); and legal staff of international financial institutions or development agencies assisting the country or the SOE with the privatization program.

Governments and SOEs rarely possess in-house legal staff with the requisite privatization qualifications and experience. This is true in industrial as well as in developing or transition countries. Countries as diverse as Argentina, Côte d'Ivoire, France, Germany, New Zealand, the United Kingdom, and most of the central and eastern European countries therefore have made wide use of private law firms or legal consultants to advise them in their privatization operations.

Legal staff of the World Bank and other donors and assistance agencies often help prepare and implement privatization programs, in particular by drafting the terms of reference of legal advisers recruited under World Bank-supported projects and by supervising their work. Their role is not to act as primary legal advisers to governments or SOEs but to help governments of eligible countries, at their request, select advisers and finance their services.

Local or foreign lawyers? Although the use of foreign lawyers is often unavoidable, it can pose political difficulties. It may clash with the interests of local lawyers who, while they may not always possess the required experience, are nonetheless eager to obtain these prestigious and often lucrative commissions. It may also give the appearance that the government is acting under pressure or control from abroad, especially when the

Box 6.3   Advisory Fees in Privatization Transactions

Fees of investment bankers often run 2–5 percent in large public offerings. In the United States there is "a well-established fee schedule," which ranges from 7 percent for small initial public offerings (IPOs) to 2 percent or less for large secondary-block trades (*Euromoney*, February 1996, p. 40). The first offering of Telmex, the Mexican telephone company, in 1991 brought the investment bank 4.5 percent, but the second, a year later, only 3 percent. YPF, the Argentine oil company, was done for 4 percent in 1993. The subscription and administration premium in the public offering of shares in Lufthansa, the German airline, was apparently 1.5 percent, and the placement fees 2.1 percent of the transaction amount. For the public flotation of the second tranche of the privatization of the Peruvian tele-communications company, the government selected investment banks based on the lowest commission level requested; the winning bidder asked for 2.42 percent.

In 1995 total advisory costs represented about 5 percent of total privati-zation revenue in Poland. The public flotation in November 1995 of a 15 percent stake in ENI, the Italian energy company, generated over $200 million in advisory fees, or about 5.3 percent of gross proceeds. High advertising expenses accounted for a significant part of this amount. Advi-sory costs represented 3.9 percent of proceeds from the first tranche of the British Telecom privatization, though only 1.8 percent for the third tranche.

When the assignment requires significant upfront work to prepare the company (and sector) for privatization, two separate fees are typically agreed upon: a structuring fee, which may be a fixed retainer or a time-based fee (or a combination), for example; and a placement or under-writing fee, typically a percentage of the transaction, which compensates the investment bank for its research and corporate finance staff, placement efforts (sales force, road shows, and so on) and involvement in making markets for the shares once issued.

Secondary offerings are often easier and less staff-intensive than IPOs, because the preliminary structuring has already been accomplished, the company is already under private management, and its shares are already traded on the stock exchange. Consequently, secondary offerings usually command lower fees. Similarly, public offerings tend to be more costly than private placements and trade sales. These two points are well illus-trated in the privatization of the Italian insurer INA: advisory costs for the IPO amounted to 4.25 percent of gross proceeds, whereas for the second tranche, which was sold through private placement, costs were about 0.25 percent.

Finally, on the placement side, firm underwriting involves an additional risk and thus higher fees.

Sources: Euromoney, Gravy train gets bogged down, February 1996, pp. 40–43; *Financial Times,* 10 October 1994 and 31 January 1996; *Privatisation International,* March 1996.

private expertise is financed by donors. The costs associated with foreign law firms tend to be very high, with hourly fees often exceeding the weekly salary of official counterpart staff. Finally, hiring reputable international lawyers may constrain governments in their privatization approaches; indeed, such lawyers or firms may not want to be associated with dubious transactions.

Prudent precautions can reduce this sensitivity to foreign advice. First, because the law is an expression of national sovereignty and therefore particularly susceptible to the appearance of foreign influence, it will often be preferable not to recruit foreign lawyers to draft legislation. Foreign advisers can, however, give governments and parliaments valuable information about legislative experience in other countries. They can also offer comments and suggestions about legal instruments drafted by local officials. A good privatization law is not necessarily an elegant law, but it should be a law perceived as the expression of the national will. Second, it is important that the government clearly explain to the officials concerned and the general public why it is calling on foreign advisers and why this in no way impairs the independence of the country. Subordinated texts and contractual agreements generally provoke less sensitivity to foreign advice than does the privatization law itself.

It is not uncommon for local and foreign law firms to work together on privatization cases: the local firm contributes its knowledge of the country and its legal machinery and business practices, and the foreign firm offers its experience with similar operations in other countries. In practice, privatization tends to stimulate demand for the services of local private lawyers in important areas of business law, areas in which they had previously lacked the opportunity to gain much experience.

Because local lawyers in many countries are unlikely to be familiar with the technical aspects of privatization operations, it may be useful to organize basic and developmental training programs. These programs can address the specific needs of local lawyers, thus arming them with the skills necessary to make a positive contribution to the implementation of privatization.[45]

Legal contribution to strategy formulation. Lawyers need to be involved in the early stages of preparation of the privatization program, particularly so that they can identify obstacles that could obstruct privatization and devise ways to eliminate or circumvent them. Unfortunately, however, governments, privatization agencies, SOE managers, and bilateral and multilateral assistance agencies are not unfailingly aware of the importance of upstream

---

45. Pertinent legal training is offered as part of the continuing education programs of many universities and by specialized legal training institutions, such as the Rome-based International Development Law Institute, and the Washington-based International Law Institute.

involvement of qualified and experienced lawyers who fully measure up to the demands of these complex tasks.[46]

A single group of legal advisers could conceivably possess the qualifications and experience to provide the range of services required throughout the privatization process. The skills for assisting with the preparation of a comprehensive program, however, are likely to differ from those needed for executing the privatization operations.

Upstream, governments seek lawyers with a good understanding of societal choices and their economic and political implications. Since the advice these lawyers provide is factored directly into strategy formulation, they need to have a clear perception of local conditions and difficulties. To assess the propitiousness of the general environment for business activity and the specific measures that will need to be taken to facilitate privatization, legal advisers will usually have to take an empirical and inductive approach, starting by identifying day-to-day difficulties that hamper private business activity or any constraints on the government's choice of privatization techniques. In practice, as pointed out earlier, governments should not strive to create the perfect legal environment before starting privatization operations. Such an approach would give rise to endless delays and eventually doom the entire privatization process.

Some lawyers, accustomed to a more theoretical or deductive approach, undertake a relatively exhaustive examination of all major legislative instruments, their objective being to recommend changes to bring those instruments into line with international standards. This approach can easily mask specific privatization problems in the country in question, which might stem from inability to ensure effective application of and compliance with the legislation, customary practices not codified by law, or restrictions imposed by unusual laws or regulations, to cite only a few examples. Lawyers involved in the development of strategy will therefore need to have a sharp awareness of the realities of business life and the political, administrative, and other constraints in the privatizing country. They will need to work in close collaboration with nonlegal advisers also involved at that stage and, if they are foreigners, with local lawyers.

Legal assistance in privatization transactions. A law firm should normally be retained to represent the government in each transaction, especially if a large enterprise or an enterprise in a regulated sector is to be sold. This is undoubtedly an arduous task, and one that calls for relevant experience in the field. Many law firms across the world have extensive privatization experience, often acquired in several countries. Preferably, the law firm

---

46. "Qualified and experienced legal counsel should be able to identify and anticipate obstacles, both legal and nonlegal, and, more importantly, devise ways to get around such obstacles and achieve the desired objective. Legal advisers that merely identify obstacles are of little value and, indeed, may be counter-productive in transactions of the complexity of most privatizations" (Quale 1991, p. 25).

selected will also possess experience in the sector in question. This is particularly important for privatization in the infrastructure sectors, which are governed by special legislation and regulations presenting specific problems.

It will sometimes be desirable for the SOE to have legal advisers of its own, especially if the transaction relates to only part of its assets; in this case the SOE, as seller of part of its assets, has an interest in the transaction that is independent of that of the government as owner of the SOE. Whatever the situation, the role of outside legal advisers is to fully protect the interests of the seller and to ensure that the objectives of the seller are achieved to the extent possible. Privatizing a large enterprise is one of the biggest and most complex commercial operations a government can undertake. Private buyers will often be assisted by attorneys highly skilled in the negotiation of transactions of this kind; the seller should be able to rely on equally qualified and experienced legal counsel.

Conflicts of Interest Facing Advisers

Investment bankers (or other financial advisers) and law firms could join forces with the aim of winning a contract to provide comprehensive advice on privatization. There are arguments both for and against such an association.

On the one hand, conflicts of interest can arise when lawyers work for or as part of a team with the financial advisers (the investment bank), rather than for the seller (the government or the SOE). The terms of reference of legal advisers sometimes include advising the government in connection with the negotiation or execution of a contract with the investment bank. This role will not necessarily be performed independently and impartially where the lawyers are subcontractors or joint-venture partners of the investment bank. Moreover, the government's interest may be better served by seeking differing points of view concerning the transaction.[47]

On the other hand, an integrated team can be useful in some aspects of the negotiation of transactions, for example by compelling the various advisers to present the government with a single approach. Conflicts of interest are less likely to arise, and the structuring of the advisory team becomes less important, when the assistance concerns upstream questions of strategy and legislation, provided the same team is not responsible for downstream transactions. In these circumstances, multidisciplinary teams comprising lawyers, economic and financial advisers, and other consultants will often be better placed to advise the government on a comprehensive strategy and action plan encompassing all aspects of privatization. Governmental resources (or lack of them) also can argue in favor of an alliance of legal and financial advisers: many governments have found that

---

47. It would not be untypical for one group, either the lawyers or the investment bankers, to be selected first and then assist the government in the selection of the other group, however.

they are unable to adequately monitor and coordinate the activities of separate consulting firms.[48]

Another factor can complicate an alliance of advisers: financial and legal advisers are remunerated in different ways. Investment bankers are typically paid, at least in part, on the basis of a success fee (a percentage of the selling price) and lawyers are compensated for time spent on a project. The practice of billing solely on the basis of time may present incentives to raise as many questions and problems as possible when lawyers review privatization legislation and when they prepare and negotiate transactions and contracts for privatization. This overcautious approach is a way to protect themselves from being accused of shoddy work (and from possible lawsuits), but it is also a way to boost their billings.

The investment bankers' success fee is not without problems either, and it too may create perverse incentives and conflicts of interest. This is particularly the case where investment bankers advise the government on basic policy issues underlying the transaction: their incentive may be to suggest the option that would yield the highest sale price and the largest success fee. It is not uncommon for investment banks to advise governments to maintain high protection or long exclusivity periods when such policies are economically unjustified. Examples include granting telephone companies to be privatized a monopoly on basic services (see the section in chapter 7 on increasing competition in telecommunications) and granting the privatized industry protection from imports or domestic competition (see the section in chapter 3 on protecting and promoting competition). The fee structure could also influence investment bankers to opt for the sector structure and reforms requiring the least work on their part to generate the fixed or success-based fees.

Investment banks may face other conflicts of interest, which lawyers should point out to their clients. For example, a bank may represent several governments whose privatizations could compete with one another on the capital market, as would happen if two large telecommunications companies were offered to the public around the same time; the bank would then have to choose which one of its clients would get the better time slot; its representation of multiple clients with competing interests could also affect the terms and conditions it suggests for the transactions. A conflict of interest can also arise if a bank acts as general financial adviser to the government on a privatization transaction while being in charge of underwriting the issue and placing the shares for that same transaction (see Graham and Prosser 1991, p. 92). As a firm underwriter it may, for instance, argue for a lower sale

48. In the process of privatizing the Buenos Aires Water Company, the Argentine government, which had split the assistance contracts among lawyers, technical consultants, and financial consultants, experienced difficulty in coordinating these different teams. The Venezuelan government ran into the same problems during privatization of CANTV (the national telecommunications company); four different teams of advisers (on the economic, financial, legal, and telecommunications aspects) assisted in the privatization operations.

price so as to ensure full placement of the issue and minimize the risk of being left with unsold shares.

Yet even these conflicts may pale compared with the more fundamental and worrisome conflicts that have emerged in the context of privatization transactions. For example, in the much publicized loans-for-shares program carried out in Russia in 1995–96, the banks that managed the tender process emerged as winners in those same tenders.[49]

Conclusion

The formulation and implementation of a privatization program is a complex and lengthy undertaking. Successful execution calls for inputs from many participants with a variety of skills. It also requires that suitable institutions be set up to implement and monitor the program and that opposition to the program, if it exists, be overcome.

Finding the right balance in the relationship between parliament and the executive has been a common problem in privatizations. Many parliaments are reluctant to delegate broad powers to the government, but parliamentary micromanagement comes at a cost: it can slow or even block the process. Broad delegation of powers usually requires either a strong executive or a wide-ranging consensus between parliament and the executive on the policies to be pursued.

Specific institutions are often set up to act as executing agencies for large national privatization programs. The experience of the countries that have carried out such programs shows that these agencies can take various forms. There is no such thing as an ideal or universal model or blueprint; institutions have to be tailored to specific needs and environments.

---

49. Under the loans-for-shares scheme, the Russian government organized auctions in which banks competed to give the government loans backed by shares as collateral. The loan was to be repaid by September 1, 1996; if it was not, the bank would have to sell the stake by December 1998, reimburse itself for the loan amount and keep 30 percent of the resulting capital gains, and return the other 70 percent to the state. The best-known example may be that of Norilsk Nickel, the world's leading nickel, cobalt, and platinum producer, with annual sales of about $3 billion and earnings of almost $700 million. Uneximbank organized the auction for Norilsk Nickel, disqualified the highest bidder on the basis that it did not provide adequate guarantees, and won the stake for a $170 million loan, less than half of the $355 million offered by the highest bidder. "Tactics are primitive," reports *Euromoney*: "To thwart rival bidders (including Rossiyski Kredit, which offered to pay twice as much), the company insisted that those making an offer do so at the company's offices in Russia's hinterland. The company then proceeded to close the local airport so that no other bidders could meet the requirements—hardly a model of transparency." Uneximbank thus gained control over 38 percent of Norilsk Nickel's shares and 51 percent of its voting shares. The management and new shareholders of Norilsk Nickel soon fell out, however, and by June 1996 Uneximbank had installed one of its own board members as acting chief executive. See *Privatisation International*, March 1996, p. 23; *Business Central Europe*, February 1996, p. 16; *Wall Street Journal*, 14 February 1996; see also note 66 in chapter 3.

Nevertheless, some common lessons can and should be drawn from the privatization experience of other countries. Whatever the chosen institutional structure, certain conditions always have to be met. For example, to avoid the risk of gridlock, responsibilities should not be dispersed among many separate entities, and the allocation of overlapping responsibilities to competing agencies should be avoided.

Creation of a separate group or agency with extensive powers and a clear mandate to manage the implementation of privatization operations seems to be the best solution, at least for countries with extensive privatization programs. The choices range from a small team that manages the process but delegates execution of the transactions (such as the privatization unit in the Mexican ministry of finance) to large agencies with vast resources and a mandate to implement the program directly (such as Germany's Treuhandanstalt). The German approach, although successful, will prove difficult to replicate; it relied on a strong and shared sense of urgency, strong political commitment, and a huge and powerful privatization agency endowed with considerable human and financial resources.

The choice of a small, central government team that delegates or contracts out important tasks to external experts, institutions, and firms will often be better suited to the needs of the privatization program and to the country's administrative capacity. Some call this the privatization of the privatization process.

Central privatization ministries, agencies, and committees are not the only institutions to play a key role in privatization programs. Local authorities, government holding companies, enterprises to be privatized, financial institutions, or other agencies can also be called upon to manage certain operations. Small privatization projects are often carried out by municipalities or other decentralized bodies; such local privatizations may nevertheless be part of an overall policy decreed by national authorities and implemented under their supervision.

To be effective, agencies in charge of privatization need to have adequate and timely financing to hire outside advisers, prepare SOEs for divestiture, settle outstanding claims (where necessary), bring the companies to market, and so on. That funding should not be provided ad hoc for each transaction; it should largely be exempt from the burdensome a priori controls so common for public expenditures. Allowing those in charge of privatization to use sale proceeds to cover these expenditures, subject to a posteriori controls, has proven useful in many countries.

Whatever the institutional structure, staff working on privatizations will need to have the right incentives (financial rewards as well as penalties) and must be held accountable for their actions. Accountability requires clear objectives and mandates and transparent procedures. The privatization programs of many countries owe their sluggish progress to uncertainty about the mandate or policy to be carried out. Furthermore, an ambiguous mandate is likely to fuel dissension and power struggles among the various parties to the privatization.

A clearly defined mandate that assigns the necessary powers to the privatization agencies can emanate only from the country's highest authorities. The fact is that even the best institutions, like the best strategies or the best legislation, can be effective only if they are backed by broad consensus and political commitment. Privatization programs are surrounded by controversy in many countries, and civil servants will rarely dedicate themselves to designing and implementing such programs unless the signal to do so comes unambiguously from the top. The president or prime minister—as head of the executive and the civil service—and the ministers and heads of privatization agencies or committees must give clear instructions to the responsible entities and staff, delegate the necessary powers to them, and publicly support the initiatives they take to implement the privatization policy and the legislation adopted by government and parliament.

Mechanisms to minimize fraud or corruption are also needed, but care must be given not to burden the new institutions with a multitude of bureaucratic constraints and procedures. Greater disclosure and publicity in the decisionmaking and implementation processes, for example, can contribute to the transparency required to establish and maintain a reputation for integrity without bogging down the entire process. In addition, resources will have to be set aside for monitoring the effective implementation of the program (including, for example, the compliance of buyers with the obligations they have assumed).

The privatization process has given birth to new institutions. Privatization funds, for example, were established in many transition countries to avoid the atomization of shareholding, give small shareholders greater voice in corporate bodies, improve corporate governance, and develop financial intermediaries and markets. Similarly, new regulatory institutions have been set up in the context of infrastructure privatization programs, as discussed in chapter 7.

Creating new institutions naturally involves the risk of their entrenchment. Institutions tend to perpetuate their existence even after their justification has disappeared, in this case after the substantial completion of the privatization program. This risk can be mitigated. The law can include a provision stipulating that the entity shall be dissolved after a specified number of years or upon completion of the core program. The German example springs to mind: the Treuhandanstalt took early action to reduce its staff and close many offices as a prelude to its own demise at the end of 1994. The risk of entrenchment will also be lower where the main privatization body is a small central unit that contracts out much of its work.

Finally, the importance of recruiting competent external experts to advise governments cannot be overemphasized. As a rule, the staff of the privatization agency or bodies cannot be expected to muster the range of technical, economic, financial, legal, and other expertise necessary for executing the privatization program. Accordingly, external experts must help the government not only to negotiate the specific technical modalities of each privatization operation but also to formulate the overall reform strategy.

The legal dimensions of privatization deserve special note. The range and complexity of the legal issues to which a privatization program can give rise are almost unlimited. In each country, for each major operation, governments must retain the services of qualified, experienced, and independent lawyers to help them identify and resolve the legal problems that turn up at all stages of the process, from design to implementation and monitoring. It is the responsibility of these lawyers to facilitate the divestiture process by identifying difficulties before they lead to gridlock and by suggesting ways to eliminate or alleviate those problems. Legal advisory assistance is necessary also to protect the interests of the seller in the negotiation and conclusion of major privatization operations.

The economic angle also deserves attention. The privatization of sectors and enterprises offers a unique opportunity to remove barriers to entry and competition. The first step in preparing for a privatization will often have to be the design of sector reforms that promote greater efficiency and a better environment for economic activity. Advice from economists is thus often critical at the early stages of the process, in particular when dealing with protected sectors.

In short, privatization is a complex and multidisciplinary undertaking that calls for close cooperation among economists, financial advisers, lawyers, and other experts, as well as between these advisers and the officials they advise.

7

Privatization of Infrastructure

The preceding chapters covered privatization operations in general, without differentiating between sectors and enterprises. Specific approaches and techniques need to be applied in some sectors, however, especially highly regulated ones. Infrastructure sectors such as power, gas, water, telecommunications, and transport are cases in point.[1] All these infrastructure sectors are, or were, usually thought to exhibit monopoly characteristics; that is, one operator should be able to provide these services more efficiently than could several operators acting separately. Consequently, the fate of any one of these sectors became inextricably entangled with that of the public enterprise that dominated it, which raises special issues for privatization. This chapter explores those issues and refers the reader to previous chapters for discussions of more general privatization issues that also apply to infrastructure enterprises.

The paradigm of the monopolistic public enterprise has been losing ground and relevance since the early 1980s in the face of technological progress (which has, for example, substantially reduced sunk costs, and therefore economies of scale and barriers to entry, in many sectors), advances in economic research, and lessons from successful demonopolization and privatization programs in the United Kingdom and other countries. In particular, such factors as the contestability of these sectors (or of some of their segments), the potential capture of regulators, the adverse effects of lack of competition, and the inefficiencies inherent in many public management systems were rarely taken into account in cost-benefit analyses of monopoly retention.[2] It is becoming increasingly difficult to argue that the telecommunications or power generation sectors, for example, are intrinsically monopolistic.

---

1. Special rules may also be necessary to facilitate privatization of other sectors not covered here, such as natural resources (mines, hydrocarbons, and so on) and the financial sector, for example.
2. Two seminal pieces in the economic literature on demonopolization and privatization are Baumol, Panzar, and Willig 1982 on the theory of contestable markets and Stigler 1971 on the capture of regulators.

These economic, political and technological developments, combined with increasingly severe constraints on public finances, have generated a dual movement of demonopolization and privatization of infrastructure sectors. This movement has not been uniform, however. One set of countries—mainly industrial countries (New Zealand, United Kingdom) and better-off developing countries (Argentina, Chile, Malaysia, Mexico), typically with a relatively well-developed system of private ownership, at least embryonic capital markets, a liberal economic philosophy, and good standing among foreign investors—privatized major infrastructure sectors relatively early on as part of broader privatization programs. Another group—most transition countries, most poorer developing countries (Bolivia and Côte d'Ivoire are among the exceptions), and those industrial countries that still apply relatively nationalistic or statist economic policies—has so far focused their privatization programs mainly on the commercial, industrial, and financial sectors.

A brief historical overview of private sector participation in the infrastructure sectors follows. Issues that arise in the context of infrastructure privatization, and in particular market structure and competition, special privatization techniques, and regulation, are examined next.

Historical Overview of Infrastructure Sectors

It is important to bear in mind that many large infrastructure services across the world have not always been public (see, for example, Foreman-Peck and Millward 1994; Klein and Roger 1994). In a few countries, infrastructure companies have always been and remain today in private hands. This is the case in the United States, which largely escaped the nationalization waves of this century. With a few exceptions such as water supply and sanitation services (which are often run directly by municipal enterprises), some electric utilities, and some railways taken over by the government following their bankruptcy, most infrastructure companies have always been private.

Water

In Paris, the brothers Perrier distributed water through wooden pipes in what was one of the first modern water systems (1782). The concession technique became prevalent in France in the nineteenth century, which saw the establishment of two large, private water companies which still dominate the French and international scene (Compagnie Générale des Eaux, founded in 1853, and Lyonnaise des Eaux, in 1880). The fact that France, a country that has championed the cause of public services and public enterprises, is among the few countries in which this sector has remained largely private is indeed noteworthy. Private water concessions were also granted in England and in many other European cities, such as Berlin (1856) and Barcelona (1867). "In 1800, private firms owned fifteen out of the sixteen waterworks that had thus far been constructed to serve the few and small cities of predominantly rural United States."[3]

Private provision of water services was in no way limited to industrial countries. In Morocco, for example, the water distribution system was developed on a private basis starting around 1914, but after independence in 1956 concessions with private (French) operators were not renewed and municipal utilities were set up to take over the systems. A private company still provides more than one-third of Casablanca's bulk water supply, however, based on a 50-year concession granted in 1949 and is negotiating for a concession to distribute water and power in Casablanca. In Côte d'Ivoire, the water sector has been and remains private (on a lease, or *affermage*, basis). In Guinea, it was run privately before the government took over, then it was reprivatized (also on an *affermage* basis) in 1989.

Argentina, Belgium, Bolivia, Chile, Guatemala, Italy, Macao, the United Kingdom, and the United States are among the countries that have private water distribution companies at present, some of them privatized recently. Australia, Malaysia, and Mexico are among those with private water treatment and sewerage stations.

Energy

Gas utilities were established in the first half of the nineteenth century, primarily for lighting and heating purposes. London was the first city to install gas street lighting (in 1813). The Imperial Continental Gas Association, established in 1824 in London, soon spread to the continent. In 1818 Brussels gave a concession to a private company to build the first public gas lighting system on the continent. Other cities soon followed. In addition to street lighting, gas became a major source of industrial and household energy. The strategic importance of the gas industry started to wane with the advent of the power industry, only to regain some importance in the 1970s and afterward with the introduction of natural gas (see Brion and Moreau 1995).

The invention of the generator by Zenobe Gramme in 1869 and of the light bulb by Thomas Edison in 1879, as well as the introduction of alternating current by Westinghouse in the late 1880s, all contributed to the development of franchises for street lighting, electric street cars, and power distribution in the United States and Europe. In Belgium, Russia, and other countries, private tramway companies, which converted from horse-drawn or steam carriages to electric power in the 1880s, used existing networks to bid

3. Jacobson and Tarr 1995, p. 11. Local governments rapidly took over, though, and their share rose from about 6 percent of waterworks in 1800 to 53 percent in 1896. "By 1900, all but one of the eleven cities in the United States with a population of more than 300,000 had acquired or constructed a municipally owned waterworks" (p. 11). Part of the reason for this shift toward municipal provision resulted from conflicts between cities and private waterworks about the latter's public service obligations to provide hydrants and adequate water volumes and pressure for fire fighting.

for lighting and later power distribution concessions, hence becoming the precursors of the electric power industry. Private gas distribution companies in Belgium, France, and Portugal, to name a few, were also quick to enter this new business, because it was a direct threat to their established franchises.[4]

In the late nineteenth and early twentieth centuries, most electricity companies started out private.[5] They have to a large extent remained private in Belgium, the United States, and some other countries. Colombia (in several stages, beginning in the 1930s), France (1945), Indonesia (1953), and Jamaica (1971), however, subsequently nationalized their power companies, while India and the Philippines opted to nationalize some, but not all, private power companies. In Argentina, Chile, Côte d'Ivoire, and the United Kingdom, events have come full circle: their power companies were initially private, then nationalized, and finally reprivatized.

Nationalizations typically either represented a response to excessive fragmentation of the electric power industry, which prevented integration of networks and the achievement of technically feasible economies of scale, or resulted from a failure in regulation or from ideological or nationalistic trends (see Klein and Roger 1994; Wells and Gleason 1995). The recent privatizations, for their part, came about for a number of reasons, headed by the huge investment requirements in this sector, estimated at over $100 billion a year for the developing countries alone, requirements that exhausted public treasuries cannot afford to finance.

Transport

The railways have a similar history of private involvement. In the United Kingdom, private companies built and operated the railways under charters granted by parliament. Horse traction was initially used until the Stockton and Darlington railway, inaugurated in 1825, introduced steam locomotives; it was also the first to carry freight as well as passengers and to operate as a common carrier railway open to all shippers. The railways were nationalized in 1914 for war-related reasons, privatized in 1921, renationalized in 1948 under British Rail, then finally unbundled and privatized in 1995–96. The U.S. railways were developed in the nineteenth century by private industrialists (in many cases with international bond financing), and they are mostly still private. A few were nationalized as a result of the bankruptcy of private operators; of those, Conrail has since been privatized

4. In 1894 the private company Gaz Belge offered the French city of Cambrai a substantial reduction in its gas tariffs in exchange for the city's award of a monopoly power distribution franchise (see Brion and Moreau 1995, p. 130).

5. This was the case with power companies in Argentina, Belgium, Brazil, Bulgaria, China, Colombia, France, Greece, India, Indonesia, Italy, Jamaica, the Philippines, Poland, Romania, Russia, Spain, Sri Lanka, Syria, Thailand, Turkey, the United Kingdom, the United States, and Venezuela, among others. See Roth 1987; Kessides 1993; Covarrubias and Maia 1994; Brion and Moreau 1995.

again, and Amtrak is still state-owned. Many concessions in the Austro-Hungarian Empire were granted to the private sector from 1836 onward, but the sector was nationalized in 1891 by the Hungarian government and in 1891 by the Austrian government (see Cameron 1961, pp. 209–21).

In France, railway lines were also developed and operated by private interests in the nineteenth and early twentieth centuries, but were based on a national system established by the state as early as 1842; the basic infra-structure of the main lines was planned and financed by the state, whereas the superstructure (including ballast, tracks, signaling system, stations, and rolling stock) was provided and financed by private companies operating under a concession scheme. The whole system was nationalized in 1937, when the Société Nationale des Chemins de Fer Français was established. In Belgium, private investors were the dominant players in the early stages of railroad development, but the state gradually took over.[6]

Private French and British companies, among others, obtained concessions to build and operate railways around the world. In Argentina, the railways were by and large built and financed by British and French companies starting in 1854, when the first concession was granted; they were nationalized against compensation by the Peronist regime in 1946–47 and reprivatized beginning in 1991 (see Kopicki and Thompson 1995, pp. 138–39). Uruguay also granted concessions to British companies toward the end of the nineteenth century. In Mexico, the first railroad between the Pacific and Atlantic coasts was developed in 1906 by a private British company. Various rail concessions were granted by the former Ottoman empire, including a 1891 concession for a line between Beirut and Damascus (completed in 1895). Finally, a number of African railways were privately developed and operated, including the Benguela railway in Angola, completed in 1928 based on a 99-year concession granted in 1902 by the Portuguese government.

The nineteenth century also saw the creation of tramway (streetcar) and subway companies. The first rail networks for streetcars were developed in the United States in the first half of the nineteenth century. Tramways were initially horse-drawn; steam engines started replacing them in the 1870s, followed by electricity in the 1880s and 1890s. By the turn of the century, private companies had developed and were operating tramways in many cities, including Richmond (Virginia), London, The Hague, Warsaw, Odessa, Salonika, Cairo, Rio de Janeiro, and São Paulo, to name but a few (see Brion

6. The state was active in the sector as early as 1834. In 1870, it operated 869 km out of the 2897 km network, or 30 percent, but by 1880 that percentage had increased to 68 percent, or 2792 out of 4112 km. Many concessions were bought back by the state following public dissatisfaction, including accusations of cherry-picking, inadequate investments, and high private profits, but also for nationalistic or strategic reasons. "In 1868–69, a French group tried to take over some lines of the Belgian railway network. This transaction was voided by the public authorities which created a diplomatic incident. The risk of seeing a key sector of the national economy under foreign control haunts from then on Belgian public opinion" (see Brion and Moreau 1995, p. 22).

and Moreau 1995). In the United States, streetcar lines, as well as elevated lines and bus lines, were largely private until the late 1940s.[7]

In ports, the public sector tradition has been long established and is still widespread. Port infrastructure has traditionally been financed and owned by the public sector, but in many ports commercial activities have historically been performed by private operators. In England, however, privately owned and operated ports were established starting in the late seventeenth century and reached their peak in the nineteenth century. Around the turn of this century the public sector started taking over control of these ports. Most U.K. ports were reprivatized after the 1981 transport act. In the United States, the nineteenth century also witnessed rapid expansion of private port activity (especially by railway companies), which led to certain abuses of dominant position, restrained by a Supreme Court ruling of 1892. In France, local chambers of commerce were assigned a major role in port management from the nineteenth century on. In India, many ports were built and run by the East India Company, while the ports of Tangiers in Morocco and Beirut in Lebanon were developed by the private sector under the concession system (see Grosdidier de Matons 1995).

Mention should also be made of the construction of private tollroads in the United States in the early nineteenth century. Most of these were taken over by the states and counties by the 1860s, because canals and railways offered stiff competition, users could not be prevented from evading toll booths, and developers (unlike state and local governments) were unable to capture the benefits of rising property values attributable to their road development efforts.[8] Similarly, in some countries canals and aqueducts were built by private interests exercising the right to levy tolls on users of these infrastructures.

A few large infrastructure works stand out, such as the 363-mile-long Erie Canal in the United States (1825), the Suez Canal (1860), and the Channel Tunnel (1994), which were built and operated by the private sector. Investors in the Erie canal were hurt by a recession that started in 1837, the Suez canal was nationalized in 1956, and Eurotunnel, the owner-operator of the Channel Tunnel, is on the brink of bankruptcy. The Panama Canal, for its part, was to be built and operated under a concession contract by the Panama Canal Company, founded in 1880. The company went bankrupt in 1889, however, and a new company set up in 1894 proved unable to raise the nec-

---

7. Because of their complexity and capital intensity, subway lines were publicly financed in most cities, including Boston, New York, and Philadelphia, but they were leased to private operators. See Jacobson and Tarr 1995, pp. 9–10.

8. See Jacobson and Tarr 1995, p. 5, referring to Bruchey 1965, pp. 124–40. Jacobson and Tarr (p. 6) also point out that from the late nineteenth century, private real estate developers built streets as well as water and sewerage systems as part of residential developments in many U.S. cities. These were most often turned over to the local government upon completion of the development, though in some instances the streets remained private and were maintained by homeowner associations.

essary capital to complete the works. The concession was finally sold to the United States; a treaty with the newly constituted state of Panama granted the United States full sovereignty until 1999 over a ten-mile-wide zone along the canal.[9]

Telecommunications

The first telegram was sent in 1844 from Baltimore, Maryland, to Washington, D.C., by Samuel Morse. Private companies established telegraph links beginning in the mid-nineteenth century and telephone links toward the end of the nineteenth century. The period 1849–59 saw the birth of at least half a dozen private companies whose purpose was to link different countries by telegraph cable laid under the English Channel, between England and Ireland, and under the Mediterranean, the Atlantic, and the Red Sea, to cite only a few examples.[10] Most international telegraphy concessions awarded in the second half of the nineteenth century were for an unlimited duration, but included fixed-term exclusivity rights. Whereas development of the international network was undertaken mainly by the private sector, in many countries (including Japan) domestic telegraph links were run by a state entity from the start.

The telephone was patented by Alexander Graham Bell in March 1876. By 1887, only a decade after its commercial introduction, this new communications device was already in use in many countries; there were over 150,000 phones in the United States, 26,000 in the United Kingdom, 9,000 in France, and 7,000 in Russia, among others. While many telecommunications services were launched by private companies, others were provided by the public sector from the outset (as in Japan, for example). Private telecommunications companies were often subsequently nationalized, as was the case in China and France, and in some cases finally reprivatized, as in Argentina, Chile (see box 7.1), Jamaica, Mexico, and the United Kingdom.[11] Some countries, however, including the

9. Many other public works concessions and BOO (build, own, operate) or BOT (build, operate, transfer) projects are under negotiation or implementation in all infrastructure sectors, including roads and airports, all over the world.

10. See Barty-King 1979, p. 10. The author mentions that of the world total of 8,000 miles of telegraph cable in 1855, some 4,500 miles (56 percent) were operated by the Electric Telegraph Company and 2,200 miles (27 percent) by the English and Irish Magnetic Company.

11. The United Kingdom is a particularly interesting case because two of the major telecommunications companies passed through this cycle. First, Cable and Wireless, whose origin dates back to the mid-nineteenth century, was nationalized in 1946–47 and reprivatized following a 1981 law. This company currently runs, directly or through subsidiaries, all or part of the telecommunications services in many countries, including several Caribbean countries, several Pacific islands, Hong Kong, Macao, Australia, Sierra Leone, Latvia, and Sweden. Since the 1981 telecommunications law, Cable and Wireless has been authorized to operate in the United Kingdom in direct competition with BT, and it set up the Mercury company for that purpose. The telecommunications sector was in fact largely private in the United Kingdom until it was nationalized in 1912, when BT became the national monopoly public operator. The sector became private again following the 1984 telecommunications law authorizing the privatization of BT (see Barty-King 1979).

Box 7.1   Telecommunications in Chile, 1880–1996

Telephone service was introduced in Chile by the Compañía de Teléfonos de Edison in 1880. The company was acquired by International Telephone and Telegraph Corporation (ITT) in 1927. At that time there were 26,205 telephones in Chile, but the only intercity links were between Valparaiso and Santiago.

In 1930, with the aim of promoting expansion of the network and integration of the various regions of the country, the government enacted Law no. 4791, which spelled out the rights and obligations of the telephone company newly set up under the name Compañía de Teléfonos de Chile (CTC); ITT held 80 percent of CTC shares. In exchange for a nonexclusive 50-year concession, CTC was required to modernize the network and interconnect certain regions. The law also provided that upon expiration of the concession, the government could buy back the company, failing which the concession would automatically be extended for 30 years. CTC duly carried out the investments to which it had committed itself. Subsequently, however, the pace of expansion of the network slowed and CTC was accused of inflating its costs; this led the government to renegotiate its agreements with the company in 1958 and 1967, including new investments to be carried out. Meanwhile, in 1964 the government created ENTEL, held by the state holding company CORFO, to provide long-distance and international services.

The Allende government intervened directly in the management of CTC from 1971 to the 1973 coup. Law no. 4791/1930 was later repealed, and in 1974, despite the laissez-faire policy generally favored by the military government, CORFO acquired the shares of ITT in CTC. The government, having thus become the owner of both CTC and ENTEL, allocated the local communications market to CTC and the long-distance and international market to ENTEL, while the cross-subsidies between local and long-distance services strengthened the integration of the two companies. Rate increases during this period were often held below the inflation rate, and the two companies lacked revenue to develop the network and acquire new technologies.

The year 1982 marked the start of sector restructuring that led to privatization of the two companies, broad liberalization, and introduction of a new regulatory framework. The General Telecommunications Law no. 18168/1982 promotes competition, allowing restrictions only on technical grounds to the number of enterprises that may be granted concessions. This law was amended in 1987 to prepare for the privatization of CTC and ENTEL. New provisions were added, defining the criteria to be used in determining telephone service charges and installing new regulatory agencies. Finally, in 1988 a majority of the government's shares in CTC and ENTEL were transferred to the private sector. Noteworthy is that Telefónica of Spain became shareholder of CTC (44 percent) and ENTEL (20 percent). A ruling of the Chilean courts given pursuant to antitrust provisions forced Telefónica to divest one of its two participations. As a result, Telefónica exchanged its ENTEL shares for shares of Cointel, the consortium controlling 60 percent of Telefónica de Argentina.

After having been shared between the public and private sectors (from 1964, when ENTEL was created, to 1974, when CTC was nationalized) and after a period entirely under state control (from 1974 to 1988), the telecommunications

(box continues on the following page)

Box 7.1 *(continued)*

landscape has changed dramatically. "Chile, which two decades ago began-boldly experimenting with free market economics, has become the world's proving ground in another field—fiber optics, personal phones, digital switching, and other advances in telecommunications. More than any place in the world, Chile is the testing ground for how to succeed in telecommunications" (*Journal of Commerce*, 1 December 1995).

Chile has one of the most competitive telecommunications markets in the world. CTC and ENTEL were privatized without monopoly. In long distance and international services, eight companies, five of them major players, are vying for customers. For each call customers dial a three-digit number to get access to the carrier of their choice. After a fierce price war pushed the price of an off-peak call from Santiago to New York down to about 23 U.S. cents per minute at the end of 1995, prices rose to about 75 cents in January 1996, which was still slightly cheaper than calls from New York to Santiago, and significantly cheaper than the $3 charged in neighboring Argentina for similar calls. Although competition has reduced margins, it has also led to a rapid increase in number of subscribers (penetration or teledensity rates have increased from 5 percent to over 12 percent since privatization in 1988) and to much higher volume, leaving most carriers with higher than expected profits.

Sources: Galal and others 1994; Galal 1994; *Financial Times*, 18 August 1994; Reuter, 21 January 1996.

United States and the Philippines, have never nationalized their telecommunications sectors. The present decade is clearly marked by increased liberalization and privatization of this sector, a trend that, fueled by accelerating technological innovation, is bound to spread even further.

These examples from the water, energy, transport, and telecommunications sectors illustrate that private participation in infrastructure is hardly a new phenomenon. Many public enterprises that have recently been privatized or that are up for privatization were, in fact, initially private. Infrastructure sectors that are now being opened up to competition often started out open to competition and private investment in the nineteenth or early twentieth century. Meanwhile, lessons can be drawn from history to avoid some of the mistakes that were made and that led in many instances to the nationalization of these sectors.

Market Structure, Competition, and Divestiture

After a brief general discussion of the need to rethink the infrastructure sectors by unbundling them, and of the use of yardstick or benchmark competition as a regulatory tool, this section examines how competition and private participation have been introduced in the water, energy, transport, and telecommunications sectors, with a particular emphasis on recent experience in reforming telecommunications. As Yarrow 1986 pointed out ten years ago, "such structural reforms should be evaluated and decided *before* any final decisions are taken on the ownership question: it is easier to change the framework of competition and regulation before privatization" (p. 364).

Unbundling a Sector

Privatizing a major public infrastructure monopoly is tantamount to privatizing the sector in which it operates. Strategic and policy issues should take precedence over the more transactional aspects of the privatization. Every infrastructure reform strategy should rest on a thorough analysis of the existing and potential market structures and the extent to which competition can and should be introduced; the costs and benefits of a breakup of the existing monopoly also must be assessed. The benefits will derive mainly from competition (direct and indirect). The costs may include transition costs, higher transaction costs, and coordination costs (in particular, more complicated network planning, more difficult technical standardization, thorny conflicts between participants, and so on). One will need to determine whether the advantages of a more competitive system—investments, quality, price, choice, satisfaction of demand, and so on—outweigh these costs. Similarly, advantages deriving from economies of scale generated by a monopolistic sector structure will need to be weighed against cost of inefficiency caused by lack of competition and bureaucratic inertia (see World Bank 1994c; Kessides 1993).

To determine those costs and benefits, it may be useful to break a sector or an enterprise down into its component parts to examine which activities are essentially monopolistic and which are of a competitive nature. Unbundling can be done through vertical separation, which refers to a breakup in the production chain between upstream and downstream activities, or between infrastructure and services. In the power sector, such unbundling translates into three or more distinct activities, namely generation, transmission, and distribution (as well as supply). In railways, it may lead to a separation in responsibility between track and transport services. Unbundling can also take the form of horizontal separation, which results from dividing a single activity of the incumbent monopolist, say, power generation or distribution, into separate companies, which may either compete directly in the market (as is increasingly the case in power generation) or retain a geographic monopoly and compete only indirectly (as is mostly the case for power distribution).[12]

---

12. Where the power sector is broken up into generation, transmission, and distribution components, there is usually no direct competition for customers, though distribution companies would normally compete against each other in buying power from generators or intermediaries. Where competition is expanded to reach customers, as is already the case in the United Kingdom for large customers and soon for all customers, the distribution company becomes in effect a downstream transporter of power with the obligation to supply power provided by any other source. In such instances, supply becomes a fourth distinct component of the unbundled sector.

The unbundling of infrastructure activities is presented in figure 7.1. It provides a highly simplified view of sectoral situations which may vary substantially in space and in time. The table's grid structure forces the classification of every activity into one of four boxes, but some activities may shift to different places within the grid or overlap two boxes, depending on the specific circumstances of the market or country. Thus, long-distance communications is competitive in nature, whether analyzed from the standpoint of the physical infrastructure or the service. Electric power generation will often be monopolistic in a small market and competitive in a large one. Solid waste collection (not included in the table) is basically a transport service and therefore has competitive elements, but it also has strong economies of contiguity which give it monopolistic characteristics. Specific circumstances and policy preferences must determine whether a single provider or multiple providers should serve a given area; in view of limited economies of scale in waste collection, most cities can, however, be divided into zones served by companies competing for the right to provide the service.

As figure 7.1 illustrates, physical infrastructures tend to have monopolistic characteristics, and services competitive ones.[13] To the extent that infrastructure and services can effectively be unbundled or separated, this analysis opens the door to solutions that otherwise may not have been identified. Indeed, the monopolistic characteristics that typically derive from the high sunk costs (fixed investment costs) of infrastructure do not necessarily carry over to the use of the infrastructure, that is, to services. For example, whereas telephone and electricity distribution or rail networks may have strong monopolistic characteristics, their use may be organized on a competitive basis.

The figure also suggests that where there is competition in the market, government intervention can be limited to ensuring that the market functions properly. This is typically done through provisions governing compliance with competition rules and technical standards. On the other hand, where the monopolistic element predominates, the government will have to choose between public and private supply of the service. By considering the private route, the government introduces the possibility of organizing competition not *in* the market but *for* the market through competitive bidding.[14] A private takeover (and, where an incumbent SOE is allowed to bid for the contract, the simple threat of such takeover) may yield significant improvements in productivity, among other benefits. Consumers will benefit from this competition for the market, especially where the lowest service price or tariff governs the selection of the operator. Where selection is based on the price the operator is prepared to pay the government for the right to provide the service (through a concession

13. See also World Bank 1994c, fig. 3.1, p. 62, and tables 6.3 and 6.4, pp. 126–27. For a cross-country overview of market structure in the power, gas, railways, telecommunications, and water sectors, see Gray 1996. For a literature survey on privatization, deregulation, and competition in infrastructure sectors, see Kwoka 1996.

14. For an analysis of the concept of competition for the market as opposed to competition in the market, see Chadwick 1859. On competition in network industries, see Klein 1996.

Figure 7.1   Unbundling Sectors into Their Component Activities

	Competitive components	*Monopolistic components*
Physical infrastructure	Power stations Wireless and long-distance networks Warehouses, terminals	Power transmission and distribution Water transport and distribution Roads, rail track Port quays and channels Airport runways
Service	Telecommunication services Passenger and freight transportation (all modes) Stevedoring, handling Equipment supply	Port or river dredging Traffic safety (all modes)
Market options	Normally private Competition in the market No special regulation	Choice between private and public Competition for the market Detailed regulation

or license fee or divestiture proceeds, for example), competition for the market transfers these monopoly rents (or part of them) from the monopoly holder to the public authority. A well-structured bidding process should allow existing or expected monopoly rents to be extracted right from the start.[15]

Yardstick Competition

Unbundling the provision of monopolistic services horizontally among different regional companies multiplies sources of information on the sector, new technologies, and ways of reducing operating costs. The regulator can thus control the operations of the regulated enterprises more effectively and benchmark one operator's performance against that of others. Unbundling may help to leverage additional financial and human resources, diversify technological and managerial approaches, and spread risk. It may also make it easier to enforce bankruptcy against a defaulting public service provider, because other national companies with relevant expertise could easily take over operations.

Argentina, which together with Chile and the United Kingdom has been at the forefront of infrastructure reform, used this technique in several sectors. In addition to introducing competition in the market where it was deemed feasible, Argentines decided also to break up existing monopolies on a geographic basis to create benchmark (or "yardstick") competition in most infra-

15. Competitive tenders or auctions do not, however, preclude the need for future regulation to address developments in the sector, behavior of the monopolist, other unforeseen events, or the enforcement of the terms of the concession or licenses. Activities or market segments run on a monopoly basis should in particular be subject to regulation, regardless of whether the services are provided by a public or a private enterprise. See the section in this chapter on the regulatory framework.

structure sectors. In the telecommunications sector, for instance, it was decided that direct competition should not be introduced immediately for basic telephone services previously provided by ENTEL. ENTEL was split between two geographic areas (north and south, with Buenos Aires divided into two zones), served by two separate privatized companies.[16] Although direct competition is (initially) not authorized for basic services, this geographic division allows the regulator and the public to compare the performances of the two companies and exert pressure on the less efficient operator. The same principle was applied to power and gas distribution companies.

It had also been envisaged for the water supply sector, with the city of Buenos Aires to be divided into two areas for which separate concessions would be awarded to different consortia.[17] The idea had to be abandoned, however, owing to the technical difficulty of separating the two existing interconnected networks and the delays in the privatization process that would have resulted. Nevertheless, comparison is still possible between the private management performances of Aguas Argentinas (the concessionaire for the Greater Buenos Aires) and the water companies of Argentina's other cities, as well as with international norms.

Structural Reforms in the Water Sector

Water is probably the most monopolistic of all infrastructure sectors, which does not in itself imply that structural reforms have no role to play. There is no general consensus, however, about what the right structure may be with respect to unbundling water production, transport, distribution, treatment, and sanitation services (sewerage network and treatment plants). Nor is there a consensus on broader issues of water management and pricing.[18] In some cases a single enterprise handles all these services; in others, different enterprises are in charge of different segments. Where different providers operate in the same

16. Four companies succeeded ENTEL: Telecom for the northern network and Telefónica de Argentina for the southern network, each enjoying a temporary monopoly; and two companies held jointly by Telecom and Telefónica—Telintar for international telecommunications, which also enjoys a temporary monopoly, and another company for the supply of value-added services operating in competition with other operators. See also notes 52, 53, and 73.

17. Note that in Paris water distribution is divided into two zones for which lease (*affermage*) contracts were awarded to different private companies: the Left Bank network is run by SPE, a subsidiary of Lyonnaise des Eaux-Dumez, and the Right Bank network by CEP, a subsidiary of Compagnie Générale des Eaux. The two networks are interconnected and transfers between them are metered and billed accordingly.

18. See, for example, Hunt and Lynk 1995, who looked at the separation of the production and regulatory functions of the regional water authorities before privatization. Production functions were privatized and a national Rivers Authority was established "to oversee water resource management, controlling both pollution and abstraction." The authors conclude that the lost economies of scope between the regulatory and production functions are considerable, perhaps even higher than the dynamic efficiency gains achievable under a privatized water industry. On water privatization, see also Bhattacharyya, Parker, and Raffiee 1994; Ogden 1994; Spulber and Sabbaghi 1994; Idelovitch and Ringskog 1995; Rivera 1996.

market, as may be the case for water treatment plants, they rarely compete directly for business; instead, they tend to be linked by long-term contracts with the water utility. So even though there may be a multiplicity of companies operating in the sector, those companies usually do not compete directly in the market. Competition does exist in the award of contracts, however, and yardstick competition can also be fostered, as discussed above.

In the United Kingdom, private water supply companies existed before the 1989 privatization of the ten regional water companies of England and Wales; these smaller companies were called statutory water companies. The 1989 privatization was preceded by far-reaching restructuring that gave rise to independent, regional companies for water and sanitation.[19] The price regime put in place was a variation of the price cap formula used in telecommunications.[20] Water utilities were allowed to increase their rates by more than the rate of inflation, so that they could make the huge investments required to upgrade capacity and bring water and sanitation quality up to the standards set by the European Commission directives on drinking water quality, bathing beaches, and urban waste water treatment. Water prices therefore rose sharply in the first five years following privatization. At the 1996 review, however, OFWAT (the regulator) imposed tighter price caps. Also noteworthy is the authorization that OFWAT granted in 1996 to Anglian Water to supply water to a customer outside its geographic area, in what amounts to the first major dent in the monopoly of a water company.[21]

19. The water act of 1989 enabled privatization and established OFWAT (the Office of Water Services), headed by the director general of water services. Further regulation of the industry is found in the licenses, or "instruments of appointment," issued to each company ("undertaker"). See also the water industry act of 1991 for economic regulation, and the water resources act of 1991 on the National Rivers Authority (for details, see Armstrong, Cowan, and Vickers 1994).

20. The tariff formula is described as RPI + K, where RPI is the retail price index and K the allowable price increase above inflation; the net allowable increase is a reflection of the required new capital investments minus the productivity improvements to be achieved by the operator. "The K-factors for the privatized . . . Water and Sewerage Companies vary between 3 percent for Yorkshire to between 6.5 percent to 11.5 percent for South West, and for the water only (previously statutory) companies, between 3 percent for York to 22.5 percent for Tendring. The K-factors for the Water and Sewerage Companies are lower on average than for the Water Companies due to the capital restructuring undertaken by the Government at privatisation. Generally this consisted of cash injections which enabled the companies capital expenditure programmes to be funded with smaller tariff increases. Since the Water Companies were already in the private sector this rendered capital restructuring infeasible. The Government, therefore, granted higher K-factors. The K-factors were set initially for ten years with a five year periodic review in 1994. There is also provision for interim determinations or reviews on K on an annual basis where significant deviations of the companies capital programmes from those expected occurs. The results of these determinations may involve either clawback of allowance or additional passing through of unavoidable costs" (Hunt and Lynk 1995, p. 374).

21. Anglian Water would be allowed to supply a chicken farm currently served by neighboring Essex and Suffolk Water. This would require construction of a pipe three miles long. Authority was granted under the inset appointment scheme, which was designed to foster competition between water companies for large users, namely, those using over 250 megaliters of water per year. See *Financial Times*, 17 June 1996.

In 1993, after an international competitive bidding process, Argentine authorities privatized the Buenos Aires water supply company.[22] Five international consortia, each headed by a strong European water operator, were prequalified. Two of them joined forces, and four bids were eventually received. The consortium led by Lyonnaise des Eaux, having bid a price 27 percent below the tariff charged by the former SOE, was awarded the contract. All water supply and sanitation assets of Greater Buenos Aires were transferred to Aguas Argentinas, the concessionaire company formed by the winning consortium; Aguas Argentinas holds a concession for thirty years, after which the sectors, including the new investments made by the private operator, would revert to the owner, the Argentine government (see Idelovitch and Ringskog 1995).

Structural Reforms in the Energy Sector

Unbundling of the sector, introduction of competition, and privatization have become common in electricity as well as gas.

Electricity. To instill competition, mobilize private capital, and take advantage of recent technological advances, many countries have decided to unbundle the power sector.[23] Recent international experience has demonstrated that it is possible to introduce competition in the market, especially on the generation side. In other segments—distribution in particular—the case for natural monopoly may appear stronger, though competition can be introduced by separating the commercial (selling) function from the wire or transport business. This is illustrated by the still unfolding liberalization program in the United Kingdom, which should result in competition in all segments of the electricity markets except for the wire business, as well as by experiments in New Zealand and elsewhere.

In the United Kingdom, privatization of the power sector in the early 1990s was preceded by sectoral restructuring that led to new, independent companies.[24] Different privatization formulas were applied in Scotland, Northern

22. See Decree 1443/91, which authorized the concession scheme and schedule, and Decree 2408/91, which adjusted the schedule.

23. Technological innovations include efficient medium-capacity turbines (particularly combined-cycle gas turbines), which allow plant standardization and reduce risks and economies of scale in power generation and thereby make it easier for independent producers to enter the sector. Moreover, advances in computing power and data processing—which facilitate the dispatch of electricity across the network and vertical separation of the electric power industry—and in metrology (more sensitive and efficient meters) make the electricity distribution sector more attractive to private operators. On power sector reform, see Tenenbaum, Lock, and Barker 1992; Covarrubias and Maia 1994; Newbery 1994; Ruff 1994; Bacon 1995; Gray 1995. See also table 7.1.

24. The electricity act of 1989 enabled privatization and competition in the sector; it also established the post of director general of electricity supply, heading the office of electricity regulation (OFFER).

Ireland, and England and Wales. The need for differentiated approaches stemmed mainly from the distinct characteristics of those networks.

In England and Wales, the former Central Electricity Generating Board and Area Distribution Companies were restructured into a National Grid Company (NGC), two power generation companies (National Power and PowerGen), and twelve regional electricity companies (RECs). The RECs were privatized in December 1990 and the generators in March 1991 (with a second tranche of 40 percent sold in March 1995). Shares in NGC were initially handed over to the RECs, which later divested them through a public flotation raising about $6 billion (NGC had been valued in 1990 at about $1.5 billion, or a quarter of the sale price five years later).

Breaking up generation into only two large private companies controlling nearly 90 percent of generating capacity (the next largest producer being British Energy, the nuclear producer privatized in 1996) has not introduced sufficient competition in the market. Because he considered prices to be excessively high, the director general of electricity supply has been trying to boost competition in power generation in England and Wales.[25] In his 1995 five-year review, the regulator imposed a one-time reduction of 11 to 17 percent in electricity distribution prices (the percentage varied according to the circumstances of each REC), while limiting future increases to 2 percentage points below the inflation rate.[26]

Full competition is being introduced gradually to the British power market. It started with competition to supply the pool, then expanded to compe-

25. In fact, an increase of over 20 percent in the "pool" price (the pool being the market mechanism where supply and demand are equalized) was largely responsible for an investigation by the regulator, which culminated in February 1994 with an agreement under which National Power and PowerGen would sell or divest some capacity and accept price controls. In return, the regulator would not refer the two companies to the Monopolies and Mergers Commission (MMC). In particular, National Power and PowerGen undertook to sell or divest power stations equivalent to a capacity of 6000 megawatts (approximately 10 percent of installed capacity in England and Wales) and to reduce their selling price to the pool by 7 percent for a period of two years, which ended on April 1, 1996. Many observers felt that these concessions were unlikely to be sufficient to create a true competitive market. Since the producer price caps have just ended, it is still too early to evaluate the impact of this agreement on competition in the market. However, during the time that "voluntary" price caps were in effect, the market saw substantial price volatility, which the regulator cites as evidence of the market power exercised by the two generators. Recent attempts at vertical integration by National Power and PowerGen through the proposed takeovers of, respectively, Southern Electric and Midlands Electricity has raised additional concerns about the degree of competition in the U.K. power generation market. The MMC did recommend that the proposed transactions be cleared, largely on the basis that they would help British firms compete abroad, but the government (wisely) decided on April 24, 1996, to block these mergers. Such mergers would have abolished the separation between major generation and distribution companies decided upon at privatization, made the regulator's job much more difficult, and threatened already weak competition. See *Financial Times*, 12–13 February, 14 February, 17 February, 4 March, 26 April, all in 1994, and 25 April 1996; see also *Journal of Commerce*, 16 December 1993; *Energy Utilities*, April 1996; and the section in this chapter on the regulatory framework.

26. This decision became extremely controversial, because it overrode an earlier announcement on future price caps, to which the stock exchange had reacted favorably, by considerably

tition to supply very large customers, and later to medium-sized customers and, as of 1998, all retail customers.[27]

These broad reforms were implemented only in England and Wales. Scottish Power was privatized in 1991 as a vertically integrated company. Because Northern Ireland's network was not interconnected and was deemed to be too small to justify reforms of the type applied in England and Wales, it was decided not to separate transmission and distribution. Privatization of power generation was effected by the sale of power stations to investor consortia (and not by public flotation to the general public); the power stations privatized in this way rely on long-term power purchase agreements rather than on the short-term pool system of England and Wales.

In Argentina, the power sector was restructured radically in 1992 by separating generating, transmission, and distribution activities and organizing them under separate companies.[28] The generating capacity of the federally-owned enterprises was shared among some 20 new companies, which were sold to competing private groups. These power generators, as well as new entrants, now compete vigorously in selling electricity. In fact, the transfer of (often poorly maintained) existing power stations to private investors led to very quick improvements in efficiency and to a shift from excess demand to excess capacity. In addition, open entry allowed other investors to build new gas-fired plants close to Argentina's gas fields, providing even greater competition in the power supply market. As a result, wholesale electricity prices dropped substantially before stabilizing at a level 40 percent lower than at the time of privatization.

Argentina has a competitive wholesale spot market for power administered by Cammesa, a nonprofit entity controlled by the government, the power companies, and major users. Large users (initially those who used over 5 megawatts, since lowered to 1 megawatt, and then to 0.1 megawatt) are allowed to bypass the distributors and contract directly for their power

---

tightening the caps. The positive reaction of the markets, as well as information the regulator uncovered that had been withheld by some of the companies, contributed to the tightening. The shares of the RECs dropped by 23 percent following the final decision, and those of the private generators by 4 percent. Part of the controversy arose from the timing of the decision, which fell only one day after the state had sold its remaining shareholdings in National Power and Power-Gen through a public flotation. See also box 7.4.

27. Until March 1994, only about 5,000 customers with a peak demand in excess of 1 megawatt had access to the competitive market; this represented about 30 percent of electricity consumption. The limit was dropped from April 1994 to 100 kilowatts, adding about 50,000 new customers to the market, or about 20 percent of total demand. All customers would join the competitive market in 1998. However, "the timetable for introducing competition into Britain's domestic electricity market in 1998 is being threatened by a dispute over who should meet the estimated £300m ($474m) bill for new computer systems" required to manage the extension of competition to all 22 million domestic customers (*Financial Times*, 13 November 1995).

28. See Law no. 24065 of January 1992 on electricity and Decree 1398/92 (regulation). See also *Wall Street Journal*, 19 June 1996.

needs. Transmission companies earn a fixed fee for power transported. The concession for the high-voltage transmission network covering 14 of Argentina's 24 provinces was assigned on a monopoly basis to a new privatized company (Transener), and five smaller transmission companies were further divested in 1993. Distribution is provided by companies with a regional monopoly, some of which, including Edelnor and Edelsur, distributors to Greater Buenos Aires, were also privatized in 1992 under 95-year concessions. Several provincial power companies have since been sold off as well. Retail tariffs are subject to a price cap formula. The Argentine experience has, by and large, been more profitable for distributors than for producers.

Hungary opted to unbundle its power sector into seven nonnuclear power generation companies, whose privatization was initiated at the end of 1995; a transmission company (MVM), which also operates the country's only nuclear plant and is slated for privatization in 1997; and six distribution companies privatized in late 1995.[29]

International experience, as illustrated above, indicates that governments must carefully study how to open up the power sector to private investors. Should they, for example, separate generation, transmission, and distribution and privatize them separately? If so, should they prohibit any company or group from controlling more than one of these market segments, as the Argentine and Peruvian authorities have done?[30] Or should shareholdings be authorized in more than one segment, as is the case in Belgium, Chile, and to a lesser extent England and Wales?[31] Or should governments limit

29. The electricity privatization drive at the end of 1995 was only partly successful. The process was marked by tight timetables, last-minute changes in tender conditions, disagreements with local governments on their rights in these companies, as well as ambiguities in the license or concession terms and conditions and in the overall regulatory framework; all these factors contributed to lackluster demand and postaward litigation. Five of the seven generating companies found no responsive bidders, partly as a result of the government's insistence of linking their sale with that of coal mines and of regulatory uncertainty. The sale in 1995 of a 24 percent stake in MVM was subsequently canceled by APV RT (the privatization agency) and its privatization had to be postponed to 1996 and later to 1997 because of continuing uncertainty regarding key regulatory issues (pricing, in particular) and delays in adopting a law on nuclear electricity.

30. See articles 30 to 33 of the Argentine electricity Law no. 24065. Article 122 of Peruvian Decree-Law no. 25844 on electric concessions of November 1992 stipulates that generation, transmission, and distribution activities cannot be exercised at the same time by the same person or company, with the exception of specific cases provided in the law.

31. *Belgium:* The power sector has always been predominantly private. One company (Tractebel and its affiliate Electrabel), though not protected by a legal monopoly, supplies 92 percent of generation, controls the transmission network, and is a major shareholder (together with municipalities) in many distribution companies, which are usually managed by Electrabel. In addition, Tractebel has a joint venture with SPE, the second largest generator, a municipally owned company supplying about 5 percent of power. The European Commission has raised concerns about the lack of competition in the Belgian power market, in particular about Electrabel's practice of offering the municipal (or jointly owned) distribution companies shares in Electrabel in exchange for extensions of up to 30 years of their almost exclusive power supply contracts with Electrabel.

competition and maintain more vertical integration? This may be done by divesting the existing SOE with its monopoly, as was the case in eastern Germany.[32] Vertical integration is also maintained by limiting the role of new private power companies to supplying the national utility, as China, Malaysia, Thailand, and other Asian countries are doing.[33]

Or, conversely, should the priority be to expose the sector to new entry and competition or to divest? Norway, for example, has a competitive power market, though Statkraft, the largest generator, remains state owned; Statnett was established as a separate state-owned transmission company owning and operating the grid and operating the pool system. In New Zealand, the distribution market was deregulated and competition allowed in 1992. In 1995–96 the state-owned ECNZ was split up into a transmission company (Transpower) and two generating companies, all state-owned. Prices have

---

The competition commissioner wrote the company that he had serious concerns that this would prevent the entry of new competitors in the market and he requested that they submit modifications to these contracts within one month. See *Financial Times*, 12 March 1996 and 4 June 1996.

Chile: The holding company Enersis controls the main distribution companies (particularly Chilectra) and the major generating company, Endesa (which accounts for about 65 percent of installed capacity), which itself controls the central Chile transmission company. This situation, together with the weakness of the regulatory framework, creates conflicts of interest and discourages new companies from entering the sector. It has also led to lawsuits between electric power-generating companies. See Bitran and Serra 1994.

England and Wales: The regional electricity distribution companies were the shareholders of the transmission company until 1995, when the latter was listed separately and floated on the stock exchange. This demerger was decided for corporate financial reasons, not regulatory ones. On the other hand, the attempted takeover of RECs by National Power and PowerGen was blocked by the government, despite endorsement of the MMC (see note 25 above). In 1995, however, Scottish Power, a vertically integrated company supplying a limited amount of electricity to the English market, was allowed by the government to take over an English REC (Manweb) without prior referral to the MMC, which had been recommended by the regulator. See *Financial Times*, 13–14 April 1996.

32. The privatization in 1994 of the East German power sector came in for sharp criticism on this score; the public sector's monopoly was shifted to the private sector, thereby enlarging the area of domination of the private West German power utilities instead of breaking up the sector and introducing competition. In 1996 the German federal cartel office (competition commission) urged the government to press ahead with liberalization, and, referring to the power utilities that are positioning themselves for the liberalization of the telecommunications market, the commission stressed that competition in the German telecommunications market would be effective only if companies such as RWE, VEBA, and VIAG no longer had regional electricity monopolies. In March 1996 the federal cartel office ruled against a contract giving RWE the exclusivity to supply power to Nordhorn, a town in Lower Saxony, and in so doing threatened to undermine the local monopolies that have prevailed in Germany for the last 50 years. The German utility companies and municipalities fear that deregulation would dent the monopolies and privileges they enjoy in energy distribution; municipalities get handsome fees from the utilities in exchange for long-term exclusive supply contracts. See *Financial Times*, 31 January 1996 and 5 March 1996.

33. In these cases, although there is new private entry, there is neither divestiture nor real competition among operators. Instead, independent power producers supply the (public) utility based on long-term power purchase agreements; in effect, the private generators are subcontractors of the utility company, which retains its monopoly.

been deregulated and legal restrictions to entry and competition in all seg-ments of the power sector have been removed. Limited divestitures of power stations were scheduled starting in 1996; some distribution compa-nies had already merged, opened up their capital, or been taken over by pri-vate companies.

Issues of sequencing also arise. Australia, Peru, and the United Kingdom have, for example, privatized distribution first and generation soon thereaf-ter, whereas other countries have started with generation (Bolivia, for exam-ple) or have managed both processes simultaneously (as in Argentina and Hungary).[34] Finally, specific characteristics of a power system, in particular its size, may influence the choice of market structure; in a small system, for example, unbundling the sector and introducing competition may not be an efficient solution (see Bacon 1995).

The current trend is clearly toward unbundling and greater competition, although vested interests in many parts of the world are trying to block or delay this transition. As competition moves from the generation side to the wholesale or even retail side, issues of third-party access will more and more come to the front. Where an integrated public (or private) enterprise still controls the network, access rules are needed to force it to allow third parties to transmit electricity from a producer to a consumer over its grid and to stop it from charging exorbitant, deterrent rates for such access or engaging in other anticompetitive practices.

The successive reform proposals tabled by the European Commission for the domestic gas and electricity markets since 1989 illustrate the current debate rather well. In the power sector, the objective of the reforms was to liberalize the sector, notably by separating generation, transmission, and distribution activities and granting large consumers the right to buy their power from the suppliers of their choice (the grid company would be obli-gated to provide access to the network). These proposals have been met with strong opposition, especially from the French government and its state-owned, vertically integrated monopoly (EDF), which insisted on restricting cross-border electricity trade within the European Union by channeling all transactions through a single national grid company. To overcome this opposition, the commission threatened to use its special powers to fight monopoly abuses. On the other hand, faced with worsening international competitiveness conditions, European industrialists, German ones in partic-ular, were pushing to liberalize the energy markets; European energy costs

34. The United Kingdom first sold the 12 RECs in 1990 before selling National Power and Power-Gen in 1991. Similarly, the government of the state of Victoria in Australia decided to first priva-tize its distribution companies. The state "stunned financial markets by raising A$8.4 billion (US$6.2 billion) from the sale of its five regional power distribution authorities over just four months" in the second half of 1995 (*Privatisation International*, December 1995). Two large genera-tors were sold in 1996, raising another US$3.8 billion. Competition is to be introduced gradually, starting immediately with the state's 50 largest power users; by 2000 it should reach all residential customers. See also *Financial Times*, 8 November 1995; *Privatisation International*, September 1995.

are, indeed, estimated to be about 40 percent higher than in the United States (see *Journal of Commerce*, 18 January 1996). In June 1996 an agreement was finally reached requiring a gradual opening of the power markets of member states, while leaving each country the choice between a competitive third-party access model and a single-buyer model under which cross-border contracts would have to be concluded with the national monopoly transmission company (vertically integrated monopolies would be required to unbundle their activities into separate generation, transmission, and distribution businesses).

It is becoming more and more difficult for established SOEs to defend the concept of public monopoly, especially when the public operator is unable to meet the demand, as is the case in many developing countries, and third parties (industrialists, for example) are ready to contract with independent power producers on mutually agreed terms. Similarly, the transition of the power sector from what was seen as a natural monopoly into an increasingly competitive and market-driven field undermines those who try to oppose private power deals; the pretext that the price of private electricity may be higher than a long-run marginal cost estimated by some national planning agency no longer holds water.

Gas. The trend in gas is also clearly toward unbundling, privatization, and, to a lesser extent, competition. British Gas was privatized in 1986 with only a limited upfront attempt to establish a competitive sector, however.[35] This has produced several referrals to the Monopolies and Mergers Commission and regulator decisions. Postprivatization regulatory pressure has fostered greater competition and lower prices (a reduction of more than 20 percent in real terms since the privatization of British Gas). The culmination of these protracted battles between the company, its regulator, the MMC, and the government was the government's decision to allow full competition in the gas market by 1998, and the decision of British Gas in February 1996 to split itself into two companies, separating its trading business from its pipeline, exploration, and international activities.[36]

35. The gas act of 1986 enabled privatization and established OFGAS (the office of gas supply), which is headed by the director general of gas supply, and the Gas Consumers' Council. Yarrow 1986 noted that "the most worrying case is that of British Telecom and the projected privatization of British Gas where little thought has been given to limiting the abuse of monopoly power. Rather the regulatory environment has been tailored to the needs of the existing management and to ensuring a successful share flotation" (p. 323). The competition and service (utilities) act of 1992 rectified the absence of any requirement to promote competition in the gas market. See, for further details, Armstrong, Cowan, and Vickers 1994.

36. The 1988 MMC report found that British Gas was practicing extensive discrimination; it led to the opening of the industrial market to new competitors. The 1991 Office of Fair Trading Gas Review concluded that the remedies implemented after the 1988 MMC report had been ineffective at introducing competition. The 1993 MMC report concluded that self-sustaining competition required complete separation between trading and transportation and recommended the end of British Gas' domestic monopoly by 2002. The government did not follow these recommendations.

(continued on the following page)

In Belgium and Russia, privatization has not yet been accompanied by unbundling or greater competition. The Belgian natural gas transport and distribution network was developed by the state through Distrigaz, a joint venture with Tractebel (a private energy and public services company); in 1994 the state sold its 50 percent share, giving Tractebel full control over the company.[37] Gazprom was also privatized in 1994 and managed—pursuant to a special 1992 order of President Yeltsin—to escape breakup, the fate of most other huge Russian monopolies; it remains a vertically integrated company, from exploration all the way to distribution, and has been described as a state within the state.[38]

Argentina and Hungary, on the other hand, have chosen to unbundle the sector before privatization. Argentina split its national monopoly SOE, Gas del Estado, into two transportation companies (one serving northern, the other southern, Argentina) and eight distribution companies, which were privatized in 1992.[39] Hungary sold five regional gas distribution companies

---

(continued)

Instead, it decided that full competition had to be introduced by 1998 and that the company, rather than break up, had to introduce an internal separation between its trading and pipeline businesses. The company's decision to break up was in part motivated by the hope that this action would reduce the regulatory pressure it was facing and place it in a better competitive position. As a result of new entry and competition in the industrial market, the market share of British Gas had fallen to 35 percent by 1995. See *Financial Times*, 6 February 1996; Armstrong, Cowan, and Vickers 1994.

37. In September 1994 the Belgian government sold SNI (the state-owned holding company, which held the government's 50 percent participation in Distrigaz) to a consortium that included a financial holding company and Tractebel, the private joint-venture partner in Distrigaz; the understanding was that this participation would be transferred from the consortium to Tractebel, which in turn would be obligated to transfer part of this stake to the intercommunal gas companies (the local distribution companies, some of which are owned by the municipalities only, others in joint venture with Tractebel) and to float 16.6 percent of Distrigaz on the stock exchange. This transaction has been criticized for its complexity and lack of transparency. See Vincent 1995, pp. 9–11.

38. About 35 percent of the shares were auctioned as part of the voucher privatization program, 15 percent were sold for a song to Gazprom employees, and 10 percent were bought by Gazprom, primarily to be sold by management to foreign investors. After earlier failed attempts, about 9 percent was to be sold to foreign investors in late 1996, while the remaining 1 percent held by the company was being floated on the Russian market to establish a benchmark price for the planned international offering. As Gazprom had kept the right to veto secondary resale of its shares, it was one of the least liquid Russian stocks. The rest of the shares remain state property until at least 1999. Gazprom profits amount to over $6 billion a year, on revenues of $20 to $25 billion. It controls over a third of the world's known gas reserves and supplies over half of Russia's hard currency reserves. The privileges granted to Gazprom and its management are attributed by many observers to the fact that the Russian prime minister, Victor Chernomyrdin, used to head the company. See *Wall Street Journal*, 5 March 1996; *Financial Times*, 5 September 1996.

39. See Law no. 24076 on the privatization of Gas del Estado and articles 2 and 3 of Decree no. 1189/92 of July 1992. The decree established the new companies, transferred the assets to these companies, and defined the sale process. Decree no. 1738/92 (as amended by decree no. 2255/92) regulates transportation and distribution of natural gas as a public service, prices, import-export, enforcement authority, and general policy principles applicable to the privatized companies. Decree nos. 2451–2460 of 1992 set the service conditions for gas distribution, including tariffs. Decree no. 1186/93 provides measures to secure free competition in the marketing of natural gas. The gas exploration and production business was already separate and part of YPF, the hydrocarbons company privatized in 1993.

to separate groups of investors in late 1995, as well as a stake in MOL, the national oil and gas company.

These and other issues of market structure and competition need to be addressed in any privatization program dealing with the energy sector. The options that are chosen will be reflected in the privatization legislation, license and concession terms, and other privatization agreements.

Structural Reforms in the Transport Sector

Technology is driving change in the transport sector, too. Multimodal transport, containerization of shipments, and innovations in telemetry and signaling are all having a profound impact on the organization of the transport sector. Furthermore, the competition that a transport operator faces often comes more from another mode of transportation than from a competitor in the same subsector. In tollroad concessions, it is not uncommon to see restrictions imposed on the construction of roads that could compete with the tollroad, as well as clauses dealing with competition from other modes (rail subsidies, for example). Railways face strong competition from trucking, as the deregulation of the rail and trucking industries in the United States following the Staggers Act and the Motor Carrier Act (both of 1980) clearly demonstrated.

Rail. The considerable advances made in the field of telemetry and signaling are radically transforming the organization and management methods for railway companies by allowing them, in particular, to substantially reduce their fixed investments through greater use of single-track lines, which in turn reduces the size of sunk costs and the monopolistic characteristics of the sector. They make it possible to keep track of a shipment when it moves from boat to train or truck, facilitating intermodal transport and just-in-time management.

In only a few countries is there effective competition between railway companies, but they compete almost everywhere with road, waterway, sea, and air carriers.[40] Canada, the United States, and a few other countries do have competing railway lines.[41] In the United Kingdom, however, the object of the ambitious (and controversial) privatization program launched by the railways act of 1993 is to create competition between railway carriers, notably by separating infrastructure from transportation

40. For further reading on railway reform and privatization, see Kopicki and Thompson 1995; Cavana 1995; Eichengreen 1995; Kessides and Willig 1995.

41. There are two major railroads in Canada, the privately owned Canadian Pacific and Canadian National Railways, privatized in November 1995 through a $1.6 billion public offering on the Toronto Exchange. The government has been implementing a parallel, gradual program of deregulation of the railways, reducing subsidies and other forms of protection.

activities.[42] In Sweden also, competition has been introduced for rail services based on the separation of infrastructure and services.

The Argentine government decided to privatize many railway lines to end the enormous losses suffered in this sector, which exceeded $1 billion a year between 1987 and 1990. The sector was radically restructured following a 1989 decree. Concessions were granted on the basis of competitive tendering for most of the potentially profitable services, including five freight networks privatized between 1991 and 1993 and four concessions for the metropolitan Buenos Aires passenger transit service. The latter were awarded to those who submitted the lowest annual operating subsidy to provide the public service stipulated in the concession contracts; concession agreements were signed in January 1994. Many unprofitable lines and activities were closed down or transferred to the provinces, and a large part of the company's real estate and other assets were sold off.[43]

New Zealand's loss-making rail company was sold in 1993 to a consortium of U.S. and New Zealand investors, and it has since returned to profitability. In the same year, Japan sold 62.5 percent of its shares in one of its regional rail companies (East Japan Railways) through a public offering yielding close to $9 billion. Other recent privatizations include railway companies privatized through concessions in Côte d'Ivoire and Burkina Faso (December 1994), Bolivia (November 1995), and Brazil (March 1996). Fepasa, the freight division of the national railways, was privatized in Chile in 1995. In Mexico, a major rail privatization law was enacted in May 1995 and the first tenders for the privatization of lines were launched in 1996.

Ports. In ports, containerization, door-to-door multimodal transport, and the rapid growth of international merchandise trade are among the factors that have forced ports to adapt. Two major institutional models have tradi-

---

42. A new company, Railtrack, owns, operates, and maintains the rail infrastructure (including track and signaling system) and was privatized through a public flotation in May 1996. The three freight companies and the postal carrier were bought by the same consortium led by Wisconsin Central, which paid a monopoly premium; the merger was approved on the basis that road haulage provides adequate competition to rail freight. Passenger services were broken down into 25 franchises, some of which have already been privatized. In addition, British Rail was further broken down into three rolling stock leasing companies, 13 rail infrastructure services companies, several engineering companies, and various other companies, all of which have been or are scheduled to be privatized. British Rail's noncore businesses were sold off separately, including its telecommunications subsidiary privatized in December 1995. In a separate move, the U.K. government awarded a 999-year concession to a consortium to build and operate the channel tunnel rail link with London (see note 70 below).

43. Donaldson and Wagle 1995, p. 43, cite the case of FEPSA, one of the five freight concessions, which was privatized in 1992. FEPSA has a 30-year concession for a 5300 km network. Productivity improvements were considerable following privatization; staff was reduced from 3,000 to 780 for the same freight volume. This renewed competition from rail led the trucking industry to lower its own hauling tariffs by 20 to 30 percent, which clearly benefits consumers. See also Alexander and Corti 1993, pp. 13–14; Kopicki and Thompson 1995, pp. 153–64; and ministry of economy resolutions nos. 1386/92, 1457/92, 68/93, and 69/93 on railway concessions. A railroad commission was established to regulate the sector (see Decree nos. 1863/93 and 455/94).

tionally dominated, namely, the landlord port, where a separate entity—almost always a public-sector entity—is responsible only for the infrastructure and not for services (which may be performed by private or public-sector companies, in competition or not), and service ports, where the port authority is an integrated entity responsible for infrastructure as well as services. Ports are prime candidates for unbundling and introduction of competition; this has clearly been the trend over the last decade.[44]

By separating the responsibility for basic infrastructure (such as piers, quays, and access channels) from service delivery, as landlord ports do, private-sector entry can be encouraged in commercial activities. The private sector can also be put in charge of some major fixed investments, including the construction and operation of container terminals. But the largest efficiency gains will be achieved by opening all or most activities (depending on the characteristics—size, in particular—of the port) to competition. In large ports, competition can be introduced between terminals; towage and cargo handling (stevedoring, warehousing, forwarding, and so on) are fundamentally competitive services.

Airports. Similar forces are at work in other transport sectors, including airports. The successful privatization of British Airports Authority (BAA) in 1987 was the first major airport privatization. It is now being criticized on competition grounds: airports could have been sold separately to stimulate competition, in particular in the London market. Moreover, the airports act of 1986 did not give the civil aviation authority (the regulator) the mandate to promote competition. Competition should in general be encouraged between airports, as well as within an airport, not only for handling, catering, restaurants, duty free shops, and other services but also between terminals.[45]

Privatization can be, and has been, introduced even in activities that are still seen in many countries as basic state functions. Canada, which has forceful policies for overall transport liberalization and privatization, sold its air traffic control system for $1.1 billion to Nav Canada, a nonprofit corporation that on July 1, 1996, took over seven regional air traffic control centers, 44 airport control towers, training facilities, and contracts with over 6,000 employees. Nav Canada is governed by a board that includes representatives from the airline industry, federal government, employee unions, and general aviation, as well as members elected by these representatives. After a two-year

44. Examples of unbundling of port activities or of port privatization can be found in Argentina, Australia, Canada, Colombia, Hong Kong, Malaysia, Mexico, New Zealand, Pakistan, Philippines, Sweden, Thailand, and the United Kingdom (see Baird 1995; Thomas 1994), among other countries.
45. Examples of airport privatization can be found in Austria, Canada, Colombia, Denmark, Greece, Jamaica, Spain, the United Kingdom, and Venezuela. Cameroon, France, Guinea, and Togo all have privately managed airports. For further reading on airport privatization, see Kapur 1995 and Juan 1995. And Argentina, Australia, and Mexico, among other countries, have recently launched ambitious airport privatization programs.

transition period, the federal air transportation tax will gradually be replaced by fees and user charges set by the board of Nav Canada.[46]

In all transport sectors, the first step is to break the monopoly down into its separate components, analyze each component or activity separately, determine which ones are truly of a monopolistic nature, and decide where competition can be introduced and what the effects of that introduction would be.

Structural Reforms in the Telecommunications Sector

The radical reforms that are under way in the telecommunications sector are driven largely by rapid technological innovation, increasing globalization, stiffer competition, and huge capital requirements. These and other forces have led most countries to open their telecommunications sector to competition and private investment and to divest. After an overview of these broad themes, some of these country experiences are examined more closely, starting with the United Kingdom, which set the trend in more than one way, and the European Union, which illustrates how supranational norms may drive the liberalization of this sector. After a discussion of the U.S., Canadian, and New Zealand experiences and a review of the first major telecommunications privatization of the former East bloc (Hungary), this partial review closes with a case study of a smaller country (Venezuela). The influential privatizations carried out by Argentina, Chile (see box 7.1), and Mexico, as well as reforms in other countries, are described elsewhere in this chapter.[47]

Increasing globalization. Recent developments in the telecommunications sector indicate that external factors are now playing a decisive role in setting government policies, leaving national authorities only limited room for maneuver.[48] Technological breakthroughs—new wireless communications (cellular, microwave, radio), worldwide satellite and fiber-optic networks,

---

46. See *Washington Post*, 4 May 1996. This shift was motivated in part by the government's desire to withdraw from operational activities and in part by the large investments that will be required to move air traffic control toward satellite-based guidance systems.

47. *Argentina*: The government raised $214 million in cash and $5 billion in debt securities (face value) for the sale to two consortia of 60 percent of the two successor companies to ENTEL in 1990. In addition, it raised $830 million for 30 percent of Telefónica in a 1991 IPO, and $1.2 billion for 30 percent of Telecom in a 1992 IPO; 10 percent of the shares were reserved for company personnel. See also, in this chapter, notes 16, 52, 53, and 73 and table 7.3.

Mexico: Telmex was privatized in 1990 with a seven-year exclusivity period. The company already had private shareholders before 1990. The government raised about $7.5 billion through the Telmex sale, including nearly $1.8 billion in 1990 for the initial sale of 20.4 percent to the consortium headed by Grupo Carso; $2.4 billion for a public offering of 15.7 percent of the shares in 1991; $1.4 billion for 4.7 percent in 1992; $1 billion for a 3 percent tranche in 1993; and $550 million for convertible bonds relating to 1.5 percent of the shares in 1994. See also notes 76 and 99.

48. For further reading on liberalization and privatization of the telecommunications sector, see Ambrose, Hennemeyer, and Chapon 1990; Berenson 1991; Takano 1992; Chamoux and Stern 1993; Herrera 1993; Hill and Abdala 1993; Levy and Spiller 1993; Smith and Staple 1994; Wellenius and Stern 1994; Galal and others 1994; Parker 1994b; Ramamurti 1996.

expanding Internet access and services, vastly enhanced data compression techniques, and integration of communications and data processing—lead to much lower unit costs, fading of the distinction between voice and data transmission, and, more generally, a move toward highly competitive sector structures.[49] This makes the retention of monopolies increasingly untenable.

These technological advances also underlie the globalization and diversification of the industry. Telephone companies are expanding toward other communications subsectors, such as cable television and data processing. New companies are providing services (cellular and satellite, for example) complementing those furnished by the fixed network. Enterprises from other sectors are entering the telecommunications sector; these include, on the one hand, companies with an existing fixed network that can be used (given certain investments) to transmit communications, such as cable TV operators, power and water companies, and railways; and on the other, media companies and other content providers.[50]

The survival of many telecommunications companies depends in part on international alliances that state-owned enterprises cannot easily form. Such alliances involve cross-shareholdings, designed to ensure their stability, that are difficult to bring about without private incorporation and management style. In addition, companies operating in countries that have already liberalized their telecommunications markets have a clear lead over others in an increasingly competitive international marketplace. Operators that combine a monopolistic situation and state control are thus handicapped from the outset in this race.

Increasing competition. In response to new developments, most countries are opening up their telecommunications sector.[51] They have allowed or will soon allow increased competition through the issue of new wireless licenses, in some cases in competition and in others in collaboration with the fixed-network telecommunications company or companies. The monopoly enjoyed by the dominant companies in value-added services, such as supply of terminals, paging, data services, or e-mail, is coming to an end in most

49. The recent invention of the callback switch has permitted the rapid emergence of companies offering callback services from countries with low international rates (United Kingdom and United States) to users calling from high-rate countries, thereby circumventing the national operator and often forcing it to lower its international rates. Another recently commercialized technology is fixed wireless, which makes it possible to compete with or supplement the local wire network at much lower costs than mobile cellular telephony. PT Ratelindo, an Indonesian company with private majority shareholding, is currently developing such a system in Jakarta.

50. Established companies with existing networks that have entered the telecommunications sector include Energis, the telecommunications subsidiary of the U.K. National Grid company; BR Telecommunications, a British Rail subsidiary privatized in December 1995 (bought by Racal); Télécom Développement, subsidiary of the French railways; DBKom, a subsidiary of Deutsche Bahn (railways), in which Mannesmann took a 49.8 percent share in July 1996; and subsidiaries and joint ventures formed by the German electric utilities RWE, VEBA, and VIAG.

51. See Wellenius and Stern 1994, pp. 587–674, for an analytical overview of the legal and regulatory framework, operator ownership, and level of competition in the telecommunications sector in more than 80 countries.

countries. Even basic wireline local phone service (the local loop), which until recently was considered a natural monopoly, has been opened up to competition in the United Kingdom since 1981, and more recently in Australia, Canada, Chile, New Zealand, and the United States.

To the extent monopolistic conditions or characteristics persist, the introduction of competition must usually be accompanied by special provisions to neutralize the dominant position exercised by the established operator through its control of essential bottleneck facilities. Such provisions will, for example, foster fair access to the network by third parties or force the main operator to lease lines to third parties on reasonable terms and conditions. To be successful, cellular operators or long-distance service providers have to be connected to the principal operator's fixed network; the technical details and the cost of that interconnection often determine the viability of third-party service. Rules need to be in place providing for nondiscriminatory access to the network, which implies in particular that where the dominant operator provides some of its services in competition with other operators, it must grant them such access on the same technical and financial terms and conditions that it applies to its own use of the network.

Whereas full monopolies covering most segments of the market were the rule until recently, the changes outlined above will most likely lead to the abolition of exclusivity rights in telecommunications. As a transition measure, most telecommunications privatizations have, however, granted the privatized dominant operator some type of time-bound exclusivity. Such exclusivity typically covers basic telephone services and is limited to a fixed period, at the end of which the exclusivity expires and competition is authorized. The concept of basic service varies from country to country and may include, in addition to the local wired loop (which is its core), all or part of other voice telecommunications services, particularly long-distance and international communications. Where governments wish to grant temporary protection to basic services, the scope of such services should be defined as narrowly as possible. Furthermore, the dominant operator should be held accountable for meeting minimum targets for providing these protected services; failure to perform could then lead to suspension or early termination of its exclusivity rights. Indeed, the incumbent, dominant operator should not be allowed to keep new entrants from providing services that it does not, or cannot, provide (see Smith and Staple 1994).

The duration of exclusive rights is often shorter than the term for a concession or license, which means that double time limits are imposed: at the end of the first time limit, the monopoly protection is abolished; the second time limit marks the expiration of the concession contract or license itself (unless, of course, the license has been granted in perpetuity). The United Kingdom did not grant an exclusivity period, though BT remained protected until 1991 by a duopoly on basic services. In other countries, exclusivity periods have ranged from five years in Peru, seven to ten years in Argentina (where the license is of indefinite duration), eight years in Hungary (twenty-five-year concession), and nine years in Venezuela (thirty-five-year concession), all the way to twenty-five years in Jamaica, where the concession term and the monopoly period are the same (see the 1988 telephone act).[52] The scope of the monopoly also varies, from the local network only (some local concessions in Hungary) through all basic services (Argentina, Mexico), to all services, including value-added services (Jamaica).

The grant of temporary exclusivity is often explained by the need to rebalance the tariff structure to phase out cross-subsidization of local services by long distance and international services. Such rebalancing, it is argued, has to be done over time to avoid tariff shock and popular opposition to the privatization. If monopoly protection were abolished before tariff restructuring, the dominant operator could not compete with new operators while continuing internal subsidization of local services. The argument is not convincing, however. A similar result could be obtained by adding a premium to the interconnection fees charged to other operators to compensate the dominant operator for money-losing public service obligations; or the state could pay the dominant operator for these services in some fashion. The terms and conditions of interconnection are the crux of the matter. They can be designed to withdraw protection gradually, if that is deemed necessary.

Another reason often cited to justify an exclusivity period is that it is needed to finance the large investments required in many countries; such investments could not be financed as easily, some argue, under a liberalized regime, which would generate uncertainty. Yet again the experience of countries that have liberalized belies the argument; some even fear that competition will lead to overinvestment.

The fact that telecommunications privatizations have been implemented without exclusivity periods or with only limited, timebound ones underscores the fast changes that are occurring in the sector. The exclusivity may be granted not because the sector is monopolistic but because, for political, social, technical, financial, or other considerations, a transition period is thought necessary to bring about changes gradually. The high sale prices fetched in telecommunications privatizations indicate the large size of the monopoly rents resulting from sector regulations.

International experience also illustrates the benefits of competition on prices: "According to the OECD, business tariffs in countries where telephone

52. In Argentina, the monopoly (the exclusivity period) was initially set at only two years, to be automatically extended to seven years when the two companies fulfilled their commitments, which included the implementation of an investment program of about $5 billion and certain service quality standards; the monopoly period could be extended by an additional three years if even higher targets are achieved. The seven-year period expires in November 1997 and many in government would prefer not to grant the extension. Indeed, though the firms may meet their investment and other commitments, tariffs remain very high by international standards and are hampering the competitiveness of the Argentine economy. Meanwhile, competing countries like Chile, where privatization has gone with strong competition in the market (see box 7.1), have seen telephone tariffs plummet and have increased the penetration rate (teledensity) much faster.

service is still monopolised fell by 3.1 percent between 1990 and 1994; but they fell by 8.5 percent in countries that had introduced competition" (*The Economist*, 9 December 1995). In summary, privatizing governments should clearly try to introduce as much competition as possible into the sector, as early as possible, even at the cost of a lower sale price.

Private capital requirements. Most developing and transition countries face huge investment needs stemming from the low density of the existing networks (which are reflected in low market penetration rates and large, unsatisfied demand) and from the rapid economic growth that the more vibrant of these countries are experiencing (with annual GDP growth rates exceeding 10 percent in some cases). Promoting new investments to speed up development of the network is therefore a matter of high priority. The experience of the last few decades demonstrates that the typical monopolistic public enterprise is not up to this challenge.

The privatization of telecommunications companies in Argentina, Hungary, Indonesia, Mexico, Peru, and Venezuela required in each case heavy new investments, together with improvements in service quality and productivity gains.[53] The main purpose of regulation of the sector in such countries should be to foster investment rather than to control prices per se, which may be a more appropriate priority for countries with mature markets and high penetration rates.

Divestiture. The important technological progress achieved in the telecommunications sector, the emergence of dynamic international private operators and major global alliances, and the impressive track record of countries that have liberalized and privatized the sector are leading an increasing number of countries toward privatization. Thus, as box 7.2 and table 7.1 show, in addition to the countries that have always had private telecommunications operators, such as the Philippines and the United States, many countries have recently privatized or partially privatized their telecommunications companies, while others are currently preparing such

---

53. *Argentina*: See article 10.1.8 of Decree no. 62/90, and Decree no. 677/90, as well as the terms and conditions of tender documents for privatizations.

Hungary: Notably, an increase in the line stock by 15.5 percent a year over six years, connection of all applicants within six months by 1997, automation of the entire network, and development of Hungary as a regional telecommunications hub.

Indonesia: Collectively, the five consortia selected to operate basic telecommunications service in five of seven regions under concession-type arrangements had to install 2 million new lines over a four-year period; their contract, signed in October 1995, requires them to meet increasingly tight targets for service quality and performance.

Peru: Notably, investments of the order of $1.5 billion over five years for the purpose of tripling the number of lines in service from the current 630,000 to 1.8 million, and the introduction of telephone service in all villages of over 500 population (see *Financial Times*, 1 March 1994).

Venezuela: See the section below on the privatization of the Venezuelan telephone operator.

Box 7.2   Recent Privatizations in the Telecommunications Sector

In one group of countries, state-owned telecommunications companies have been privatized and control (though not always a majority of shares or even a majority of seats on the board) transferred to the new private owners. These include Argentina, Barbados, Belgium, Belize, Bolivia, Chile, Congo, Cuba, Czech Republic, Denmark, Estonia, Gibraltar, Guinea, Guyana, Hungary, Ireland, Jamaica, Latvia, Mexico, Mongolia, the Netherlands (KPN was the first post and telecommunications company privatized without prior separation of these two activities), New Zealand, Peru, Senegal, Spain, the United Kingdom, and Venezuela (see tables 1 and 2 in the introduction for details on the largest of these transactions carried out between 1991 and 1996). Additional divestitures have pertained to long-distance, international, or satellite communication companies in Australia (Aussat), Canada (Teleglobe and Telesat), Puerto Rico (TLD), South Korea (Daecom), and Yemen (TeleYemen International, in 1971), among other countries, as well as cellular telecommunications companies, notably in South Korea (Korea Mobile Telecom).

In other countries, divestiture of the dominant operator has been partial, with the government continuing to be the controlling shareholder. This was the case with Japanese operator NTT, 35 percent of whose shares were sold in three tranches between 1986 and 1988 for a total of over $70 billion; Telekom Malaysia, with a public flotation of 25 percent of the shares in 1990; Singapore Telecom, where nearly 11 percent of the capital was sold in October 1993; Pakistan Telecommunications Corporation, for which the government issued coupons in September 1994 that represented 12 percent of the capital (these were eligible for conversion into shares of the company following its corporatization and privatization); Korea Telekom, with an offer of 10 percent of the capital limited to Korean investors in February 1993 (only 3 percent found takers), and a 5 percent tranche placed with domestic investors in 1994; Indosat, the Indonesian international operator, 32 percent of whose shares were sold through a public flotation on the New York and Jakarta exchanges (October 1994); PT Telkom, the domestic operator, whose international initial public offering had to be curtailed at the last minute because of weak demand (19 percent of shares sold in November 1995); Portugal Telecom, with an initial public offering in June 1995 and a second tranche in June 1996, leaving the state with a 51 percent shareholding; Greece, where the government finally managed to sell about 8 percent of OTE's stock in March 1996, after several more ambitious attempts had failed; Israel, where 23 percent of Bezeq has already been sold; and Germany, where 26 percent of Deutsche Telekom was floated in November 1996.

Finally, many countries have indicated their intention to privatize their dominant operator. These include (in addition to countries planning to sell second, third, or further tranches of telecommunications companies already partially privatized) Albania, Australia, Brazil, Bulgaria, Colombia, Côte d'Ivoire, Croatia, Ecuador, El Salvador, France, Gabon, Ghana, Guatemala, Honduras, India, Italy, Jordan, Kenya, Lithuania, Madagascar, Moldova, Morocco, Nicaragua, Panama, Poland, Romania, Russia, Rwanda, Slovenia, South Africa, Sri Lanka, Sweden, Thailand, Turkey, Uganda, and Uzbekistan.

privatization operations. Most of these have been accompanied by at least some form of sector liberalization.

The British approach. In telecommunications, as in most other infrastructure sectors, the United Kingdom has been a pioneer. The privatization of British Telecom (BT) in 1984 had added significance in that it set important precedents for future U.K. infrastructure privatizations, including use of public flotations instead of strategic sales, creation of a golden share, establishment of a regulatory framework centered on an independent regulator for the sector, development of the price cap formula, and so on.[54]

The major shortcoming of this process was that insufficient attention was given to the creation of a competitive environment at the time of privatization. BT had a legal monopoly on telecommunications services until the British Telecommunications Act of 1981 established it as a corporation separate from the General Post Office, privatized Cable & Wireless (C&W), allowed C&W to set up a subsidiary (Mercury) in the United Kingdom to compete with BT in all segments of the market, and liberalized terminal equipment. Limited competition had thus been introduced even before BT's privatization in 1984. A second cellular license was issued in 1983 to compete with BT's Cellnet. Value-added services were also opened to competition. The duopoly policy, which was confirmed at the time of BT's privatization, never provided strong competition to the incumbent monopolist, however, and came to an end in 1991.[55] Since then, cable companies, foreign telecommunications firms, and others provide competition in all segments of the market, including the local loop, with one notable exception: until 1996, international operators other than BT and Mercury were not allowed to own and operate their own circuits for international calls; they had to lease circuits from the former duopolists or pay them a fee for each call carried. The removal of this restriction allows other operators to connect their calls directly to satellites, build their own international cables, and negotiate agreements with overseas operators.

About 150 telecommunications licenses have now been granted and BT faces competitors in all segments of the telecommunications market. Under combined pressure from increasing competition and the regulator (OFTEL), telecommunications prices have fallen by over 30 percent in real terms since 1984.

54. Some of these features had already been introduced by the telecommunications act of 1981. The telecommunications act of 1984 enabled privatization of British Telecom and established the regulatory body, the office for telecommunications, headed by the director general of telecommunications. Further regulation of British Telecom is found in the network operating license granted to BT under the act. See also the sections below on public flotation, golden shares, the tariff regime, and the regulatory framework.

55. See the duopoly review White Paper: *Competition and Choice: Telecommunications Policy for the 1990s,* Department of Trade and Industry 1991. See for details Armstrong, Cowan, and Vickers 1994.

The policy of the European Union. In Europe, a series of legislative instruments have been enacted by the European Commission and European Council providing for phased deregulation of the telecommunications sector. Measures began in 1988 with terminal equipment (including computer modems and telephone handsets; Commission Directive 88/301/EEC of May 16, 1988), followed by value-added services in 1990 (Commission Directive 90/388/EEC of June 28, 1990, on competition in the markets for telecommunications services). Telecommunications markets were further liberalized through open network provision in 1990 and 1992, and access through alternative infrastructure (such as railway and power utility networks and cable television) for commercial services as of July 1996. The reforms will culminate with the introduction of full competition through opening up markets in voice telephony and public network infrastructure, effective January 1, 1998.[56] Although article 222 of the Treaty of Rome requires that policies adopted by the European institutions remain neutral with respect to member states' choice of type of ownership (private or public) of their enterprises, in practice few SOEs are likely to be able to resist the onslaught of competition and the greater efficiency it requires.

State-owned operators will not be able to hold on to their market share at the European level without radical reforms in the structure and modus operandi of their enterprises, a change that will almost inevitably mean they will have to open up their capital base to private partners and tap the capital markets. What is more, European Union (EU) rules concerning state aid sharply curtail the option of using public funds to help a national operator get back on its feet, EU competition rules limit mergers that reduce market competition, and European policies increasingly require the separation of regulatory and operational functions. These and other factors explain the radical transformation of this sector, in particular the gradual abandonment of the national, monopolistic public enterprise paradigm. This evolution still needs to be rounded out by detailed rules governing mutual recognition of licenses by EU member countries, interconnection, and dispute settlement between European operators; even the establishment of a European regulatory agency might be contemplated.

It is noteworthy also that, within the same EU framework, member countries have adopted very different strategies. At one extreme is the United

---

56. See, on open network provision, Council Directive 90/387/EEC, June 28, 1990; Council Directive 92/44/EEC, June 5, 1992 on the application of open network provision to leased lines, amended by Commission Decision 94/439/EC; and Council Recommendation 92/383/EEC, June 5, 1992. The reforms to be introduced by July 1996 and January 1998, respectively, are set forth in Commission Directive 96/19/EC, March 13, 1996, amending Directive 90/338/EEC with regard to the implementation of full competition in telecommunications markets. This directive (as well as the earlier ones) was issued by the Commission using its powers under article 90 of the Treaty of Rome, which allows the commission to give directives to member states to fight and overhaul anticompetitive features of public monopolies and other exclusive rights in member countries.

Kingdom, which has been the pioneer and remains the front-runner in European telecommunications privatization and liberalization; at the other are Greece and France, where the public monopoly model still has strong and vocal supporters. Between these two endpoints lie a whole range of reforms pertaining to sectoral structure, ownership, competition rules, and institutional and regulatory structures, represented by the following, for example: Sweden, which has a very open, competitive, and dynamic telecommunications sector with multiple operators (including cable companies), though Telia is still owned by the state and remains the dominant operator; the Netherlands, where privatization was through public offering of KPN, which is in charge of telecommunications as well as postal services; Belgium, where a consortium of international telecommunications operators has acquired a controlling stake in Belgacom; Spain, where the state's shareholding in Telefónica has dropped to 20 percent; Portugal, where state-owned or controlled operators were merged before privatization; and Germany, with its high-profile, public offering of Deutsche Telekom.[57] For most member states, convergence of national policies will be forced by the 1998 deadline. Member states with "less developed networks," such as Greece, Portugal, and Spain may, however, at their request be granted an additional five years (until 2003) to fully open up their telecommunications sector, whereas states with "very small networks" may get an extra two years.

Telecommunications reform in other industrial countries. One of the most interesting and unusual features of recent U.S. telecommunications history is that it was a judge who took the decision to restructure the entire telecommunications sector in 1982. Judge Greene's "consent decree" called for divestiture in 1984 by AT&T, the private monopolistic operator, of its local service monopoly to seven new, independent regional companies, known as the Baby Bells.[58]

---

57. The German program has been sharply criticized by the German competition commission, which felt that the program largely retained the monopolistic structure of the industry, skewed competition, restricted the range of services offered, and would keep prices artificially high and threaten the international competitiveness of German telecommunications by postponing the deadline for deregulation of basic service to the latest date authorized by the European Commission (1998). See *Financial Times*, 8 July 1994.

58. See (Roger) Noll and Owen 1994. One of the main purposes of the breakup of AT&T was to foster competition and lower prices in long-distance and international services. Most observers agree that this objective has been largely accomplished. For a contrary point of view, see Michael Noll, who maintains that the reductions in long-distance rates achieved since January 1984 (when the divestiture became effective) are attributable to technological developments and the abolition of cross-subsidies for local services, not to strong competition among AT&T, MCI, Sprint, and other operators. In his view the cost of this competition, mainly in the form of higher advertising expenditures, may well have pushed these rates higher today than they would have been if the reforms had not been introduced. He explains this in part by the existence before 1984 of a relatively enlightened monopolist company (AT&T) governed by a regulatory system that operated in the public interest (Noll 1994, pp. 355–62).

Not until February 1996 was a new telecommunications law enacted; the law goes much further than the consent decree by expanding the scope of competition in all segments of the telecommunications market and removing the barriers that separated the telephone, cable, and broadcasting industries. In ending the separation between the telecommunications and audiovisual sectors, which had been artificially maintained through regulation, this law should foster the development of new technologies and services. A key feature of the new legislation is that it allows long distance operators and cable companies to enter the local market and local Baby Bells to enter the long distance market, provided they have adequately opened up their networks to competitors. The law entrusts the Federal Communications Commission (FCC, the agency responsible for telecommunications regulation) with broad responsibility to implement the legislation; among other requirements, it gave the FCC six months to enact detailed interconnection rules.[59]

Similarly, the Canadian Radio-Television and Telecommunications Commission (CRTC) took the important decision in September 1994 to open up the local telecommunications sector to competition by cable TV companies and other applicants. The local-service monopoly enjoyed by the telephone companies would end, but they would be allowed to provide audiovisual services. Regulations reflecting this decision had not yet been enacted, however.

In New Zealand, the 1988 telecommunications law abolished the monopoly of Telecom New Zealand (privatized in 1990), with effect from April 1, 1991. This opened the door to competition in all segments of the sector, including the public switched network, and made the New Zealand telecommunications sector one of the most open in the world.[60]

Telecommunications reform in Hungary. Hungary adopted a highly innovative approach when, in November 1992, it enacted a new telecommunications law promoting competition and innovation and authorizing privatization of

59. Long-distance companies are paying the local telephone companies about $28 billion a year in interconnection charges. These are at the center of the current telecommunications debate in the United States: all parties agree that they exceed the cost of providing access to the local networks, but there is no agreement about how much and how fast they should be reduced. The first rules adopted by the FCC to implement the new law did not alter the level of theses charges, but focused on access to the network of the incumbent local monopolists. The FCC issued federal guidelines mandating the Baby Bells to grant access to those individual components of their network or services that service providers wish to access, at a price consistent with the costs an efficient firm would incur in providing the service. The FCC guidelines will be supplemented by more detailed regulations adopted at the state level. See *Wall Street Journal*, 24 June 1996; *New York Times*, 5 August 1996.

60. The telecommunications amendment act of 1988 removed the statutory monopoly over basic services; the telecommunications act of 1987 had already provided for progressive deregulation. Competition was effectively introduced in New Zealand in 1991 with the entry of Clear Communications, a consortium comprising MCI, Bell Canada, the railway company, and a local radio broadcasting company (see Donaldson 1994, p. 259).

the sector. In December 1993, following a call for bids prescribed by the tele-communications law (articles 4 and 5), the government sold a controlling block of shares in MATAV, the national telecommunications company, to the Magyarcom consortium (Deutsche Telekom and Ameritech) for $875 million.[61] In addition, the European Bank for Reconstruction and Development and the International Finance Corporation together hold about 3 percent of the company's shares; these shares result from the conversion of debentures they bought to support the reform process and supply the company with urgently needed capital before its privatization. Although the government initially intended to include a second tranche of MATAV shares in its mass privatization program, it proceeded in December 1995 with the sale of an additional 37 percent to the Magyarcom consortium for $852 million; the private partners undertook to reduce their stake from 67 percent to about 51 percent by floating shares on the stock exchange at a later date.

The MATAV concession runs for 25 years, including an exclusivity period of eight years, and covers basic service in 29 of the 54 national regions as well as long-distance and international services throughout the country. The municipalities were given the option of keeping the telephone services for their region within MATAV or offering them as separate concessions. A majority of municipalities in 25 regions chose the second option. The concessions for 23 of the 25 regions not covered by the initial MATAV concession were awarded to the highest bidders in February 1994. Eight of these were awarded to MATAV and 15 to other companies; there were no takers for two of the regions.[62] These concessions have a twelve-and-a-half year term, grant exclusive rights to provide local telephone service for eight years, and make the concession holder eligible for a cable television license covering the same territory. Hungary's approach is described by some observers as a resolutely modern approach that takes account of strategic and technological developments in the telecommunications sector during the last few years; others think of it as a political compromise to overcome the municipalities' opposition to MATAV's monopoly.

61. This block of shares (30.2 percent) did not, in fact, give them effective control of the company. Indeed, the consortium did not have majority representation either on the board of directors or in the general shareholders meeting. An executive or management committee was, however, set up in which the investors had two of the four seats plus a casting vote. This committee, which reported to the board of directors, was responsible for day-to-day management of the company and implementation of its annual program. The sale proceeds were allocated as follows: $400 million for a capital increase, $342 million paid to the public holding company for the purchase of preexisting shares, and $133 million paid to the ministry of communications as a concession fee (see *Privatisation International*, January 1994, p. 4, and January 1996).

62. These contracts were awarded to several consortia, led by, among others, the Compagnie Générale des Eaux, Alcatel, and several American companies. They paid a total of $80 million for these 15 concessions and undertook to invest nearly $200 million during the first three years of their concession (see *Financial Times*, 1 March 1994 and 11 March 1994). MATAV continues to provide the service in the two regions that did not find takers, though not under a concession. As a result of this process, MATAV, which used to operate the whole national system, had to divest itself of the regional businesses for which it did not win the concession and transfer each one of them to the competing bidder or consortium that won.

The privatization of the Venezuelan operator. CANTV, the national telephone company of Venezuela, was set up in 1930 by private investors.[63] In 1964 it was nationalized, merged with Venezuela's other telecommunications enterprises, and granted an operating monopoly. It was privatized in December 1991 by the sale of 40 percent of its shares for nearly $1.9 billion, involving transfer of its management to a consortium comprising GTE, Telefónica de España, AT&T, the Caracas power company, and a local bank.[64]

Why was the sale limited to 40 percent of the shares? First of all, the government wanted to sell only to a top-grade international operator capable of executing the ambitious investment and management program set forth in the privatization documents. This meant a foreign company. Sale of a majority of the capital to a foreign consortium had been ruled out for political reasons. Some mechanism therefore had to be devised to assure private investors that they could control the company with less than 50 percent of the shares.[65]

CANTV holds a 35-year concession, which can be extended another 20 years, and enjoys a nine-year monopoly over the basic wired network and

63. The following sources were used for the case study on CANTV: Gizang and Sabater 1994; Pisciotta 1994; Taylor and Vidal 1994; *Financial Times*, 29 September 1994 and 26 October 1995; *New York Times*, 21 June 1995.

64. Before submitting their financial bid, bidders had to deliver all the privatization contracts and related agreements (including the agreement establishing the bidding consortium), the revised bylaws of CANTV, bid and performance bonds issued by approved banks, and any other document related to the transaction, the whole duly signed. This made it impossible to equivocate or negotiate more favorable clauses after winning the contract. All these documents, however, together with the concession contract, had been prenegotiated with two consortia selected after a prequalification process (see table 7.3 for a list of preselection criteria). One consortium was headed by GTE, the other by Bell Atlantic and Bell Canada. The final bid related solely to price, all the other factors having been set in the bidding documentation; any condition or reservation expressed in a bid rendered it null and void. The bidding rules called for all prequalified contenders (both consortia, in this case) to submit an envelope in the final round, whether or not it included a bid. This was done to keep a bidder from learning how many remained in competition for the concession; indeed, if a bidder were to find out that it was the only one planning to make a formal offer, it might lower its bid.

65. CANTV shares were divided into four classes. Class A comprises the 40 percent transferred to the winning consortium and confers the right to appoint five out of nine members of the board of directors (up to the year 2001); specific clauses limit the ability of the winning consortium to resell all or part of its shares, or of GTE to reduce its participation in the consortium. Class B represents the 49 percent held by the government and confers the right to two seats on the board; the government can sell its shares, for example by public flotation (such an offering occurred in late 1996). The remaining 11 percent are Class C shares in trust for the benefit of CANTV employees and retirees, who may subscribe a specified number of shares (based on length of service and salary) and pay for them in installments spread over nine years or more; two directors are appointed by the employees. One percent of the class C shares was to be bought by CANTV and held in trust to create a bonus program under which free shares would be awarded to certain employees based on performance. Upon subsequent transfer, class A, B, and C shares automatically become class D shares, that is, ordinary shares without special privileges. To make certain changes in the bylaws a double majority of class A and class B shareholders is required. By falling below the critical threshold of 50 percent public shareholding, CANTV is no longer subject to the laws governing public enterprises.

long-distance and international communications. This temporary monopoly was granted to rebalance rates and gradually phase out internal cross-subsidization, whereby long-distance and international services supported costs of local services. The substantial margins realized in long-distance and international services were deemed necessary for the financing of the ambitious investment program required under the terms of the concession. The high selling price points to the existence of high monopoly rents and suggests that the exclusivity term could have been shorter. All other services, notably terminals, private networks, value-added services, satellite links, and cellular, are excluded from the monopoly. The government had, in fact, already granted a nationwide nonexclusive cellular concession for 20 years (renewable) in May 1991 to the Telcel consortium for $107 million. A subsidiary of CANTV provides cellular services in competition with Telcel.

The concession agreements require CANTV to renew the network by installing new digital lines, converting old lines to digital, and increasing the number of public phones, among other obligations; this means that 3 million new lines and 600,000 replacement lines had to be installed during the first nine years of CANTV's concession. The agreements also require CANTV to upgrade the service quality, especially by reducing the time needed to get a dial tone, shortening repair times, and raising the call completion ratio (the percentage of calls going through on the first attempt). Two years after privatization, CANTV had already invested more than $1 billion, installed 850,000 lines (an increase of about one-third), and connected 460,000 new subscribers, thus exceeding the requirements of its concession contract. Between 1991 and 1995 the penetration (teledensity) rate increased from less than 8 percent to over 11 percent. Service quality also improved greatly, as did the company's productivity, but profits did not. Economic crisis and other factors discussed below caused CANTV to lose money in 1994. In four years, through the end of 1995, CANTV investments exceeded $2 billion, or about $500 million a year; annual investments in telecommunications averaged about $80 million in the last three years of state ownership.

Time constraints led the government to incorporate most of the regulatory framework into the concession contract, which was approved by the Venezuelan congress; it also issued a decree creating Conatel, the regulatory agency established as an "autonomous service" of the ministry of transportation and communications with limited powers and no autonomous source of financing. Parliament never adopted the telecommunications law submitted by the government, which called for a new regulatory framework and a regulatory agency with greater autonomy and wider powers. Consequently, the sectoral regulations established by decree remained in force. Tariffs were to be adjusted quarterly, following a formula linked to the price index and applied to three baskets of services. These periodic adjustments have to be proposed by CANTV, recommended by Conatel, and approved by the minister of transportation and communications.

The lack of a regulatory organ with adequate institutional and financial autonomy probably remains one of the major weaknesses of this transaction. In 1994 relations between CANTV, on the one hand, and the regulator and government, on the other, became very tense. New foreign exchange controls and government actions did not allow the company to buy dollars to service its debt, which led to defaults and debt rescheduling. Other macroeconomic policies taken from 1994 by the government, including the devaluation of the bolivar and the resulting galloping inflation (about 60 percent), as well as a general recession, further aggravated the plight of CANTV. Public sector and government customers accumulated substantial arrears toward CANTV with bills exceeding 400 days, on average; unpaid public sector bills amounted to about $60 million; high inflation in the country (over 50 percent) made the situation even worse for CANTV. It appears that the regulator blocked the rebalancing of rates and did not meet deadlines to authorize some rate increases provided for in the privatization agreements; one of the quarterly increases was even, apparently, denied. Moreover, Conatel granted licenses to third parties despite the monopoly accorded to CANTV. The government's replacement of the chairman of Conatel was yet another indication of the fragility of the regulatory framework.

The arrival in 1995 of a new regulator (appointed by government) and of a new Venezuelan CEO (appointed by CANTV) seems to have introduced a period of more harmonious and constructive relations between the private operator, the government, and the regulator. Periodic rate adjustments are again applied, CANTV's foreign debt has been restructured, and the company was in the black again in 1995. The government sold the state's remaining 49 percent shareholding in November 1996 through an IPO (40 percent) and an employee allocation (9 percent), raising over $1 billion.

Toward international norms. As already discussed, EU norms are having a forceful impact on domestic European telecommunications companies and markets; many countries, especially in southern Europe, would not be liberalizing their markets were it not for these directives. The increasing globalization of the telecommunications industry has also been discussed; international mergers and alliances require the approval of regulators in the countries concerned, who may condition their approval on stipulations that have a direct impact on sector structure and competition in countries outside their jurisdiction. The U.S. FCC, for example, imposed conditions on the $4.2 billion investment by France Télécom and Deutsche Telekom for a 20 percent stake in Sprint. The new alliance cannot increase the number of lines to France and Germany until the two countries meet a series of demands related to the liberalization of their telecommunications markets. In addition, FCC approval may be revoked at any time if France and Germany do not comply with various undertakings, including liberalization of alternative infrastructure by July 1, 1996, and removal of restrictions on foreign investment. Interestingly, most of these undertakings simply mirror obligations Germany and France already have pursuant to existing EU norms. The threat of withdrawal of FCC approval in this case boosts commitment to effectively implement the agreed reforms.

Other signs attest to growing international norms in telecommunications. As a follow-up to the Uruguay Round, for instance, the World Trade Organization is hosting talks on telecommunications liberalization. This is a solid indication that competition rules and basic regulatory safeguards in the telecommunications sector are increasingly moving toward internationalization.

Range of Organizational Options

Examples from the infrastructure sectors discussed in the previous sections and summarized in table 7.1 illustrate the wide range of sector structures and privatization schemes, which must be tailored to the specific circumstances and constraints of each country and sector, as well as to specific government objectives and strategy. In most cases no track record exists yet, because most of these reforms have only recently been implemented and their costs and benefits are still being evaluated. Preliminary results, however, demonstrate the promise of the procompetitive approach and its superiority over the earlier paradigm of state-owned monopolies. The privatization of infrastructure sectors is not an exact science, and it will almost always involve adjustments and corrections. Countries like Argentina, Chile, and the United Kingdom have been pathbreakers; other countries should take advantage of the lessons of their experience.

Special Issues in Infrastructure Privatization

The general developments discussed in the first six chapters of this book apply also to the infrastructure sectors. They will not be reviewed here. A few issues, however, arise either differently or more acutely in these sectors, usually as a corollary of their unique characteristics. Special privatization techniques, specific constitutional and legislative issues, prior restructuring requirements, and various transactional matters that apply to infrastructure privatization are examined in turn.

Techniques for Infrastructure Privatization

As discussed above, one of the specificities of infrastructure privatization is the priority that needs to be given to matters of sector structure and competition. Additional and country-specific features may derive from the public service nature of infrastructure activities and from the special legal status that may be attached to sector assets. These special features have led to the development of specific privatization techniques.

The term "privatization" is used to refer to a range of different though often overlapping situations, each of which has several variations and covers, among other things, divestiture or privatization *sensu stricto*, which implies the permanent transfer of the ownership of sector assets to the private sector; concessions and other fixed-term privatizations, which typically limit the scope and duration of the rights transferred and imply a return of the sector assets to the public authority at the end of the concession period; and new entry following demonopolization of the sector and introduction of competition.[66]

Divestiture and fixed-term privatization are transactional in nature. They involve the transfer of an existing enterprise to the private sector, which runs it at its own risk. In both cases the most valuable asset offered is not the physical infrastructure itself but the operating license, the right to provide the service.

The terms "license" and "concession" are often used interchangeably, though they may have specific and different meanings in given countries or legal systems. Concession often refers to a contract that grants an operating license, but it also includes a range of other special features. In many countries, for instance, concessions give the private operators only limited rights over the sector assets, falling short of legal ownership. This type of concession is particularly well suited to situations where, for constitutional, legal, political, or other reasons, it is not possible to transfer ownership of strategic sectors to private parties. In other countries, the ownership restriction applies only to foreigners and can be similarly circumvented. Concessions of this type can be constructed in a way that mimics the features, and particularly the incentives, of full private ownership.

Moreover, the term concession often implies, especially in countries with a French-inspired legal tradition, the return of the enterprise or sector assets to the public authority (a return that could be postponed indefinitely by extending or renewing the contract). In Argentina and Chile, for example, concessions have been granted on a permanent basis, however.[67] Within concessions, a distinction is sometimes made depending on whether the operator is responsible for new investments in the sector or whether that responsibility remains with the public sector; the latter case is sometimes referred to as leasing, or *affermage*.[68] Finally, concessions may be deemed to

66. See also the definition of privatization given in the introduction. This book focuses on privatization in the sense of transferring existing enterprises or assets from the public to the private sector; build, own, operate (BOO) or build, operate, transfer (BOT) contracts, greenfield public works concessions, and other such private infrastructure schemes therefore fall outside its scope.

67. See, in particular, article 30 of Chilean Decree-Law no. 1 of June 1982 concerning the electric power sector, which provides that "definitive" concessions shall be granted with indefinite duration. In Argentina, indefinite concessions have been granted in the telecommunications sector.

68. In addition to the specific features of concessions found in some legal systems, there may be a difference in form between a license and a concession; the first is a unilateral act and the second is a bilateral or consensual contract. This difference may be devoid of real implications, however, because the unilateral amendment of a license by a public authority generally requires the licensee's agreement (article 11 of the 1989 U.K. electricity act, for example, provides that the license may be amended with the holder's consent), whereas French case law, for example, gives the public authorities the right to alter the terms of a concession contract unilaterally when circumstances so require (the principle of adaptation of service). In the United Kingdom, provisions governing unilateral amendment of licenses vary from sector to sector; if the regulator and the licensee disagree, the matter is usually referred to the minister or to the MMC.

be administrative rather than commercial contracts, which may have a wide range of important implications.[69]

Introduction of competition and new entry represent a third type of privatization, which results from the adoption of new sector structures and policies, as discussed in the previous section. In all three cases, private operators are given an operating license, that is, the right to provide the service. The three techniques often coexist in one privatization program. In Argentina, for example, the power sector was unbundled and liberalized, power stations were divested, and transmission and distribution companies were privatized through concessions. In Indonesia, PT Telkom, the main telephone operator, was partially privatized in November 1995, a few weeks after having entered into "joint operations schemes" (akin to 15-year concessions) for the operation of five of its seven regions with private consortia; previously, a minority stake in Indosat, the international carrier, had been floated on the market and new entry had been allowed in most segments of the market. In the United Kingdom, in addition to the unbundling and privatization of the railway system, the government awarded in March 1996 a 999-year concession to a private consortium to build and operate the high-speed rail link between London and the Channel Tunnel; as part of the deal, the U.K. government agreed to provide subsidies and to divest and transfer to the private consortium large areas of railway land as well as its ownership interest in European Passenger Service, a joint venture of British Rail and the Belgian and French railways operating the Eurostar trains from London to Brussels and Paris.[70]

Table 7.1 shows the instruments that have been chosen in various sectors in several countries. As pointed out above, the distinction between divestiture

69. The Turkish government tried to avoid the application of administrative law to BOT projects by submitting a bill to parliament that stated that a BOT contract was a nonconcessionary contract governed by private law; this text was adopted and became law (article 5 of the BOT law of June 1994). But this provision was struck down in 1995 by the constitutional court (decision no. 1995/23, published in the Turkish official gazette no. 22586 of March 20, 1996). The court ruled that this provision violated article 155 of the constitution and that BOT contracts were in fact concessions and thus administrative contracts, not private contracts. BOT contracts thus become subject to Turkish administrative law; disputes cannot be submitted to international arbitration. This ruling also has adverse tax implications for BOT projects. This decision dealt yet another setback to the Turkish BOT program and will make it more difficult for the government to attract private sponsors and lenders. Since then, the government has adopted a new BOO (build, own, operate) model, which no longer implies the return at the end of the contract's term of the facilities built by private investors; the government hopes to escape the classification of projects developed under this new model as concession contracts subject to administrative law and other public law constraints. See *Middle East Executive Reports*, June 1996; *Project & Trade Finance*, September 1996.

70. The concession was awarded on the basis of the lowest level of cash subsidies demanded. The selected consortium bid £1.4 billion ($2.1 billion), which was apparently £500 million less than its rival. See *Financial Times*, 1 March 1996; see also note 42 above.

Table 7.1 Infrastructure Networks: Privatization Mode and Sector Reform in Selected Countries

Sector	Divestiture	Concession and leasing	Introduction of competition in the market
Telecommunications (wireline voice)	Argentina; Chile; Cuba; Guinea; Hungary; Jamaica; Mexico; New Zealand; Peru; United Kingdom; Venezuela	Cook Islands; Guinea-Bissau; Indonesia; Madagascar	Australia; Chile; European Union; Hong Kong; Mexico; New Zealand; Philippines; Sweden; United Kingdom; United States
Electric power (generation)	Argentina; Australia; Bolivia; Canada; Chile; Germany; Hungary; Pakistan; Peru; United Kingdom	Côte d'Ivoire; Guinea	Argentina; Australia; Bolivia; Chile; New Zealand; Norway; Peru; United Kingdom
Gas transport and distribution	Australia; Belgium; Hungary; Latvia; Russia; United Kingdom	Argentina	Argentina; United Kingdom; United States
Water distribution	United Kingdom	Argentina; Brazil; Central African Republic; Chile; Colombia; Côte d'Ivoire; France; Guinea; Macao; Malaysia; Senegal	United Kingdom
Railways	Bolivia; Canada; Japan; New Zealand; United Kingdom; United States	Argentina; Brazil; Chile; Côte d'Ivoire-Burkina Faso; Mexico	Sweden; United Kingdom; United States

Note: The table includes only countries that have privatized by transferring existing public-sector facilities to the private sector, not those that that have opened up the sector in question through greenfield concessions or BOT and BOO contracts only, such as Thailand (telecommunications) and China (power generation). For some countries and sectors it was not possible to ascertain precisely whether privatization (in the broad sense) had been effected by means of a permanent divestiture or a concession implying the return of sector assets to the granting authority. See also box 7.2 for additional examples of divestiture in the telecommunications sector.

and concession is somewhat artificial and arbitrary.[71] Listed as concessions are mainly those transactions in which sector assets continue to belong to the state or another public entity (a municipality, for example) and revert to the state without market-based compensation at the end of the concession contract. A different criterion might distinguish between transactions where the public sector remains responsible for major new investments in the sector (some, but not all, examples from the concession and leasing column of table 7.1) and those where this responsibility rests with the private sector (all the examples in the divestiture column, plus some of the ones in the concession and leasing column).

What matters in the end is not what the transaction is labeled but what its terms and conditions are, in particular, the specific rights and obligations conferred, as well as the operator's incentives to improve the quality and efficiency of service delivery.

Constitutional and Legislative Restrictions

National constitutions often contain specific provisions concerning the infrastructure sectors, notably railways, telecommunications, and electric power (see table 7.2). Such provisions fall mainly into five categories. Some constitutions preclude any private ownership or operation of infrastructure sectors. Others enable the legislator to reserve certain activities to the public sector but do not spell out which ones. A third class of provisions does not allow the transfer of control over specific infrastructure sectors or enterprises to the private sector, while permitting noncontrolling private shareholdings. In a fourth group of countries, the constitution reserves these sectors to the state but does not prohibit the government from granting concessions to the private sector. A fifth type limits (or excludes) foreign participation in infrastructure sectors.

Similar restrictions are sometimes found in laws or subordinate instruments.[72] For example, although the Turkish constitution authorizes the

---

71. One would have to check, in particular, whether the right to operate is limited in time and, if so, what happens at the end of the prescribed concession or license term if it is not renewed (return of the sector assets to the public authority; sale to the new concession holder or licensee; free disposal by the company); the conditions that could lead to such failure to renew would have to be investigated, too. This information was not available for some of the country and sector examples mentioned in table 7.1.

72. In *Italy*, four concessions have been granted to public or joint-venture companies under the telecommunications and postal services code, approved by Presidential Decree no. 156 of March 29, 1973. These concessions provide (article 4) that the public holding company IRI must hold a majority of the voting shares in each of the concession-holding companies. The creation of Telecom Italia as a subsidiary of STET and the planned sector privatization require the amendment of these concession contracts (see Gioscia 1993). In *Japan*, the telecommunications law was amended in May 1992 to authorize participation by foreign investors in the capital of NTT (up to 20 percent). U.S. legislation limits foreign participation in telecommunication and air transport companies to 25 percent. Finally, *Romania*'s enterprise restructuring law of July 1990 prescribes that autonomous public-law units (rather than corporations) be set up in strategic sectors, including energy, postal services, and telecommunications; these units may, however, delegate the operation of those sectors to private companies under concession contracts.

government to grant concessions, subject to approval by an administrative tribunal, the foreign investment law prescribed that foreigners may not hold concessions; this created serious problems for the government when it attempted to privatize the power and telephone companies. The restriction was abolished by the 1994 privatization law. In Indonesia, the telecommunications law authorizes private participation in the sector, but states that, with respect to basic services (local, long-distance, and international communications), only companies in which the public operator is a shareholder can be given a license. That is, the dominant operator is required by law to be a shareholder of its potential competitors, hardly a situation that is likely to foster sound competition (see article 12 of Indonesia's Law no. 3 of 1989 on telecommunications). Until May 1995, Mexican law prohibited foreign investment in the transportation, storage, and distribution of natural gas. Until August 1995, Italian law required that airports be operated by public or public-sector-controlled enterprises.

Although restrictions on infrastructure privatization usually derive from constitutions or laws, Uruguay provides an interesting exception: it held a popular referendum on December 13, 1992, which led to suspension of part of the October 1991 privatization law, particularly the provisions authorizing privatization of ANTEL, the telephone company.

Legislation for Infrastructure Privatization

Only in rare cases are large infrastructure sectors or companies privatized without special legislation or regulations. Indeed, telecommunications, electricity, gas, water, and transport privatizations are usually the subject of specific legislation, which may take the form of sector- or enterprise-specific privatization laws or amendments to existing laws.[73] In addition, some countries have enacted cross-sectoral concession or BOT laws to govern the way in which concessions can be awarded to private operators.[74] Whereas the industrial and commercial sectors lend themselves to an omnibus privatization law, infrastructure sector privatizations generally demand specific provisions dealing with market structure, competition, and regulation, as well as provisions enabling the privatization.

73. See the examples cited in the appendix. Most of Argentina's large infrastructure companies, for instance, were privatized pursuant to specific privatization laws, with the notable exception of ENTEL, the telecommunications company; that privatization was governed by provisions of the state reform law of August 1989 and by a series of decrees, most of which were specific to the telecommunications sector.

74. See, for example, the concession laws of Albania (1995), Brazil (1995), Bulgaria (1995), Chile (1988, 1991), Colombia (1993), Djibouti (1989), Hungary (1991), the Kyrgyz Republic (1992), Panama (1986), Peru (1991, 1996), and Turkey (1908, 1932); the Thai Royal Act on private participation in state affairs (1992); the BOT legislation of the Philippines (1990), Turkey (1994), and Viet Nam (1993); and the French law on transparency and prevention of corruption in economic activities and public procedures (*loi Sapin* of 1993).

Table 7.2 Constitutional Restrictions on Infrastructure Privatization

Restriction	Country and sector	Example
No private ownership or operation	Germany; post and tele-communications	Article 87 of the German constitution (concerning areas of direct federal administration) provided that post and telecommunications were federal government undertakings; this provision was amended on August 30, 1994, and a new article 143b was added; the separation of the postal services from the telecommunications company and their privatization were authorized
	El Salvador; post and tele-communications	Article 110 of the constitution of El Salvador refers to post and telecommunications as services that have to be provided by the state or autonomous public bodies
Option to reserve activities to the public sector	Italy; public services and monopolies	Article 43 of the Italian constitution provides, for instance, that certain activities or categories of activities relating to essential public services, energy, or monopolies may, in the public interest, be reserved by law to the public sector (or to worker or consumer associations)
Public sector to retain control	Germany; railways	Article 87e of the German constitution (privatization of federal railways) stipulates that railways must be run directly by the federal administration or by federally owned or controlled companies
	Brazil; telecommunications	Article 21 of the Brazilian constitution defines the powers of the federal government and prescribed (section 11) that telecommunications fall within the competence of the national authorities, which may contract their operation under concession to companies controlled by the government. The government control provision was removed by constitutional amendment 8 of August 15, 1995, to permit the privatization of Telebras, but a law was still required to implement this new provision
State retain controls but private concessions are allowed	Mexico; railways, telecommunications, and other sectors	Article 28 of the Mexican constitution was amended in 1983 to authorize the government to grant concessions; this provided the basis for the privatization of Telmex in 1990. It was further amended in February 1995 to allow the award of concessions in the railway sector to private investors

Limit on foreign ownership or operation	Brazil; power, air transport, railways, waterways, roads, ports	Section 12 of article 21 of the Brazilian constitution prescribes that the right to operate electric power, air transportation, railways, navigable waterways, interprovincial and international roads, and ports are reserved to the federal government, which may, however, delegate their operation via a concession, authorization, or permit. This provision deals more with allocation of federal and provincial responsibilities than with divisions between public and private responsibilities
	El Salvador; ports, railways, canals and other public works	Article 120 of the Salvadoran constitution states that concessions granted for port (quays or jetties), railways, canals, or other public works cannot be granted for more than 50 years, and that said public works have to be returned to the state in perfect operating condition and without indemnity at the end of the term
	Philippines; public utilities	Section 11 of article 12 of the Philippine constitution reserves the operation of public utilities to Philippine citizens and to corporations or associations organized under Philippine law, provided that at least 60 percent of their capital is owned by Philippine citizens. It further provides that foreign participation in the governing body of any such corporation or association be limited to the foreign investor's proportionate share in the capital and that all the executive and managing officers be Philippine citizens. Act no. 108, known as the antidummy law, prohibits the use of front men or corporations to circumvent this constitutional restriction. The provision became an obstacle for the planned privatization of the Manila water system, although government officials and their advisers hoped to circumvent the problem by granting an operating concession without ownership rights over the sector assets (see *Financial Times*, 30 January 1996). In the case of the independent power plants, Executive Order 215 provided that this nationality requirement was not applicable to generating companies that sold their power to the National Power Corporation or another government distribution agency (see *Independent Energy*, November 1994, pp. 35–38).

The choice of legal instrument to define the new framework and rules governing the sector may depend largely on the country concerned, its traditions, and any constraints (constitutional or other) that may exist with respect to the proposed reforms. Many investors feel more reassured when the key elements of the applicable regime are defined in a law as well as in privatization-related agreements. A law offers them the advantage of explicit political endorsement, which is not negligible, given the often politically contentious nature of infrastructure privatization, while a contract offers them precise remedies and means for exercising their rights.

Prior Restructuring and Corporatization

The privatization of large public infrastructure enterprises generally calls for prior restructuring measures, whether to reflect the new market structure, to take account of public-law characteristics of the entity to be privatized, or to address other issues.[75] The U.K. electricity law of 1989 illustrates this well. The first part of the law establishes the new sector framework, including sector structure, competition, and regulation. The second part deals with the reorganization of the power industry. It addresses the creation of new companies organized under company law, whose shares are initially held by the government; transfer of the assets of the former public enterprises to the new companies; winding up of the old entities and treatment of their debts and other obligations; management of the new companies before they are privatized; and other transitory provisions. It also includes provisions on the flotation of the power companies. The third part contains miscellaneous provisions concerning, for example, nuclear liabilities and pension schemes.

In Germany, the partial privatization of Deutsche Telekom in 1996 required, in addition to an amendment to the German constitution, radical restructuring of Deutsche Bundespost. It had to be split into three new companies responsible for telecommunications, postal services, and financial services; many other issues were settled, too, such as the responsibilities of the new companies for employee retirement (see the law of September 14, 1994, on reorganization of postal services and telecommunications).

In summary, many issues are bound to arise, and have, as infrastructure enterprises are readied for privatization. These include not only the general enterprise-level preprivatization measures discussed in chapter 4 (including financial, corporate, management, and labor restructuring) but also the enterprise restructuring measures needed to make the sector more competi-

75. The infrastructure service may have been organized as a central administration agency or as a public-law enterprise, or as an enterprise governed by some public-law provisions. Corporatizing such an enterprise—that is, transforming it into a company organized under company law—before privatization can pose special problems, as discussed in chapter 4. See also chapter 1 and box 1.3 on the legal status of public enterprises. Preprivatization labor and pension issues are discussed in chapter 3.

tive (including breakup of monopolistic enterprises and establishment of successor companies), as discussed in the section on market structure, competition, and divestiture in this chapter.

Choice of Strategic Partners

The placement of a controlling block of shares with strategic investors, usually including an experienced operator, is a common technique in the privatization of infrastructure companies. The main purpose is to put the management of the enterprise in the hands of companies with a proven track record in the sector. Many privatizations of telecommunications companies, for example, have been carried out through a two-tranche share issue: a first tranche is earmarked for strategic investors, followed by a second tranche offered to the general public. This was the formula planned by, for example, Argentina, Hungary, Mexico, Peru, and Venezuela. In four of these five cases, the private consortium acquired only a minority shareholding but nevertheless obtained control of the company's management.[76] Whereas Argentina, Mexico, Peru, and Venezuela have proceeded with public offerings, the Hungarian government in the end sold its second tranche to the strategic investors with an undertaking on their part to float part of that tranche at a later date.[77] Similar two-stage privatizations are found in other infrastructure sectors also, including energy (Argentina and Peru, for example) and airlines.[78]

This two-stage approach has many advantages: it allows the selected investors to restructure the company and enhance its profitability by giving

76. This applies to MATAV (Hungary), where in a first stage the private consortium has had to accept more risk in holding only 30 percent of the shares and a proportionate number of board seats, while playing a more important role in the day-to-day running of the company (see the section above on telecommunications reform in Hungary); Telmex (Mexico), in which the government sold the private consortium 20.4 percent of the capital, corresponding to 51 percent of the voting shares, that is, control of the company (the government had in fact restructured Telmex's capital, of which 44 percent was already in private hands, before the December 1990 privatization, and only 40 percent of the shares carried voting rights; see Galal and others 1994, p. 419); Telefónica del Peru, in which the strategic investors acquired 35 percent of the shares in 1994; and CANTV (Venezuela), in which the private consortium held 40 percent of the shares, but five out of nine seats on the board of directors (see the section on the privatization of CANTV, above). In Argentina, however, the two winning consortia each held 60 percent of the shares in the acquired company from the onset.

77. See also the section on foreign legislation in chapter 3 and, in this chapter, note 47 and the section on telecommunications reform in Hungary.

78. Following an international competitive bid, British Airways was selected as strategic investor in Qantas, the Australian carrier, and acquired 25 percent of its stock. The Australian government sold its remaining shares (75 percent) on the Australian Stock Exchange in 1995. In August 1995, 50.1 percent of Ecuatoriana, the Ecuadoran airline, was sold to a consortium led by VASP (Brazil); in addition, the Ecuadoran law instructed the government to sell an additional 24.9 percent of its shares through a public offering within six months after the sale of the control block.

them corporate control; it gives the government the opportunity to benefit from the upside potential through a higher sale price in a second tranche. It limits the amounts of funds investors need to raise up front and allows local investors to become shareholders of the privatized enterprise. This approach also presents some risks, however. Experience has shown that in quite a few cases the second-tranche public offering did not materialize as planned. Indeed, if the privatized company is doing well after the first tranche is sold to strategic investors, these investors often pressure the government for a larger share, and the government itself may be tempted to keep its shares. If it is not doing well, a second tranche would probably have to be postponed for fear that the public offering would fail.

The Bolivian capitalization program is a variation on the two-stage theme. Strategic investors are selected competitively to subscribe to a capital increase, and existing shares are transferred from the government to a trust fund that holds shares while the new mechanism for managing the citizens' pension funds is set up.[79]

In other cases, notably power companies in Argentina, Chile, and Germany, privatization took the form of sale of all or almost all the shares to strategic investors or groups of investors. New Zealand used a hybrid formula: following an international call for bids, all shares of Telecom New Zealand were sold in September 1990 to a U.S. consortium, with the stipulation that the consortium reduce its shareholding to a maximum of 49.9 percent within three or four years, partly by means of a public offering on the New Zealand market.[80]

The procedure for choosing a strategic investor in advance usually comprises two stages: the stage of declaration of interest or prequalification, and the actual bidding stage. The selection rules normally include minimum selection or prequalification criteria that allow the authorities to eliminate weak or unproven candidates, limit the number of eligible bidders, and ensure that the company selected has the necessary technical and financial resources to fulfill its commitments. Governments typically limit the number of prequalified bidders to three or four, because the costs associated with more bidders often exceed the benefits of additional competition. These include, for the bidders, the high cost of preparing bids, carrying out a rigorous due-diligence process, and negotiating the transaction; and, for the government, the cost of scarce time availability of key decisionmakers and officials and the escalating fees of

---

79. See box 5.1. The strategic investors selected in 1995 were STET of Italy for the telecommunications company; VASP of Brazil for the airline; three consortia headed by Dominion Energy, Energy Initiatives, and Constellation Energy of the United States, respectively, for the power generation companies; and, in early 1996, the Chilean company Cruz Blanca for the railways.

80. The sale in 1990 of all the shares of Telecom Corporation of New Zealand to Bell Atlantic and Ameritech brought in more than $5.25 billion (NZ$4.5 billion). The consortium also included New Zealand interests, which undertook to buy back nearly 10 percent of the shares by September 1993. By that date the two Baby Bells each held only 24.9 percent of the shares and the above-mentioned New Zealand interests only 3.3 percent. Part of the balance was held by a U.S. group (5 percent) while the rest was distributed in the market following IPOs in New Zealand, New York, London, and Sydney (see Donaldson 1994, pp. 255–56).

legal, financial, and other advisers. A high number of bidders reduces the likelihood for each one of them of winning the bid, and hence reduces their willingness to invest in the preparation of a proposal.

Table 7.3 summarizes the prequalification criteria used in the privatization of some telecommunications companies, chiefly in Latin America.[81] In every case the seller clearly wanted to exclude, right from the start, any candidate that did not combine great telecommunications experience and an excellent track record for performance and quality of service. Notable also is the alternative offered by Peru between the criterion of a minimum number of service lines and of minimum annual telecommunications revenues; this made it possible, for example, to avoid excluding companies like AT&T and MCI, which have great experience in long-distance and international services, but did not operate local telephone networks.

Strict criteria of the type outlined in table 7.3 make it easier to dismiss less qualified firms with good political connections. Not all countries are as precise as those in table 7.3 in their requirements, however. In selecting operators for concession-type telecommunications contracts, Indonesia issued broad prequalification criteria, giving the selection committee discretion to decide which firms should be allowed to bid.[82]

Only the prequalified companies will be invited by the selling government to submit formal bids. After prequalification and before the issuance of formal bidding documents (or requests for proposals), governments may wish to consult the prequalified bidders on the proposed terms and conditions. The complexity of many infrastructure sectors, the lack of experience of privatizing governments, the uncertainty that may surround the existing facilities and operations, new technologies, and differing approaches and business methods of bidders are among the reasons to seek the input of bidders at this stage, as the governments of Argentina, Guinea, Jamaica, Peru, and Senegal, among others, have done for their infrastructure privatizations. It is then up to the government and its advisers to decide how to take the suggestions of bidders into account in the final bidding documents.

A broad range of final selection options are available, based at one extreme solely on the bid price and at the other on a combination of the bidder's technical and financial proposals. Since the transaction relates to infrastructure services, the government cannot remain indifferent to the way the new owners plan to discharge public service obligations; an award to the highest bid-

81. As mentioned above, the decision to privatize ANTEL of Uruguay was submitted to a popular referendum in December 1992, and was defeated. As a result, the company was not privatized.

82. The 1994 prequalification document stated that the applicant "must be able to show that his group has the required technical capacity and capability, by providing evidence of their experience with projects of similar complexity and size, as well as the availability of human resources and equipment." It also required evidence of financial strength. Although such criteria may sound overly vague and could have led to prequalification of weak firms, most consortia prequalified by the Indonesian government included as a key member a major international telecommunications operator; all five contracts were awarded to consortia with such strategic partners.

Table 7.3 Prequalification Criteria for Privatization of Telecommunications Companies

Criterion	Argentina (ENTEL)	Hungary (MATAV)	Peru (Entelperu and CPT)	Uruguay (ANTEL)	Venezuela (CANTV)
Number of lines[a]		≥ 1 million	> 2 million[b]	≥ 2 million	> 6 million
Share of local digital exchanges					> 25%
Share of successful international calls			> 95%	> 95%[c]	> 65%
Waiting time for connection			≥ 85% within 30 days	≥ 90% within 30 days	< 1 month
Average repair time			≥ 75% within 24 hours	≥ 80% within 24 hours and 95% within 48 hours	< 16 hours
Contribution to capital by foreign operator	≥ 4.9% of capital		≥ 51% of voting rights in consortium		
Assets of consortium partners	≥ $1 billion; $300 million for domestic partners				
Credit rating for long-term debt			≥ A+ (Moody's) or BBB+ (S&P)	≥ A+ (Moody's)	
Annual gross revenue		≥ $1 billion[d]	> $2 billion[b]	≥ $3 billion[d]	> $5 billion

a. Installed or in service (or number of subscribers).

b. Candidates had to meet either number-of-lines criterion *or* annual gross revenue criterion.

c. Including domestic long-distance calls.

d. Annual gross revenues from telecommunications services.

Sources: Argentina: terms and conditions for privatization of the public telecommunications service, adopted by Decree no. 62/90 of January 5, 1990; *Hungary: PFI,* April 16, 1993; *Peru:* merit and background prequalification document, July 1, 1993; *Uruguay:* Herrera 1993; *Venezuela:* public announcement in local press.

der, irrespective of qualifications or business plan, would thus not be appropriate. In one scenario, the buyer will be required to operate within a very strict framework laid down in the bidding documentation. This framework, which may be embodied in a concession contract or a schedule of conditions, for example, will generally be nonnegotiable to ensure that all bidders address a single, common set of specifications, the only variable being the bid price. Alternatively, the government could confine itself to enumerating the objectives to be achieved by the privatized company and leave it up to the bidders to determine how and under what financial conditions they propose to achieve them. The first approach offers the advantage of transparency and ease of appraisal, and the second that of greater flexibility and enhanced use of private-sector resources and solutions. Other variations abound; describing them all is beyond the scope of this work.

Public Flotation

A number of large infrastructure companies have been privatized by means of a public flotation to the general public, effected in several tranches and without any prior or concomitant strategic share placement. Most of these were relatively well-run telecommunications companies of industrial countries, such as Nippon Telegraph and Telephone (NTT), British Telecom (privatized in three tranches between 1984 and 1989), and Koninklijke PTT Nederland (KPN, two tranches in 1994 and 1995), as well as companies of dynamic developing countries, such as Chile, Malaysia, and Singapore.[83]

On the other hand, such attempts to privatize tend to be doomed unless an adequate regulatory framework is set up and the company is thoroughly prepared (or, where necessary, completely restructured) for the flotation. Examples include Sui Northern in Pakistan (whose failed public flotation is discussed in box 7.4), Korea Telekom (out of the 10 percent offered in February 1993, the Korean government found buyers for only 2 or 3 percent), and, to a lesser extent, PT Telkom in Indonesia.[84] Similarly, in November 1994, the Greek government had to postpone the public offering of about 25 percent of OTE, the telephone company, in view of the weak interest on the part of international investors. Indeed, because OTE lagged technologi-

---

83. See box 7.2. In the power sector, 21 percent of Korea Electric Power was sold in 1989, and 23 percent of Tenaga Nasional Berhad (Malaysia) in 1992, through public flotations yielding about $ 2.1 billion and $1.2 billion, respectively. In Chile, the full privatization of Chilgener 1985–88 and Enersis 1985–87 was carried out through gradual sales to employees and pension funds and through the stock exchange (see Galal and others 1994).

84. In November 1995, the government had to cut the size and the price of its initial public offering down at the last minute in response to weak market interest. This was caused in part by the uncertainty surrounding the fate of the concession contracts for the operation of the telecommunications networks in five of Indonesia's seven regions, which had only recently been awarded to international consortia. Because a large part of PT Telkom's cash flow and profits was expected to be generated by these concessions, uncertainty depressed the stock's prospects. Many observers attributed this flop to adverse market conditions following the Mexican crisis

(continued on the following page)

cally, quality of service was mediocre, and the company would remain under public control, the Greek government would have had to accept a price below that of other recent telecommunication privatizations.[85]

Governments that privatize their infrastructure companies in several tranches typically do so in the hope that the later tranches will bring in higher receipts, reflecting performance improvements achieved by the new shareholders and better prospects for returns on investments. The chances that such a strategy will prove successful, however, depend in large measure on changes in the management and running of the company. Out of all the public flotations mentioned in this section, only the BT and KPN share offerings and the Chilean power privatizations have led to the transfer of corporate control from the public to the private sector; they were also the most successful public flotations of this group. The mere flotation of a minority block on the stock exchange without transfer of control of the company to the new private shareholders is unlikely to substantially improve performance.

Golden Shares

The U.K. privatizations have, as a rule, used the "golden share" technique. The creation of this special share was expressly provided for in the statutes of the company to be privatized, which had been amended before privatization (see also the section on golden shares in chapter 5). Generally speaking, a golden share gives the government the right to intervene to block changes in corporate control, takeovers, or foreign participations, as it did in the cases of Cable & Wireless, British Telecom, British Gas, British Airways, and BAA, for example.[86] For these, and for power generating and transmission companies,

---

(continued)

of December 1994 and a flooding of telecommunications issues on international markets, but these were known and already discounted factors. Another factor contributing to this problematic IPO was the institutional arrangements for the flotation, in particular the excessive number of global coordinators and financial advisers involved in the transaction; the crowd included four foreign global coordinators and four Indonesian ones, as well as two advisers.

85. See *Journal of Commerce*, 9 November 1994. An earlier attempt in 1993 to place 35 percent of OTE shares with strategic investors and 14 percent with the public was blocked by union opposition. A public share offering of 8 percent finally took place in March 1996, raising about $400 million. See also note 53 in chapter 3.

86. The 1984 prospectus for the sale of shares of British Telecommunications Plc described the rights attached to the golden share in the following terms: to attend and speak at shareholder meetings; to appoint up to two directors with the right to vote on issues of concern to the government; no right to share in the company's capital or profits; and repurchase value of one pound sterling. Similar provisions appear in the 1988 prospectus for British Gas Plc, except for the right to appoint directors; in addition, the government's prior written approval must be obtained for the amendment of some provisions of the company's articles of association, particularly the one prohibiting any person from holding more than 15 percent of the company's capital. The 1987 prospectus for British Airways Plc describes how the golden shares will limit the right of foreigners to acquire shares in the company, because foreign control could lead to loss of the right to operate certain international routes. Finally, in the case of British Airports Authority, the sale of an airport by the company (privatized in 1986) is subject to approval by the holder of the golden share.

the golden share has no expiration date. In other instances, it expired on a specified date: December 31, 1994, for the regional water distribution companies, for example, and March 31, 1995, for the regional electricity distribution companies. The flurry of takeover activity following the lapse of the golden share in the power and water distribution sectors attests to the strength of the rights given to the government by the golden share.[87] The main motivation for indefinite golden shares was often national security, whereas fixed-term golden shares were intended primarily to allow time (about five years) for the management of the privatized companies to restructure their company without having to worry about possible takeovers.

In New Zealand, the articles of Air New Zealand and Telecom were similarly amended to allow the government to retain a "Kiwi share" conferring special rights. The articles of Telekom Malaysia provide for a golden share entitling the government to oppose any decision that substantially affects the composition of the company's shareholding. In Italy, a decree-law introduces a provision into the statutes of public service companies granting the government a special share entitling it to oppose the acquisition or buildup by any person (or group) of shares exceeding 10 percent of the corporate capital of the company (or such lower percentage as may be determined by decree of the minister of the treasury).[88] Other countries have also utilized this technique, including Belgium for the privatization of the gas distribution company (see Royal Decree of June 16, 1994, reserving a golden share in Distrigaz for the government) and Hungary for the privatization of power and gas companies.[89]

Where golden shares are needed, they should be defined in the narrowest sense possible by limiting the scope of extraordinary rights they confer to the government to what is strictly necessary, and by restricting the duration of those rights. Golden shares—especially where they are held by governments without solid, credible track records—otherwise unduly restrict privatization and reduce privatization benefits, whether in the form of lower proceeds or less-efficient service providers.

---

87. This included, in the water sector, a $1.3 billion takeover of Northumbrian Water by Lyonnaise des Eaux in 1995 and the takeover of Southern Water by Scottish Power in 1996 (see note 117). In the electricity distribution sector, 1995 saw the $3.8 billion takeover of Eastern Electric by the Hanson conglomerate, the $1.7 billion takeover of Manweb by Scottish Power (an integrated utility), the $1.7 billion takeover of South Western Electric by Southern Company of the United States, the $2.4 billion takeover of power distributor Seeboard by Central & South West of the United States, the $1.3 billion takeover of South Wales Electricity by Welsh Water (now called Hyder), the $2.5 billion acquisition of Norweb by Northwest Water (since renamed United Utilities), as well as various other bids (see also above notes 25 and 31 and *Financial Times*, 13–14 April 1996).

88. See Decree-Law no. 389 of September 27, 1993, which had to be confirmed by means of an ordinary law within 60 days after its promulgation.

89. In Hungary, the golden shares in the privatized utilities were transferred after privatization by the privatization agency to the ministry for industry and trade, which will exercise the related rights on behalf of the government (see *Privatisation International*, March 1996, p. 21).

The Regulatory Framework

As noted before, the privatization of infrastructure companies offers a unique opportunity to introduce reforms in market structure, competition, and regulation. The discussion of regulation in this section will focus on important regulatory issues that arise in the context of privatization. A brief review of who should be regulated for what activities will be followed by discussions of specific regulatory instruments, consistency between regulatory reform and privatization, and regulatory institutions.[90]

Objectives of Regulation

Public service regulation may have multiple objectives. These include the promotion of efficiency; the satisfaction of demand, notably by promoting investment; the protection of consumers and users, in particular, against monopolistic or other abuses by the operator(s); the protection or even promotion of competition, including protection of those competing with a dominant operator; the prevention of discrimination; and the protection of investors against opportunistic government action. The primary purpose of economic regulation is to make up for the shortcomings of the marketplace. It should be distinguished from technical, safety, environmental, and other forms of regulation, although in practice these may often be intertwined.

The regulatory focus in many OECD countries has traditionally been on prices or profits, the objective being to limit monopoly profits through regulation of price or rate of return, which is not an unreasonable objective in mature markets. This approach was often relatively static, however, without taking due account of dynamic efficiencies and with few or no built-in incentives for efficiency. The U.K. privatization experience has vividly illustrated the extent to which public monopolies lead to vast inefficiencies; the size of the productivity enhancements obtained by allowing the privatized companies to keep the bulk of their cost savings has been surprisingly large (see the section below on the tariff regime).

The objectives of regulation ought to be different in most developing and transition countries, though. The level of profits of the private operator should be only a second order of importance. The main challenge is to meet existing and latent demand for services. Hence, the primary objective of regulation should be to ensure that the operators (public or private) meet minimum performance standards, leading to an accelerated closing of the gap between supply and demand. Consumers in most of these countries prefer a high-priced service to no service at all. Furthermore, distributional objectives or concerns can, if needed, be addressed through subsidies or other mechanisms.

---

90. For a more in-depth treatment of regulatory issues, see Beesley and Littlechild 1989; Train 1991; Veljanovski 1991, 1993; Beesley 1992; Laffont and Tirole 1993; Levy and Spiller 1993; Lipworth 1993; Bishop, Kay, and Mayer 1994; Armstrong, Cowan, and Vickers 1994; Laffont 1994; Tenenbaum 1996.

Depending on the objectives to be met, regulation may focus on tariff policy; direct and indirect subsidies; access to bottleneck facilities, including interconnection or network access by third parties; investment levels; performance targets; service quality and continuity; and so on. Most countries use a range of regulatory instruments (including specific stipulations in concession agreements or licenses and general rules) to govern the award of licenses, the oversight of the licensees, and, more generally, the rights and obligations of users, competitors, and other parties.

Enterprises Subject to Regulation

Economic activities can be regulated in different ways. Under public ownership, which is the most intrusive form of regulation, the state takes over the operation of the activity, enterprise, or sector. Under private ownership, the state regulates private economic agents through various legal instruments (laws, regulations, licenses, contracts, and so on). Recourse to monopoly public enterprises has not proven to be a very successful form of regulation, largely because of principal-agent problems. Where a public enterprise operates in a competitive sector, however—even if it is in a monopolistic segment of that sector—its public nature should in no way exempt it from the same arms-length regulation that applies to private enterprises.

Many have argued that where a monopoly is to be maintained, whether because the activity is a natural monopoly (a shrinking variety) or for some other reason, a public monopoly is in itself better than a private monopoly. Yet neither this nor the contrary thesis has ever been proven empirically, although limited attempts have been made.[91] Some private monopolies, such as the Philippines telecommunications company until recently, are notoriously inefficient, while others, such as the predivestiture AT&T, are relatively efficient.[92] Even a private monopoly operating without oversight by a regulator may sometimes be preferable to the former public monopoly or to a (poorly) regulated private monopoly.[93] In fact, the efficiency and

91. For a study confirming the dominant view that private enterprises tend to be more efficient, see, for example, Galal and others 1994, which covers primarily infrastructure companies (see also box 1 and note 7 in the introduction to this book). For a contrary view, see Bhattacharyya, Parker, and Raffiee 1994 who claim that their econometric study of the cost behavior of 225 public and 32 private water utilities in the United States provides "evidence that public water utilities are more efficient than private utilities on average, but are more widely dispersed between best and worst practice."

92. The liberalization of the Philippine telecommunications market that started in the early 1990s has resulted in a drop in PLDT's market share from about 97 percent in 1991 to about 80 percent five years later. "Yet the sector is now growing so rapidly that PLDT's business is set to triple, from about 1m telephone lines in 1994 to an estimated 3m by 2000" (*The Economist*, 11 May 1996). Interestingly, deregulation and the resulting growth prospects have made it easier for PLDT to attract foreign investment than was the case in the days the company was protected by a monopoly. See also Levy and Spiller 1993. On AT&T, see note 58 in this chapter.

93. See Roth 1987, p. 91, in which the author refers to a 1959 study that found that some unregulated private power companies in Latin America performed better than the regulated companies.

behavior of a monopolistic enterprise, whether private or public, depends much on the framework in which it operates, and especially on the existence of performance-enhancing incentives and penalties.

Regulation should be imposed on infrastructure service providers (public or private) where a market failure exists and the benefits of regulation exceed its costs. SOEs should thus be subject, by and large, to the same regulatory framework as private enterprises.[94] This becomes even more important when most infrastructure sectors are being opened to competition and new entry. If a sector is opened up to new entry but the incumbent SOE retains monopoly power in one or more market segments (large or small), the SOE will have to interact or compete with other operators. This should be done on a level playing field, with a common set of rules, regulations, and enforcement mechanisms.

Activities Subject to Regulation

The scope of regulatory intervention is largely determined by market structure and competition policy, which in turn depend on the specific characteristics of the sector and country concerned. While some activities or sector segments will be opened up to competition, others may remain monopolistic and will normally need to be regulated (see World Bank 1994c; Kessides 1993). Competitive activities will often be governed by the competition laws examined in chapter 3. In the transition from monopoly to competition, however, an active regulator may be needed to nurture nascent competition (maybe even by tilting the playing field in favor of new entrants) and to ensure that the (publicly or privately owned) dominant operator does not abuse its position.

Where some activities of a privatized company are competitive and others are subject to regulation, the competitive activities are sometimes covered by the regulatory framework established for the monopoly activity. This ensures, among other things, that the regulated activities do not subsidize the unregulated ones.

Award of Concessions and Licenses

Privatization of large infrastructure companies typically requires the issuance by the government or a regulator of concessions, franchises, licenses, authorizations, or permits to investors. These terms for the authority to operate are often used interchangeably, though they may have specific and different meanings in given countries or legal systems (on licenses and concessions, see also the section above on techniques for infrastructure privatization). The most

94. France (the general directorate for regulation) and Germany have established regulatory frameworks for the oversight of their monopolistic SOEs, but more as a prelude to demonopolization of the sector than as a way to deal with any perceived shortcomings of the SOE. In Australia, Chile, New Zealand, and other countries, corporatization of SOEs has been accompanied by arms-length regulation of the corporatized enterprises.

valuable asset offered for sale in an infrastructure privatization is not so much the physical infrastructure itself as the right to provide a service.[95] The conditions governing the award of the concession or license may be prescribed either in the privatization law, a concession law, or the regulations governing access to these sectors, where such regulations already exist. They will normally be detailed in the bidding documentation, where such licenses are awarded competitively. The award of a privatization contract following a bidding process should automatically include the grant of the operating license; indeed, ownership of sector assets without the authorization to provide the service would be pretty much worthless (see also the section below on the powers of regulators).

Similarly, the right granted by a license or concession to provide a public service sometimes requires access to other state-controlled resources or assets, which will need to be awarded as part of the license or concession or separately. This is especially so for the spectrum needed for wireless communications. Recent auctions held by the FCC in the United States show how valuable these spectrum rights are: the treasury raised over $1 billion in two narrow-band PCS (personal communications services) auctions and close to $18 billion in two broad-band PCS ones, organized as simultaneous, multiple-round auctions between 1994 and 1996.[96] The highest bidders got an operating license, as well as exclusive rights over a specific part of the radio spectrum, in their geographic area. Although no physical assets were transferred, this privatization of a portion of the airwaves counts among the largest privatization operations worldwide. Before these PCS auctions, licenses were awarded free of charge following an often lengthy administrative procedure in which firms competed for licenses and the embedded rents; firms that obtained licenses often sold them later at a handsome profit.

New EU rules call for free entry in telecommunications, unless there are resource constraints, spectrum in particular, in which case individual licenses (in addition to the operator's general telecommunications license) will be required to get the right to the spectrum. Other examples of access rights that need to be guaranteed to give a licensee the full benefit of the license include the award of airport slots, which are necessary complements to airline routes, and, more generally, third-party access or interconnection rights in network-type sectors.

---

95. In some instances, however, including some port or railway privatizations, land available for development may be more valuable than the infrastructure business itself.

96. Narrow-band licenses are used for paging, data services, and similar applications, while broad-band licenses are suitable for cellular services. The first broad-band auction ended in March 1995 following 112 rounds of bidding for 99 PCS licenses and raised $7 billion; three pioneer licenses had been awarded earlier without competition for about $700 million. The second broad-band auction ended in May 1996 following 184 rounds of bidding and yielded the treasury over $10 billion for 493 PCS licenses covering all the country in smaller geographic areas; they included preferential payment terms for small businesses, which had to pay only 10 percent down with the rest due over a ten-year period at a low treasury bill rate; the estimated discount embedded in these terms was 40 to 60 percent from cash terms. See *Washington Post*, 17 February 1996 and 7 May 1996; Cramton 1995.

Content of Concessions or Licenses

The concession (or license) entitles the holder to provide a public service under defined terms and conditions, including price. The terms of a concession should define the rights and obligations of the concessionaire (or licensee) and limit the possibility of arbitrary or political interference in the day-to-day management of the enterprise. They should clearly specify the scope of the license (services covered, time period, and so on).[97] In view of the chronic inefficiency and endemic underinvestment that characterizes infrastructure sectors in many countries, licenses will often require performance improvements as well as specific investment levels (see the section above on private capital requirements). By and large, though, the concession (or license) should focus on the results to be achieved by the service provider and on the incentives and sanctions linked to the achievement of those results; the means of achieving the results are generally better left to the judgment of the private operator.

The concession (or license) will also reflect (or even determine) the degree of competition in the sector and the rules governing such competition, including in many cases the scope of exclusivity rights, if any (see the section above on increasing competition in telecommunications).

Third-party access. In many infrastructure sectors, particularly in network industries, the most important part of the licensing terms and conditions may pertain to third-party access and interconnection. A major consideration in opting for unbundling the gas or power sector (through vertical separation of production, transmission, and distribution), for instance, is to simplify the regulators' task and the definition and enforcement of interconnection terms and conditions.[98] In the United Kingdom, the complexity of third-party access and interconnection issues and their importance to create competitive markets were underestimated at the design stage of the power, gas, and telecommunications privatizations; they remain one of the most difficult and controversial aspects of the regulatory system.

In most telecommunications reform programs the dominant operator loses its monopoly but radical unbundling does not usually take place. Following liberalization the dominant operator is at the same time operator of the network and main competitor of would-be entrants asking for intercon-

---

97. See, for example, article 23 of the Brazilian concession law of 1995, which outlines the essential clauses to be included in concession contracts.

98. See the special issue of *Oil & Gas-Law and Taxation Review*, 13 (1), January 1995, on third-party access in the EU power and gas sectors. See also European Council Directive no. 91/440/EEC of July 29, 1991, on community railway development, which includes provisions for third-party access to railway infrastructure; and European Commission decisions in *Sealink/B&I-Holyhead* (November 8, 1988) on third-party access to port facilities, and *London European/Sabena* (OJ 1988 L317/47) on access to a computerized reservation system for air transport services. See also Laffont 1994.

nection. In this context, how will new entrants be able to gain fair access to the network? Technical and financial issues are at the core of this question and must be addressed.

Important technical matters include the specific locations where competitors can interconnect, the signalization scheme used to allow the interface between operators, the numbering plans (including the access codes given to various operators, the ease with which consumers can switch between carriers, and the portability of telephone numbers), and so on.

The financial conditions of interconnection are also crucial. Access to the network or to bottleneck facilities should normally be granted on terms and conditions not less favorable than those that apply for internal use. Interconnection prices may also include a public service fee or surcharge, so that other operators contribute financially to the public service obligations imposed on the dominant carrier or local monopoly; this has been the case in the United States, where interconnection charges billed to long-distance companies subsidize local services provided by the Baby Bells (see note 59 above). In Mexico, the negotiations between Telmex and new entrants on these issues illustrate the difficulty of this process and its huge economic and financial stakes.[99] So do the many appeals filed by operators around the world against the access charges of the dominant operator.[100]

Regulatory provisions. Concessions and licenses are regulatory instruments; they set a priori the key regulatory parameters for the sector. They may be revoked if the licensee fails to meet its obligations. They provide for oversight, by the public administration or a regulatory agency, of the way in

99. Terms and conditions of interconnection between Telmex and the new entrants were to be negotiated between these parties in preparation of the liberalization of basic services in January 1997. In view of the impasse in negotiation, it was up to the Mexican ministry of communications to set the interconnection conditions. Cost was the most critical point in these discussions. Telmex had proposed a connection fee of 14.7 U.S. cents per minute, while competitors initially suggested a fee between 1 and 1.5 cents. The ministry finally settled on an average of 5.32 cents in 1997, 4.69 cents in 1998, and 3.15 cents thereafter. Executives from competing firms feared that, as this is an average for three different types of interconnection (local, long distance in, and long distance out), Telmex would keep international rates significantly higher and local rates lower (see *Journal of Commerce*, 25 April 1996 and 29 April 1996). The delays in coming to an agreement are to a large extent a result of the government's failure to adopt binding interconnection principles and rules, as well as of the absence of a regulator who could impose a binding settlement on the parties. The establishment of a new federal telecommunications commission was planned for late 1996.

100. In France, for example, following a complaint submitted to the director general of postal services and telecommunications (DGPT) by SFR (an affiliate of the Compagnie Générale des Eaux which became the second operator of mobile telephones) against the interconnection charges billed by France Télécom, the minister of postal services and telecommunications ruled in June 1994 in favor of the private operator, compelling the public operator to reduce its public network access charges and also its line lease charges by 41 to 62 percent (*Le Nouvel Economiste*, 949, 10 June 1994, p. 45). See also note 118 for a U.K. example.

Box 7.3   Basic Features of a Telecommunications License or Concession

The clauses of concessions or licenses vary substantially, of course, depending on the scope of services covered, the intensity of competition, and other country and sector characteristics, but they do have some common features. The following are typically found in concessions or licenses granted to the operator of a public telecommunications network.

- Definition of the network to which the concession or license applies, clearly distinguishing between this network and, where appropriate, other public networks, private networks, and terminal equipment
- Definition of the services covered: for example, local exchange, long distance and international communications, wireless services (cellular or other), trunk radio, paging, Internet access, satellite communications, packet-switched data network, leased lines, private networks, telex, telegram, and so on
- Definition of scope and duration of exclusivity, where exclusivity is granted
- Qualitative and quantitative performance obligations, namely geographic coverage, number of new connections, number of public telephones, maximum percentage of faults tolerated, maximum repair time, and so on
- Obligation to publish tariffs and to meet consumer demand on a nondiscriminatory basis
- Social or public service obligations, such as free emergency numbers, information services, and services to the physically handicapped and hearing impaired
- Prohibition of anticompetitive practices, such as linked sales, cross-subsidies, discrimination, and selection of subcontractors without prior public call for bids
- Obligation to connect approved terminal equipment without discrimination and rules concerning the supply of equipment manufactured by the operator
- Obligation to grant connection to other networks (interconnection) on reasonable conditions; formula to calculate the interconnection tariff, taking into account the cost of such service and, where applicable, a contribution to help finance the main operator's public service obligations
- Tariffs and adjustment formulas, including determination of the baskets of services to which they apply
- Code of good practice with respect to suppliers and consumers, including rules of confidentiality
- Billing, metering, and recordkeeping requirements
- Prohibition on dealing with a single foreign carrier when several operators are authorized to provide international services
- Rules concerning the allocation, change, and portability of telephone numbers
- Rights of way; use of or access to public or private properties allowing the operator to install and maintain cables and equipment; application of eminent domain rules, where applicable
- Payment by the operator of license or concession fees
- Disclosure requirements; information to be provided to the regulatory agency; right of agency to perform controls as needed, including onsite verifications
- Accounting and auditing rules and regulations

- Award to operator of necessary permits, authorizations, and so on
- Rules on assignment of concession or licenses, including (where applicable) limitations on foreign investment
- Rules concerning the investigation of complaints
- Action to be taken in the event of service interruptions or of default of the operator
- Operator's responsibility and liability
- Guarantees, warranties, performance bonds, and so on
- Penalties
- Conditions pertaining to termination, revocation, amendment, and renewal of the license or concession.

Source: Adapted from Smith and Staple 1994, p. 68, who based their checklist primarily on the licenses or concessions of the dominant operating companies in the United Kingdom (BT), Mexico (Telmex), and Sri Lanka (SLT). The first two were already private, while SLT was still an SOE (it is being prepared for privatization).

which the company is fulfilling its obligations, and they specify how rights and obligations may be amended to take account of new circumstances.[101]

Box 7.3 lists common clauses found in basic telecommunications concessions and licenses. Similar clauses may be found in concessions or licenses in other infrastructure sectors and for other telecommunications services. Depending on specific legal and administrative traditions, some of these clauses may be found in related agreements or instruments rather than in the license or concession itself; additional items will invariably be covered by the license or concession.

Tariff Regime

The pricing system, particularly the tariffs and their adjustment formula, is typically the cornerstone of the regulatory mechanism. It will determine the returns investors can expect and the incentives they may receive to provide a quality service. This section deals primarily with the tariff level and formula. Often of equal importance will be who will apply this tariff regime, what discretionary powers are given in this context, and how such discretion will be managed (see the section below on regulatory institutions).

Most infrastructure sectors are not as monolithic as was once thought (see the section on market structure, competition, and divestiture). Some activities

101. See, in particular, the theories of *imprévision* (circumstances unforeseen) and *fait du prince* (right of government to act unilaterally) in French concession law. Article 12 of the Philippine constitution limits franchise or license rights to a maximum of 50 years and allows congress to unilaterally amend or repeal such authorizations when the common good so requires. See also articles 14 through 17 of Colombian Law no. 80 of 1993 on contracts with the state, which provide for unilateral termination and modification of state contracts, including concession contracts. See also note 68 above.

in a sector may be of a competitive nature, whereas others remain fundamentally monopolistic. Normally, only the prices of noncompetitive services should be regulated, and restrictions should be imposed prohibiting an enterprise from subsidizing its competitive activities with revenues from its regulated activities.[102] The introduction of separate cost accounting is often a first step in this direction.[103]

The chosen tariff formula must be one that can be effectively applied by the competent authority. This presupposes, in particular, that the information needed by the authority to perform its function is available, that the authority can force the regulated enterprises to disclose such information, and that it can check its accuracy and reliability. The degree of complexity of the price adjustment mechanism should thus take account of the regulatory agency's technical resources and capacity. In other words, the regulatory mechanism should be tailored to the specific characteristics and constraints of the country and sector concerned.

RPI–X. The following paragraphs explore the tariff formula adopted by the U.K. government in most of its infrastructure privatizations (see Beesley and Littlechild 1989; Lipworth 1993). That formula merits special attention for its innovative nature, for its key role in the U.K. infrastructure privatization process, and for the considerable influence it has had on regulatory thinking and on the design of regulatory schemes in privatizing countries.

The U.K. formula—better known as the price cap or RPI–X formula—sets a cap or ceiling on the authorized periodic price adjustment of a specified basket of services at RPI–X, where RPI represents the inflation rate as measured by the retail price index and X the productivity factor initially stipulated in the privatization prospectus. In the case of British Telecom, for example, the value of X was set originally (1984) at 3 percent, then raised by OFTEL (the regulator) to 4.5 percent in 1989 (at the end of the initial five-year period prescribed in the license), 6.25 percent in 1991, and 7.5 percent in 1993.[104] BT has thus been compelled by the regulator to pass more and more

102. BT's license contains clauses prohibiting BT from using its profits from regulated services to subsidize unregulated activities, such as the sale of telecommunications equipment. The purpose is to prevent BT from competing unfairly with other equipment suppliers. The terms of the license similarly prohibit BT from charging third parties (competitors) a higher price for access or other intermediate services than it costs BT to provide for its own services.

103. EU regulation no. 1893/91 (modifying regulation no. 1191/69 dealing with public service obligations in the transport sector), for example, establishes the principle of suppression of public service obligations and their replacement with contracts negotiated by the government and the transport company in instances where nonprofitable transport services are to be maintained for public policy reasons; it further requires separate accounting for such public service activities.

104. Indexing is to a basket of services, which was modified at each formula adjustment. BT is free to alter the prices included in this basket, provided that the price of the overall basket, as a (weighted) average, declines in real terms at least by the value of X, the set productivity factor. Some services not included in the basket are subject to other productivity factors (different value of X), while the price of yet another category of services is freely set by the operator. The percentage of BT's receipts subject to price control rose from 55 percent in 1984 to 80 percent in 1993.

of its productivity gains on to subscribers. Since the 1991 adjustment, the price cap formula has led to annual reductions not only in real prices but also in nominal prices.

At the time of the first adjustment in 1989, BT agreed that the next review would be held in 1993, that is, a year earlier than initially planned, with a possible mid-term review in 1991 to reflect any exceptional circumstances outside BT's control. The 1991 interim adjustment did take place to take account of, in particular, accelerated technological developments in the telecommunications sector.

The value assigned to a productivity factor should be neither too high (to avoid discouraging potential buyers or the investments they may be prepared to make, or deterring the entry of new competitors) nor too low (to avoid either excessively low productivity gains or excessive profits, high consumer prices, and reduced competitiveness of the national economy). Although the productivity adjustment should normally be negative (positive productivity factor, preceded by a minus sign), it may be outweighed by some other factor, such as the extra cost of capital required when large new investments have to be made, as was required in the U.K. water sector to bring standards up to EU norms.[105]

Choosing the level of productivity gains to be achieved is particularly difficult at the time of privatization, because there is not enough information available to ascertain the productivity gains the privatized enterprise can obtain. The U.K. government in fact underestimated the inefficiency of the infrastructure SOEs to be privatized, or, more precisely, the potential productivity gains the privatized companies would be able to achieve. Because it limited competition in the market (see the section above on competition, market structure, and divestiture) and did not create competition for the market, that is, for the right to buy the enterprises to be privatized, the government was not able to extract the monopoly rents that remained in these sectors at privatization. Where competition cannot be introduced in the market, the best way to extract these rents is to use a competitive mechanism for the sale of the enterprise or of its shares, leaving it up to the bidders or to the marketplace to assess potential productivity gains. The first tranche of BT was, however, sold in November 1984 by means of a public offering of three billion shares (50.2 percent of the capital), at the fixed price of £1.30 per share; the offer was three times oversubscribed. A similar mechanism was used in most U.K. infrastructure privatizations that followed.

The factor X was scheduled to be revalued every four to five years, depending on the specific license provisions in each sector. The regulator may, however, decide at any time to amend the terms of a license, including the value of X, with the agreement of the regulated enterprise. In the event

---

105. The formula used in the water privatization is referred to as RPI+K, where K represents the increase in the tariff needed in real terms to finance the sector's huge investment program. See the section above on water, and note 20.

that the privatized company (BT, for example) opposes this adjustment, the matter may be submitted to the Monopolies and Mergers Commission; if the MMC declares the regulated enterprise to have acted contrary to the public interest, and if the minister of industry and trade does not object, the regulator may amend the license (see sections 12–15 of the telecommunications act of 1984; see also notes 25, 36, and 68 in this chapter).

In the United Kingdom, a certain amount of bargaining can take place between regulator and regulated enterprise concerning not just the value of X but also the degree of competition in the market, the conditions of interconnection, the information to be furnished, and even the very survival of the enterprise as such, as the regulator can threaten to go to the MMC asking that the enterprise be split into smaller entities.

By allowing the enterprise to keep the benefits of any cost reductions it achieves between two relatively distant adjustments, the price cap formula provides real efficiency incentives which tend to be higher than under rate-of-return regulation (even when taking regulatory lag into account). The periodicity of the X factor modification may, however, bring this formula closer to the rate-of-return formula. Indeed, as part of the preparatory analysis leading to the setting of a new X value, the regulator will assess the enterprise's rate of return; an "excessive" rate of return will inevitably lead to a higher X factor (that is, lower permissible rate increases); the profitability of the enterprise is thereby reduced to a rate the regulator deems reasonable in light of information obtained from the capital markets (industry averages for rate of return on equity, bond yields, and so on) and other sources.

Another difference between RPI–X and the rate-of-return formula is that the administrative burden of the former is lighter, because it is less dependent on information supplied by the regulated enterprise itself, requires less verification on the part of the regulator, and allows the regulator's discretionary interventions to be spaced more widely. Some argue, on the other hand, that the administrative burden of price caps may be higher rather than lower, because in the end regulators need to perform the same analysis as that required for rate-of-return regulation, and they must forecast productivity improvements over the next four or five years.

Price caps may be better suited to industries experiencing constant technological change, where the regulated enterprise will be able to benefit from productivity and profitability gains generated by the accelerated introduction of new technologies. It is still too early, however, to pass final judgment on the respective advantages and disadvantages of these formulas. But it is clear that the price-cap formula is not without shortcomings and risks. Tenenbaum, Lock, and Barker (1992, pp. 27–28) note three such risks: (a) the regulator may try to reduce tariffs if the companies post profits that are higher than expected, and thereby reduce the incentive to cut costs; (b) the regulated enterprises may try to increase their profits by lowering service quality; and (c) the formula may not provide the desired incentives to carry out new investments. In addition, price caps tend to expose investors to greater regulatory risk.

These risks are amplified in developing or transition countries whose regulatory organs may not have developed a solid reputation for independence and professionalism. The main risk in these cases is that investors may not be prepared to accept a discretionary adjustment of X that could lead to heavy losses, or they may consent to invest only if the expected yield is very high, enabling them to recoup investments before the first adjustment of the X factor. Any long-term private investment in these sectors will be conditional on the existence of a reasonable and credible price adjustment mechanism that limits the risk of "administrative expropriation." From this point of view, a four- or five-year lag between regulatory reviews of the formula tends to be preferable to discretionary annual price adjustments. Moreover, investors may seek protection from arbitrary revisions by having rules or principles included in the applicable regulation or license to guide such revisions; they may also ask for provisions in their contracts allowing them to go to arbitration in the event a regulatory decision significantly alters the terms of the license or the balance of the contract with adverse effect on the company.

Excess tariffs. In most countries, the posting of extraordinary profits—profits much higher than risk-adjusted market yields—by enterprises that enjoy some degree of monopoly will usually be politically untenable over the long term, regardless of the applicable contractual or regulatory provisions. The row over the profits and the compensation packages of senior executives of privatized water and power companies in the United Kingdom provides a recent illustration. It also points to new directions in regulatory design, in particular toward formulas that allow efficiency improvements to be shared between the operator and the users, which might make large profits more palatable politically. In response to this heightened sensibility, some British water utilities decided in 1995 to use part of their profits to offer voluntary rebates to their customers.

Finally, as pointed out earlier, excessive importance should not be attached to the level of prices in countries where the priority is to stimulate investment and network expansion. In these countries it may indeed be preferable to have relatively high tariffs. An enterprise could then self-finance a large part of its investment program, and contractual or regulatory mechanisms could compel it to reinvest the "excess" tariff in the sector to meet demand.

Consistency between Regulatory Reform and Privatization

The regulatory framework governing the activities of the privatized enterprise should be put into effect before or, at the latest, at privatization. Regulatory reform and privatization processes thus need to be closely coordinated.

Impact of regulation on potential investors. Before they can calculate the price they are prepared to offer, investors will want to know the regulatory system under which the company will be operating.[106] They will also have to form a view on how this regime can be expected to evolve in the years ahead. To meet these objectives, it may be desirable to anchor the regulatory framework securely in a law, which would give it greater stability than an executive instrument. In Venezuela, the lack of such a law has probably been a factor in the relative instability of the regulatory system, as discussed above in the section on the privatization of the Venezuelan telecommunications operator. The regulatory framework can be spelled out in a sector-specific privatization law, in a special regulatory law, or in the law organizing the sector. Key provisions can be further stabilized by inclusion in the privatization or concession contracts, which require the consent of the investors to be modified. A tradeoff exists, however, between stability and flexibility. A rigid framework, legislative or contractual, may reduce uncertainty, but it may also entail a cost, because mistakes are harder to correct and evolving circumstances harder to take into account.

To reassure investors, reduce the risk premium they factor into every investment decision, and obtain the best possible price for the enterprise or activity to be privatized, the government may have to promise not to alter the regulatory system substantially, or at least not to do so to the detriment of the investors. To be effective, however, this commitment needs to be credible. Credibility could be enhanced by provisions in the privatization agreements or the license allowing the company to automatically adjust its tariffs based on a given formula, or by an undertaking that the government will compensate the operator (through a subsidy or tax break, for example) for any negative impact that results from governmental rejection or delay of a contractually agreed tariff increase. Failing this, the promise is unlikely to be

---

106. "How much should regulators reveal about their plans for industries under their supervision?" asks *The Economist*. "Too little, and the regulated firms' managers, investors and competitors are obliged to make long-term decisions based on loose guesswork. Too much, and regulators find themselves prejudging issues they have had too little time to consider. In Britain these questions are politically sensitive right now, because the government is about to sell half its remaining 49% stake in BT, the near-monopoly telephone company. Potential investors know that what BT's regulator, OFTEL, decides over the next few years will affect its profitability much more than anything BT's management is likely to dream up. So they want to know more about OFTEL's intentions. . . . The silence is the result of conflicting interests. As seller and policymaker, the government is pulled two ways. It wants to raise as much as it can for its shares, partly to curb its expanding borrowing requirement and partly to avoid accusations of a giveaway. To do that, it needs to talk BT up. At the same time, it wants to be seen to be promoting competition in Britain's telecommunications industry, and to be equipping the regulator it created with the means to do its job. OFTEL itself is in a similar bind. Sir Bryan wants both to assert his independence from the government and to avoid controversy that might lose him his job when he comes up for reappointment next June. The same forces act upon any government, and any regulator, when state-owned industries go private" ("The Regulators' Bind: When Governments Sell Their Stakes in Industry, Frankness is Best," *The Economist*, 2 November 1991, p. 18). In the end, OFTEL did break the silence and made a statement prior to flotation.

taken seriously and bidders will submit lower bids. Governments with low credibility and an inadequate track record hence will usually have to offer more guarantees to attract private investors.

Impact of regulation on buyers. Coordination between regulatory approach and privatization objectives extends to the very close link that exists between the key features of the concession and the behavior of the winning bidder. Imposition of excessively severe obligations with respect to the quality of the service to be provided by the privatized company (for example, very short repair times, or very high dial tone requirements or call-completion ratios for the telecommunications sector) or excessively low rates could compromise expansion and increased penetration of the network, which are prime objectives for most developing and transition countries.

Impact of regulation on the value of the privatized company. The tariff or regulatory formula also may be a function of the chosen privatization objectives and techniques. Where, for example, an enterprise is regulated by reference to a rate of return on capital invested, user charges may simply be jacked up to achieve the authorized (regulated) rate of return and maximize privatization receipts (this would not be the case if the rate of return were calculated on the historic book value of the company, for example, which may differ widely from the price paid).

The scope and nature of the controls that will be exercised after the government withdraws will necessarily have a direct bearing on the value of the company. Stricter regulation or lower protection against competition will inevitably reduce profits and therefore share value, which, as indicated earlier, is not necessarily a bad thing. Box 7.4 illustrates the fluctuations in the share price of regulated companies caused by amendments to the regulatory framework. A similar link between regulatory framework and share price can be seen in the poor results of privatization operations launched in the absence of a well-defined and credible regulatory framework, as demonstrated, for example, by the less than successful privatization of Hungarian power companies at the end of 1995; prices were lower than expected, and five of seven generation companies found no buyer at all (see *Privatisation International*, December 1995, p. 25, and March 1996, p. 21).

Regulatory Institutions

As shown in the preceding section, the establishment of a regulatory framework is a prerequisite for the success of an infrastructure privatization program. This section focuses on the regulatory agencies and the regulators.[107]

107. It is, however, impossible in this book to examine all of the possible institutional and regulatory alternatives. For a more thorough review of issues of regulatory design and institutions, see Helm 1994; Neven, Nuttall, and Seabright 1993; Phillips 1993; Smith 1996.

Box 7.4   Impact of Regulatory Changes on Share Price

Regulatory decisions often have an immediate and sometimes dramatic impact on the stock market performance of the regulated enterprises. For example, the shares of BAA (British Airports Authority) rose by 5 percent on November 18, 1991 (to the highest daily trading volume since share flotation in 1987), in response to an improvement in BAA prospects due to adoption of a new formula for the calculation of traffic user fees by the Civil Aviation Administration. Similarly, British Gas shares fell by some 3 percent on December 21, 1993, after the government announced the abolition (partial from 1996 and total from April 1998) of the monopoly held by this company, privatized in 1986.

The decisions of OFFER (the power regulator) have had a major impact on the share quotations of the companies affected. Thus the market capitalization of the 12 electricity distribution companies of England and Wales rose from £14.8 billion to 15.9 billion (an increase of about 7.5 percent) following announcement by the regulator on August 11, 1994, of the new pricing system, which the market perceived as better than had been predicted; some people had expected the regulator to impose appreciably bigger price reductions. When the same regulator announced on March 7, 1995, that the price regime would be tightened further than announced in August 1994, shares of the regional electricity companies lost nearly 23 percent of their value. This surprise announcement came the day after the U.K. government had completed the sale of its second and last tranche of shares of the two large power generators (PowerGen and National Power); those shares "tumbled more than 4% in London trading, infuriating investors who bought the shares Monday, before Mr. Littlechild's bombshell" (*Wall Street Journal*, 8 March 1995 and 30 March 1995).

Finally, the share price of the Chilean telephone company CTC fell by 14 percent in one day following downward revision of its tariffs by the Chilean regulator in March 1994. The New York stock exchange had to suspend quotation of CTC.

The privatization of Sui Northern Gas Pipelines Ltd., a gas distribution company in Pakistan, affords another illustration of the importance of setting up a clear regulatory framework before privatization. In 1992 the government launched the privatization of this company with a private placement of 20 percent of the shares with a strategic investor (gas operator) and 40 percent by a public offering underwritten by MCB, a local commercial bank. The shortcomings of the regulatory framework were partly responsible for the failure of both the private placement and the subscription, and MCB found itself with a large block of shares on its hands. The government and MCB tried to interest multinational companies in the purchase of these shares, but the negotiations broke down for the same reason—namely, the share price was deemed too high in light of the uncertainty surrounding the regulatory system. Potential buyers were prepared to pay the asking price provided that sectoral regulations were satisfactorily amended before the purchase; without such amendment, they were not prepared to offer more than 40 to 60 percent of the asking price.

Sources: See also *Financial Times,* 19 November 19, 1991, 22 December 1993, 9 March 1994, and 13–14 August 1994; *Oxford Analytica,* 8 April 1994; Beesley and Littlechild 1989, p. 457.

Tailoring the institutional and regulatory framework to national conditions. The telecommunications sector has a rich fund of experience in privatization and regulation. As in other sectors, the United Kingdom created an interesting precedent when it privatized BT by establishing an autonomous, independent regulatory organ with decisionmaking powers (OFTEL). Autonomous regulatory commissions find their origins in the mid-nineteenth century in the United States and the United Kingdom. They started out as advisory railways commissions, and the first autonomous regulatory commissions with decisionmaking powers were established by several American states in the 1870s.

The U.K. model, and in particular the decisionmaking powers given to individual and independent regulators, should be seen in the proper context: the United Kingdom is a sophisticated industrial country with very strong, well-established legal practices and traditions. In many developing and transition countries, the difficulty of designing an appropriate regulatory framework is amplified by civil service regulations, practices, and salary scales; political intervention; weakness of the judicial system; scarcity of trained managers; lack of relevant regulatory experience; and other such constraints.

It should also be noted that the U.K. model is currently being reassessed there. Many observers feel that the regulatory process lacks transparency; that it has been excessively personalized; and that the powers of the regulators are too broad, while regulators themselves are not subject to control and many of their decisions are not open to appeal (see Veljanovski 1993, pp. 60–62). Some have proposed that the regulators be subject to parliamentary control to give the process more democratic legitimacy. Others feel that the increasingly competitive nature of regulated sectors erodes the justification for separate sectoral regulatory agencies, and suggest that merger of these agencies, or even their absorption by the competition agencies, would in the longer run be a better solution (see Lipworth 1993, p. 57; Helm 1994).

Levy and Spiller 1993 compared the performance of private telecommunications operators in five countries. The authors concluded that the major determinant of telecommunications performance is a good fit between the mode of organization and regulation of the sector in a given country, on the one hand, and the country's administrative, judicial, and legislative practices and traditions, on the other. In addition to rules that are clear and tailored to these practices and traditions, good systems have three other characteristics: basic rules limiting the discretionary powers of the regulatory body, restrictions on the power to modify the existing system, and mechanisms for ensuring effective implementation of and compliance with these rules and restrictions.

The study notes high private investment levels where these requirements are met, as in Chile (since 1987), Jamaica (before 1962 and since 1987), and the United Kingdom (since 1984), and low private investment if one or more of the conditions is not met, as in Chile (in the 1950s), Jamaica (between 1966 and 1975), and the Philippines. The authors postulate that the strong growth of private investment following the 1990 privatization of ENTEL in Argentina, despite the lack of a clear regulatory framework, is attributable to the confidence inspired by the scope and success of the Menem administration's overall economic reform program. Another conclusion of the study is that a given system of regulation can be perfectly effective in one country and totally ill suited for another; a thorough analysis and understanding of a country's administrative, judicial, and legislative practices and traditions is essential to the design and implementation of an efficient regulatory scheme.

Powers of regulators. The authority or powers of regulatory bodies vary widely. The range goes from purely advisory bodies to bodies that award and police licenses, adjudicate disputes, and oversee the sector in general.

Advisory bodies should not be discounted too easily as regulatory instruments.[108] They offer a degree of transparency and inject analysis and debate in discussions that previously would have taken place in the secrecy of a ministerial cabinet. The advisory body can see its role and influence increased when the authority that is competent to make a specific decision (a minister, for example) is not only forced to seek its advice and take it into account, but also to justify any departure from such advice; furthermore, for certain matters, the competent authority may not be allowed to reach a decision going against the opinion or advice received.

In a privatization context, the issuance of licenses is usually left to the government as part of the divestiture process.[109] Indeed, the sale of a utility or infrastructure company without the licenses and permits needed to provide the public service would not make much sense. The postprivatization award of licenses, or modifications in existing licenses, may be left either to the government agency that issued the original license, to that agency upon recommendation of the regulator, to the regulator, or to some other mechanism. The power to modify or adapt the terms of concessions or licenses, if given to a regulator, is usually restricted, as discussed in the sections above on award and content of concessions or licenses.

Regulators typically have the power to adjudicate disputes between operators or between users and operators. This may be the most important func-

---

108. As mentioned above, U.S. regulatory commissions were initially established as advisory commissions, the Rhode Island Railway Commission being the first one in 1839. The creation of the Hungarian energy bureau pursuant to the gas law of 1994 provides a more recent example of a regulator that can recommend but not set tariffs.

109. An exception is Bolivia, where even the initial licenses were granted by the regulatory agency. Capitalization (privatization) agreements signed by the government and the investors promised that such licenses would be issued. This approach is not recommended, however, because it adds an unnecessary element of uncertainty to the privatization process. If the regulator does not issue the promised license, investors would not be totally unprotected, however; they would still have contractual recourse against the government.

tion of a regulator when a sector is being liberalized and a dominant operator controls bottleneck facilities and tries to use them to keep competitors out or at a significant disadvantage. Disputes on technical, financial, or timing aspects of interconnection are cases in point.

Regulators are also normally in charge of verifying compliance with the legislation in force as well as with the terms and conditions of concessions or licenses. To facilitate this task, legislation imposes strict disclosure requirements on regulated enterprises and gives regulators broad investigative powers. They may also have the power to impose sanctions and penalties. Finally, regulatory bodies may be given the power to prepare and enact general norms and regulations applicable to the enterprises operating under their watch.

Autonomy and independence of regulators. The independence of a regulatory body is worth little unless it is upheld against incursions by the regulated industry. Cases of capture of the regulator by industry are indeed not uncommon. The problem is particularly acute where regulatory agencies are set up as part of the civil service in countries where this system (especially its personnel rules) does not allow for adequate remuneration of staff. In these cases, the independence of the regulatory staff is likely to be rapidly eroded by practices which, while undoubtedly illegal, are nonetheless common. By removing regulatory staff from civil service constraints, governments may remunerate them in ways that better protect them from industry capture and that allow the agency to attract qualified candidates, hence enhancing the professionalization of the regulatory function.

In addition, rules need to be laid down concerning conflicts of interest (for example, by prohibiting former staff of the regulatory agency from working for a regulated enterprise for a specified period after they leave the agency). Independence from industry also requires that, where SOEs are operating in the sector, the regulatory function be clearly separated from the exercise by the government of its SOE ownership functions. Where sectors were run as a public monopoly the confusion of operating and regulatory powers in a single entity or person was not uncommon; as the sector starts to open up to new entry, however, this situation quickly becomes untenable. An institutional setup that allows the same senior official to be regulator and representative of the state's ownership interests in an SOE would not pass muster.[110]

Ministerial regulation has been the tradition in numerous countries, including Indonesia, Japan, Malaysia, and many continental European countries.[111] It is losing ground, however, even in countries such as France and Germany where the regulatory function had typically been entrusted to a department or

---

110. For an extreme example, consider Pakistan, where in 1995 the chairman of the board of the Pakistan Telecommunications Corporation was assigned the additional responsibility of chairman of the Pakistan Telecommunications Authority.

111. In Japan, for example, the ministry of postal services and telecommunications has to approve the tariffs of NTT, the dominant and partially privatized telecommunications operator.

agency of the central government.[112] The trend is clearly toward more autonomous regulatory setups, separating regulatory agencies from government ministries. This is illustrated, for example, by conditions placed by the European Commission on the approval of the alliance between Deutsche Telekom and France Télécom, and by the regulatory principles being negotiated at meetings of the World Trade Organization on telecommunications.[113]

Independent, autonomous regulatory agencies with decisionmaking powers may not be suitable for all countries, however. This may be especially true of countries with authoritarian governments, where in practice the head of state takes all important decisions affecting the country, whether legally empowered to do so or not. If the political independence of the regulatory organ cannot be ensured, creating a new agency with decisionmaking powers may needlessly complicate the management of the sector and the life of the operators by introducing an additional actor and yet another level of uncertainty.

112. In France, the ministry of industry and telecommunications has been in charge of regulating telecommunications, including settling disputes between operators, even though it was also the supervisory ministry of France Télécom, the national telecommunications SOE. This setup is likely to change, however. Indeed, although the French government has traditionally been opposed to autonomous regulatory bodies, it is now moving in that direction. In a recent public consultation document on telecommunications, it stated, "While the experience acquired by the DGPT since its foundation confirms the potential and the advantages inherent in the current transition towards a competitive market, the complete opening up of the French market to competition makes a new approach necessary. There appear to be two feasible solutions: the first is to entrust to an autonomous body the tasks of carrying out arbitration and imposing penalties, while regulation (i.e. regulation arising from the application of market ground rules) would be handled directly, as is the practice today, within a ministerial organisation; the second would involve giving the regulatory body more independence from the Government to enforce the ground rules, to act as arbitrator and to impose penalties. . . . To set up an autonomous regulatory body would be to adopt a similar approach to most of our partners. The independence of such a body would be guaranteed by the manner of appointment of its director(s), i.e. for a fixed term of office and not renewable. That body would also enjoy all the guarantees necessary to its proper operation. . . . Powers related to regulation (settlement of disputes arising from network interconnection and licences, application of the schedules of terms and conditions, allocation of essential resources, monitoring of universal service provision) would fall within the remit of the regulatory authority by delegation under law or by decision of the Minister. Licences could be granted by the Minister on the basis of reports submitted by the regulatory body (as in the UK) or directly by the regulatory body itself (as intended in Germany)" ("New Ground Rules for Telecommunications in France," Ministère des Technologies de l'Information et de la Poste, October 1995, pp. 21–23). The government later submitted a bill to parliament that called for an independent regulatory commission to rule on competition issues and settle disputes between operators (public and private), while leaving the licensing of operators to the government (Law no. 96-659 of 26 July 1996 on regulation of telecommunications).

113. Conditions imposed by the commission for its approval of the Atlas alliance between Deutsche Telekom and France Télécom, and of the Global One alliance between these two operators and Sprint, included the effective liberalization by France and Germany of alternative infrastructure provision (and award of the first licenses to such providers), the sale by France Télécom of its German data network services subsidiary, nondiscriminatory access by competing operators to their networks and facilities, separate accounting systems for the new alliances, and the prohibition of cross-subsidies (see *Financial Times*, 18 July 1996; see also the section above on EU policy in the telecommunications sector).

The same does not hold for regulatory commissions with an advisory mandate. To the contrary, creation of an autonomous, independent commission in this case may well constrain the arbitrariness of the political decisionmakers. By requiring that such a body make recommendations on all key regulatory decisions, the ultimate decisionmaker may indeed make better-informed decisions and be more reluctant to rule in a way that demonstrates arbitrariness, discrimination, or cronyism. Publicity of recommendations can further strengthen the commission's influence and the decisionmaker's accountability.

The specific institutional setup of a regulatory agency also may affect its independence. Design issues include choices between a regulatory body responsible for several or all infrastructure sectors and a separate one for each sector; and between a single regulator and a collegial regulatory commission. The U.K. model, for example, provides for a single regulator, called director general, who heads an office with numerous staff. The U.S. model provides for a commission of regulators acting as a council; examples are the public service commissions that exist in most states, as well as the Federal Communications Commission and Federal Energy Regulatory Commission (FERC). Multimember commissions often provide greater safeguards against undue influence or lobbying and may limit the risk of rash or radical regulatory decisions; in many developing and transition countries this consideration will outweigh the relative costs in terms of slower decisionmaking and lesser accountability of regulators.

Another design issue is the way in which regulatory activities are financed: autonomy is strengthened by granting the regulator financing sources independent of the general budget, typically in the form of charges, fees, or levies on the enterprises or services subject to regulation. Publicity, transparency, and disclosure rules reinforce and protect the independence of the regulator.

Finally, regulators are typically appointed by the government, although they often have to be confirmed by the legislature. In Bolivia, regulators are appointed by the executive from a list presented by the legislature.[114] In some American states, such as Tennessee and Georgia, they are elected by the general population (this gives a large influence on regulatory matters to one specific group, namely, residential users of public services). Appointment by the executive with legislative involvement (initiation or confirmation) gives the process more stability and authority. In order to avoid undue governmental interference in the regulatory business, the law often specifies that, once appointed to a fixed term (most often between four and seven years), regulators cannot be removed at the government's discretion.

---

114. Article 4 of Law no. 1600 (October 28, 1994) on the establishment of Sirese, the regulatory institution for the infrastructure sectors, stipulates that the president appoints the general superintendent in charge of Sirese from a list of candidates proposed by the senate voting with a two-thirds majority. Article 8 specifies the same appointment procedure for the sectoral superintendents.

More or less discretion? In countries with administrative and judicial systems short on resources or credibility, the use of detailed and relatively inflexible concession agreements backed by international arbitration procedures may be more likely to reassure investors than the creation of an autonomous regulatory agency with rulemaking powers. Guinea and Côte d'Ivoire both opted for this approach in privatizing their water supply and electric power sectors; the concession agreement was accompanied by a detailed schedule of obligations and conditions, leaving few aspects to be decided or agreed upon during execution of the contract. Detailed a priori regulation is better suited to relatively stable, technologically mature, and monopolistic sectors, such as water and power distribution, than to sectors undergoing rapid technological evolution, such as telecommunications.

A balance has to be found for each country and each sector between prior definition of rules that can turn out to be highly restrictive and adoption of a more flexible framework that allows for evolution of the rules under the authority of a regulator but adds uncertainty. In certain circumstances (where regulatory institutions are weak, for example) and in some sectors (such as water), fairly precise upfront regulation may be preferable to more flexible rules subject to more discretion on the part of the regulator. Care must be taken, however, not to trim the powers of the legislator or regulator too much. In practice, whichever regulatory framework is adopted, protection of the public interest will sometimes call for unilateral amendments. The challenge is hence to strike a healthy balance between the legitimate interests of the private operator and those of the community. In countries with weak institutions or poor track records, the tradeoff has to lean toward less discretion, lest investors decide to stay away. As a positive track record is built up, the regulatory framework can evolve toward more flexibility.

Single or multisector agency? Should governments set up a regulatory body for each sector, as has been done in Argentina and the United Kingdom; a single agency for closely linked sectors such as gas and power, as in Hungary and the United States (at the federal level, FERC); or one multisectoral agency for all or most infrastructure sectors, as in Bolivia and the United States (public utilities commissions at the state level)? On the other hand, perhaps there should be no special regulatory body at all, as in New Zealand, where the Commerce Commission, the national competition agency, is in charge of economic regulation of the infrastructure sectors on the basis of the country's general competition rules.[115]

A multisectoral regulatory agency should contribute to a greater degree of coherence or consistency in the regulation of different sectors; it also allows

---

115. The commerce act of 1986 (section 53) provides, however, that the government can, under certain circumstances, control the prices of goods or services "in a market in which competition is limited or is likely to be lessened," provided such controls are "necessary or desirable ... in the interests of users, or consumers, or, as the case may be, of suppliers."

lessons from one sector to be applied to others, creates administrative economies of scope, and may limit the risk of corruption or undue influence by a particular enterprise or ministry. It is particularly well suited for countries that lack the necessary financial, human, and administrative resources to equip separate agencies. Some argue that it does not promote the development of in-depth sector expertise, but this can be addressed by a degree of technical specialization within the agency. Basic legal, economic, and financial skills and experience are, in fact, largely common to the various infrastructure sectors.

Appeal procedures. Whatever the regulatory mechanism in place, one should consider whether appeal procedures should be provided. In the United Kingdom, which has the longest and broadest postprivatization experience, the Monopolies and Mergers Commission—whose powers derive from privatization laws and general competition legislation—has several times been asked to hear disagreements between privatized companies and their regulators concerning amendments to the terms or conditions of licenses.[116] The regulator has to take the recommendations of the MMC into account but is not required to follow them (except for certain submissions to the MMC concerning enterprises in the water and sanitation sector).[117]

British Gas and other companies complain that their regulators have developed the habit of broadening the subject of an appeal to the MMC well beyond the original dispute, for example, by questioning the very structure of the sector when the disagreement concerned only a tariff adjustment (see Lipworth 1993; Veljanovski 1993). Since the MMC can recommend that the private company be broken up, regulated companies tend to avoid involving it in their disagreements with the regulator. The threat of such recourse is hence a formidable weapon in the regulator's arsenal. Courts, on the other hand,

116. The regulators may refer companies to the MMC. In addition, the director general of fair trading (OFT) is also allowed to refer privatized utilities to the MMC for anticompetitive or monopoly practices. The secretary of state (the minister) has similar powers in the water sector, for example. One should also add that, in the case of the four main airports, the MMC is automatically required to rule on the five-year tariff adjustments proposed by the Civil Aviation Authority (see McEldowney 1995).

117. Mergers of companies in the water sector always have to be referred to the MMC. This was done following the bid launched in March 1995 by Lyonnaise des Eaux on Northumbrian Water. The MMC report issued in July threatened to block the bid unless it guaranteed price cuts of up to 20 percent. This report was used by the trade and industry secretary as a basis for further inquiries by the water regulator. In the end, Lyonnaise's $1.3 billion takeover was allowed, provided it guaranteed a reduction of 15 percent in customer's water bills over six years. In addition, "Lyonnaise has given undertakings not to bid for another U.K. water company for 10 years. It must float at least 25 per cent of its U.K. water interests, which includes Essex and Suffolk Water, by 2005" (*Financial Times*, 24 November 1995). Following this takeover, Northumbrian will be merged (under a single amended license) with North East Water, the statutory water company that was already controlled by Lyonnaise. See also notes 25 and 31 on the role of MMC in power sector takeovers.

have so far played a relatively minor role in the United Kingdom.[118] The U.K. appeals regime, with its role for the MMC, the OFT, the minister (or secretary of state), and, to a lesser extent, the courts, is rather idiosyncratic, however. It is, in part, a reflection of the decisionmaking powers of U.K. regulators.

The design of an appeals regime should be a function of the specific institutional setup and legal traditions of a country; courts may play a role where they have or can reasonably acquire the expertise, integrity, and efficiency needed to settle appeals on regulatory matters. More generally, in the design of a regulatory framework, the interests of speed and certainty (which lead to denying appeals against regulatory decisions or limiting the grounds and timeframe for filing such appeals) should be balanced against those of fairness toward regulated entities (and consumers) and accountability of the regulator.

Privatization of the regulatory function. Conciliation and arbitration procedures play a very important role in private infrastructure contracts. They substitute for or complement the formal appeal or recourse mechanisms to higher-level government authorities, courts, or special bodies. Most contracts include mechanisms for the prompt amicable settlement of problems or disputes that may arise in the course of their implementation (see chapter 3). Failing this, contractual provisions typically assign the settlement of disputes between the operator and the state or conceding party to arbitration, most often international arbitration. Because contracts often include regulatory commitments such as future tariff increases, specific regulatory action or inaction could become a breach of contract by the state or conceding authority, which justifies recourse to arbitration. The threat of recourse to arbitration may be a powerful incentive to force compliance, although actual arbitration proceedings may also sound the end of the contract.

Furthermore, much of the work traditionally performed by regulators lends itself very well to contracting out to private experts. Opponents of privatization sometimes take refuge behind the complexity of regulation and the paucity of national capacity in many developing or transition countries to justify a continuation of public-sector provision of infrastructure services. Complex regulatory functions need to be performed professionally; where limited administrative capacity is indeed a binding constraint, at least in the short and medium term, privatization of regulatory tasks should be considered.[119]

---

118. One of the few suits was filed in December 1993, by Mercury, the largest competitor of British Telecom, against OFTEL, which had just announced its determination on the interconnection between BT and Mercury; it asked the court to define a new formula for calculating the network access charge it has to pay BT for transmitting its calls to their final destination (see *Financial Times*, 21 December 1993).

119. Moreover, even if regulatory tasks cannot be discharged adequately (whether by regulators, private auditors, or otherwise), keeping a public-sector monopoly may not be the best policy. First, as already argued, contracts and licenses can be designed to increase the operator's incentives to act in the public interest; second, regulation is needed for private as well as public operators; and third, even if regulatory capacities are weak or nonexistent, a private monopoly is not necessarily worse than a public one.

Governments and regulators can, and often do, hire consultants, advisers, and experts to assist them in all aspects of their regulatory tasks. Such contracting out can also be taken one step further and formalized through, for example, performance audits or certifications performed by independent verification companies under contract with the regulator. Auditors could be asked to certify that the information provided by the regulated companies to the regulator (including performance targets) is, in their opinion, fair and reliable, based on the checks they have performed and on their assessment of the systems the companies established to produce the required information. In addition, they could be asked to certify that the regulated company is in compliance with the legislation in effect, as well as with the terms and conditions of its license or concession, and, if it is not so, determine the degree of noncompliance and the factors that may have contributed to it. Their task could also include surveys of user satisfaction.

Finally, auditors could measure the regulated companies' performance against key parameters, prepare time series showing trends, and compare these results with international norms. None of the listed functions implies any discretionary decisionmaking. What such audits would do, however, is provide the decisionmakers with a sound analytical basis for their decisions. By introducing a degree of transparency or publicity in this process, while respecting private and confidential information, the scope or likelihood of arbitrary decisions could be limited. Auditors would be subject to ethical standards and liability, just as financial auditors or verification companies are. Their fees could be funded from the regulatory levy on the regulated industries.

The degree of delegation of regulatory tasks to private companies can be pushed even further, as decades of experience in the aviation area show. Some countries have delegated their sovereign power to certify the airworthiness of aircraft to private companies. In Morocco, for example, the ministry in charge of civil aviation has delegated this function to Bureau Veritas, a private company of international repute.[120] This company delivers airworthiness certificates to all Moroccan aircraft, including those of the national airline but excluding military aircraft. The company, which is remunerated from fees paid by the controlled companies, makes periodic checks on such aircraft, as well as on aircraft maintenance workshops and parts manufacturers established in Morocco. Final authority still rests with the civil aviation authorities, but Bureau Veritas is authorized to take protective or preventive measures, such as temporarily withdrawing the airworthiness certificate and immobilizing the aircraft, pending decision from these authorities.

Self-regulation. As mentioned above, regulation is a delicate and political undertaking, especially when it comes to the regulation of monopolies. The

120. See Decree no. 2-61-161 of July 10, 1962, on the regulation of civil aviation, and ministerial order no. 364-67 of May 3, 1967, designating Bureau Veritas for the control of aircraft airworthiness, including the issuance, renewal, and validation of airworthiness certificates.

reputation of firms also is an important regulatory mechanism. Indeed, international infrastructure companies cannot afford to abuse their dominant position in some countries, lest their reputation and chances of winning new contracts be impaired in that country or abroad. In high-growth sectors, this type of self-regulation may sometimes be more effective than formal regulatory mechanisms. A free and critical press, as well as consumer and user associations, may further contribute to the effectiveness of the overall regulatory process.

Balancing the costs and benefits of regulation. This overview of the regulatory issues that arise or should be considered while preparing an infrastructure sector for privatization cannot do full justice to this complex issue. There is no single blueprint for regulation. Regulatory reform must always be based on an analysis of the cost of regulation, which should not exceed its expected benefits.

The concept of regulatory bodies independent of the industry and the government is undoubtedly attractive and worth pursuing. The fact remains, however, that in many countries it is difficult, if not impossible, to achieve that independence in practice, at least in the short run. Where this is the case, a gradual approach—which starts by giving an autonomous regulatory body advisory powers and eventually other powers, as its track record, independence, and the confidence it inspires mount—may often be the preferred approach.

Generally speaking, the regulatory framework must be able to reconcile profitability of the operator, continuity, and quality of the service while meeting two other often contradictory requirements. On the one hand, it must ensure compliance with the commitments entered into by the parties and hence reduce the inherent risk of investments of this kind; this calls for only limited discretionary powers. On the other hand, it must have enough flexibility built in to make adjustments when changing circumstances so require; this calls for a greater measure of discretion on the part of the regulator.

Recent developments in U.K. regulatory policies and practices illustrate this difficult tradeoff. High profits and generous compensation packages for senior executives of regulated infrastructure companies have sparked protests and become politically very controversial, particularly in the water sector where the price cap formula adopted at privatization has led to significant tariff increases. These high profits, dividends, and bonuses result partly from efficiency gains achieved by the companies since privatization and partly from regulatory design mistakes (generous price caps and insufficient competition in the market). U.K. regulators have tried, especially in 1995 and 1996, to correct some of these problems by tightening the pricing formulas, sometimes considerably, while leaving the regulated companies the opportunity to make reasonable returns and the incentives to innovate and pursue additional productivity gains.

The difference between a priori assumptions used to set the regulatory framework and the a posteriori assessment of how that framework has lived up to reality is inherent in the regulatory process. Governments designing a privatization program, and regulators thereafter, will never have all the information they need to make their decisions, while regulated enterprises will always tend (at least publicly) to underestimate the productivity gains that can be achieved and to withhold, to the extent they can get away with it, information to the contrary.

Finally, regulatory capacities may also affect the choice of market structure and competition rules. A difficult balance may need to be struck between a theoretically optimal structure and one that is manageable in light of the country's traditions and institutional and human capabilities. The introduction of competition into a sector may simultaneously facilitate and complicate the regulator's task. It facilitates it by, for example, creating different operators with differing interests who will be quick to denounce any abuses committed by their competitors; multiple operators also give regulators more reference points for evaluating operators' performance and possible productivity improvements. Yet the introduction of competition complicates regulation by requiring the regulator to monitor a larger number of companies and to arbitrate disputes among these operators concerning access to the network, predatory pricing, and other matters; in addition, there may be a positive correlation between the number of operators and the number and complexity of these disputes.

Conclusion

The quality and competitiveness of infrastructure services is increasingly becoming a key factor in the competitiveness of countries, which can no longer afford to be dragged down by underperforming public monopolies. Privatization of infrastructure sectors has thus become a high priority for an increasing number of governments around the world. It raises specific issues, which have warranted this special chapter. The discussion has focused on how issues of market structure, competition, and regulation may affect the privatization process, given recent and ongoing developments. The economic policy choices made in these areas are crucial in deciding on the legislative and regulatory frameworks that will govern infrastructure privatizations.

Infrastructure sectors are subject to rapid changes in technology, ideology, economic conditions (notably through the introduction of growing competition), geopolitics (the artificial barriers between protected national territories are steadily falling), and so on. These sectors relied until recently almost entirely on public funds to finance their investments, but the public finance crises in many countries, combined with huge investment requirements (especially in high-growth countries), have made private-sector participation indispensable. Furthermore, the poor performance of most public enterprises and their inability to offer a quality service and meet demand have encouraged many governments to turn to the private sector for the provision of infrastructure services. These and other developments have led to the need for radical reforms, encompassing both privatization and demonopolization of infrastructure sectors.

The pendulum has swung more than once over the choice between public or private ownership in these sectors. The recent trend toward privatization and demonopolization, though, is not likely to be a passing fancy. It is a phenomenon that reflects profound ideological, technological, and economic changes. Moreover, the largely positive experience of pioneering countries should encourage other countries to promote greater private participation and increased competition in these sectors.

The privatization trend should be further strengthened by the emergence of a global industry for infrastructure services. This industry, which did not exist ten years ago, owes its existence to the reforms discussed in this chapter. These reforms have generated and then amplified the demand for private infrastructure services. They have also helped create the supply, first by forcing enterprises that previously enjoyed a national monopoly in a given sector to compete and become more efficient, and by allowing them to diversify geographically and sectorally and, second, by encouraging new operators to enter these previously highly protected sectors. The early reformers, such as Chile and the United Kingdom, have given their national infrastructure services companies a lead in the international markets. Finally, international infrastructure groups have a reputation to protect, so that they can maintain and develop their activities in the countries where they operate and win new contracts elsewhere. This is a valuable form of self-regulation.

Experience with privatization in infrastructure sectors indicates that clear definition of objectives from the very outset is even more important here than elsewhere. Where the objectives are to improve service levels, satisfy a growing number of users, and boost the international competitiveness of infrastructure services and hence of the national economy, divestiture (with the receipts it brings in) will very often be less important in itself than effectively demonopolizing and opening up the sector to new enterprises that compete with the hitherto dominant (public, private, or privatized) operator as well as with other new entrants. A recent report of the European Competitiveness Advisory Group, chaired by former Italian premier Carlo Ciampi, expressed this in the following terms: "What matters most is not so much that the ownership—and management—of public utilities moves from the state to the private sector, as that competition is introduced and extended wherever possible" (*Financial Times*, 13 December 1995).

The emphasis and priority should thus be on opening the sector to private entry and competition (privatization of the sector), rather than on the transactional aspects of the divestiture of one or more SOEs. Legal monopolies and other barriers to entry will need to be abolished; constitutional provisions may need to be amended or abolished. The privatization of large infrastructure companies offers the government a unique opportunity to rethink the entire organization and structure of the sector. Activities or services that were provided by an integrated, monolithic enterprise will be unbundled and competition introduced in those segments that can sustain it. Such reforms have to be implemented up front; it is indeed much more difficult to alter the structure and operating rules of the sector after privatization, because such changes would inevitably affect private ownership rights.

Introducing competition in the market presupposes, however, that governments are willing to accept that such competition may lower the selling price of an SOE. This immediate shortfall in earnings for the public treasury will usually be made up rapidly through the effects of faster economic growth resulting from more efficient infrastructure sectors and, more directly, through the elimination of SOE subsidies and the collection of taxes and levies on the activities and profits of the enterprises operating in the privatized and liberalized sector.

Where competition cannot be introduced in the market, as tends to be the case for water supply, for example, it should at least be introduced for the market—that is, for the right to supply the service on an exclusivity basis. Properly structured tenders or auctions will allow the government to extract part of the monopoly rents for the benefit of the treasury and the consumers. Yardstick competition can then be used as a regulatory tool to compare the performance of the monopoly operator with that of operators in other regions of the country and with international norms; the regulator can use such comparative information to justify tougher performance targets or tariff adjustments at the time of regulatory review.

The importance of good coordination and sequencing of the sectoral reform and privatization programs cannot be stressed too strongly. This may be particularly difficult where different government agencies are responsible for privatization and sector reform. Such consistency is needed in the period leading to privatization, as well as after privatization.

Because infrastructure investments tend to be of a long-term nature, investors need guarantees even more than in other sectors. One of the best guarantees is a good regulatory framework, preferably established by legislation and backed by strong political commitment. This framework will have to be known before the bidding process starts and licenses or concessions are awarded, and it must effectively be in place before or at privatization. Investors will often seek additional comfort by including key regulatory features (such as the price regime) into their contractual agreements with privatizing governments. Governmental failure to comply with such rules as stipulated would give investors recourse rights, often through international arbitration.

Design of the regulatory framework needs to take into account institutional capacities, as well as administrative and judicial traditions. Choices have to be made between regulatory bodies with decisionmaking powers and those with only advisory powers, between multisectoral and single-sector agencies, between agencies headed by a director and those led by a commission. The integrity of the regulatory process must be protected by rules guaranteeing due process, transparency, and accountability. Many countries, particularly developing and transition countries with little or no regulatory track record, may wish to adopt a light-handed system of regulation with limited discretionary powers and to contract out much of the regulatory control and verification work to reputable private auditors.

It is the government's task to introduce the degree of competition and market access best suited to the country and sector and to strike the proper balance between highly detailed licenses or concessions and a more flexible regime in which the regulatory agency has wider discretionary powers. These country and sector characteristics must therefore shape an approach that deals harmoniously with the scope for competition within the sector (structure), the competition rules (laws and regulations), and the country's institutional capacities and traditions (institutions).

Governments will rarely hit upon the ideal design or solution in the first go-around. Some trial and error should be expected, as illustrated by the history of infrastructure privatizations in the United Kingdom. The government has to decide on an approach that takes due account of the factors discussed in this chapter, and then take the plunge, so to speak, leaving any necessary adjustments for later when the reform is implemented.

As stressed earlier, particularly in chapter 6, external experts have a valuable contribution to make as advisers on privatization. Their assistance is even more important in the reform of strategic sectors. Very few governments have experts on staff to handle demonopolization, competition, restructuring, privatization, and regulation in these sectors. Governments that have successfully privatized large infrastructure enterprises have done so with the assistance of economists, lawyers, financial experts, and sector specialists. The complexity of the necessary market structure studies, the legislation and regulatory framework to be put in place, the bidder selection procedures, the drafting and negotiation of licenses and contracts, and the design of effective incentive mechanisms, as well as the multiple and often contradictory interests at play, are all factors that point to the need to recruit high-level advisers right from the start of the reform program.

Infrastructure privatization is a relatively new and still evolving field, and it would be premature to venture definitive conclusions. The various approaches tried over the past fifteen years need to be evaluated and compared to determine which ones promise the most under what circumstances for efficiency, service quality, innovation, satisfaction of demand, and public service generally. Whatever the result, the fact is that many factors discussed in this work—the explosion of investment needs in the infrastructure sectors worldwide, the poor state of public finances in most countries, the rapid growth of large private infrastructure companies operating on an international scale, and the steady breakup of activities traditionally regarded as natural monopolies—are fundamentally changing the way in which infrastructure services are delivered and managed. The picture in five, ten, or fifteen years will most likely be very different from the present one, but it will surely feature much greater private-sector participation and sharper competition.

8

Meeting the Privatization Challenge

Since the launch of the U.K. privatization program in the early 1980s, the privatization wave has swept over the world, touching every continent, every political system, and every sector. Its emphasis has moved gradually from the industrial, commercial, and financial sectors to the infrastructure sectors and then to municipal services; it has only recently started to reach education, health, and administrative activities. This book seeks to shed light on this global trend and to draw preliminary lessons from the experience acquired so far. Its focus has been the strategic, legal, and institutional aspects of privatization, with the legal framework as the common backdrop for much of the analysis.

A Strategic Challenge

The real challenge of privatization is not just to sell an enterprise or shares. Much more, it is to seize the opportunity to refocus the role of government and public administration, increase economic efficiency, and adapt an enterprise, a sector, or the economy as a whole to the fast-changing requirements of the international economy. This challenge is inherent in all privatization programs, though its magnitude and intensity differ from case to case. More radical reforms are often needed, for instance, in developing and transition countries.

A privatization program may offer an excellent opportunity for strengthening and deepening financial markets, for example. In sectoral privatizations the breakup of monopolies and the introduction of competition will often rank as high priorities. The privatization of a specific enterprise may call for the unbundling of its activities and for its piecemeal privatization. A privatization strategy can, and should, meet challenges of this type. It should not be bound by the static view of privatization as a zero-sum game in which some win and others lose, without any net gain in overall social welfare. To the contrary, privatization should be seen as a dynamic process whose objective is precisely to yield this net gain.

Three Tiers of Privatization

This book identified three main tiers of privatization and many different approaches. The first tier is divestiture, the mechanism by which ownership or control of an enterprise is transferred from the public to the private sector. This micro approach focuses primarily on the privatization transactions and the legal and institutional framework needed to facilitate them. The main divestiture issues were discussed in chapters 5 and 6, mainly from legal and institutional perspectives.

Other challenges arise in the privatization of infrastructure sectors; these were examined in chapter 7. Here, the government must not only prepare a given enterprise for privatization but also reconsider the entire structure of the sector. The aging paradigm of public enterprise monopolies will have to be discarded and replaced by a sector structure that is more dynamic, competitive, and open to the private sector. Rapid changes are taking place in the infrastructure sectors, particularly in the telecommunications sector, which is undergoing a radical revolution leading to intensified competition and increased private participation, but also in the energy and transport sectors. Ports, airports, railways, and power companies can no longer be seen as monolithic, monopolistic entities; rather, they represent a range of separable activities (infrastructure and services). Parts of this unbundled whole may well still have natural monopoly characteristics that make direct competition uneconomical, but most of the constituent activities (services, in particular) can generally be organized on a competitive basis. Prior sector restructuring is an essential precondition for privatization of most large infrastructure enterprises.

Finally, after privatization at the enterprise and sector levels, follows privatization of the economy. The strongest case, of course, is the systemic conversion from a command to a market economy that followed the collapse of the centralized planning system developed by the former U.S.S.R. and copied by its satellites. Privatization of the economy is not limited to the so-called transition countries, however. Indeed, many developing countries also had heavily centralized and bureaucratic economic management styles, which have increasingly come under attack. Even in industrialized countries, there is rarely ground for complacency. Substantial reforms may be needed to make these economies more flexible and dynamic, as convincingly demonstrated by the economic reform and privatization program launched in 1984 by the Labor government of New Zealand. The lackluster performance of many European economies in the first half of the 1990s illustrates the cost of not seizing the opportunity to strengthen market mechanisms.

Privatization should be viewed against the backdrop of the internationalization of the economy, which further restricts the options for resolving the chronic difficulties of SOEs. This globalization, which is reflected in new norms of international law, is broadening the very definition of the relevant market for goods or services. It increasingly renders illegal the subsidies and tariff protection enjoyed by many SOEs, and it fosters the development of flexible enterprises able to adjust quickly to constantly evolving international markets.

These three tiers of privatization, with the added opportunities and constraints stemming from the internationalization of economies, are separate yet at the same time interlinked: separate, in that the problems arising at each level differ in nature, and interlinked, in that the success of reforms at each level helps determine success at the other levels. By and large, the truly effective programs are the ones in which the government introduced and coordinated the necessary reforms at each level in a coherent and mutually supportive way.

The very term "privatization" is broad and flexible: privatization of an enterprise is not the same thing as privatization of an economy. Some countries prefer not to use the term publicly at all, even though the policies they follow are undoubtedly privatization policies; others apply the term to programs that do not directly involve the private sector but only mimic its incentives. The dividing line between public sector and private sector is becoming increasingly blurred. Joint-venture (public and private) enterprises have long existed in many countries, and special techniques for private participation in the delivery of "public" services—concession, lease (*affermage*), contracting out, management contract, and other forms of partnership between the public and private sectors—are flourishing.

Changing the Role of the State

Privatizing does not in any way imply putting a country's entire economy in the hands of the private sector and abdicating the role of the state. On the contrary, privatization offers governments a unique opportunity to refocus their action by shifting the emphasis from activities perceived to be strategic (a concept that has been used to justify the nationalization of agriculture or bakeries, for example) to core governmental responsibilities. Examples are national defense, security, justice, foreign affairs, and taxation, although in each of these cases governmental responsibility should not rule out private sector participation. The creation of an enabling environment that nurtures the physical and social infrastructures essential to economic growth and social well-being remains another important role of the state. As they withdraw from the role of producer and refocus, governments are increasingly becoming catalysts, promoters, regulators, and redistributors (of wealth). Meanwhile, the responsibility for production of goods and services is shifting to those who have a comparative advantage in this area, namely, the private sector.

The state's withdrawal from productive activities accompanies its assumption of responsibility for other, often new, activities. The regulation of infrastructure sectors previously run as public monopolies is a case in point. These new responsibilities are quite different from those of a producer or service provider, however. Transforming an operational or planning service into a regulatory entity may be problematic: the needed skills are different and so is the culture. Regulation is an intrinsically delicate task, involving, as it does, difficult tradeoffs between often divergent interests.

Setting up efficient and independent regulatory mechanisms is a major challenge in the privatization of regulated sectors. Establishing this function at arms length not only from the regulated industry but also, as much as possible, from political and bureaucratic interference should enhance its effectiveness. Although autonomous and independent commissions may be worth pursuing in most countries, in some cases they might be given an advisory rather than decisionmaking role. In countries with authoritarian regimes where independence from the government or head of state may exist on paper but not in fact, for instance, this approach may be appropriate; it can also be a first step to establish the credibility of such commissions. Regulatory issues and analyses tend to converge across infrastructure sectors, and multisectoral commissions or agencies should be considered, particularly in countries with limited administrative capacities. Attention should also be given to the design of a transparent regulatory system open to inputs from key stakeholders.

In this context, most countries may wish to consider privatizing at least some regulatory activities. Government officials are not necessarily well suited to perform many of the rather technical control and verification functions on which regulation of infrastructure sectors rests. Much as independent private auditors are called upon to audit the finances of companies, or inspection companies to check on import and export transactions, most of the actual regulatory controls could be delegated to private auditors. This could include verification of information provided by regulated enterprises (public or private), compliance by such enterprises with their licenses or concessions, achievement of performance targets or other indicators, and so on. Auditors could also usefully evaluate the performance of such enterprises relative to others in the sector, nationally as well as internationally, and recommend actions to be taken by the regulator or government. Private regulatory auditors could be hired and paid from the proceeds of a regulatory fee levied on private and public operators.

The regulatory task can be facilitated in noninstitutional ways, such as the introduction of domestic competition and the globalization of the economy. To maintain or strengthen the competitiveness of their economies, countries are opening up protected domestic markets and exposing them to competition. By creating a greater number of economic agents with typically divergent interests, this may considerably lighten the regulatory burden. Investments by international companies that have a reputation to protect may further contribute to a healthy regulatory environment.

Redefining the role of the state may often require amendments to the constitution, as discussed in chapters 2 and 7. This has happened in all transition countries but also in many other countries, on every continent and with governments of every persuasion. It requires broad political support and may be a lengthy, although often essential, process.

Defining Objectives

All too often the objectives of a privatization program are not clearly spelled out. Lack of transparency in government policymaking or disagreements over the objectives to be pursued are among the causes. Defining and agreeing on objectives is an essential stage in the process, however; to omit it is to court failure or, at the very least, to risk poor policy choices and suboptimal outcomes. Privatization objectives should form an integral part of the broader objectives of the economic reform program.

Many privatization programs appear to focus more on revenue generation than on the longer-term gains that more radical restructuring of the enterprise or sector concerned would bring. Although preoccupation with the budget is understandable, revenue generation should be a major privatization objective only in competitive and nonprotected sectors. For infrastructure and other public services, the primary objective should be to provide the consumers and the economy with more competitive services, whether in terms of quality, range of services, price, or volume. Social objectives also often have high priority, but they may be pursued more effectively through appropriate complementary measures and programs than through the privatization process itself.

Decisions Based on Thorough Analysis

The process of transferring enterprises from the public to the private sector calls for skilled analysis and judgment at every stage. If a privatization operation is to succeed, the main obstacles and constraints must first be identified and then eliminated, as discussed in chapters 2, 3, and 4.

Once the government's objectives have been defined, a broad range of legal instruments will need to be analyzed to determine whether they allow privatization and fit with its objectives or whether they need to be amended, suspended, or repealed to allow or facilitate privatization. Public enterprise laws and the legal status of the SOEs to be privatized must, for instance, be conducive to privatization or be amended. The rules governing the creation and operation of public agencies (which may apply to the privatization agency), civil service regulations, public finance legislation, legislation on state or public property, and other aspects of public and administrative law also deserve attention.

Where the ownership of certain public enterprises or assets is in dispute, as is often the case with formerly nationalized enterprises, the rights of the various parties will have to be determined. To succeed, privatization must take place in a legal and institutional environment characterized by respect for the rule of law and proper recognition and protection of the rights of citizens and private economic agents, especially private property rights which are the cornerstone of a market economy. Discrimination between the private and public sectors must be eliminated to create a level playing field for all.

A country's business climate, its legislation, and its track record with investors are decisive factors in investment decisions, foreign or domestic. A good business environment can only facilitate privatization and enhance its chances of success. To create this environment it may be necessary to abolish a monopoly, protect and promote competition, enforce compliance with contracts, regulate (or deregulate) a sector, reduce import and export restrictions, streamline procedures for incorporating companies, facilitate foreign investment, simplify the tax system, guarantee foreign exchange convertibility and repatriation, and speed up the settlement of disputes, to cite only a few critical issues. It will also be necessary to take stock of existing business norms and practices and their applicability to the proposed privatization operations. Of particular importance is legislation governing mergers and acquisitions, liquidation, insolvency, bankruptcy, financial transactions, and securities markets. Elements of a country's basic legal framework that are not directly connected with privatization may nonetheless have far-reaching effects on its implementation.

A thorough analysis is even more important when it comes to highly regulated sectors, such as infrastructure. In addition to the overall assessment of the business environment, an economic analysis of the effects of the existing sector structure and regulations on sector performance will be required. Where such review indicates, for example, that the lack of competition hampers the sector's (and, more important, the economy's) performance, privatization will need to be preceded by reforms in sector structure and competition rules. The size and technical characteristics of the sector may be an important factor in such an analysis; this would be the case, for example, in the power sector where small networks that are not or are poorly interconnected may not allow for immediate introduction of competition in the market.

Relevant country comparisons are a useful tool for such investigations and should include countries that have successfully implemented reforms in the relevant areas. Nevertheless, analysis and further study should not become a pretext for inaction or timid reforms. Reforming governments will never have all the information at their disposal that one would ideally wish to have before reaching a decision. Nor will they be able to remove all existing constraints and obstacles to create a perfect environment. An empirical approach to this analytical or investigative task starting from an assessment of the most binding constraints and obstacles will often yield more relevant and useful results than a systematic review of all relevant laws and regulations.

A Clear Strategy and Clear Priorities

Ideally, a legal and regulatory framework fostering private sector activity in general and privatization in particular will already be in place. In most developing and transition countries, however, this will not be the case. Reform must focus on those legal instruments that absolutely have to be in place if privatization is to succeed. To proceed in any other way would result in endless delays. The content of the basic reform program will depend on the specific situation of each country, including the legal framework in place, the scope and nature of the privatization program, the administrative and other capabilities to implement the program, and the political context.

Imprecise property rights, arbitrary application of the law, and weak financial markets, to take only a few examples, can hinder the smooth execution of privatization operations. The elimination of these constraints should therefore be part of the package of basic reforms. Where they cannot be eliminated, the government may need to find creative ways to achieve its objectives despite these legal obstacles. An example is the leasing technique, which allows a private operator to use state assets that the government cannot transfer immediately, either because it is not allowed to transfer ownership or because its ownership rights are disputed.

Similarly, where the SOEs to be privatized include enterprises protected by monopolies, the government's strategy should be to open the sector to competition and private entry. In the case of natural monopolies (such as water distribution), a reform strategy may include horizontal unbundling: a regulator's task will be made easier if information on costs, service levels, technology, and other relevant parameters can be obtained from several operators, each with regional exclusivity.

Ranking these obstacles, with the most constraining ones at the top of the list, is a first step. Reform priorities have to be set in light of the ultimate objectives. Those reforms that are essential to the success of privatization and are consistent with the general economic reform program should be undertaken first; the others may be implemented in parallel with or after privatization, but they should generally not hold up the process.

Proper sequencing of the reforms is important. Deregulation and liberalization of prices and foreign trade, for example, will have to precede privatization, especially in countries where private initiative is hamstrung by compulsory licensing, protectionist trade policies and practices, or price controls. If investors cannot freely set their prices and operate their own enterprise, few of them will be interested in buying an SOE. On the other hand, if a public enterprise were to be sold despite this unfavorable environment, any subsequent price deregulation or liberalization could yield the investor a windfall profit; the privatization authorities would probably be accused of having sold off the SOE at a bargain price, however, which could harm the entire program. The converse will often happen when foreign trade is liberalized after privatization: the disappearance of protection can instantly lower the value of the privatized enterprise, unfairly harm the buyer's interests, and undermine the credibility of the government and its privatization program.

Regulatory reform and privatization also have to take place in the correct sequence. To be able to calculate the price they are prepared to pay, investors will need to know under what regulatory system and rules the company will be operating. This means that these will have to be established before privatization. Uncertainty about the applicable regulations will inevitably cool investor interest and lower the selling price. In addition, in the case of privatization in a regulated sector, investors will want to know not only the structure of the sector, degree of competition, and regulatory system at privatization but also how these are likely to evolve. Stability of the regulatory system, enshrined in a law and guaranteed, where appropriate, by a credible undertaking on the part of the government not to substantially alter the system (at least not to the detriment of the privatized company) for a specified period, can help attract investors.

The effectiveness of a privatization program may be a function of the pace of its implementation. Speed is of the essence: windows of opportunities often do not stay open very long. An attempt to go too fast may backfire, however, as a result of inadequate preparation and design, lack of response from investors, or lack of support from key constituencies. A drawn-out process, on the other hand, may lead to the deterioration of the SOEs slated for privatization, the loss of momentum and support for sometimes painful reforms, and the scuttling of the overall program.

Protecting Stakeholder Interests

The role of government in a privatization operation cannot be reduced to that of a holding company selling some of its assets. Indeed, the state's interests as seller may conflict with its obligations to protect the public interest or to promote economic efficiency. Where that happens, the public interest and economic efficiency should prevail. Issues arising in the context of corporate mergers and acquisitions are thus only a subset of those that characterize SOE privatizations.

The attitude of private investors and their response to a privatization program—and hence the success of the program—will depend to a large extent on how well the government prepares and implements the program. This implies, among other things, that legislation must support and reflect the program's overall strategy, allow and facilitate its implementation, and foster the development of an overall environment conducive to private investment. It is no secret that capital, being mobile, moves to those countries with a sound business environment. A major objective, then, of the privatization program ought to be to reduce the uncertainty that potential private investors face.

New investors are not the only stakeholders, however. Because privatization programs are part of the process of refocusing or reinventing government, they can be expected, like all reforms, to meet with opposition from those who fear they may lose by the change. Such programs entail adjustment costs which, while they cannot be avoided entirely, can often be mitigated through complementary policies. Many countries have taken ancillary measures of this kind to soften the impact of privatizations on the more vulnerable groups of the population.

Privatization experience has highlighted the importance of i and labor-law reforms. Where public enterprises are overstaffed, appropriate measures (such as recruitment freezes, severance, and reassignment) must be taken right from the start to deal with this issue, lest the privatization program be delayed or compromised. Officials from sector ministries and SOE managers may feel that privatization threatens their influence and perhaps even their jobs. Measures may have to be taken to give the affected employees, managers, and officials incentives to press forward with implementation of the reforms or, where appropriate, to defuse their opposition; severance bonuses and free or preferential shares are among the most common incentive measures. Privatization may also have to be accompanied by amendments to labor legislation and structural reforms in social security and pension regimes. A well-prepared privatization strategy should include a social component.

Similarly, where the government wishes to bolster the confidence of the private sector, it will have to take care to preserve the rights of SOE creditors. This may be particularly complex where the debt is owed to private creditors or where the privatization affects the discount at which it trades. Responsibility for obligations and acts of commission or omission on the part of the SOE before its privatization, such as pollution, may need to be clarified. Should they be incumbent on the government (as the former owner) or on the enterprise and its buyers? Finally, the government must ensure that the legitimate interests of other parties are protected; for example, private shareholders may have preemptive rights when the government sells its shares in a joint-venture company.

A Political Process

Privatization is a political process managed (or at least supervised) by government and politicians. It is often also a controversial policy. Unconditional and unwavering commitment from the highest political authorities, including the president (or head of state) and the prime minister, is thus a prerequisite for the success of a privatization program. The political nature of this process requires that it be conducted with integrity and transparency to avoid both possible abuses and accusations of favoritism or fraud.

The design and implementation of privatization programs are typically the responsibility of civil servants. Difficulties encountered in privatization programs are often a consequence of weak institutional capabilities in the legislative, executive, or judicial branches of government. The importance of establishing efficient institutional structures and mechanisms and of providing involved officials with the right set of incentives to ensure effective implementation of privatization programs was stressed in chapter 6. Many countries have established privatization agencies or teams to that effect.

There is, however, no blueprint for institutional design and different solutions have worked well in the context of different countries or programs. International experience shows that clear responsibilities and mandates, streamlined processes, access to resources and advisory services, political support, and accountability of privatization officials may matter more than the organizations themselves.

Public sector agencies and jobs will often disappear; overcoming bureaucratic hostility and inertia may be a precondition for success. Remaining staff need to be motivated and those leaving may be offered compensation or reassignment. A certain degree of realism should prevail when it comes to setting expectations for speed and success in administrative reform. Institutions—large, public-sector bureaucracies, in particular—do not change overnight; in many countries, it may be advisable, at least initially, to contract out part of the privatization process itself.

Because privatization is a political program, it needs support not only from the groups directly affected but also from the general public. This requires, among other things, that the program yield benefits for consumers (shorter waiting times for telephone connections, for example, or better service quality or introduction of new services) and for taxpayers (as a result of, for example, abolition of SOE subsidies and reduction of public debt). These benefits need to be explained to all the parties concerned, including the general public. A good public information campaign, explaining in particular the costs and benefits of the proposed privatization program and how it fits into the government's overall economic reform program could contribute substantially to the success of the policy.

Is a Privatization Law Necessary?

Whether a country needs to enact a privatization law or can do without one depends on several factors: the political situation and legal traditions of the country, the scope of its privatization program, and the nature of the enterprises to be privatized. Two different issues have to be addressed: does legislation need to be enacted to authorize or facilitate privatization, and if so, should the new provisions take the form of amendments to the pertinent laws or be grouped together in a specific privatization law?

Some countries have opted to enact privatization laws even when privatization could have been implemented without amending the existing legislation. This may have the advantage of mobilizing explicit political support and commitment in favor of privatization from the very start. It may confer a stronger, clearer mandate on the government and agencies in charge of implementing privatization and make them more accountable. A privatization law also provides an opportunity to introduce changes in legislation that, although not required for commencing the process, may substantially facilitate it. On the other hand, a privatization law involves risks, including potentially long delays in getting parliament approval, the sometimes excessively restrictive scope of legislative provisions, and a tendency on the part of some parliaments to interfere too much in the implementation of privatization transactions. Furthermore, special legislation may not be needed for the transfer of the subsidiaries, participations, or assets of SOEs or public holding companies.

Where a law is necessary or desirable, it may be preferable to limit its provisions to the minimum needed to ensure efficient privatization. New legislation will be required for operations that cannot be executed (or cannot be executed efficiently) under existing law. Privatization laws will often embody provisions designed for remedying the main gaps in the rules regulating the market economy or the functioning of the public sector or for introducing support measures deemed necessary for the success of privatization. Provisions of this kind represent what may be called facilitating provisions, as opposed to the enabling provisions authorizing the privatization process itself.

The scope of the necessary legislative amendments is much broader when it comes to privatizing sectors that were under public monopoly. In such instances, provisions establishing the old monopoly will need to be repealed and replaced by a new sectoral organization; new rules governing the entry of operators into the sector and the terms of their access to any remaining bottleneck facilities; and new institutions and mechanisms to regulate the demonopolized sector. The complexity and sector-specificity of many of these provisions have often led to sectoral privatization laws.

The privatization law proper should reflect the broad political lines of the privatization strategy and program. It should also endow the government or privatization agency with the required implementation powers, and it should avoid restrictions that may unduly tie the hands of the executing agencies and slow down the process. The legislation must allow adequate flexibility (for example, in the choice of the privatization technique best suited to each case), while providing basic safeguards guaranteeing the integrity and efficiency of the process. Success of the program hinges on, among other things, a basic consensus among parliament, government, and head of state on the scope and broad lines of the program; a clear mandate given to the executing agencies along with the powers necessary for fulfilling that mandate; and unambiguous, flexible, and competitive privatization procedures applied in a transparent manner by officials accountable for their actions.

Furthermore, subordinate legal instruments should be used where they are equally or better suited, leading to greater latitude in actual implementation. Examples of subordinate instruments include not only decrees, implementing regulations, directives, and administrative decisions but also contractual agreements negotiated with buyers. The danger is, however, that under similar circumstances different deals might be struck with different buyers, which could undermine the legitimacy of the process.

A final important point is to guard against legislative optimism. Even if the legislator could correctly predict the major problems that might arise during execution of the privatization program and set up the optimal legal framework for handling privatization, the program's success would not be guaranteed. The legislation would still need to be applied effectively, which assumes that the necessary institutions and resources exist or are put in place and that each operation is prepared, structured, negotiated, and executed competently and with integrity. The institutional challenge of privatization is hence twofold: to develop good strategies and good programs, and to set up efficient institutions and mechanisms through which to implement them. These strategies, programs, institutions, and mechanisms, as well as the underlying legal framework, need to be adaptable and able to respond to lessons of experience and changing circumstances.

Role of Advisers

The broad range of policy and legal issues that shape and affect the privatization process are, by and large, new for governments. Government administrators rarely have all the skills and experience required to analyze these new issues and to address them effectively. Outside experts with specialized skills and knowledge of the experience of other countries are almost always called for. Economists, lawyers, financial advisers, and other consultants have thus played an important role, and worked toward a common goal, in privatizations in most countries.

Proper coordination and integration of these advisory inputs is important and often difficult. Infrastructure privatization affords a good illustration. Economic analysis should normally set the stage for strategy formulation, although legal and other technical input is also needed from the outset. Once the broad strategy, including breakup of monopolistic sectors and introduction of competition, has been adopted, lawyers and financial advisers will tend to take the lead from economists and policy advisers as the privatization transactions are implemented.

A multitude of laws and regulations need to be taken into account or amended as part of the preparation of a privatization program, and lawyers have a creative role to play in this exercise. Their job is to find ways to implement privatization despite any obstacles, not just to draw attention to those obstacles without recommending ways to address them. Lawyers will, of course, also have a central, and more traditional, role to play in drafting documents and advising the seller and the buyer in negotiations on the reams of agreements and contracts pertaining to privatization transactions. Many of the special provisions of privatization laws discussed in this book have been addressed in these contractual documents rather than through legislation.

Once a privatization operation has been completed, guarantees are required to ensure compliance by all of the parties with the terms of the privatization agreements. Efficient enforcement mechanisms will be needed, disputes will have to be settled, and noncompliance penalized. The new regulatory framework may need to be fine-tuned and amended to better tailor it to new or unexpected developments. All of this will require inputs from experts.

In brief, the scope and complexity of the legal issues to which privatization programs can give rise are practically unlimited; they concern both public and private law and domestic, international, and foreign law. To meet this challenge, privatizing governments must secure the services of qualified, experienced, and independent lawyers to help them identify and resolve critical problems for each operation. This is a necessary but not a sufficient prerequisite for success: necessary, because law is at the heart of the privatization process, though not sufficient in itself, because the legal aspects of privatization are only one component among many others to be taken into consideration.

A Multidisciplinary and Empirical Approach

Political, administrative, legal, economic, financial, technical, social, and other dimensions of privatization are equally important and directly affect the design of the privatization program, the content of the privatization legislation, and the way program and law are implemented. Law is not an end in itself; it is a reflection of social and political values and priorities.

The purpose of this book is to contribute to a better integration of the strategic, economic, political, legal, and institutional aspects of privatization. Law was used as the common thread throughout, though greater emphasis was placed on economic analysis in discussing the reform and privatization of infrastructure sectors. Most economic liberalization and privatization programs require amendment of existing legal norms to make them suitable for new strategies and policies. The analysis was based not on a review or comparison of privatization-related laws but on the actual experiences of many countries, the problems encountered, and the solutions applied, the good ones as well as the not-so-good ones.

This multidisciplinary and comparative overview of privatization experience has shown that each country needs to tailor its approach to its specific objectives and constraints. This means that there is no universally applicable model privatization program or law. Nevertheless, the process can be substantially enriched by examining the lessons drawn from other countries' experience. This book contributes to the dissemination of these lessons of experience.

Appendix
Privatization Legislation, by Country

This list of privatization legislation is not exhaustive. It encompasses laws, decrees, and regulations currently in force and others that have since been abrogated or amended. Wherever possible, the references contain the correct title and the date of the instrument; some titles are translations, while others describe the content of the instrument. Some references are taken from newspapers or journal articles and are not necessarily accurate.

Albania

Law no. 7512 authorizing and protecting private ownership, freedom to engage in independent private activities, and privatization (August 10, 1991)

Decree no. 22 promulgating Law no. 7512 of August 10, 1991 (August 15, 1991)

Council of Ministers Decision no. 307 on the rights and duties of the National Privatization Agency and the Commission for Preparation of the Privatization Process (August 29, 1991)

Council of Ministers Instruction no. 3 on the organization of the work and implementation of the transition from public to private ownership through auction sales (August 30, 1991)

Law on commercial companies (November 19, 1992)

Law no. 7698 on restitution of property to and compensation of former owners (April 15, 1993)

Law no. 7699 on compensation to former owners of agricultural land (April 15, 1993)

Decree no. 248 of the Council of Ministers on the acceleration of privatization (April 1993)

Decree no. 47 of the Council of Ministers on evaluation of state-owned property (May 1993)

Land Law (June 1993)

Law on foreign investment (November 1993)

Decree no. 93 of the Council of Ministers on the transformation of state-owned enterprises into commercial companies (February 1994)

Decision no. 234 on measures for the acceleration of privatization of small and medium-sized enterprises (May 24, 1994)

Decree on the issuing and distribution of privatization vouchers (March 1995)

Law no. 7971 on public procurement (July 26, 1995)

Law no. 7973 on concessions and participation of the private sector in public services and infrastructure (July 26, 1995)

Law no. 7979 on investment funds (July 26, 1995)

Algeria

Decree no. 87.266 on the creation and organization of the National Planning Council (December 8, 1987)

Law no. 88.01 on public enterprises (January 12, 1988)

Law no. 88.02 on planning (January 12, 1988)

Law no. 88.03 on Participation Funds (January 12, 1988)

Ordinance no. 95.22 on the privatization of public enterprises (August 26, 1995)

Argentina

Law no. 22177 authorizing the national government to privatize state-owned enterprises and assets (March 4, 1980)

Law no. 23696 on state reform (August 18, 1989)

Law no. 23697 on the state of economic emergency (September 15, 1989)

Decree no. 1105/89 implementing Law no. 23696 of August 18, 1989 (October 1989)

Decree nos. 377/89, 570/89, 769/89, and 824/89 implementing Law no. 23697 of September 15, 1989 (1989)

Decree nos. 731/89, 59/90, 60/90, 61/90, 62/90, 420/90, 575/90, 636/90, 677/90, 1130/90, 1185/90, 1229/90, 1230/90, 1948/90, 1967/90, 1968/90, 2096/90, 2332/90, 2344/90, 2345/90, 2346/90, 2347/90, 2762/90, and 778/91 on privatization of ENTEL

Decree nos. 575/90, 105/90, 1948/90, and 2074/90

Law no. 23883 on the creation of a national fund to finance private production activities (October 24, 1990)

Decree nos. 1443/91 and 2408/91 on the privatization of the Buenos Aires water supply company (1991)

Decree no. 2515/91

Law no. 24045 (December 31, 1991)

Law no. 24065 on electricity (January 16, 1992)

Law no. 24076 on regulatory framework for the gas industry and privatization of Gas del Estado (June 12, 1992)

Decree no. 999/92 on potable water supply and sanitation services concessions (June 18, 1992)

Decree no. 1189/92 on establishing new gas companies (July 1992)

Decree no. 1398/92 implementing Law no. 24065 of January 16, 1992 (August 11, 1992)

Decree 1738/92 implementing Law no. 24076 of June 12, 1992 (September 18, 1992)

Law no. 24145 on privatization of YPF S.A. (hydrocarbons) (November 6, 1992)

Law no. 24155 on privatization of the National Savings and Insurance Bank and the National Development Bank (1992)

Decree no. 2108/92 on privatization of Aceros Paraná S.A. (1992)

Decree 2255/92 regulating the transportation and distribution of natural gas (December 7, 1992)

Decree no. 2339/92 creating the National Railways Regulatory Commission (December 4, 1992)

Decree nos. 2451/92 through 2460/92 on the transportation and distribution of natural gas (1992)

Decree nos. 51/92, 214/92, 839/92, and 2514/92

Decree no. 2792/92 approving the by-laws of Encotesa (December 1992)

Resolution no. 551/92 (as amended by Resolution no. 873/92) setting the conditions and procedures for debt-for-shares swaps (1992)

Ministry of Economy resolution nos. 1386/92, 1457/92, 68/93, and 69/93 on railway concessions

Decree no. 1108/93 implementing Law no. 24145 of November 6, 1992 (May 31, 1993)

Decree no. 1186/93 on measures to secure free competition in the marketing of natural gas (June 9, 1993)

Decree no. 1863/93 on the creation of the National Commission of Railway Transportation (September 1, 1993)

Decree no. 454/94 on the creation of the Arbitral Tribunal of Railway Transportation (March 24, 1994)

Decree no. 455/94 on the jurisdiction of the National Commission of Railway Transportation (March 24, 1994)

Armenia

Law on ownership (October 31, 1990)

Decree of the Supreme Soviet on the principles of privatization (February 13, 1991)

Law on privatization and denationalization of state-owned enterprises and projects under construction (August 27, 1992)

Australia

Law on public enterprises of the State of New South Wales (1989)

Austria

Amendment to the second nationalization law (July 2, 1987)

Azerbaijan

Law on divestiture and privatization (January 1993)

Law on enterprises (July 1994)

Law on privatization (July 21, 1995)

Bahamas, The

Public Utility Commission Act (1993)

Belarus

Law on property ownership in Belarus, and implementing decree (November 9, 1991)

Law on divestiture and privatization of state-owned property (January 19, 1993)

Supreme Council decree on implementation of the law on divestiture and privatization of state-owned property (January 19, 1993)

Law on registered privatization vouchers (July 7, 1993)

Regulation defining the methods of sale of shares and other state property (May 1994)

Belgium

Law on the organization of the public credit sector and standardization of the supervision and conditions of operation of credit establishments (June 17, 1991), as amended by royal decree of September 27, 1993, by law of December 27, 1993, and by royal decree of April 7, 1995

Royal decree on the State Property Valuation Commission (October 8, 1992)

Law containing fiscal and financial provisions (July 22, 1993), as amended by law containing various social and other provisions (December 21, 1994)

Royal decree approving amendment of the bylaws of the Société Nationale de Crédit à l'Industrie (May 30, 1994)

Royal decree instituting a golden share in Synatom reserved to the government (June 10, 1994)

Royal decree instituting a golden share in Société Nationale de Transport par Canalisations reserved to the government (June 10, 1994)

Royal decree establishing the Société Fédérale d'Investissement (June 10, 1994), as amended by Royal decree of September 16, 1994

Royal decree instituting a golden share in Distrigaz reserved to the government (June 16, 1994)

Royal decree containing various provisions pertaining to the Société Fédérale d'Investissement and privatization of the Société Nationale d'Investissement (June 16, 1994)

Royal decree regulating the procedures for transfer of government-held shares in the Société Nationale d'Investissement to the Caisse Générale d'Epargne et de Retraite-Holding (July 20, 1994)

Royal decree on the acquisition of quoted shares of Distrigaz (July 20, 1994)

Royal decree amending the bylaws of Société Nationale de Crédit à l'Industrie and regulating the transfer of government-held shares in the Société Nationale de Crédit à l'Industrie to the Caisse Générale d'Epargne et de Retraite-Holding (July 20, 1994)

Benin

Law no. 88-005 on the creation, organization, and functioning of public and semipublic enterprises (April 26, 1988)

Decree no. 88-351 defining privatization techniques, procedures, and responsibilities (1988)

Decree no. 89-15 setting up a privatization bids appraisal commission (1989)

Law no. 92-023 (replacing Decree no. 88-351) laying down the basic principles of denationalization and transfer of ownership of enterprises from the public to the private sector (August 6, 1992)

Decree no. 92-340 on the composition, organization, and functioning of the technical commission on denationalization and transfer of ownership of enterprises from the public to the private sector (December 7, 1992)

Bolivia

Supreme Decree no. 21060 (August 29, 1985)

Supreme Decree no. 22836 on public enterprise reorganization and state participation in mixed enterprises (June 14, 1991)

Law no. 1330 on privatization (May 1992)

Supreme Decree no. 23170 on implementation of Law no. 1330 (June 1992)

Law no. 1544 on capitalization (March 21, 1994)

Law no. 1600 on the system for sector regulation (SIRESE) (October 28, 1994)

Supreme Decree no. 23985 on implementation of Law no. 1544 (March 30, 1995)

Electricity Law (December 1994)

Supreme Decree no. 23991 on public enterprise reorganization (April 10, 1995)

Law no. 1732 on private pension funds (November 29, 1996)

Brazil

Decree no. 91991 containing provisions on the process of the privatization of enterprises under the direct or indirect control of the federal government, and other measures (November 28, 1985)

Decree no. 95886 on the Federal Divestiture Program (March 29, 1988)

Law no. 6629 authorizing the executive of the State of São Paulo to transfer control of the capital of Viacão Aerea São Paulo S.A. (December 27, 1989)

Law no. 8018 on privatization vouchers (April 11, 1990)

Law no. 8031 authorizing the National Destatization Program (PND) (April 12, 1990), as amended and consolidated by Decree no. 724 (January 19, 1993) and further modified by provisional measures no. 327 (June 24, 1993), no. 415 (January 21, 1994), and no. 432 (February 23, 1994)

Decree no. 99463 appointing BNDES for implementation of the PND (August 16, 1990)

Decree no. 99464 on privatization of Usiminas (August 16, 1990)

Decree no. 99469 regulating the privatization procedure (August 1990)

Provisional measure no. 299 interpreting Law no. 8031 of April 12, 1990 (October 1, 1991)

Law no. 8250 on PND (October 24, 1991)

Law no. 8630 on port operations (February 25, 1993)

Decree no. 1068 (1994)

Law no. 8987 on public services concessions (February 13, 1995)

Law no. 9074 on the modernization of public service regulation, especially in the electric sector (July 5, 1995)

Bulgaria

Decree no. 56 on economic activity (January 9, 1989)

Decree no. 36 on the development of private and individual initiative in commerce, tourism, and services (April 10, 1990)

Decree no. 16 establishing the privatization agency (February 8, 1991)

Decree no. 42 on the adoption of regulations for auctioning state and municipal property (March 14, 1991)

Law on the conversion of state-owned enterprises into private companies (June 27, 1991)

Law on the restitution of nationalized real estate property (February 5, 1992)

Law on the restitution of property expropriated under the aegis of previous laws (February 5, 1992)

Law on transformation and privatization of state and municipal enterprises (April 23, 1992)

Decree no. 105 on the adoption of regulations for the auction sale and valuation of assets subject to privatization (June 15, 1992)

Law regulating small-scale privatization (January 1993)

Decree on preferential participation (1993)

Decree for the establishment of a fund to cover privatization expenditures (1993)

Law on mass privatization (June 9, 1994), as amended on December 1, 1995

Law on concessions (1995)

Burkina Faso

Ordinance no. 91-0042/PRES (1991)

Ordinance no. 91-0044/PRES authorizing privatization of 12 enterprises and creating the Privatization Commission (July 17, 1991)

Decree no. 91-0385/MCIM on the composition, organization, and functioning of the Privatization Commission (September 26, 1991)

Burundi

Decree-Law no. 1/027 defining the organic framework of public-law companies and private-law joint-venture companies (September 28, 1988)

Decree-Law no. 1/21 on the privatization of state-owned enterprises (August 12, 1991)

Decree-Law no. 100/133 on appointment of the Inter-Ministerial Privatization Committee (August 13, 1991)

Ministerial Ordinance no. 120/321 prescribing the competitive bidding procedures for the privatization of state-owned enterprises (October 4, 1991)

Cameroon

Law no. 89/030 authorizing the president of the republic to legislate by ordinance with respect to the privatization of public and semipublic entities (December 29, 1989)

Ordinance no. 90/004 on the privatization of public and semipublic enterprises (June 22, 1990)

Decree no. 90/1257 on implementation of Ordinance no. 90/004 of June 22, 1990 (August 30, 1990)

Decree no. 90/1423 on the privatization of certain public and semipublic enterprises (October 3, 1990)

Canada

Canada Development Corporation Act (June 30, 1971)

Atlantic Fisheries Restructuring Act (November 30, 1983)

Financial Administration Act (June 29, 1984)

Act authorizing divestiture of Northern Transport Company Ltd (June 28, 1985)

Canada Development Corporation Reorganization Act (December 20, 1985)

Act authorizing divestiture of Canadian Arsenals Company Ltd (May 1, 1986)

Act authorizing divestiture of Canadair Ltd (December 19, 1986)

Act authorizing alienation of assets of the Northern Canadian Energy Commission located in the Yukon (March 26, 1987)

Teleglobe Canada Reorganization and Divestiture Act (April 1, 1987)

Eldorado Nuclear Ltd Reorganization and Divestiture Act (July 28, 1988)

Act concerning public participation in the capital of Air Canada (August 18, 1988)

Nordion and Theratronics Divestiture Authorization Act (January 30, 1990)

Petro-Canada Public Participation Act (February 1, 1991)

Canada Reorganization and Divestiture Act (December 17, 1991)

Debt Service Account and Debt Reduction Act (June 18, 1992)

Cape Verde

Law no. 52/III/89 demarcating ownership in economic sectors (July 13, 1989)

Law no. 47/IV/92 on privatization (July 5, 1992)

Decree no. 116/92 creating an advisory agency to the government on privatization (September 17, 1992)

Chad

Ordinance no. 017/PR/92 authorizing divestiture of state enterprises (August 29, 1992)

Decree no. 460/PR/MCDI/92 concerning the technical commission on the organization and functioning of divestiture (1992)

Chile

Decree-Law no. 2564 on civil aviation (March 1979), as amended by Law no. 18243 (September 1983)

Decree-Law no. 1 on electricity services (June 22, 1982)

Law nos. 18398 and 18401 on popular capitalism (1985)

Law no. 18747 on labor capitalism (1988)

Decree-Law no. 381 on concessions (1988)

General Law no. 18168 on telecommunications (October 2, 1982), as amended by Law
   nos. 18482 and 18591, Decree-Law no. 1 of 1987, and Law nos. 18681 (December 31,
   1987) and 18838 (September 30, 1989)

Decree-Law no. 382 on sanitation services (June 21, 1989)

Law no. 18922 on electricity services (January 30, 1990)

Decree-Law no. 164 on infrastructure concessions (July 22, 1991)

Supreme Decree no. 240 on regulation to Decree-Law no. 164 of July 22, 1991 (April
   1992)

Law on electric concessions (November 6, 1992)

Law no. 19252 modifying Decree-Law no. 164 on infrastructure concessions (October
   11, 1993)

China

Regulation implementing on an experimental basis the registration of Chinese
   business groups (May 4, 1992)

Standard Opinion of the State Committee on Economic Restructuring on joint-stock
   companies (May 15, 1992)

Measures on implementing the transformation of the operational mechanism of
   state-owned commercial enterprises, promulgated by the Ministry of Commerce,
   the State Economic and Trade Office, and the State Commission for Restructuring
   the Economic System (November 6, 1992)

Provisional regulations promulgated by the State Council on the issue and sale of
   shares (April 22, 1993)

Addendum to the Standard Opinion issued by the State Committee on Economic
   Restructuring (May 24, 1993)

Colombia

Decree nos. 2132, 2139, 2140, and 2142 (1992)

Law no. 35 on the privatization of financial-sector entities (January 5, 1993)

Law no. 37 authorizing shareholding by private investors in the cellular mobile
   telephone service (1993)

Law no. 80 on contracts of the public administration (October 28, 1993)

Law no. 142 on residential public services (1994)

Law no. 143 on electricity (July 1994)

Law no. 226 on alienation of state-owned shares (1995)

Congo

Law no. 21-94 on the framework for privatization (August 10, 1994)

Decree no. 94-424 on the organization and functioning of the Privatization
   Committee (September 1, 1994)

Decree no. 94-425 on the implementation procedures for the privatization of public
   enterprises (September 1, 1994)

Decree no. 94-426 on valuation of enterprises (September 1, 1994)

Decree no. 94-427 on the level of participation by the state and other subscribers (September 1, 1994)

Decree no. 94-428 on the conversion of debt into shares (September 1, 1994)

Decree no. 94-429 on the conditions of eligibility for participants in the privatization program (September 1, 1994)

Decree no. 94-430 on exceptions to the cash payment principle (September 1, 1994)

Costa Rica

Law no. 6955 on public-sector financial equilibrium (February 24, 1984)

Law no. 11060 on the Regulatory Authority for Public Utilities (national electricity services transformation) (October 31, 1990)

Côte d'Ivoire

Decree no. 87-197 authorizing transfer of the government's holding in the capital of Société Ivoirienne des Tabacs (February 6, 1987)

Decree no. 90-1610 authorizing transfer to the private sector of shares and participation held by juridical persons under public law, creating entities responsible for the program of privatization and restructuring of the parastatal sector, and defining the implementing procedures for that program (December 28, 1990)

Order (*arrêté*) no. 002 appointing the members of the Parastatal Sector Privatization and Restructuring Committee (June 3, 1991)

Law no. 94-338 on the privatization of state-owned shares and assets in certain domestic public enterprises and establishments (June 9, 1994)

Decree on implementing procedures for Law no. 94-338 of June 9, 1994 (1994)

Decree no. 94-520 on the composition, functioning, and responsibilities of the Privatization Committee (September 21, 1994)

Croatia

Law on the transformation of enterprises with social capital (April 18, 1991), revised 1993, 1994

Czechoslovakia

Law no. 105/90 on private enterprise by citizens (and supplement thereto) (April 18, 1990)

Law no. 403/90 on the alleviation of certain injustices with respect to property (October 2, 1990)

Law no. 427/90 on the transfer of ownership of certain state-owned assets to other juridical or natural persons ("Small-Scale Privatization Law") (October 25, 1990)

Czech National Council Law on the jurisdiction of the institutions of the Czech Republic with respect to the transfer of state property to other juridical or natural persons (November 15, 1990)

Law no. 87/91 designed to redress results of injustices committed during the period 1948-89 ("Extra-Judicial Rehabilitation Law" or "Restitution Law") (February 21, 1991)

Law no. 92/91 on the conditions of transfer of state property to other persons ("Large-Scale Privatization Law") (February 26, 1991)

Czech National Council Law no. 171/91 on the jurisdiction of the agencies of the Czech Republic with respect to the transfer of state property to other persons, and on the Czech Republic Assets Fund (April 23, 1991)

Law no. 172/91 on transfer of ownership from the government of the Czech Republic to municipalities (April 24, 1991)

Law no. 229/91 on adjustments to ownership rights pertaining to land and other agricultural assets (May 21, 1991)

Slovak National Council Law no. 253/1991 on the jurisdiction of the agencies of the Slovak Republic with respect to the transfer of state property to other persons, and on the Slovak Republic Assets Fund (May 24, 1991)

Government Decree on the issue and use of investment coupons (September 5, 1991)

Law on the conditions of transfer of state property to other persons, amending and supplementing Law no. 92/91 of February 26, 1991 (February 18, 1992)

Law no. 248/92 regulating privatization investment funds and investment companies (April 28, 1992)

Czech Republic (see also *Czechoslovakia*)

Law no. 222 on energy (1994)

Djibouti

Law on economic and social objectives, 1990–2000

Company Law (1988)

Law on exclusive concessions (1989)

Law authorizing the privatization of specified public enterprises

Dominican Republic

Law no. 14-90 authorizing private-sector participation in electric power generation and distribution (February 1990)

Ecuador

Law no. 50 on modernization of the state, privatization, and delivery of public services by the private sector (October 21, 1993)

Executive Decree no. 1335 establishing the Ministry of Finance unit responsible for modernization of the state (January 5, 1994)

Egypt, Arab Republic of

Law no. 230 on joint-venture companies (1989)

Law no. 203 on public-sector commercial enterprises (June 19, 1991)

Prime Minister Decree no. 1590/1991 on the implementing regulations for Law no. 203 of June 19, 1991 (1991)

Law no. 95 on capital markets (June 1992) and executive regulations (April 1993)

El Salvador

Amendment to the 1983 constitution, allowing private enterprises to manage public services (1994)

Estonia

Law on privatization of state-owned enterprises in the service, trade, and food sectors (December 13, 1990)

Law on the principles of property reform (with implementing decree) (June 20, 1991)

Law on land reform (November 1991)

Law on foreign investment (1991)

Resolution signed by the chairman of the Supreme Council prescribing the conditions and procedures for the privatization of state and municipal property (August 13, 1992)

Resolution of the chairman of the Supreme Council on commencement of the sale of shares of state-owned enterprises (August 13, 1992)

Law on bankruptcy (November 1992)

Decree no. 36 on the procedure for the restitution of illegally expropriated property (February 5, 1993)

Law on privatization (June 17, 1993)

Decree on the issue of privatization vouchers (November 1993)

Law on securities market (September 1993)

Property Law (December 1993)

Accounting Law (July 28, 1994)

Government decree on procedures for public offering of shares in state-owned enterprises (August 1994)

Government decree on investment funds (August 1994)

Finland

Guidelines of the Council of State on the capitalization of state-controlled companies (June 23, 1994)

France

Constitutional Council Decision no. 86-207 on the enabling law authorizing the government to take various economic and social measures (June 25 and 26, 1986)

Law no. 86-793 authorizing the government to take various economic and social measures (July 2, 1986)

Law no. 86-912 on the procedures for implementation of the privatization decided on by Law no. 86-793 of July 2, 1986 (August 6, 1986)

Decree on the appointment of members to the Privatization Commission (September 9, 1986)

Decree no. 86-1067 on freedom of communications (September 30, 1986)

Decree no. 86-1140 on the application of Law no. 86-912 of August 6, 1986 (October 24, 1986)

Decree no. 86-1141 on the application of article 10 of Law no. 86-912 of August 6, 1986 (October 25, 1986)

Instruction no. 4 B-5-86 on privatization, portfolio, and shares of enterprises (November 12, 1986)

Instruction no. 5 G-15-86 on system governing private capital gains on the transfer of securities and social rights with respect to privatization (December 15, 1986) of the Privatization Commission (January 14, 1987)

Order (_arrêté_) prescribing the procedures for privatization of Compagnie Financière de Paribas (January 16, 1987)

Order (_arrêté_) setting the exchange values of debt paper assigned in payment for the shares of Compagnie Financière de Paribas transferred by the government by public offering for sale of January 19, 1987 (January 16, 1987)

Instruction no. 2 O-3-87 on stamp duty and assimilated duties, and powers of representation of shareholders at general meetings on the privatization of certain enterprises (March 6, 1987)

Instruction no. 5 F-15-87 on benefits accorded to employees under privatization operations and other issues relating to exempted salaries, wages, pensions, and annuities (August 24, 1987)

Instruction no. 2 O-7-87 on stamp duty and assimilated duties, and transfer of the national program company "Télévision Française 1" (September 1, 1987)

Decree no. 88-1054 on the Public Enterprises Valuation Commission (November 22, 1988)

Law no. 89-465 amending Law no. 86-912 of August 6, 1986, on implementing procedures for privatization (July 10, 1989)

Law no. 90-560 on corporatization of the Régie Nationale des Usines Renault (July 4, 1990)

Decree no. 91-332 on minority opening of public enterprise capital (April 4, 1991)

Law no. 93-122 on prevention of corruption and transparency in economic activities and public procedures (_loi Sapin_) (January 29, 1993)

Law no. 93-923 on privatization (July 19, 1993)

Decree no. 93-930 on the application of Law no. 93-923 of July 19, 1993 (July 21, 1993)

Order (_arrêté_) setting the swap value of government debt paper (6 percent, July 1997) assigned in payment for the shares of Banque Nationale de Paris transferred by the government through public offering on October 5, 1993 (October 4, 1993)

Order (_arrêté_) prescribing the procedures for privatization of Banque Nationale de Paris (October 4, 1993)

Decree no. 93-1190 on the election of the members of the bid opening commission for the award of local public service concessions (October 21, 1993)

Opinion of the Privatization Commission on the minimum value of Rhône-Poulenc (November 10, 1993)

Order (_arrêté_) prescribing the procedures for privatization of Rhône-Poulenc S.A. (November 15, 1993)

Order (_arrêté_) setting the swap value of government debt paper (6 percent, July 1997) assigned in payment for the shares of Rhône-Poulenc transferred by the government through public offering on November 16, 1993 (November 15, 1993)

Decree no. 93-1296 on the application of article 10 of Law no. 86-912 of August 6, 1986, as amended, on privatization procedures and certain rights pertaining to golden shares (December 13, 1993)

Decree no. 93-1297 amending Decree no. 86-1141 of October 25, 1986, on application of article 10 of Law no. 86-912 of August 6, 1986, on privatization procedures (December 13, 1993)

Decree no. 93-1298 instituting a golden share reserved to the government in Société Nationale Elf Aquitaine (December 13, 1993)

Circular on jurisdiction (*saisine*) for application of article 10.1 of Law no. 86-912 of August 6, 1986, on privatization procedures, as amended by Privatization Law no. 93-923 of July 19, 1993 (April 5, 1994)

Opinion of the Privatization Commission on the minimum value of Union des Assurances de Paris (April 21, 1994)

Order (*arrêté*) prescribing the procedures for privatization of Union des Assurances de Paris (April 25, 1994)

Law no. 94-679 on various economic and financial provisions, particularly articles 17 and following, on company law and Air France (August 8, 1994)

Law no. 95-127 on public procurement and concessions (February 8, 1995)

Decree no. 95-635 on annual reports on price and quality of water and sewerage services (May 6, 1995)

Law no. 96-659 on regulation of telecommunications (July 26, 1996)

Gabon

Law on privatization (February 13, 1996)

Georgia

Law on the privatization of state enterprises of the Republic of Georgia (with implementing decree) (August 9, 1991)

Government decree on the sale by auction of state-owned property (May 28, 1992)

Decree of the State Council on the government program of privatization of state-owned enterprises of the Republic of Georgia (August 18, 1992)

Government decree on the government program of privatization of state-owned enterprises of the Republic of Georgia (August 25, 1992)

Presidential decree on large-scale privatization (May 1994)

Decree on widening employee rights upon the transformation of state entities into joint-stock companies (May 1994)

Law of the Republic of Georgia on foreign investment (1995)

Germany

Law on privatization and reorganization of publicly owned assets (Treuhandgesetz, or Trusteeship Law) (June 17, 1990); this law was adopted by the East German parliament before reunification.

Unification Treaty (August 31, 1990), particularly article 25, incorporating the Treuhandgesetz (Trusteeship Law) into German law and amending it; and annex containing the law on the settlement of outstanding ownership questions (amended in March 1991)

Omnibus Law on the elimination of obstacles to the privatization of enterprises and on investment promotion (March 22, 1991)

Law on the restructuring of enterprises under Treuhandanstalt administration (Spaltungsgesetz of April 5, 1991)

Law on the finalization of the privatization activities of the Treuhand agency (August 9, 1994)

Law modifying the Basic Law (Gesetz zur Anderung des Grundgesetzes) with an insertion on public oversight and ownership of post and telecommunications (August 31, 1994)

Law on the construction and financing of federal roads and motorways by private enterprise (August 1994)

Law on the new organization of postal services and telecommunications (September 14, 1994)

Ghana

Divestiture of state interests (implementation) Law 1993 (January 5, 1993)

Greece

Law no. 1892/90 (1990)

Law no. 2000/91 on denationalization (1991)

Law on the privatization of telecommunications (1994)

Guinea

Ordinance no. 306 PRG-85 on the privatization of industrial-type public enterprises (December 12, 1985)

Ordinance no. 318 PRG-85 applying the reorganization measures cited therein to certain specified enterprises (December 21, 1985)

Decree no. 194-PRG-86 on liquidation of commercial-type public enterprises (October 7, 1986)

Ordinance no. O/91/025 on the institutional framework of public enterprises (March 11, 1991), as amended by Ordinance no. O/92/022/PRG/SGG (May 26, 1992)

Decree no. D/92/133 prescribing the conditions of application of Ordinance no. O/91/025 of March 11, 1991 (May 26, 1992)

Law no. L/92/016 on the general regulation of telecommunications (June 2, 1992)

Law no. L/93/037 prescribing the rules for privatization of public enterprises (August 20, 1993)

Decree no. D/93/208 on application of the public enterprises privatization law (October 21, 1993)

Guinea-Bissau

Council of Ministers decree creating the public enterprises reform management unit (UGREP) (February 28, 1990)

Honduras

Decree no. 161-85 on privatization covering procedures applicable to four institutions (October 10, 1985), as amended by Decree no. 178-92 of October 30, 1992

Decree nos. 03-93 and 04-93 on the extension of the application of Decree no. 161-85 and its regulations to all public institutions and on the creation of the Consultative Commission for Privatization (September 7, 1993)

Decree no. 135-94 mandating the government to propose a plan for the privatization of Hondutel and a framework for managing telecommunications in Honduras (1994)

Decree-Law no. 153-94 containing the framework law for the electricity sector (November 26, 1994)

Hungary

Law no. 24 (company law) (1988)

Law no. 13 on conversion of management organizations and business associations (May 30, 1989)

Law no. 5 on private enterprise (1990)

Law no. 7 establishing the State Property Agency to manage and utilize state property (January 26, 1990), amended by Law no. 53 of July 25, 1990

Law no. 8 on the protection of property entrusted to state enterprises (January 26, 1990)

Law no. 18 amending Law no. 13 of May 30, 1989 (1990)

Law no. 72 amending Law no. 13 of May 30, 1989 (September 11, 1990)

Law no. 74 on privatization (alienation, utilization) of state-owned companies engaged in retail trade, catering, and consumer services (September 18, 1990)

Law no. 16 on concessions (1991)

Law no. 25 on partial compensation for damage caused by the state to citizens' property (compensation law) (June 26, 1991), as amended by Law no. 50 of 1991

Law no. 69 on financial institutions (November 30, 1991)

Law no. 24 on partial compensation for confiscation of citizens' property by the state pursuant to laws enacted between May 1, 1939, and June 8, 1949 (April 7, 1992)

Law no. 39 on concessions in the field of transport and water management (1992)

Law no. 44 on employee's share ownership program (June 1992)

Law no. 54 on the sale, utilization, and protection of assets of which the state is provisional owner (1992)

Law no. 72 on telecommunications (November 23, 1992)

1993 budget law regarding use of privatization receipts (December 28, 1992)

Law no. 41 on gas supply (March 29, 1994)

Law no. 48 on the production, transport, and supply of electric energy (April 6, 1994)

Law no. 39 on the sale of state-owned enterprises (May 9, 1995)

India

Sick Industrial Companies (Special Provisions) Act (1985), as amended in December 1991

Indonesia

Law no. 3 on telecommunications (April 1, 1989)

Presidential Decree no. 37 on private participation in the electricity sector (1992)

Government Regulation no. 8 on private participation in the telecommunications sector (1993)

Government Regulation no. PP 20 on foreign investment (May 19, 1994)

Iran, Islamic Republic of

Decree no. 5283/T 109H on the policy of transfer of government-owned shares and public enterprises and organizations (June 19, 1991)

Decree no. 61164/T 466H on privatization of industrial enterprises (February 9, 1992)

Decree no. 1213/T 18H amending Decree no. 5283/T 109H of June 19, 1991 (April 24, 1992)

Decree no. 8456/T 87H on privatization of mines (May 13, 1992)

Resolution no. 113 DSh on privatization of agricultural enterprises (June 15, 1992)

Decree no. 34/785 on privatization of the tourism industry (August 9, 1992)

Decree no. 51021/T 490H replacing the Privatization Commission set up by Decree no. 5283/T 109H of June 19, 1991, by a Secretariat (December 27, 1992)

Israel

Law amending the law on state-owned companies (August 1993)

Italy

Law no. 218 on privatization of banks (July 31, 1990)

Decree-Law no. 356 on privatization of banks (November 20, 1990)

Law enabling BOTs in electricity generation (1991)

Decree-Law no. 386 on the conversion of public enterprises (December 1991)

Law no. 35 on conversion of government holding companies, liquidation of government holdings and transfer of public assets that may belong to the private sector (January 29, 1992)

Law no. 58 on reorganization of the telecommunications sector (January 1992)

Law no. 149 (February 18, 1992)

Decree-Law no. 333 (July 11, 1992), ratified by Law no. 359 on the corporatization of public enterprises (August 8, 1992), as amended by Decree-Law no. 332 (May 31, 1994)

Decree-Law no. 340 on liquidation of EFIM (Ente Partecipazioni e Finanziamenti Industria Manifatturiera) (July 18, 1992)

Decree-Law no. 365 (August 14, 1992)

Decree-Law no. 124 creating private retirement funds (April 21, 1993)

Decree of Chairman of Council of Ministers establishing the Standing Consultative and Guarantee Committee on Privatization (June 30, 1993)

Law no. 344 creating mutual securities investment funds (August 14, 1993)

Decree-Law no. 350 (September 10, 1993)

Decree-Law no. 389 on privatization (September 27, 1993), renewed by Decree-Law nos. 486 (November 29, 1993), 75 (January 31, 1994), and 216 (April 1, 1994)

Law no. 422 converting Decree-Law no. 350 of September 10, 1993, into a law (November 8, 1993)

Decree-Law no. 332 on rules for acceleration of procedures for the retirement of share holdings of the State and public authorities in public limited companies (May 31, 1994)

Law on the establishment of regulatory authorities (November 1995).

Jamaica

Telephone Act (1988)

Law on employee's share ownership program (1994)

Japan

Telecommunications Business Law (December 1984)

Law restructuring the national railways (November 1986)

Kazakstan

Law of the Kazak Soviet Socialist Republic (SSR) on denationalization and privatization (with implementing resolution) (July 1991)

Presidential decree on the program of denationalization and privatization of state property for 1991–92 (first stage) and the voucher scheme for privatization of state property in the Kazak SSR (1991)

Resolution no. 101 of the State Committee of the Kazak SSR on state-owned property (August 1, 1991)

Law on protection of and support for private initiative (March 1993)

Presidential decree on the program of denationalization and privatization of state property for 1993–95 (second stage) (March 5, 1993)

Law amending the law of the Kazak SSR on denationalization and privatization (April 1993)

Presidential Decree-Law no. 2721 on privatization (December 23, 1995)

Kenya

Decree prescribing the institutional framework for the Parastatal Reform and Privatisation Programme (1992)

The State Corporations (Privatization Exemptions) Order (1992)

Korea, Republic of

Law on the management of enterprises in which there is public shareholding

Kuwait

Decree no. 131 establishing the Kuwait Telecommunications Company (1992)

Kyrgyz Republic

Law on sale by competitive bidding and sale by auction (August 7, 1991)

Decree of the president on denationalization and privatization of state-owned property (August 7, 1991)

Law on general principles of denationalization, privatization, and private initiative in the Kyrgyz Republic (December 20, 1991)

Decree on urgent measures to speed up denationalization and privatization (January 27, 1992)

Law on concessions and foreign-concessioned enterprises in the Kyrgyz Republic (March 6, 1992)

Law on the State Property Fund (July 1, 1992)

Law on denationalization and privatization of state-owned property in the Kyrgyz Republic (January 12, 1994)

Decree of the president on the establishment of the Enterprise Reform and Resolution Agency (May 1994)

Lao People's Democratic Republic

Council of Ministers Decree no. 17/PCM on the conversion of state-owned enterprises to some other form of ownership (March 16, 1990)

Decree of the Prime Minister no. 47/PM on the establishment of a permanent privatization committee (March 9, 1993)

Latvia

Law on entrepreneurial activity (September 26, 1990)

Law on state enterprises (December 12, 1990)

Law on the privatization of agricultural enterprises and fishery collectives (with implementing decree) (June 21, 1991)

Supreme Council resolution on the concept of privatization of state and municipal property and the preparatory program (March 3, 1992)

Law on the order of privatization of state and municipal property (June 16, 1992)

Law on the transformation of state and municipal property into statutory companies (September 1992)

Law on state and municipal privatization funds (December 1992)

Law on privatization of state and municipal property (February 1994)

Law on the state property fund (February 1994)

Law on state and municipal privatization commissions (February 1994)

Lithuania

Law on the initial privatization of state-owned property (February 28, 1991)

Enabling decree to the law of February 28, 1991 (March 14, 1991)

Decree no. 238 on reorganization into smaller units of state enterprises and state stock corporations which are being privatized (June 19, 1991), amended in part on June 24, 1992

Law on the privatization of unprofitable state enterprises (July 23, 1991)

Law on privatization of the property of agricultural enterprises (July 30, 1991)

Law on the privatization of primary wealth (1991), as amended on December 18, 1991

Law on foreign investment (November 1991)

Law on employee participation in privatization (May 1992)

Law on the terms and conditions of restitution of ownership rights (1993)

Law on mutual funds and investment companies (1993)

Law on state enterprises not to be privatized or corporatized before the year 2000 (December 1994)

Law on special purpose companies and their sphere of activities (February 1995)

Law on privatization of state and municipal property (July 1995)

Macedonia, former Yugoslav Republic of

Law on the transformation of enterprises with social capital (June 1993)

Madagascar

Law no. 93-001 on institutional reform of the telecommunications sector and the postal services sector (postal, money order, and checking services) (January 21, 1994)

Malaysia

Federal Roads (Private Management) Act (1984)

Amendment to the Telecommunications Act of 1950 (1985)

Electricity Supply Act (1990)

Ports Privatization Act (1990)

Airport and Aviation Services (Operating Company) Act (1991)

Postal Services (Successor Company) Act (1991)

Railways (Successor Company) Act (1991)

Slaughterhouses Privatization Act (1993)

Sewerage Services Act (1993)

Mali

Decree no. 88-21/P-RM establishing a fund for laid-off employees of public enterprises (1988)

Decree no. 88-34/AN-RM authorizing opening up the capital of state-owned and joint-venture companies (February 27, 1988)

Ordinance no. 91-014/P-CTSP laying down the basic principles of the organization and functioning of industrial and commercial-type public establishments and state-owned companies (May 18, 1991)

Decree no. 91-051/AN-RM prescribing the standard form and content of the bylaws of industrial and commercial-type public enterprises and the procedures for their legal dissolution (1991)

Mauritania

Ordinance no. 90-90 containing the bylaws of public establishments and public corporations and governing relations between these entities and the state (April 4, 1990)

Mexico

Federal Law on parastatal entities (May 14, 1986)

Enabling regulations to the law on parastatal entities of May 14, 1986 (January 1990)

New charter law of Pemex (July 16, 1992)

Law amending the law on electric power (December 1992)

Law regulating railway services (May 12, 1995)

Law on telecommunications (May 1995)

Amendments to article 28 of the constitution on the removal of government monopolies in the areas of railways and satellite communications (January 1995)

Regulation on natural gas (November 8, 1995)

Moldova

Law no. 627/XII on privatization (July 4, 1991)

1993–94 privatization program (March 12, 1993)

Decree on measures to prevent illegal privatizations (March 12, 1993)

Law on privatization (March 14, 1993)

Decree approving the list of government assets to be offered for sale in the Republic of Moldova in 1993–94 (March 16, 1993)

1995–96 Privatization Program (March 1995)

Mongolia

Law on privatization (May 31, 1991)

Law on economic entities (June 1991)

Law on foreign investment (May 1993)

Law on banks (June 1993)

Law on securities (October 1994)

Montenegro

Law on transformation of property and management (1992)

Morocco

Law no. 39-89 authorizing the transfer of public enterprises to the private sector (April 11, 1990)

Decree no. 2-90-402 implementing article 5 of Law no. 39-89 of April 11, 1990 (October 16, 1990)

Decree no. 2-90-403 on the powers of the minister responsible for implementing transfers of public enterprises to the private sector (October 16, 1990)

Decree no. 2-90-577 issued in application of article 7 of Law no. 39-89 of April 11, 1990 (October 16, 1990)

Decree no. 2-90-578 prescribing the working conditions for the Transfer Commission provided for in article 2 of Law no. 39-89 of April 11, 1990 (October 16, 1990)

Amendment to Law no. 39-89 of April 11, 1990 (January 1995)

Mozambique

Decree no. 21/89 allowing for the sale of state-owned assets through public competition and establishing the administrative organization for these sales (May 23, 1989)

Law nos. 13/91 and 14/91 on transformation of state enterprises (August 3, 1991)

Law no. 15/91 establishing norms for the restructuring, transformation, and reorganization of the state-owned enterprises sector, including privatization and sale of enterprises, establishments, installations, and shareholdings of the state (August 3, 1991)

Law no. 17/91 instituting public companies (August 3, 1991)

Decree no. 27/91 setting up an interministerial commission for enterprise restructuring (November 21, 1991)

Decree no. 28/91 issued in application of Law no. 15/91 of August 3, 1991 (November 21, 1991)

Decree no. 30/91 containing a list of enterprises to be privatized (November 26, 1991)

Law no. 17/92 clarifying article 16 of Law no. 15/91 of August 3, 1991 (October 14, 1992)

Decree no. 20/92 on the creation of the Fund for Support of Economic Rehabilitation (August 5, 1992)

Decree no. 3/93 listing enterprises to be privatized under article 14 of Law no. 15/91 of August 3, 1991 (April 21, 1993)

Decree no. 20/93 on the sale of shares to white-collar and manual employees (September 14, 1993)

Decree no. 4/94 listing enterprises to be privatized under article 14 of Law no. 15/91 of August 3, 1991 (1994)

Nepal

Act no. 2050 on privatization (January 3, 1994)

New Zealand

State-Owned Enterprises Act 1986 (December 18, 1986), as amended

Telecommunications Act (1987)

Telecommunications (Amendment) Act (1988)

Telecommunications Regulations—International Services (1989)

Telecommunications Regulations—Communication of Information (1990)

1991 Budget Act, Chapter 5 (Privatization Strategy)

Nicaragua

Decree-Law no. 7-90 on the creation of Junta General de Corporaciones Nationales responsible for privatization of state companies (May 2, 1990)

Decree-Law nos. 11-90 and 23-91 on the procedure for claims filed by individuals whose property was confiscated by the previous regime (May 11, 1990 and 1991)

Presidential Resolution no. 291-92 on instructions for privatization (October 15, 1992)

Law no. 169 regulating the disposition of public/state property and the public services controlling entity (December 2, 1993)

Niger

Decree no. 86-120/PCMS/MTEP/SEM approving the model bylaws of public administrative establishments (September 11, 1986)

Decree no. 86-121/PCMS/MTEP/SEM approving the model bylaws of public industrial and commercial establishments (September 11, 1986)

Decree no. 86-122/PCMS/MTEP/SEM approving the model bylaws of public corporations (September 11, 1986)

Decree no. 86-123/PCMS/MTEP/SEM approving the model bylaws of joint-venture companies (September 11, 1986)

Nigeria

Decree no. 25 on privatisation and commercialisation (July 5, 1988)

Decree no. 78 establishing the Bureau of Public Enterprises (1993)

Pakistan

Order on the transfer of establishments (1978, amended in 1990)

Notification no. F.5 (1)-Adm-I/91 on the setting up of a Privatization Commission (January 22, 1991)

Ordinance on the protection of economic reforms (1992)

Notification no. F.5 (13)-Adm-I/93 on the reconstitution of the Privatization Commission (August 28, 1993)

Ordinance no. 26 on the Debt Retirement Fund (1993)

Ordinance no. 51 on telecommunications (July 13, 1994)

Panama

Law on concessions (1986)

Law no. 16 on privatization (June 14, 1992)

Executive Decree nos. 197 (December 15, 1993) and 352 (August 17, 1994) on implementing regulations to Law no. 16 of June 14, 1992

Paraguay

Law no. 126/91 on privatization (December 30, 1991)

Decree no. 13461 on implementing regulations to Law no. 126/91 of December 30, 1991 (May 8, 1992)

Law no. 320 authorizing privatization of Lineas Aereas Paraguayas S.A. (March 29, 1994)

Law no. 433 on privatization (September 27, 1994)

Law no. 548 on the reappraisal and regulation of the assets of enterprises (April 21, 1995)

Peru

Decree-Law no. 647 authorizing the private sector to hold a minimum of 51 percent of the shares of Centromin, Hierro Peru, and Minero Peru (July 1991)

Decree-Law no. 674 on the promotion of private investment in public enterprises (September 25, 1991)

Decree no. 675 authorizing privatization of Minpeco S.A. (October 2, 1991)

Decree-Law no. 758 on the promotion of private investments in public works and utilities (November 13, 1991)

Supreme Resolution no. 071-92-EF/10 authorizing use of debt for privatization (June 1992)

Decree-Law no. 25570 amending Decree-Law no. 674 of September 25, 1991 (June 19, 1992)

Decree-Law no. 25604 on protection of the assets of public enterprises in process of privatization (July 8, 1992), clarified in Supreme Decree no. 8-95-PCM of February 22, 1995

Decree-Law no. 25618 on enterprises owned by regional governments (July 16, 1992)

Supreme Decree no. 070-92-PCM on implementation of Decree-Law no. 674 of September 25, 1991 (July 16, 1992), clarified in Supreme Decree no. 72-92-PCM of August 12, 1992, and modified in Supreme Decree no. 102-94-PCM of December 7, 1994

Decree-Law no. 25844 on electric concessions (November 6, 1992)

Decree-Law no. 25897 on establishment of the private system of administration of retirement funds (1992)

Decree-Law no. 26120 amending Decree-Law no. 674 of September 25, 1991 (December 28, 1992)

Supreme Resolution no. 009-93-EM implementing Decree-Law no. 25844 of November 6, 1992 (February 25, 1993)

Supreme Resolution no. 033-93-PCM amending Supreme Resolution no. 070-92-PCM (May 14, 1993)

Law no. 26286 amending Decree-Law no. 674 of September 25, 1991 (lease property) (January 12, 1994)

Supreme Decree no. 17-94-EF regulating the use of eligible obligations for the promotion of private investment in public enterprises (February 9, 1994), clarified in Supreme Decree no. 117-94-EF of September 5, 1994

Law no. 26408 on Pescaperu (December 16, 1994)

Law no. 26438 amending Decree-Law no. 674 of September 25, 1991 (January 6, 1995)

Law no. 26440 on the organizations involved in the promotion of private investment (January 20, 1995)

Supreme Decree no. 30-95-PCM on Mineral del Peru S.A. (May 11, 1995)

Decree-Law no. 839 on the promotion of private investments in public works and utilities (August 20, 1996)

Philippines

Presidential Proclamation no. 50 "Proclaiming and launching a program for the expeditious disposition and privatization of certain government corporations and/or the assets thereof and creating the Committee on Privatization and the Asset Privatization Trust" (December 8, 1986)

Presidential Proclamation no. 50-A modifying Proclamation no. 50 of December 8, 1986 (December 15, 1986)

Operating guidelines of the Committee on Privatization on the Asset Privatization Trust (January 29, 1987)

Executive Order no. 127 on reorganization of the Ministry of Finance (1987)

Executive Order no. 127-A creating the Corporate Affairs Group and for other purposes, including the Privatization Office (July 22, 1987)

Guidelines of the Committee on Privatization on the privatization of government corporations (August 12, 1987)

Republic Act no. 6957 authorizing the financing, construction, operation, and maintenance of infrastructure projects by the private sector (BOT law) (July 9, 1990)

Foreign Investments Act (1991)

Republic Act no. 7181 extending the life of the Committee on Privatization and the Asset Privatization Trust (January 17, 1992)

Administrative Order nos. 8 and 9 directing the identification of idle government properties and recommending to the president an action plan for the disposition of such properties (1992)

Executive Order no. 37 restating the privatization policy of the government (December 2, 1992)

Republic Act no. 7661 amending Republic Act no. 7181 of January 17, 1992, and extending to June 30, 1995, the completion of the privatization program (December 23, 1993)

Guidelines and regulations to implement Republic Act no. 7181 of January 17, 1992, as amended by Republic Act no. 7661 approved by Committee on Privatization of Republic of the Philippines (March 3, 1994)

Republic Act no. 7718 amending and expanding Republic Act no. 6957 (BOT law) of July 9, 1990 (May 5, 1994)

Implementing rules and regulations of Republic Act no. 6957 (BOT law) of July 9, 1990, as amended by Republic Act no. 7718 of May 5, 1994

Water Crisis Act (July 15, 1995)

Poland

Law on the privatization of state-owned enterprises (July 13, 1990)

Law establishing the Office of Minister of Ownership Changes (July 13, 1990)

Decree-Law governing the specific sphere of activity of the Minister of Ownership Changes (November 14, 1990)

Decree-Law governing the designation of state enterprises of special importance to the national economy (November 16, 1990)

Law on foreign investment (June 14, 1991)

Law on financial restructuring of state enterprises and banks (March 1993)

Law on the national investment funds (April 30, 1993)

Law on commercialization and privatization (July 21, 1995)

Law on Toll Motorways (1995)

Law on commercialization and privatization (August 30, 1996)

Portugal

Law no. 84/88 on privatization (July 20, 1988)

Law no. 11/90 laying down the framework for privatization (April 5, 1990)

Decree-Law nos. 372/93 (October 29, 1993) and 379/93 (November 5, 1993) on municipal and multimunicipal services (water and waste) concessions

Puerto Rico (see *United States*)

Romania

Law no. 15 on the restructuring of state economic units as autonomous units and commercial companies (July 31, 1990)

Land law (February 1991)

Law no. 35 on foreign investment (1991)

Law no. 58 on the privatization of commercial companies (August 14, 1991)

Government Resolution no. 643 approving the regulations governing the organization and functioning of the State Ownership Fund (October 8, 1992)

Law no. 77 on management and employee buyouts (August 1994)

Law no. 52 on securities and stock exchanges (August 1994)

Law no. 55 on the acceleration of privatization (June 1995)

Russian Federation

Law of the Russian Soviet Federal Socialist Republic (RSFSR) on ownership and property (December 24, 1990)

Law of the RSFSR on enterprise and entrepreneurship (December 25, 1990)

Law of the RSFSR on the privatization of state-owned and municipal enterprises (July 3, 1991)

Decree of the RSFSR on procedures for implementing the Law on the privatization of state-owned and municipal enterprises (July 3, 1991)

Law of the RSFSR on personal privatization accounts and deposits (July 3, 1991)

Law of the RSFSR on privatization of housing and land (July 4, 1991)

Basic provisions of the 1992 program of privatization of state-owned and municipal enterprises in the Russian Federation (January 1992)

Resolution no. 52 of the government of the Russian Federation on acceleration of the implementation of the 1992 privatization program (January 29, 1992)

Law no. 2930 revising and amending the law on the privatization of state-owned and municipal enterprises in the RSFSR (June 5, 1992)

Decree no. 2980-1 of the Supreme Soviet approving the state program of privatization of state-owned and municipal enterprises of the Russian Federation for 1992 (June 11, 1992)

Presidential Decree no. 721 on organizational measures relating to the corporatization of state enterprises and voluntary associations of state enterprises (July 1, 1992)

Decree no. 490 of the government of the Russian Federation on the procedure for implementation of the privatization vouchers scheme in the Russian Federation (July 15, 1992)

Resolution no. 547 of the government of the Russian Federation on measures for implementation of Presidential Decree no. 721 of July 1, 1992 (August 4, 1992)

Presidential Decree no. 914 on the introduction of a privatization vouchers scheme in the Russian Federation (August 14, 1992)

Presidential Decree no. 922 on the special characteristics of corporatization of public enterprises, associations, and organizations in the energy and petroleum sector (August 14, 1992)

Decree no. 708 of the government of the Russian Federation on the procedure for privatization and reorganization of enterprises and organizations of the agroindustrial complex (September 4, 1992)

Law on the reorganization and privatization of state cooperatives of the agroindustrial complex (September 4, 1992)

Law on the privatization of enterprises for initial processing of agricultural products, fish and sea products and enterprises that provide technical services, material, and support to the agroindustrial complex (September 4, 1992)

Presidential decree on measures for the organization of a securities market in the process of privatization of state-owned and municipal enterprises (October 7, 1992)

Decree no. 1186 on regulation of the voucher investment fund (October 7, 1992)

Decree of the Supreme Soviet of the Russian Federation on the process for implementing the government program of privatization of state-owned and municipal enterprises in the Russian Federation for 1992 (October 9, 1992)

Presidential decree on the development of a privatization vouchers scheme (October 14, 1992)

Presidential decree on the sale of privatization vouchers for housing, land, and municipal property (October 14, 1992)

Presidential decree on the use of privatization vouchers for social protection of the population (October 26, 1992)

Presidential decree on the sale of privatized assets in exchange for privatization vouchers (November 4, 1992)

Presidential decree on measures for implementing industrial policy during privatization of enterprises (November 16, 1992)

Presidential Decree no. 1403 on the special characteristics of privatization and corporatization of public enterprises and production and research and scientific associations in the petroleum products refining and supply industries (November 17, 1992)

Decree no. 906 of the government of the Russian Federation on the procedure for decisionmaking on the privatization of enterprises by the government and the state committee for the management of state property and its territorial agencies (November 18, 1992)

Decree no. 908 of the government of the Russian Federation on measures taken to ensure the furnishing of information to Russian and foreign investors concerning the privatization of state-owned enterprises (November 24, 1992)

Presidential Decree no. 1484 on the special characteristics of privatization of the GAZ production association (November 30, 1992)

Presidential Decree no. 1519 on the special conditions for privatization of enterprises in Bryansk Oblast (November 30, 1992)

Decree no. 969 of the government of the Russian Federation amending the law on the reorganization of *kolkhozes* and *sovkhoses* and on privatization of the agricultural state enterprises (December 11, 1992)

Decree on operational procedures for the privatization of enterprises (December 25, 1992)

Decree no. 1702 on the corporatization and privatization of coal industry associations, organizations, and enterprises (December 30, 1992)

Presidential decree on procedures for issuing 1992 privatization vouchers to certain categories of citizens (January 10, 1993)

Presidential Decree no. 216 regulating the procedure for the circulation and cancellation of privatization vouchers (February 12, 1993)

Decree of the Supreme Soviet of the Russian Federation on the implementation of the government program of privatization of state-owned and municipal enterprises for the year 1992 (April 28, 1993)

Directive no. 654-R on the corporatization of producer associations in the coal industry (April 9, 1993)

Decree no. 446 on the special characteristics of privatizing enterprises under the jurisdiction of the Ministry of Atomic Energy of the Russian Federation and managed by the said ministry, under the conditions of developing a market economy (April 15, 1993)

Presidential Decree no. 640 on government guarantees protecting the rights of citizens of the Russian Federation to participate in privatization (May 8, 1993)

Decree on execution of the public program of privatization of state-owned and municipal enterprises of the Russian Federation for the year 1992 (May 19, 1993)

Decree no. 5234-1 on the implementation of clause 5.4 of the state program of privatization of state-owned and municipal enterprises of the Russian Federation for the year 1992 (June 18, 1993)

Decree no. 5310-1 on amendments and additions to certain decisions of the Supreme Soviet of the Russian Federation concerning questions relating to the privatization of state-owned and municipal enterprises (July 1, 1993)

Presidential decree on additional measures to protect the rights of citizens of the Russian Federation to participate in privatization (July 26, 1993)

Decree of the Supreme Soviet suspending the decree of the president "on additional measures to protect the rights of citizens of the Russian Federation to participate in privatization" (August 6, 1993)

Presidential Decree no. 1238 on the protection of the rights of citizens of the Russian Federation to participate in privatization (August 10, 1993)

Presidential Decree no. 2284 on the state program of privatization of state and municipal enterprises of the Russian Federation (privatization program) (December 24, 1993)

Law no. 1832-R on supervision of special investment voucher funds (July 1, 1994)

Decree no. 1535 on supplemental measures to the state program of privatization of state and municipal enterprises (privatization program) (July 22, 1994)

Presidential (special) decree on city government powers in the privatization of municipal enterprises (February 1995)

Rwanda

Law no. 2/96 on privatization and public investment (March 11, 1996)

Presidential Decree no. 08/14 on the establishment of a National Commission for Privatization and Public Investment (May 3, 1996)

Senegal

Law no. 84-64 prescribing the procedures for liquidating public establishments, national companies, and joint-venture companies (August 16, 1984)

Decree no. 84-992 on application of Law no. 84-64 of August 16, 1984 (September 11, 1984)

Order no. 86-1370/MEF/DGT/DP setting up a special commission on state divestiture (November 8, 1986)

Law no. 87-23 on the privatization of enterprises (August 18, 1987)

Decree no. 87-1475 on the organization of the consultative committee on the parastatal sector (November 27, 1987)

Decree no. 87-1476 on the organization and functioning of the special commission to monitor state divestiture (November 27, 1987)

Decree no. 1477 on the responsibilities of the Delegation on Reform of the Parastatal Sector (November 27, 1987)

Decree no. 88-232 regulating the procedure for public flotations in the transfer of government-held shares (March 4, 1988)

Decree no. 88-233 prescribing the conditions of competitive bidding in the transfer of government-held shares in enterprises to be privatized (March 4, 1988)

Decree no. 89-179 amending Decree no. 88-233 of March 4, 1988 (February 8, 1989)

Decree no. 89-927 on procedures for transfer of government-held shares under the privatization process (1989)

Law no. 90-07 on the organization and supervision of parastatal enterprises and the supervision of legal persons governed by private law receiving financial assistance from public authorities (June 26, 1990)

Serbia

Law on privatization (1991)

Singapore

Economic Development Board (Transfer of Assets) Act (Cap. 190)
Public Utilities Act (1995)

Slovak Republic (see also *Czechoslovakia*)

Law canceling the final wave of voucher privatization (July 1995)
Law excluding strategic state-owned enterprises from the privatization process (July 13, 1995)

Slovenia

Law on privatization (November 11, 1992)
Law on denationalization (restitution of land and buildings) (1993)
Law on commercial companies (May 27, 1993)
Law on investment funds and management companies (January 26, 1994)

Soviet Union (see also successor republics)

Law on the principles of denationalization and privatization of enterprises (July 1, 1991)

Sri Lanka

Act no. 23 on the conversion of public corporations and government-owned business undertakings into public companies (May 15, 1987)

Sweden

Law no. 1991/92:69 on the privatization of public enterprises and other matters (December 1991)

Taiwan (China)

Law on the conversion of public to private enterprises (June 1991) and implementing decree (February 1992)
Regulations on the preemptive right of employees of privatized enterprises (1992)
Regulations relating to compensation granted to employees of privatized enterprises (1993)

Tajikistan

Law on property (December 5, 1990)
Law on the denationalization and privatization of property in the Tajik Soviet Socialist Republic (SSR) (February 21, 1991)

Decree on organization of the work on the denationalization and privatization of
   property in the Tajik SSR (April 16, 1991)

Tanzania

Public Corporations (Amendment) Act (1993)

Thailand

Regulations relating to the divestiture of state-owned enterprises and shares thereof
   (March 17, 1961)
Royal Act no. B.E. 2535 on private participation in state affairs (March 11, 1992)
State enterprise asset transformation act (1992)

Togo

Ordinance no. 94-002 on divestiture of enterprises by government and other legal
   persons governed by public law (June 10, 1994)
Decree no. 94-038 issued pursuant to Ordinance no. 94-002 (June 10, 1994)

Tunisia

Finance Law no. 85-109, particularly articles 79 through 84, establishing the fund for
   restructuring of the capital of public enterprises (December 31, 1985)
Law no. 87-47 on the restructuring of public enterprises (August 2, 1987), repealed by
   Law no. 89-9 of February 1, 1989
Law no. 89-9 on public portfolio and public enterprises (February 1, 1989)
Decree no. 89-376 listing the enterprises deemed to be public in light of the nature of
   their activities and their capital structure (March 11, 1989), repealed by Decree
   no. 90-1404 of September 5, 1990
Decree no. 89-377 prescribing the composition and functioning of the commission for
   rehabilitation and restructuring of enterprises in which there is government
   shareholding (March 15, 1989)
Decree no. 89-378 on representation of the government, local authorities, public
   establishments, and companies whose capital is wholly owned by the government
   in the management and decisionmaking organs of the public enterprises, and the
   procedures for exercise of jurisdiction over those enterprises (March 15, 1989)
Circular no. 33 detailing privatization implementation procedures (June 21, 1989)
Order of the prime minister prescribing the composition and functioning of the
   Public Enterprises Classification Commission (September 4, 1989)
Decree no. 90-1404 listing the enterprises deemed to be public in light of the nature of
   their activities and their capital structure (September 5, 1990)
Law no. 94-102 completing no. Law 89-9 of February 1, 1989 (1994)

Turkey

Law no. 1326 on concessions of public interest (June 24, 1908)
Law no. 2025 relating to concessions (June 25, 1932)

Decree-Law no. 233 (1984)

Law no. 2983 (1984)

Law no. 3096 on private power BOT projects (December 19, 1984)

Section 5 of Law no. 3291 on privatization of state economic organizations (May 28, 1986)

Law no. 3465 on road projects BOTs (May 28, 1988)

Statutory Decree no. 414 defining the responsibilities of the public portfolio administration (1990)

Statutory Decree no. 473 establishing the higher council of public portfolio administration (June 6, 1992)

Law no. 3974 on BOT energy projects (March 1, 1994)

Law no. 3996 on the provision of certain investments and services in the BOT model (June 8, 1994), as amended by Law no. 4047 (November 1994)

Decree no. 94/5907 implementing Law no. 3996 of June 8, 1994 (October 1, 1994)

Law no. 4046 on arrangements for the implementation of privatization and amending certain laws and decrees with the force of law (November 24, 1994)

Law no. 4107 on telecommunications (May 6, 1995)

Turkmenistan

Decree on the transfer to the Turkmen Soviet Socialist Republic of enterprises and organizations belonging to the Union within the territory of the republic (August 22, 1991)

Law on denationalization and privatization of property in Turkmenistan (February 19, 1992)

Presidential decree on voucher privatization (May 13, 1994)

Uganda

Law no. 9 on public enterprise reform and divestiture (August 4, 1993)

Ukraine

Law on property (March 26, 1991)

Law no. 2163-XII on privatization of the property of state enterprises (with implementing decree) (March 4, 1992), as amended on July 7, 1992, September 18, 1992, December 15, 1992, and February 19, 1993

Law no. 2171-XII on the privatization of small state enterprises (with implementing decree) (March 6, 1992), as amended on December 15, 1992, and February 19, 1993

Law no. 2173-XII on privatization vouchers (March 6, 1992), as amended on July 7, 1992, and in 1994

Law no. 2269-XII on leasing the property of public organizations and enterprises (April 10, 1992), as amended on December 15, 1992

Resolution of the Supreme Council of Ukraine approving the government program of privatization of the property of state enterprises (July 7, 1992), as amended on December 15, 1992, and February 19, 1993

Resolution of the Council of Representatives of the City of L'viv approving the program of privatization of the municipal enterprises of the city of L'viv for the year 1992 (September 18, 1992)

Decree of the Council of Ministers on the privatization of agricultural land (January 15, 1993)

Decree no. 51-93 on the special characteristics of the privatization of the property of the agroindustrial complex (May 17, 1993)

Decree no. 57-93 on privatization of the integrated public enterprise complexes and their structural subdivisions that have been leased (May 20, 1993)

Decree on corporatization of large enterprises (June 1993)

Presidential decree on financial funds and companies (February 1994)

Moratorium enacted by parliament on privatization and implementation of buyout by enterprises under lease agreements (July 1994)

Decree on privatization schedule for 1995 and foreign participation in the privatization of enterprises (June 27, 1995)

United Kingdom

British Aerospace Act (1980)

Civil Aviation Act (1980) for the privatization of British Airways

Transport Act (1981) for the privatization of Associated British Ports

Telecommunications Act (1981) for the privatization of Cable and Wireless

Atomic Energy (Miscellaneous Provisions) Act (1981) for the privatization of Amersham International, British Nuclear Fuels Ltd, and National Nuclear Corporation

Oil and Gas Enterprise Act (1982) for the privatization of Britoil and Enterprise Oil

Energy Act (1983)

Telecommunications Act (April 12, 1984) for the privatization of British Telecom

Transport Act (1985) for the privatization of National Bus Company

Airports Act (1986) for the privatization of British Airports Authority

Gas Act (1986) for the privatization of British Gas

British Steel Act (1988)

Water Act (1989)

Electricity Act (July 27, 1989)

Property Services Agency and Crown Suppliers Act (1990)

Water Industry Act (1991)

Water Resources Act (1991)

Competition and Services (Utilities) Act (1992)

Railways Act (1993)

United States

Law no. 5 providing resources for the education system and the development of the infrastructure of Puerto Rico by authorizing the sale of all assets of any nature, whether real property, personal property, or a combination thereof, that the Puerto Rican Telephone Authority owns in connection with operation of the communications system, excluding the Puerto Rico Corporation for Public Broadcasting; and so on (April 10, 1990)

Act on the efficiency of combined surface transport (1991)

Executive Order no. 12083 on infrastructure privatization (April 30, 1992)

Executive Order no. 12893 on private financing of infrastructure (1994)

Uruguay

Law no. 16211 on reform of state-owned enterprises (September 27, 1991)

Decree implementing Law no. 16211 of September 27, 1991, on Primeras Lineas Uruguayas de Navegación Aérea (December 30, 1991)

Decree no. 718 creating CONTEL (December 1991)

Decree no. 720 on privatization of Administración de Telecomunicaciones (ANTEL) (December 30, 1991)

Law no. 16246 authorizing the privatization of all port activities and suppressing the state insurance monopoly (April 23, 1992)

Uzbekistan

Law on ownership (October 31, 1990)

Law on denationalization and privatization (with implementing resolution of the Supreme Council, Resolution no. 107) (November 19, 1991)

Decree on the creation of a committee on state property management and privatization (February 10, 1992)

Decree of the president for the acceleration of the enterprise reform program (January 22, 1994)

Venezuela

Presidential Decree no. 1826 establishing the National Telecommunications Council (September 5, 1991)

Law on the Venezuela Investment Fund (January 15, 1992)

Law no. 4397 on privatization (March 10, 1992), as amended August 1992 and October 31, 1993

Decree no. 448 on Venezolana de Guayana (December 7, 1994)

Viet Nam

Regulations relating to major aspects of the basic procedures for the liquidation of public enterprises that suffer substantial losses, issued with Council of Ministers Decision no. 315 on improvement of production and commercial activities in the public sector (September 1, 1990)

Council of Ministers Decision no. 330 revising Decision no. 315 of September 1, 1990 (October 23, 1991)

Council of Ministers Decision no. 388 promulgating regulations governing the establishment and liquidation of public enterprises (November 20, 1991)

Council of Ministers Decision no. 462 on a plan to continue the process of management renovation in the basic economic units in 1992 (February 12, 1992)

Decisions of the Chairman of the Council of Ministers nos. 202 and 203 on the experimental corporatization of public enterprises (June 8, 1992)

Ordinance of the Prime Minister no. 84/TTG containing instructions for speeding up pilot corporatization of public enterprises (March 4, 1993)

Decree no. 87 enacting regulations on investment in the form of Build-Operate-Transfer (BOT) contracts (November 23, 1993)

Bankruptcy Law (1994)

Yugoslavia

Law on social capital circulation and management (December 1989)

Law on social capital (August 1990)

Zambia

Privatization Act (July 4, 1992)

Regulations on privatization (March 9, 1993)

Glossary

These definitions are provided for the reader's convenience only. They are not necessarily precise legal definitions and may not reflect the different meanings a term may have. Terms in italics refer to other definitions in this glossary. References to *Black's* are to *Black's Law Dictionary*, 5th ed. (St. Paul, Minn.: West Publishing Company, 1979). Many of the concepts or terms in this glossary are further described in the main text.

Act (legislative). The term "act" is often short for "legislative act" or "act of parliament" and is a synonym for "law."

Affermage. French term. Type of concession contract in which the operator leases the sector assets from the public authority, which remains responsible for major investments.

Arbitration. Extrajudicial dispute settlement procedure involving arbitrators chosen by the parties.

Articles of incorporation. Basic document establishing a company and defining its corporate governance. Also articles of association.

Auction. Public sale of property to the highest bidder.

Bankruptcy. Court-supervised procedure leading to the financial reorganization or *liquidation* of a company. Bankruptcy may be initiated by the company, its creditors, or other parties when a company is no longer able to pay its debts as they become due. See also *insolvency*.

Bid; bidding. A quotation setting forth the price that a bidder is willing to pay for an asset or share or for the right to carry out an activity. In bids for *concessions*, the price may be the tariff demanded by the bidder to provide a service. See also *tender offer*.

Bilateral agreement. Often used to refer to agreements between two sovereign nations (for example, civil aviation agreements, double taxation treaties, or investment treaties).

Build, operate, transfer (BOT). Contract by which one party (typically a private operator or consortium) agrees to build, finance, operate, and maintain a facility or system (such as a water treatment plant or tollroad) for a specified period of time, and then transfer said facility or system to the party that awarded the contract, typically the state. During the period of operation, the ownership of the facility or system may be with the public authority or with the private operator; in the latter case, the contract is sometimes referred to as a build, own, operate, transfer (BOOT) contract. A BOT contract in the infrastructure sector is in essence a public works *concession* contract.

Build, own, operate (BOO). Similar to a *BOT*, though the private party has full ownership rights over the sector assets or facility and does not have to transfer them back to the public authority.

Bylaws. "Regulations, ordinances, rules or laws adopted by an association or corporation or the like for its government" (*Black's*).

Collateral. Asset that is pledged as security for the repayment of a debt.

Commercialization. Introduction of commercial objectives and practices into the management and operations of an SOE. Commercialization does not usually imply a change in legal status. See also *corporatization*.

Company. A legal entity created by stockholders (whether individuals, companies, or other legal entities) to carry on business activities, which exists independent of such stockholders. See also *corporation* and *public company*.

Compensation. The act of giving indemnification, making whole, or giving back an equivalent or substitute of equal value (*Black's*). Monetary compensation paid to a (previous) owner for property taken by the state. See also *confiscation* and *expropriation*.

Competition *for* the market. Competition for the right to supply a service, often with exclusive rights (for example, competition for a water distribution concession).

Competition *in* the market. Competition between firms vying for consumers within a given market (for example, competition in sale of telephone equipment).

Concession. A contractual arrangement between the state (or other public entity) and a private operator (called a concessionaire) requiring the latter to operate a public service, such as a power or water distribution system, for a specified period of time and at its own risk. The concessionaire is typically also in charge of building (or expanding) and financing the related physical infrastructure, though in some concessions (sometimes referred to as *affermage*) new investments remain the responsibility of the public sector. A *BOT* is a concession for a project requiring the construction of new facilities. *Concession* is sometimes used as a synonym for franchise or *license*.

Conciliation. A form of amicable dispute settlement requiring the consent of both parties to the solution.

Condemnation. Process of taking private property for public use through the power of eminent domain (*Black's*). Many constitutions require that "just compensation" be paid if property is condemned. See also *confiscation* and *expropriation*.

Confiscation. Seizure of private property from their owners without *compensation*. Confiscation is sometimes the result of a criminal conviction of the property owner, sometimes because the use or possession of the property was contrary to a law.

Contingent liability. See *liability*.

Corporation. A legal entity created by or under the laws of a state (*Black's*). Sometimes classified as a public corporation, created and owned by the state or another public body, or as a private corporation, created by private persons for private purposes. When created by law, public corporations are sometimes referred to as statutory corporations.

Corporatization. The transformation of a state-owned enterprise or business asset into a public *corporation* organized under company law. Often also the first step in the privatization of an SOE.

Cross-subsidy. Subsidy from one product or service line to another one, often within one enterprise, such as in the cross-subsidization of rural services by urban ones, or of local telephone services by long-distance services.

Decree. An executive order, which is usually subordinated to a law. Secondary or derived legislation, as opposed to primary legislation (that is, a law enacted by the legislature). Depending on the legal regime, decrees may be issued by the president, the council of ministers, the prime minister, or another cabinet member.

Demonopolization. The process of undoing or breaking up a *monopoly* by introducing *competition in the market*. The breakup of a national monopoly into a number of smaller geographical monopolies, however, is usually not referred to as demonopolization.

Deregulation. The act or process of removing legal restrictions or regulations.

Direct negotiation. A sale negotiated and concluded privately between the buyer and the seller, and not made by *auction*, *tender*, or other competitive bidding process.

Dissolution. The termination of the legal existence of a corporate or public entity. See also *liquidation*.

Divestiture. In this book, transfer of public or state-owned property (including SOEs) to the private sector. In the United States, the 1984 breakup of AT&T (a private company) is often referred to as the AT&T divestiture.

Divestment. Liquidation or sale of parts of a firm. It is the opposite of a merger or acquisition.

Due diligence. In corporate acquisitions (including privatization), refers to investigations by potential buyers into the business of the company to be acquired.

Enabling legislation. Legislation giving the government (or another person or body) specific powers or authority. In the privatization context, legislation authorizing the government to privatize.

Expropriation. The action whereby a state takes or modifies the property rights of an individual or business entity against *compensation*, in the exercise of state sovereignty. See also *condemnation* and *confiscation*.

Going concern. An enterprise considered to be an economic unit and an operational entity. In the sale of an enterprise as a going concern, the enterprise would typically be expected to continue transacting its normal business. Sale may be on a going-concern basis even if the ownership of the legal entity as such is not transferred.

Golden share. A share in a company allowing its holder (the state) to exercise specified exceptional rights with respect to the conduct of business of the company after its (full or partial) privatization.

Initial public offering (IPO). First offering of shares of a company on the market (usually through a stock exchange).

Insolvency. The state of a person (legal entity or physical person) that is unable to pay its debts as they fall due in the usual course of business, or that has liabilities in excess of a reasonable market value of its assets. Insolvency procedure is the term used in the United Kingdom for what is referred to as *bankruptcy* procedures in the United States.

Interconnection. See *third-party access*.

Joint-stock company. A *company* with a capital (joint stock) that is divided into shares which are transferable by their owners. Used in this book to refer to incorporated *limited liability* shareholding companies equivalent to the French Société Anonyme (SA) or the German Aktiengeselschaft (AG). See also *corporation*.

Joint venture. "An association of persons jointly undertaking some commercial enterprise" (*Black's*). A joint venture may or may not be incorporated. This term is sometimes also used to refer to a *company* established jointly by the state and private partners or by domestic and foreign partners.

Juridical person. A person or entity with separate existence under law. Equivalent to legal entity.

Leasing. A contract whereby the owner of an asset (or enterprise), the lessor, provides the other party, the lessee, with the possession of and profits from such asset during a set period of time. Leasing does not transfer ownership of property unless it is accompanied by a purchase option which is exercised. See also *affermage*.

Legislation. Used in a narrow sense, this term refers to laws (that is, acts of the legislature). In a broad sense, and particularly in civil law countries, it refers to laws as well as derived or secondary legal instruments (such as decrees and executive orders).

Liability. Includes "almost every character of hazard or responsibility, absolute, contingent, or likely" (*Black's*). All the claims against a business enterprise, including wages or salaries, amounts due suppliers, dividends declared payable, taxes, long- and short-term obligations such as bonds and bank loans, and so on. A liability is contingent when its existence depends on an unknown or future event, such as the outcome of litigation or the occurrence of environmental damage.

License. Right awarded by the government or public authority to provide a service (for example, a cellular license).

Limited liability company. A company in which the owners (stockholders) are liable for the debts of the company only up to the amount of capital contributed by them to the company. In some countries, this term is used in a more narrow sense to refer to a type of limited liability company that has fewer incorporation and legal requirements than joint-stock companies, often a company whose capital is not divided into shares (equivalent in this sense to the French SARL or the German Gmbh).

Liquidation. "Winding up of corporation so that assets are distributed to those entitled to receive them. Process of reducing assets to cash, discharging liabilities and dividing surplus or loss. . . . It is to be distinguished from *dissolution* which is the end of the legal existence of a corporation. Liquidation may precede or follow dissolution, depending on statutes" (*Black's*). See also *bankruptcy*.

Management contract. Contract transferring the responsibility for managing a company to a private party, which receives a fee in exchange for its services. The management contractor does not invest in the company. The contractor's compensation may be based in part on the performance of the managed company. See also *régie intéressée*.

Monopoly. A privilege or peculiar advantage vested in one person or business entity, conferring the exclusive right or power to conduct a certain activity or trade or to control the supply or sale of a particular good or utility to a "captive" market

(*Black's*). A legal monopoly (as opposed to a de facto monopoly) is granted and protected by law. A situation of natural monopoly prevails when one producer can supply a given market at a lower cost than two or more competing producers because of heavy sunk costs or increasing economies of scale, for example (water distribution is a typical example).

Nationalization. Confiscation or expropriation of a private enterprise or asset by the state, often pursuant to a nationalization law.

Offering. "An issue of *securities* offered for sale to the public or to a private group" (*Black's*). See also *initial public offering, primary offering, secondary offering, public offering,* and *private placement.*

Ownership. *Black's* definitions of ownership include "collection of rights to use and enjoy *property,* including right to transmit it to others," "the right of one or more persons to possess and use a thing to the exclusion of others," and "the exclusive right of possession, enjoyment and disposal; involving as an essential attribute the right to control, handle and dispose."

Preemptive right. In *company* or *securities* law, the right, typically of a shareholder, to buy shares before they are offered to others.

Primary offering. An issue of new shares or *securities* by a company, typically in the case of a capital increase; proceeds of the offering go to the issuing company. See also *secondary offering.*

Private company. In this book, a *company* owned by private parties (individuals or legal entities) and not by the state or another public body. A company with mixed ownership (some private and some public owners) may be considered a private company if the public sector does not control it. Contrast a public enterprise or SOE, which is owned and controlled by a state or other public entity. See also *public company.*

Private placement. An offering made only to a limited number of persons for investment purposes and not to the public at large. Because they can be offered only to professional investors (for example, life insurance companies) and not to the public, *securities* laws often impose fewer constraints on such placements (no requirement to register the security with the securities commission, for example).

Privatization. Any measure resulting in the transfer of ownership and/or control over assets or activities from the public to the private sector. This term is much broader than *divestiture.*

Property. *Black's* definitions of property include "*ownership*; the unrestricted and exclusive right to a thing; the right to dispose of a thing in every legal way, to possess it, to use it, and to exclude everyone else from interfering with it" and "the exclusive right of possessing, enjoying, and disposing of a thing."

Public. As an adjective, this word has two main meanings in this book. It usually refers either to something related to the state or its instrumentalities, as in the case of public sector, *public enterprise,* and public corporation, or to something related to the population at large (the public), as in the case of *public company* and *public offering.* This may create some confusion: a public company, for example, is not a company owned by the public sector, but a public enterprise is an enterprise owned by the public sector.

Public company. A company whose shares are held by the public or a group of persons who do not otherwise have a common business interest. The shares are often traded on a securities market or stock exchange.

Public domain. That which belongs to the public at large and is open to common use without payment of usage fees or royalties. In France and in countries with legal systems that follow the French civil law, the state's public domain refers to state-owned property that is dedicated to public use and enjoyment. Public domain property is usually difficult to privatize, often requiring prior legislative intervention. By contrast, the state's private domain property can be more easily alienated.

Public enterprise. Enterprise owned by the public sector, including the state, municipalities, other public enterprises, or other public bodies. This term includes enterprises organized as governmental entities, public agencies, and *companies*. Though broader than *SOE*, it is often used in this book as a synonym for it.

Public flotation. See *public offering*.

Public offering. An offering of stock or *securities* to the public at large, in which any member of the public may participate, as opposed to a *private placement* or offering. Securities issued in this way are usually traded on an exchange or other *secondary market*. Public offerings are generally regulated by law.

Régie intéressée. French term. A *management contract* in which the remuneration of the contractor is based (at least in part) on performance.

Restitution. Act of restoring or returning something to its rightful owner. Differs from *compensation* in that the confiscated asset itself is returned to the (former) owner.

Secondary market. Financial market in which *securities* can be traded after their initial offering.

Secondary offering. An offering of a large block of existing stock in a company, where the proceeds of the sale go to the owner-seller of the stock (that is, to the government in the case of the divestiture of an *SOE*). In contrast, *primary offerings* are issues of new stock.

Securities. "Stocks, bonds, notes, convertible debentures, warrants, or other documents that represent a share in a company or a debt owed by a company" (*Black's*).

Self-management. Socialist SOE management scheme under which employees and management of an *SOE* exercise the ownership rights of the state in their enterprise.

SOE. State-owned enterprise. Often used interchangeably with *public enterprise* in this book.

State holding company. *SOE* confining its activities to the ownership and holding of stock in other companies and to the management and control thereof.

Strategic investor. An investor that intends to manage or control the acquired business.

Tender offer. A *bid* or offer for the purchase of shares or assets, usually stated in monetary terms, although it may include other terms and conditions. It often constitutes the basis for negotiations with the seller. Tenders may be open to all investors or limited to a specified category or group of qualified or preselected investors. Tenders may also be organized to provide a service; in this case, selection may be based on the lowest tariff offered.

Tender conditions. Seller's general conditions defining the terms under which interested parties may make an offer for the purchase of the shares or assets to be sold (or for the supply of goods or services).

Third-party access. In energy and other networks, right given to third parties (large users, for example) to use existing networks to transport electricity or gas that the user has procured independently; under third-party access rules, the network owner has the obligation to grant such access under specified conditions. In telecommunications, the term interconnection is used.

Transition country. Country in transition from a command or centrally planned economy to a market economy, such as the republics of the former Soviet Union and central and eastern European countries.

Unbundling. In reference to a sector or enterprise, segmentation or disaggregation of constituent activities into separable parts. Vertical unbundling refers to the separation of formerly integrated activities, as in the separation of power production, transmission, and distribution activities. Horizontal unbundling refers to the splitting up of a sector segment into multiple independent entities (for example, competing power generators or separate regional distribution companies). The term also refers to the separation of infrastructure services from the underlying infrastructure, as in the separation of responsibility between rail track and rail services. In reference to property rights, the delinking or separation of various attributes of property rights (for example, shares can be unbundled into voting rights and claim on cash flow).

Underwriter. Typically, an investment bank that purchases an issuer's or seller's securities for resale. Under a firm commitment contract, an underwriter assumes the risks associated with the resale of a security (that the security will be undersubscribed, for example, or that it will not sell for the anticipated price); the investment bank does not accept such risk under a best-efforts contract.

Voucher. A coupon, certificate, form, or other document indicating that its owner may apply the amount specified on the voucher against future purchases or acquisitions of certain items, such as shares in former SOEs or state assets.

Yardstick competition. Indirect competition, which compares the performance of firms not active in the same market, such as water distribution companies covering different geographical areas. Better performance by one firm can, for instance, be used to foster improved performance by its peers.

Bibliography

The following abbreviations are used in this bibliography: CFS, Cofinancing and Financial Advisory Services Department of the World Bank; EBRD, European Bank for Reconstruction and Development; EDI, Economic Development Institute of the World Bank; IFC, International Finance Corporation; OECD, Organisation for Economic Co-operation and Development.

World Bank publications are available through the Bank's local distributors outside the United States or directly from the Bank; when a department is mentioned, publications are available directly from that department; CFS publications are available from the Resource Mobilization and Cofinancing Information Services Center.

Acs, Zoltan, and Felix Fitzroy. 1994. "A Constitution for Privatizing Large Eastern Enterprises." *Economics of Transition* 2(1): 83–94.

Adam, C., W. Cavendish, and P. Mistry. 1992. *Adjusting Privatization: Case Studies from Developing Countries*. London: Ian Randle Publishers.

Ahene, Rexford A., and Bernard Katz, eds. 1992. *Privatization and Investment in Sub-Saharan Africa*. New York: Praeger.

Akuete, Ebenezer, and others. 1992. "Privatization Strategies in Africa." Center for Economic Research on Africa, Upper Montclair, N.J.

Albrecht, Barthold, and Marcel Thum. 1994. " "Privatization, Labor Participation, and the Threat of Bankruptcy: The Case of Poland." *Journal of Institutional and Theoretical Economics* 150(4): 710–25.

Alexander, Myrna, and Carlos Corti. 1993. "Argentina's Privatization Program." CFS Discussion Paper Series 103. World Bank, Washington, D.C.

Ambrose, William W., Paul R. Hennemeyer, and Jean-Paul Chapon. 1990. *Privatizing Telecommunications Systems: Business Opportunities in Developing Countries*. IFC Discussion Paper Series 10. Washington, D.C.

Anderson, Robert E. 1994. "Voucher Funds in Transitional Economies: The Czech and Slovak Experience." Policy Research Working Paper 1324. World Bank, Policy Research Department, Washington, D.C.

Andreff, Wladimir. 1992. "French Privatization Techniques and Experience: A Model for Central-Eastern Europe?" In F. Targetti, ed., *Privatization in Europe: West and East Experiences*. Aldershot, England: Dartmouth.

_____. 1993a. "Internal and External Constraints of Privatization in Eastern Europe." *History of European Ideas* 17(6): 715–23.

_____. 1993b. "Une approche comparative des privatisations: l'example français est-il transposable?" *Reflets et Perspectives de la Vie Economique* 32(3–4): 169–88.

Appel, Hilary, 1995. "Justice and the Reformulation of Property Rights in the Czech Republic." *East European Politics and Societies* 9 (winter): 22–40.

Arbess, Daniel J., and James B. Varanese. 1993. "On the Frontier: What Your Lawyer Brings to Privatization in Eastern and Central Europe." *Columbia Journal of World Business* 28(1): 212–18.

Armstrong, Mark, Simon Cowan, and John Vickers. 1994. *Regulatory Reform: Economic Analysis and British Experience.* Cambridge, Mass.: MIT Press.

Augenblick, Mark, and B. Scott Custer, Jr. 1990. "The Build, Operate, and Transfer ("BOT") Approach to Infrastructure Projects in Developing Countries." Policy Research Working Paper 498. World Bank, Policy Research Department, Washington, D.C.

Ayassor, Adji. 1990. "Privatization of Public Enterprises and Its Impact on the Promotion of the Private Sector in West African Countries: The Example of Togo." Ph.D. dissertation. University of Wisconsin Law School.

Bacon, Robert. 1995. "Appropriate Restructuring Strategies for the Power Generation Sector: The Case of Small Systems." Occasional Paper 3. World Bank, Industry and Energy Department, Washington, D.C.

Baer, Werner. 1994. "Privatisation in Latin America." *World Economy* 17(4): 509–28.

Baer, Werner, and Melissa H. Birch. 1994. *Privatization in Latin America: New Roles for the Public and Private Sectors.* Westport, Conn.: Praeger.

Baer, W., and M. Conroy, eds. 1993. *Latin America: Privatization, Property Rights, and Deregulation.* Greenwich, Conn.: JAI Press.

_____. 1994. *Latin America: Privatization, Property Rights, and Deregulation 2.* Greenwich, Conn.: JAI Press.

Baily, Elizabeth E., and Janet Rothenberg Pack, eds. 1995. *The Political Economy of Privatization and Deregulation.* Aldershot, England: Edward Elgar.

Baird, Alfred J. 1995. "Privatisation of Trust Ports in the United Kingdom: Review and Analysis of the First Sales." *Transport Policy* 2(2): 135–43.

Balasubramanyam, V. N. 1994. "The Treuhandanstalt, FDI and Employment in Germany." *International Journal of Manpower* 15(6): 72–84.

Barberis, Nicholas, Maxim Boycko, Andrei Shleifer, and Natalia Tsukanova. 1995. "How Does Privatization Work? Evidence from the Russian Shops." NBER (National Bureau of Economic Research) Working Paper 5136. Cambridge, Mass.

Barnes, Guillermo. 1992. "Lessons from Bank Privatization in Mexico." Policy Research Working Paper 1027. World Bank, Policy Research Department, Washington, D.C.

Barty-King, Hugh. 1979. *Girdle Round the Earth: The Story of Cable and Wireless.* London: Heinemann.

Baudeu, Guy. 1987. *Les privatisations: Réglementation et premières opérations.* Paris: La Revue Banque Editeur.

Baumol, W., J. Panzar, and R. Willig. 1982. *Contestable Markets and the Theory of Industry Structure.* New York: Harcourt Brace Jovanovich.

Beesley, M. E. 1992. *Privatization, Regulation and Deregulation.* London: Routledge.

Beesley, M. E., and S. C. Littlechild. 1989. "The Regulation of Privatized Monopolies in the United Kingdom." *RAND Journal of Economics* 20(3): 454–72.

Bennett, John, and Stephen Cirell. 1992. "CCT and the Transfer of Undertakings Regulations." *Solicitors Journal* 136 (July): 746.

Berenson, William M. 1991. "Developing the Regulatory Footprint for Newly Privatized Telecommunications Providers in Latin America." *Federal Bar News and Journal* 38 (September): 400–4.

Berle, A., and G. Means. 1933. *The Modern Corporation and Private Property.* New York: Macmillan.

Berlin, Dominique. 1993. "The Statutory and Regulatory Framework of Privatizations." *Droit et Pratique du Commerce International* 19(3): 371–484.

Bhaskar, V., and Mushtaq Khan. 1995. "Privatization and Employment: A Study of the Jute Industry in Bangladesh." *American Economic Review* 85(1): 267–73.

Bhattacharyya, Arunava, Elliot Parker, and Kambiz Raffiee. 1994. "An Examination of the Effect of Ownership on the Relative Efficiency of Public and Private Water Utilities." *Land Economics* 70(2): 197–209.

Bienvenu, J. J. 1993. "La liquidation des établissements publics." *Revue Française de Droit Administratif* 46: 311–14.

Bim, Aleksandr. 1994. "Privatization in Russia: Problems of the Immediate Future." *Problems of Economic Transition* 36(9): 6–22.

Bishop, Matthew, John A. Kay, and Colin P. Mayer, eds. 1994. *Privatization and Economic Performance.* New York: Oxford University Press.

———. 1995. *The Regulatory Challenge.* New York: Oxford University Press.

Bitran, E., and P. Serra. 1994. "Regulatory Issues in the Privatization of Public Utilities: The Chilean Experience." *Quarterly Review of Economics and Finance* 34 (special issue).

Bizaguet, A. 1988a. "Les privatisations boursières dans l'Europe des douze." *La revue du trésor* (May): 248–55.

———. 1988b. "Le secteur public français et les privatisations de 1986–1988." *Revue Internationale de Sciences Administratives* 54(4): 620–37.

Blaszczyk, Barbara, and Mark Dabrowski. 1993. *The Privatisation Process in Poland, 1989–1992: Expectations, Results and Remaining Dilemmas.* London: Centre for Research into Communist Economies.

Blommestein, Hans, and Michael Marrese, eds. 1991. *Transformation of Planned Economies: Property Rights Reform and Macroeconomic Stability.* Paris: OECD.

Bogdanowicz-Bindert, Christine A., and Charles E. Ryan. 1993. "The Privatization Program of the City of Saint-Petersburg." *Columbia Journal of World Business* 28(1): 150–57.

Bohm, Andreja, and Vladimir G. Kreacic, eds. 1991. *Privatization in Eastern Europe: Current Implementation Issues, with a Collection of Privatization Laws.* Ljubljana, Yugoslavia: International Center for Public Enterprises in Developing Countries.

Bolton, Patrick. 1995. "Privatization and the Separation of Ownership and Control: Lessons from the Chinese Enterprise Reform." *Economics in Transition* 3 (March). European Bank for Reconstruction and Development, London.

Borcherding, T.E., W.W. Pommerehne, and F. Schneider. 1982. "Comparing the Efficiency of Private and Public Production: The Evidence from Five Countries." *Zeitschrift für Nationalökonomie* 2:127–56.

Borish, Michael S., Millard F. Long, and Michel Noël. 1995. *Restructuring Banks and Enterprises: Recent Lessons from Transition Countries*. World Bank Discussion Paper 279. Washington, D.C.

Borish, Michael S., and Michel Noël. 1996. *Private Sector Development during Transition: The Visegrad Countries*. World Bank Discussion Paper 318. Washington, D.C.

Bornstein, Morris. 1994. "Russia's Mass Privatisation Programme." *Communist Economies and Economic Transformation* 6(4): 419–57.

Bouchard, Gilles, ed. 1991. *La réforme administrative dans les pays francophones*. Moncton, N.B., Canada: Editions d'Acadie.

Bouin Olivier. 1994. "Transférer la propriété privée par la méthode des coupons: L'expérience de l'ex-Tchécoslovaquie." *Revue Economique* 45(3): 845–56.

Bouin, O., and Ch.-A. Michalet. 1991. *Rebalancing the Public and Private Sectors: Developing Country Experience*. Paris: OECD.

Boutard-Labarde, M. C. 1987. "Droit communautaire et privatisations." *Droit et Pratique du Commerce International* 13(3): 493–504.

Bouzidi, A. 1993. "La privatisation des entreprises publiques en Algérie. *Reflets et Perspectives de la Vie Economique* 32(6): 455–61.

Boycko, Maxim, Andrei Shleifer, and Robert W. Vishny. 1994. "Voucher Privatization." *Journal of Financial Economics* 35 (April): 249–66.

———. 1995. *Privatizing Russia*. Cambridge, Mass.: MIT Press.

Brezinski, Horst, ed. 1993. *Privatization East and West*. Aldershot, England: Edward Elgar.

Brion, René, and Jean-Louis Moreau. 1995. *Tractebel: Les métamorphoses d'un groupe industriel, 1895–1995*. Antwerp, Belgium: Fonds Mercator.

Brouselle, Denis. 1993. "Les privatisations locales." *Actualité Juridique, Droit Administratif* (20 May): 323–30.

Bruchey, Stuart. 1965. *The Roots of American Economic Growth, 1607–1861*. New York: Harper and Row.

Buck, Trevor, Igor Filatotchev, and Mike Wright. 1994. "Employee Buyouts and the Transformation of Russian Industry." *Comparative Economic Studies* 36(2): 1–15.

Buck, Trevor, Steve Thompson, and Mike Wright. 1991. "Post-Communist Privatization and the British Experience." *Public Enterprise* 11(2–3): 185–200.

Button, K. 1994. "Privatisation and Deregulation: Its Implications for Negative Transport Externalities." *Annals of Regional Science* 28(1): 125–38.

Button, Kenneth, and Thomas Weyman-Jones. 1994. "Impacts of Privatisation Policy in Europe." *Contemporary Economic Policy* 12(4): 23–33.

Byrne, Peter D. 1995. "Overview of Privatization in the Area of Tax and Customs Administration." *Bulletin for International Fiscal Documentation* 49(1): 10–16.

Cameron, Rondo E. 1961. *France and the Economic Development of Europe, 1800–1914*. Princeton, N.J.: Princeton University Press.

Candoy-Sekse, Rebecca, with the assistance of Anne Ruiz-Palmer. 1988. *Techniques of Privatization of State-Owned Enterprises*. Vol. 3, *Inventory of Country Experience and Reference Materials*. World Bank Technical Paper 90. Washington, D.C.

Cartelier, Lysiane. 1992, "L'expérience francaise de privatisation: bilan et enseignements." *Revue Internationale de Droit Economique* 3: 375–402.

Castillo, Graciana del. 1995. *Privatization in Latin America: From Myth to Reality.* Santiago, Chile: United Nations, Economic Commission for Latin America and the Caribbean.

Cavana, R. Y. 1995. "Restructuring the New Zealand Railway System, 1982–1993." *Transport Reviews* 15(2): 119–39.

Caverivière, M. 1990. "La privatisation des entreprises publiques au Sénégal." *Revue Congolaise de Droit* 7–8: 102–17.

Chadwick, Edwin. 1859. "Results of Different Principles of Legislation in Europe: of Competition for the Field as Compared with Competition within the Field of Service." *Journal of the Royal Statistical Society,* series A22.

Chamoux, Jean-Pierre, and Peter-André Stern, eds. 1993. *Restructurer les télécommunications.* Paris: Le Communicateur.

Chandler, Timothy D., and Peter Feuille. 1994. "Cities, Unions, and the Privatization of Sanitation Services." *Journal of Labor Research* 15(1): 53–71.

Chaudhri, Javade. 1991. "Documents Relating to Legal Aspects of Privatization." World Bank, Legal Department, Washington, D.C.

Chen, Xavier. 1994. "La privatisation des industries électriques en Asie du Sud-Est: Causes, Modalités et Modèle." *Revue d'Economie Industrielle* 69 (3): 21–40.

Clavel, Jean-Daniel, and John C. Sloan, eds. 1991. *La nouvelle Europe de l'Est, du plan au marché: Les défis de la privatisation.* Brussels: Emile Bruylant.

Conradt, Katherine. 1993. "Another World." *LatinFinance* 46 (April): 29–37.

Conseil d'Etat, Section du rapport et des études, ed. 1985. *Les Etablissements Publics Nationaux, Catégories et Spécificités.* Notes et Etudes Documentaires 4784. Paris: La Documentation Française.

_____. 1989. *Les établissements publics: transformation et suppression.* Notes et Etudes Documentaires 4876. Paris: La Documentation Française.

Cook, Paul, and Colin Kirkpatrick, eds. 1988. *Privatisation in Less Developed Countries.* Brighton, Sussex, England: Wheatsheaf Books Ltd.

Cour des Comptes. 1990. *Rapport au Président de la République,* vol. 3. Paris: Direction des Journaux Officiels.

Covarrubias, Alvaro J., and Suzanne B. Maia. 1994. "Discussion of Issues." Vol. 1 of "Reforms and Private Participation in the Power Sector of Selected Latin American and Caribbean and Industrialized Countries." World Bank Regional Studies Program Report 33. Washington, D.C.

_____. 1994. "Appendices: Vol. 2 of Reforms and Private Participation in the Power Sector of Selected Latin American and Caribbean and Industrialized Countries." World Bank Regional Studies Program Report 33. Washington, D.C.

Cramton, Peter. 1995. "The PCS Spectrum Auctions: An Early Assessment." University of Maryland, Department of Economics. 5 December.

Crane, Keith. 1991. "Property Rights Reform: Hungarian Country Study." In Hans Blommestein and Michael Marrese, eds. *Transformation of Planned Economies: Property Rights Reform and Macroeconomic Stability.* Paris: OECD.

Crosnier, Marie-Agnès. 1992. "Textes législatifs et réglementaires relatifs à l'économie de la Russie, 1er janvier 1991 à 31 mars 1992." *Le courrier des pays de l'Est* 368 (April): 50–57.

Csaba, Laszlo, ed. 1994. *Privatization, Liberalisation and Destruction: Recreating the Market in Eastern Europe*. Aldershot, England: Dartmouth.

Czech Ministry for the Administration of the National Property and Its Privatization. 1993. *Report on the Privatization Process for the Years 1989 to 1992*. Prague: MPAC Ltd.

Dallago, Bruno, G. Ajani, and B. Grancelli, eds. 1992. *Privatization and Entrepreneurship in Post-Socialist Countries: Economy, Law and Society.* New York: St. Martin's.

Danso, Alex. 1992. "Privatization of State Owned Enterprises in Africa: The Case of Ghana." *Southeastern Political Review* 20 (fall): 335–54.

Da Silva Cornell, David S. 1993. "Transferring the People's Livelihood to the People: An Evaluation of Taiwan's Privatization Drive." *Law and Policy in International Business* 24(3): 943–92.

DeAlessi, L. 1982. "On the Nature and Consequences of Private and Public Enterprises." *Minnesota Law Review* 67:191–209.

Debène, M. 1991. "L'ouverture du capital des entreprises publiques, commentaire du décret du 4 avril 1991." *Actualité Juridique, Droit Administratif* (20 September): 623–36.

De Fraja, Giovanni. 1994. "Chicken or Egg: Which Should Come First, Privatisation or Liberalisation?" *Annales d'Economie et de Statistique* 33: 133–56.

Dehesa, Guillermo de la. 1993. "Las privatizaciones en Espana." *Moneda y Credito* 196: 131–41.

De Kessler, Ana S. 1993. "Privatization of the Enterprises of the Argentine Ministry of Defense." *Columbia Journal of World Business* 28(1): 134–43.

Delahaye, J. L. 1987a. "Certificats d'Investissement et Privatisation." *Droit et Pratique du Commerce International* 13(3): 469–84.

_____. 1987b. "La Golden Share à la Française." *Droit et Pratique du Commerce International* 13(4): 579–88.

Demougin, Dominique, and Hans Werner Sinn. 1994. "Privatization, Risk-Taking, and the Communist Firm." *Journal of Public Economics* 55(2): 203–31.

Denizer, Cevdet, and Alan Gelb. 1993. "Mongolia: Privatization and System Transformation in an Isolated Economy." Policy Research Working Paper 1063. World Bank, Policy Research Department, Washington, D.C.

De Sarrau, X. 1987. "Aspects fiscaux des privatisations en France." *Droit et Pratique du Commerce International* 13(4): 687.

Descamps, Thierry, and Cécile Digne. 1993. "Physical Persons as Privileged Subscribers." *Droit et Pratique du Commerce International* 19(4): 535–45.

Dimitriyev, S., and D. Petkoski. 1994. "Prior to Privatization" and "The First Day after Privatization." Parts A and B of "The Case of Udarnik-Stankostroitelnij Zavod." EDI Case Study. World Bank, Economic Development Institute, Washington, D.C.

Dlouhy, Vladimir, and Jan Mladek. 1994. "Privatization and Corporate Control in the Czech Republic." *Economic Policy: A European Forum* 9(19): 155–70.

Dnes, Antony W. 1991. "Franchising, Natural Monopoly and Privatisation." In Cento Veljanovski, ed., *Regulators and the Market: An Assessment of the Growth of Regulation in the UK*. London: Institute of Economic Affairs.

———. 1993. "Franchising Passenger Rail." *Scottish Journal of Political Economy* 40(4): 420–33.

Dodds, Paul, and Gerd Wächter. 1993. "Privatization Contracts with the German Treuhandanstalt: An Insider's Guide." *International Lawyer* 27 (spring): 65–90.

Donahue, John. 1991. *The Privatization Decision: Public Ends, Private Means*. New York: Basic Books.

Donaldson, David J., and Dileep M. Wagle. 1995. *Privatization: Principles and Practice*. IFC Lessons of Experience Series. Washington, D.C.: World Bank and International Finance Corporation.

Donaldson, Hunter. 1994. "Telecommunications Liberalization and Privatization: The New Zealand Experience." In Bjorn Wellenius and Peter A. Stern, eds., *Implementing Reforms in the Telecommunications Sector: Lessons from Experience*. Washington, D.C.: World Bank.

D'Ormesson, Olivier. 1987. "Le placement au Japon d'actions de sociétés privatisées." *Revue de Droit des Affaires Internationales* 3: 295–306.

D'Ormesson, Olivier, and D. Martin. 1987. "L'élaboration des lois de privatisation: présentation générale du cadre juridique." *Droit et Pratique du Commerce International* 13(3): 405–56.

Drouet, M. 1992. "Autogestion et privatisations en Yougoslavie." *Revue d'Etudes Comparatives Est-Ouest* 2–3: 59–104.

Drum, Bernard. 1993. "Privatization in Africa." *Columbia Journal of World Business* 28(1): 144–49.

Due, Jean M., and Stephen C. Schmidt. 1995. "Progress on Privatization in Bulgaria." *Comparative Economic Studies* 37 (spring): 55–77.

Duncan, Ian, and Alan Bollard. 1992. *Corporatization and Privatization: Lessons from New Zealand*. Auckland, New Zealand: Oxford University Press.

Durupty, Michel. 1988. *Les privatisations en France*. Notes et Etudes Documentaires 4857. Paris: La Documentation Française.

———. 1993. "La privatisation banalisée, commentaire de la loi de privatisation 93–923 du 19 juillet 1993." *Actualité Juridique, Droit Administratif* (20 October): 712–18.

Earle, John S., Roman Frydman, Andrzej Rapaczynski, and Joel Turkewitz. 1994. *Small Privatization: The Transformation of Retail Trade and Consumer Services in the Czech Republic, Hungary and Poland*. Budapest, Hungary: Central European University Press.

Earle, John S., and Dana Sapatoru. 1994. "Incentive Contracts, Corporate Governance, and Privatization Funds in Romania." *Atlantic Economic Journal* 22(2): 61–79.

EBRD (European Bank for Reconstruction and Development). 1995. *Transition Report 1995: Investment and Enterprise Development*. London.

EBRD and CEEPN (Central and Eastern European Privatization Network). 1993. *Management and Employee Buy-outs in Central and Eastern Europe: An Introduction*. London.

Egerer, Roland. 1995. "Capital Markets, Financial Intermediaries, and Corporate Governance: An Empirical Assessment of the Top Ten Voucher Funds in the

Czech Republic." Policy Research Working Paper 1555. World Bank, Policy Research Department, Washington, D.C.

Ehrlich, Isaac, Georges Gallais-Hamonno, Zhiqiang Liu, and Randall Lutter. 1994. "Productivity Growth and Firm Ownership: An Analytical and Empirical Investigation." *Journal of Political Economy* 102(5): 1006–38.

Eichengreen, Barry. 1995. "Financing Infrastructure in Developing Countries: Lessons from the Railway Age." *World Bank Research Observer* 10 (February): 75–91.

Ellerman, David, Uros Korse, and Marko Simoneti. 1991. "Decentralized Privatization: The Slovene ESOP Program." *Public Enterprise* 11(2–3): 175–84.

Elling, Martin. 1992. "Privatization in Germany: A Model for Legal and Functional Analysis." *Vanderbilt Journal of Transnational Law* 25(4): 581–642.

English, Richard D. 1991. "Privatization by General Fund: Economic Empowerment for Central and Eastern Europe." *George Washington Journal of International Law and Economics* 24: 527–86.

Estrin, Saul, Alan Gelb, and Inderjit Singh. 1995. "Shocks and Adjustment by Firms in Transition: A Comparative Study." *Journal of Comparative Economics* 21 (October): 131–53.

Euromoney. 1995. "Privatization: The Dithering-Away of the State." *Euromoney* 12 (April): 79–104.

European Conference of Ministers of Transport. 1993. "Railway Privatization." *Report of the Ninetieth Round Table on Transport Economics*. Paris: OECD.

———. 1995a. "Interurban Transport Costs." *Report of the Ninety-Eighth Round Table on Transport Economics*. Paris: OECD.

———. 1995b. "Transport Economics: Past Trends and Future Prospects." *Report of the Hundredth Round Table on Transport Economics*. Paris: OECD.

Ewing, Andrew, Barbara W. Lee, and Roger Leeds. 1993. "Accelerating Privatization in Ex-Socialist Economies." *Columbia Journal of World Business* 28(1): 158–67.

Feigenbaum, Harvey B., and Jeffrey R. Hennig. 1994. "Political Underpinnings of Privatization: A Typology." *World Politics* 46 (January): 185–208.

Feinberg, Robert M., and Mieke Meurs. 1994. "Privatization and Antitrust in Eastern Europe: The Importance of Entry." *Antitrust Bulletin* 39(3): 797–811.

Fleuriet, Michel. 1993. "Placement of Shares in Connection with Privatizations." *Droit et Pratique du Commerce International* 19(4): 546–52.

Flouret, Emiliano. 1994. "Private Sector Involvement in Latin American Railway Transport." *Rail International* (May): 2–11.

Fogel, Daniel S., ed. 1994. *Managing in Emerging Market Economies: Cases from the Czech and Slovak Republics*. Boulder, Colo.: Westview Press.

Foreman-Peck, James, and Robert Millward. 1994. *Public and Private Ownership of British Industry, 1820–1990*. Oxford, England: Clarendon Press.

Foster, Christopher D. 1992. *Privatization, Public Ownership and the Regulation of Natural Monopoly*. Oxford, England: Basil Blackwell.

Franks, Stephen. 1993. "Rigorous Privatization: The New Zealand Experience." *Columbia Journal of World Business* 28(1): 84–97.

French Sénat. 1992–93. *Rapport de la commission des finances, du contrôle budgétaire et des comptes économiques de la Nation*. 2d sess., no. 326.

Frydman, Roman, and Andrzej Rapaczynski. 1994. *Privatization in Eastern Europe: Is the State Withering Away?* London: Central European University Press.

Fukui, Koichiro. 1992. *Japanese National Railways Privatization Study: The Experience of Japan and Lessons for Developing Countries.* World Bank Discussion Paper 172. Washington, D.C.

Gabor, Francis A. 1991. "The Quest for Transformation to a Market Economy: Privatization and Foreign Investment in Hungary." *Vanderbilt Journal of Transnational Law* 24(2): 269-303.

Galal, Ahmed. 1994. "Regulation and Commitment in the Development of Telecommunications in Chile." Policy Research Working Paper 1278. World Bank, Policy Research Department, Washington, D.C.

Galal, Ahmed, Leroy Jones, Pankaj Tandon, and Ingo Vogelsang. 1994. *Welfare Consequences of Selling Public Enterprises: An Empirical Analysis.* New York: Oxford University Press.

Galal, Ahmed, and Mary Shirley, eds. 1994. *Does Privatization Deliver? Highlights from a World Bank Conference.* EDI Development Studies. Washington, D.C.: World Bank.

Gallo, Luis G. 1993. "The Value-Added of Investment Bankers in Privatizations." *Columbia Journal of World Business* 28(1): 196–205.

Garant, P. 1990. "Aspects constitutionnels et juridiques des privatisations d'entreprises fédérales canadiennes." *Revue Marocaine de Finances Publiques et d'Economie* 6 (first semester): 186–197.

Gates, Jeffrey R., and Jamal Saghir. 1995. "Employee Stock Ownership Plans (ESOPs): Objectives, Design Options and International Experience." CFS Discussion Paper Series 112. World Bank, Washington, D.C.

Gayle, Dennis J., and Jonathan N. Goodrich. 1990. *Privatization and Deregulation in Global Perspective.* Westport, Conn.: Quorum Books.

Gelpern, A. 1993. "The Laws and Politics of Reprivatization in East-Central Europe." *University of Pennsylvania Journal of International Business Law* 14(3): 315–72.

Générale de Banque. 1993. "Le retour en force des privatisations." *Bulletin de la Générale de Banque* 341 (July–August): 1.

Gerchunoff, Pablo. 1992. "Las privatizaciones en la Argentina." Serie de documentos de trabajo 121. Banco Interamericano de Desarrollo, Washington, D.C.

Gerchunoff, Pablo, and Guillermo Canovas. 1995. "Privatizaciones en un contexto de emergencia economica." *Desarrollo Economico* 34(136): 483–512.

Giemulla, Elmar. 1995. "Transport Sector Privatisation in the Russian Federation." *Transport Law Journal* 23(1): 99–117.

Gioscia, Marcello. 1993. "Privatization of Telecommunications: The Italian Experience." Paper presented at the International Symposium on World Privatizations. Forum International, Nice, December 2–4.

Gizang, Michael, and Juan Sabater. 1994. "A Case Study: The Privatization of the Venezuelan Telecommunications Industry." In Meridith Brown and Jiles Ridley, eds., *Privatisation: Current Issues.* London: Graham & Trotman.

Glade, William, ed. 1991. *Privatization of Public Enterprises in Latin America.* San Francisco, Calif.: ICS Press.

Glick, S. M., and W. L. Richter. 1991. "Legal Framework for Privatization in Czechoslovakia." *International Business Lawyer* 19: 353–57.

Goldenman, Gretta. 1993. "Environmental Barriers to Foreign Investment in Eastern Europe: Myths and Mistakes." *Review of European Community and International Environmental Law* 2(1): 1–8.

_____. 1994. *Environmental Liability and Privatization in Central and Eastern Europe.* London: Graham & Trotman and Martinus Nijhof.

Goldstein, R., and K. Horakova. 1993. "Investment Opportunities in Czech Capital Markets." *International Financial Law Review* 12(11): 20–22.

Gomez-Ibanez, José A., and John R. Meyer. 1993. *Going Private: The International Experience with Transport Privatization.* Washington, D.C.: Brookings Institution.

Gouri, Geeta, ed. 1991. *"Privatization and Public Enterprise: The Asia-Pacific Experience.* Columbia, Mo.: Oxford IBH Publishing Co.

Graham, Cosmo, and Tony Prosser. 1991. *Privatizing Public Enterprises: Constitutions, the State, and Regulation in Comparative Perspective.* New York: Oxford University Press.

Gray, Cheryl W. 1993a. "Bankruptcy Law and Enterprise Restructuring in Central Europe." *Transition* 4(5). World Bank, Policy Research Department, Washington, D.C.

Gray, Cheryl W., and associates. 1993b. *Evolving Legal Frameworks for Private Sector Development in Central and Eastern Europe.* World Bank Discussion Paper 209. Washington, D.C.

Gray, Cheryl W., and Rebecca J. Hanson. 1993. "Corporate Governance in Central and Eastern Europe: Lessons from Advanced Market Economies." Policy Research Working Paper 1182. World Bank, Policy Research Department, Washington, D.C.

Gray, Cheryl W., and W. Jarosz. 1993. "Foreign Investment Law in Central and Eastern Europe." Policy Research Working Paper 1111. World Bank, Policy Research Department, Washington, D.C.

Gray, Dale. 1995. *Reforming the Energy Sector in Transition Economies: Selected Experience and Lessons.* World Bank Discussion Paper 296. Washington, D.C.

Gray, Philip, ed. 1996. "Industry Structure and Regulation in Infrastructure: A Cross-Country Survey." PSD Occasional Paper 25. World Bank, Private Sector Development Department, Washington, D.C.

Greenspan-Bell, Ruth, and Thomas A. Kolaja. 1993. "Capital Privatization and the Management of Environmental Liability Issues in Poland." *Business Lawyer* 48(3): 943–61.

Grosdidier de Matons, Jean. 1995. *Public Port Administration and Private Sector Intervention in Ports and in the Port Industry.* Le Havre, France: Institut Portuaire du Havre.

Grosh, Barbara, and Rwekaza S. Mukandala, eds. 1994. *State-Owned Enterprises in Africa.* Boulder, Colo.: Lynne Rienner Publishers.

Guerraoui, Driss, and Xavier Richet, eds. 1995. *Stratégies de privatisation: comparaison Maghreb-Europe.* Paris: L'Harmattan.

Gueullette, Agota. 1992. "Le capital étranger et la privatisation en Hongrie: phénomènes récents et leçons à tirer." *Le courrier des pays de l'Est* 34 (November).

Guislain, Pierre. 1992. *Divestiture of State Enterprises: An Overview of the Legal Framework.* World Bank Technical Paper 186. Washington, D.C.

_____. 1995. *Les Privatisations: un défi stratégique, juridique et institutionnel*. Brussels: De Boeck Université.

_____. 1996. "Les privatisations dans le monde." In *Le livre de l'année 1996*. Paris: Larousse.

Guislain, Pierre, and Michel Kerf. 1995. "Concessions: The Way to Privatize Infrastructure Sector Monopolies." *FPD Note* 59. World Bank, Office of the Vice President for Finance and Private Sector Development, Washington, D.C..

Gurkov, Igor. 1994. "Privatization in Israel: The Creation of a Mature Market Economy." *Annals of Public and Cooperative Economics* 65(2): 247–79.

Hachette, Dominique, and Rolf Lüders. 1993. *Privatization in Chile: An Economic Appraisal*. San Fransisco, Calif.: ICS Press.

Haines, Lila. 1995. "Cuba's Telecommunications Market." *Columbia Journal of World Business* 30 (spring): 50–57.

Hanson, Rebecca J. 1992. "The Legal Framework for Privatization in Hungary." *Law and Policy in International Business* 23(2): 440–68.

Harder, Stephen, and Jefferson Taylor. 1993. "Swapping Enterprise Debt for Equity in Poland." *International Financial Law Review* 12 (April): 23–25.

Heald, David. 1991. "La privatisation des services publics britanniques: leçons ou mises en garde pour les autres pays membres de la CEE?" *Revue Politiques et Management Public* 9: 51–72.

_____. 1995. "An Evaluation of French Concession Accounting." *European Accounting Review* 4(2): 325–49.

Hedley, Kathryn. 1992. "Legal Development and Privatization in Russia: A Case Study." *Soviet Economy* 8 (April–June): 130–57.

Helm, Dieter. 1994. "British Utility Regulation: Theory, Practice, and Reform." *Oxford Review of Economic Policy* 10(3): 17–39.

Hensley, Matthew, and Edward White. 1993. "The Privatization Experience in Malaysia: Integrating Build-Operate-Own and Build-Operate-Transfer Techniques within the National Privatization Strategy." *Columbia Journal of World Business* 28(1): 70–83.

Herrera, Alejandra. 1993. "The Privatization of Telecommunications Services: The Case of Argentina." *Columbia Journal of World Business* 28(1): 46–61.

Hill, Alice, and Manuel Angel Abdala. 1993. "Regulation, Institutions and Commitment: Privatization and Regulation in the Argentine Telecommunications Sector." Policy Research Working Paper 1216. World Bank, Policy Research Department, Washington, D.C.

Holden, Paul, and Sarath Rajapatirana. 1995. *Unshackling the Private Sector: A Latin American Story*. Directions in Development Series. Washington, D.C.: World Bank.

Horn, Norbert. 1992. "Legal Aspects of Privatization and Market Economy: The German Experience in Comparative Perspective." Paper presented at the Eighth Colloquium of the Association Internationale de Droit Economique, Budapest, May 14–15.

Howles, Kate, and Neil Harvey. 1993. "The British Experience: Questions of Principles and Methods of Placement." *Droit et Pratique du Commerce International* 19(4): 553–64.

Huchet, J. F. 1993. "La longue marche des entreprises d'état chinoises vers le marché." *Reflets et Perspectives de la Vie Economique* 32(6): 437–53.

Hunt, Lester C., and Edward L. Lynk. 1995. "Privatisation and Efficiency in the U.K. Water Industry: An Empirical Analysis." *Oxford Bulletin of Economics and Statistics* 57 (August): 371–88.

Hyclak, Thomas J., and Arthur E. King. 1994. "The Privatisation Experience in Eastern Europe." *World Economy* 17(4): 529–50.

Hyman, Leonard S. 1995. *The Privatization of Public Utilities*. Vienna, Va.: Public Utilities Reports.

Idelovitch, Emanuel, and Klas Ringskog. 1995. *Private Sector Participation in Water Supply and Sanitation in Latin America*. Directions in Development Series. Washington, D.C.: World Bank.

Im, Soo J., R. Jalali, and J. Saghir. 1993. "Privatization in the Republics of the Former Soviet Union: Framework and Initial Results." Discussion Paper, World Bank, Legal Department, Washington, D.C.

International Finance Corporation. 1993. *L'viv: First Privatization in Ukraine*. Washington, D.C.

Intriligator, Micheal D. 1994. "Privatisation in Russia Has Led to Criminalisation." *Australian Economic Review* 106 (April–June): 4–14.

Inzelt, Annamaria. 1994. "Privatization and Innovation in Hungary: First Experiences." *Economic Systems* 18(2): 141–58.

Israel, Arturo. 1992. *Issues for Infrastructure Management in the 1990s*. World Bank Discussion Paper 171. Washington, D.C.

Israël, Jean-Jacques. 1986. "La commission administrative nationale d'évaluation des actions des banques nationalisée non inscrites à la cote officielle" (article 18 of the law of February 11, 1982). *Revue du Droit Public* 4 (July–August): 971–1013.

Jackson, Marvin, and Valentijn Bilsen, eds. 1994. *Company Management and Capital Market Development in the Transition*. Brookfield, Vt.: Ashgate, Avebury.

Jacobson, Charles D., and Joel A. Tarr. 1995. "Ownership and Financing of Infrastructure: Historical Perspectives." Policy Research Working Paper 1466. World Bank, Policy Research Department, Washington, D.C.

Jedrzejczak, Gregory T. 1991. "The Polish Capital Markets 1991: Instruments, Institutions, Perspectives." *Public Enterprise* 11(2–3): 133–40.

Jenkins, Glenn P. 1994. "Modernization of Tax Administrations: Revenue Boards and Privatization as Instruments for Change." *Bulletin for International Fiscal Documentation* 48(2): 75–81.

Johnson, S., and H. Kroll. 1991. "Managerial Strategies for Spontaneous Privatization." *Soviet Economy* (October–December).

Johnson, Simon, David T. Kotchen, and Gary Loveman. 1995. "How One Polish Shipyard Became a Market Competitor." *Harvard Business Review* 73(November–December): 53–72.

Jomo, Kwame Sundaram, ed. 1995. *Privatizing Malaysia: Rents, Rhetoric, Realities*. Boulder, Colo.: Westview Press.

Jones Day Reavis and Pogue. 1991. "New Perspectives on Investments in Eastern Germany." Comments to clients, May 17, Washington, D.C.

Jones, Leroy, and Fadil Azim Abbas. 1992. "Case Studies from Chile, Malaysia, Mexico, and the UK: Malaysia, Background, Malaysian Airlines, Kelang Container Terminal, Sports Toto." Paper prepared for the World Bank Conference on the Welfare Consequences of Selling Public Enterprises, Country Economics Department, Washington, D.C.

Joskow, Paul L., Richard Schmalensee, and Natalia Tsukanova. 1994. "Competition Policy in Russia during and after Privatization." *Brookings Papers on Economic Activity* 301–81.

Juan, Ellis J. 1995. "Airport Infrastructure: The Emerging Role of the Private Sector, Recent Experiences Based on 10 Case Studies." CFS Discussion Paper Series 115. World Bank, Washington, D.C.

Kapur, Anil. 1995. *Airport Infrastructure: The Emerging Role of the Private Sector.* World Bank Technical Paper 313. Washington, D.C.

Katznelson, I. 1990. "Une étude de cas de privatisation au Danemark: La compagnie d'assurance-vie de l'Etat." *Journées de la Société de Législation Comparée* 12: 389–401.

Kay, John, Colin Mayer, and David Thompson, eds. 1986. *Privatisation and Regulation: The UK Experience.* Oxford, England: Clarendon Press.

Kerf, Michel, and Warrick Smith. 1996. *Privatizing Africa's Infrastructure: Promise and Challenge.* World Bank Technical Paper 337. Washington, D.C.

Kessides, Christine. 1993. *Institutional Options for the Provision of Infrastructure.* World Bank Discussion Paper 212. Washington, D.C.

Kessides, Ioannis N., and Robert D. Willig. 1995. "Competition and Regulation in the Railroad Industry." In Claudio R. Frischtak, ed. "Regulatory Policies and Reform: A Comparative Perspective." Prepublication edition (December 1995). World Bank, Private Sector Development Department, Washington, D.C.

Kikeri, Sunita, John Nellis, and Mary Shirley. 1992. *Privatization: The Lessons of Experience.* Washington, D.C.: World Bank.

_____. 1994. "Privatization: Lessons from Market Economies." *World Bank Research Observer* 9(2): 241–72.

Kim, Chul, Mahn-Kee Kim, and William W. Boyer. 1994. "Privatization of South Korea's Public Enterprises." *Journal of Developing Areas* 28: 157–66.

Kiss, Yudit. 1994. "Privatization Paradoxes in East Central Europe." *East European Politics and Societies* 8(1): 122–52.

Kjellström, S. B. 1990. "Privatization in Turkey." Policy Research Working Paper 532. World Bank, Policy Research Department, Washington, D.C.

Klein, Michael. 1996. "Competition in Network Industries." Policy Research Working Paper 1591. World Bank, Policy Research Department, Washington, D.C.

Klein, Michael, and Neil D. Roger. 1994. "Back to the Future: The Potential in Infrastructure Privatization." In Richard O'Brien, ed., *Finance and the International Economy,* vol 8. New York: Oxford University Press.

Kodrzycki, Yolanda K. 1994. "Privatization of Local Public Services: Lessons from New England." *New England Economic Review* (May–June): 31–46.

Konig, K. 1988. "La privatisation en Allemagne Fédérale: problèmes, statuts et perspectives." *Revue Internationale des Sciences Administratives* 54(4): 583–618.

Kopicki, Ronald, and Louis S. Thompson. 1995. "Best Methods of Railway Restructuring and Privatization." CFS Discussion Paper Series 111. World Bank, Washington, D.C.

Kramer, Ralph M., and others. 1993. *Privatization in Four European Countries: Comparative Studies in Government, Third Sector Relationships.* Armonk, N.Y.: M. E. Sharpe.

Krawczyk, Marek, and Jose A. Lopez-Lopez. 1993. "The Role of Government in Poland's Economic Transition: Ideas and Experience from the Recent Past." *Columbia Journal of World Business* 28(1): 180–87.

Krüsselberg, Hans-Günter. 1994. "The Heavy Burden of a Divestiture Strategy of Privatization: Lessons from Germany's Experiences for Latin American Privatization." *Quarterly Review of Economics and Finance* 34 (summer): 281–99.

Kwoka, John E. Jr. 1996. "Privatization, Deregulation, and Competition: A Survey of Effects on Economic Performance." PSD Occasional Paper 27. World Bank, Private Sector Development Department, Washington, D.C.

Laffont, J. J. 1994. "The New Economics of Regulation Ten Years After." *Econometrica* 62: 507–38.

Laffont, J. J., and J. Tirole. 1993. *A Theory of Incentives in Regulation and Procurement.* Cambridge, Mass.: MIT Press.

_____. 1994. "Access Pricing and Competition." *European Economic Review* 38: 1673–710.

Laki, Mihali. 1995. "The Opportunities for Workers' Participation in Privatisation in Hungary: The Case of the Eger Flour Mill." *Europe-Asia Studies* 47(2): 317–35.

LatinFinance. Annual. *Privatization in Latin America.* Miami, Fla.: Latin American Financial Publications.

Laurin, Benoit. 1993. "Quelques aspects de la négociation de contrats d'acquisition par la Treuhandanstalt dans le cadre de la privatisation de l'economie est-allemande." *Revue de Droit des Affaires Internationales* 2: 211–18.

Lee, Barbara W. 1991. "Should Employee Participation be Part of Privatization?" Policy Research Working Paper 664. World Bank, Policy Research Department, Washington, D.C.

Lee, Barbara W., and John Nellis. 1991. "Enterprise Reform and Privatization in Socialist Economies." *Public Enterprise* 11(2–3): 101–18.

Lee, W. L., and J. M. Bartos. 1987. "Les placements privés aux Etats-Unis des titres des sociétés françaises privatisées." *Droit et Pratique du Commerce International* 13(3): 485–92.

Levy, Brian, and Pablo T. Spiller. 1993. "Regulations, Institutions, and Commitment in Telecommunications: A Comparative Analysis of Five Country Studies." In *Proceedings of the World Bank Annual Conference on Development Economics 1993.* Washington, D.C.: World Bank.

Lhomel, Edith. 1993. "Les transformations économiques en Roumanie: premier bilan." *Reflets et Perspectives de la Vie Economique* 32(3–4): 257–68.

Lieberman, Ira W. 1993a. "Privatization: The Theme of the 1990s." *Columbia Journal of World Business* 28(1): 1–17.

_____. 1993b. "Russia as an Emerging Capital Market." Paper presented at a conference on Emerging Markets, London, January 1993. World Bank, Private Sector Development Department, Washington, D.C.

_____. 1994. "Privatisation in Latin America and Eastern Europe in the Context of Political and Economic Reform." *World Economy* 17(4): 551–75.

Lieberman, Ira W., Andrew Ewing, Michal Mejstrik, Joyita Mukherjee, and Peter Fidler. 1995. *Mass Privatization in Central and Eastern Europe and the Former Soviet Union: A Comparative Analysis.* World Bank Studies of Economies in Transformation Paper 16. Washington, D.C.

Lieberman, Ira W., and Suhail Rahuja. 1995. "An Overview of Privatization in Russia." In Ira W. Lieberman and John Nellis, eds., *Russia: Creating Private Enterprises and Efficient Markets.* World Bank Studies of Economies in Transformation Paper 15. Washington, D.C.

Lieberman, Ira W., and John Nellis, eds. 1995. *Russia: Creating Private Enterprises and Efficient Markets.* World Bank Studies of Economies in Transformation Paper 15. Washington, D.C.

Lipworth, Sydney. 1993. "Utility Regulation and the Monopolies and Mergers Commission: Retrospect and Prospect." In M. E. Beesley, ed., *Major Issues in Regulation.* London: Institute of Economic Affairs, in association with London Business School.

Lissowska, Maria. 1993. "La politique économique en Pologne et le comportement des entreprises." *Reflets et Perspectives de la Vie Economique* 32(3–4): 209–22.

Liu, Zinan 1995. "The Comparative Performance of Public and Private Enterprises: The Case of British Ports." *Journal of Transport Economics and Policy* 29(3): 263–74.

Liufang, Fang. 1995. "China's Corporatization Experiment." *Duke Journal of Comparative and International Law* 5(2): 149–270.

Longueville, G., and J. J. Santini. 1986. *Privatisation: quelles méthodes pour quels objectifs?* Notes et Etudes Documentaires 124. Paris: La Documentation Française.

Looney, Robert E. 1994. "Factor Efficiency in Pakistani Industry: The Influence of Private versus Public Ownership in Affecting Capital and Labor Productivity." *Rivista Internazionale di Scienze Economiche e Commercial* 41(5): 449–70.

Lopez-de-Silanes, Florencio. 1996. "Determinants of Privatization Prices." NBER Working Paper 5494. Cambridge, Mass.

Lopez-de-Silanes, Florencio, Andrei Shleifer, and Robert W. Vishny. 1995. "Privatization in the United States." NBER Working Paper 5113. Cambridge, Mass.

Loyrette, Jean, and Olivier D'Ormesson. 1987. "L'achat par des étrangers d'actions de sociétés privatisées au regard du droit français et du droit communautaire." *Revue de Droit des Affaires Internationales* 3: 315–26.

Lüders, Rolf. 1993. "The Success and Failure of State-Owned Enterprise Divestitures in a Developing Country: The Case of Chile." *Columbia Journal of World Business* 28(1): 98–121.

Maciel, Rogelio N. 1992. "Argentina: Privatization of the Natural Gas Industry." *Journal of Energy and Natural Resources Law* 10: 371–79.

Magliveras, Konstantin D. 1991. "The Privatization of the Scottish Electricity Industry, and EC Competition Law." *Scotts Law Times* (6 December): 450.

Malaysia. 1991. *Privatization Masterplan.* Kuala Lumpur: National Print Department.

Mallon, Richard D. 1994. "State-Owned Enterprise Reform through Performance Contracts: The Bolivian Experiment." *World Development* 22(6): 925–34.

Marcilhacy, Philippe, and Frank-Emmanuel Dangeard. 1987. "Comparaison des modalités du placement international de Saint-Gobain et de British Airways." *Revue de Droit des Affaires Internationales* 3: 307–14.

Marcincin, Anton, and Sweder van Wijnbergen. 1995. *Voucher Privatization, Corporate Control and the Cost of Capital: An Analysis of the Czech Privatization Programme*. Centre for Economic Policy Research Discussion Paper 1215. September.

Martin, Greg. 1995. "Port of Brisbane Corporation: A Case Study in Corporatisation." *Economic Analysis and Policy* 25: 53–69.

Martinand, Claude, ed. 1994. *Private Financing of Public Infrastructure: The French Experience*. Paris: Economic and International Affairs Department, Ministry of Public Works, Transportation and Tourism.

Mastrangelo, Teresa, and Robert J. F. McPhail. 1993. "Serving Those Going Private: The Role of Accountancy in Privatization." *Columbia Journal of World Business* 29(1): 206–11.

McConville, James, and John Sheldrake. 1995. *Transport in Transition: Aspects of British and European Experience*. Aldershot, England: Dartmouth.

McEldowney, John F. 1992. *Electricity Industry Handbook: Law and Practice*. London: Chancery Law Publications.

_____. 1995. "Law and Regulation: Current Issues and Future Directions." In Matthew Bishop, John A. Kay, and Colin P. Mayer, eds., *The Regulatory Challenge*. New York: Oxford University Press.

McFaul, Michael. 1995. "State Power, Institutional Change, and the Politics of Privatization in Russia." *World Politics* 47 (January): 210–43.

McFaul, Michael, and Tova Perlmutter, eds. 1995. *Privatization, Conversion, and Enterprise Reform in Russia*. Boulder, Colo.: Westview Press.

McKenna & Co. 1992. "Purchase of a Company from the Treuhandanstalt." *Company Lawyer* 13(1): 31–32.

Megginson, William L., Robert C. Nash, and Matthias van Randenborgh. 1994. "The Financial and Operating Performance of Newly Privatized Firms: An International Empirical Analysis." *Journal of Finance* 49(2): 403–452.

Meheroo, Jussawalla. 1993. *Global Telecommunications Policies: The Challenge of Change*. Westport, Conn.: Greenwood Press.

Michalski, Jacek. 1991. "Privatisation Process in Poland: The Legal Aspects." *Communist Economies and Economic Transformation* 3(3): 327–36.

Millward, Robert, and John Singleton, eds. 1995. *The Political Economy of Nationalisation in Britain, 1920–1950*. Cambridge: Cambridge University Press.

Milor, Vedat, ed. 1994. *Changing Political Economies: Privatization in Post-Communist and Reforming Communist States*. Boulder, Colo.: Lynne Rienner Publishers.

Mintchev, Vesselin. 1993. "Démonopolisation et transformation des entreprises d'Etat en Bulgarie." *Reflets et Perspectives de la Vie Economique* 32(3–4): 269–80.

Mooney, Reynold, and Scott Griffith. 1993. "Privatizing a Distressed State-Owned Enterprise: Lessons Learned through Privatization Work in Argentina's Steel Sector." *Columbia Journal of World Business* 28(1): 36–45.

Moreau, Marie-Ange. 1992. "Les répercussions sociales des privatisations dans les différents systèmes juridiques." *Revue Internationale de Droit Economique* 3: 417–29.

Moreau, Michel. 1987. "L'émission d'obligations assorties de bons de souscription d'actions Elf-Acquitaine." *Revue de Droit des Affaires Internationales* 3: 327–32.

Moreau-Bourles, M. A. 1987. "Privatisations et actionnariat salarié: l'incidence de la loi étrangère." *Droit et Pratique du Commerce International* 13(4): 635–56.

Morin, François. 1992. "Les techniques de la privatisation." *Revue Internationale de Droit Economique* 3: 359–73.

Muir, Russell, and Joseph P. Saba. 1995. *Improving State Enterprise Performance: The Role of Internal and External Incentives.* World Bank Technical Paper 306. Washington, D.C.

Muller, Alberto E. G. 1994. "Tras la privatizacion: Las perspectivas del medio ferroviario argentino." *Desarrollo Economico* 34(134): 243–62.

Munoz Goma, Oscar, ed. 1993. *Despues de las privatizaciones: hacia el estado regulador.* Santiago, Chile: Cieplan.

Mwangi, Jacob N. 1986. *Towards an Enabling Environment: Indigenous Private Development in Africa.* Geneva, Switzerland: Aga Khan Foundation.

Nankani, Helen B. 1988. *Techniques of Privatization of State-Owned Enterprises.* Vol. 2, *Selected Country Case Studies.* World Bank Technical Paper 89. Washington, D.C.

Nellis, John. 1986. *Public Enterprises in Sub-Saharan Africa.* World Bank Discussion Paper 1. Washington, D.C.

Nelson, Lynn D., and Irina Y. Kuzes. 1994. "Evaluating the Russian Voucher Privatization Program." *Comparative Economic Studies* 36(1): 55–67.

Nestor, Stilpon, and Scott Thomas. 1995. "Privatisation through Liquidation." *OECD Observer* 192: 36–38.

Neven, Damien, Robin Nuttall, and Paul Seabright. 1993. *Merger in Daylight: The Economics and Politics of European Merger Control*: London: Centre for Economic Policy Research.

Newbery, David M. 1994. "Restructuring and Privatizing Electric Utilities in Eastern Europe." *Economics of Transition* 2(3): 291–316.

Noll, Michael A. 1994. "A Study of Long Distance Rates: Divestiture Revisited." *Telecommunications Policy* 18(5): 355–62.

Noll, Roger G., and Bruce M. Owen. 1994. "The Anticompetitive Uses of Regulation: United States v. AT&T, 1982." In John E. Kwoka, Jr., and Lawrence J. White, eds., *The Antitrust Revolution: The Role of Economics.* New York: Harper Collins College Publishers.

Noya, Ismael, Jorge Ossio and Jose Amado. 1992. *International Financial Law Review,* special supplement on privatization.

Nuchelmans, Didier. 1992. "Privatisation et mécanismes du marché dans le secteur des télécommunications: dérégulation . . . rerégulation?" *Revue Internationale de Droit Economique* 2: 191–204.

Nuti, Mario. 1991. "Privatization of Socialist Economies: General Issues and the Polish Case." In Hans Blommestein and Michael Marrese, eds., *Transformation of Planned Economies: Property Rights Reform and Macroeconomic Stability.* Paris: OECD.

OECD (Organisation for Economic Co-operation and Development). 1992. *Regulatory Reform, Privatization and Competition Policy.* Paris.

———. 1993. *Trends and Policies in Privatisation: Institutional Aspects of the Privatisation Process.* Paris.

_____. 1995a. "Corporate Insolvency Procedures as a Tool for Privatisation and Restructuring." *Trends and Policies in Privatisation* 2(2).

_____. 1995b. *Mass Privatisation: An Initial Assessment*. Paris.

_____. 1996. *Economic Surveys 1995–1996: New Zealand*. Paris.

Ogden, Stuart. 1994. "The Reconstruction of Industrial Relations in the Privatized Water Industry." *British Journal of Industrial Relations* 32(1): 67–84.

Oniki, Hajime, and others. 1994. "The Productivity Effects of the Liberalization of Japanese Telecommuniations Policy." *Journal of Productivity Analysis* 5(1): 63–79.

Parker, David. 1994a. "International Aspects of Privatisation: A Critical Assessment of Business Restructuring in the UK, Former Czechoslovakia and Malaysia." *British Review of Economic Issues* 16 (February).

_____. 1994b. "A Decade of Privatisation: The Effect of Ownership Change and Competition on British Telecom." *British Review of Economic Issues* 16(40): 87–113.

Pechota, Vratislav. 1991. "Privatization and Foreign Investment in Czechoslovakia: The Legal Dimension." *Vanderbilt Journal of Transnational Law* 24(2): 305-21.

Petit, B., and G. Garczinsky. 1987. "Panorama des méthodes actuelles d'évaluation lors des introductions en bourse." *Droit et Pratique du Commerce International* 13(3): 457–68.

Petkoski, D. 1994. "From State-Owned Enterprise to Joint-Stock Company" and "Waiting for Privatization: Teacher's Note." Parts A and B of "The Case of TEMP." EDI Case Study. World Bank, Economic Development Institute, Washington, D.C.

Petkoski, D., and A. Yamnova. 1994. "Conversion to the New Accounting System" and "Application of the New Accounting System." Parts A and B of "The Case of Molodoy Bolshevik." EDI Case Study. World Bank, Economic Development Institute, Washington, D.C.

Pezard, Alice. 1993. "The Golden Share in Privatized Companies." *Droit et Pratique du Commerce International* 19(4): 523–34.

Pinheiro, Armando Castelar, and Fabio Giambiagi. 1994. "Brazilian Privatization in the 1990s." *World Development* 22(5): 737–53.

Pirie, Madsen, and Peter Young. 1987. *The Future of Privatization*. London: ASI Research Ltd.

Phillips, Charles F., Jr. 1993. *The Regulation of Public Utilities: Theory and Practice*. Arlington, Va.: Public Utilities Report.

Pisciotta, Aileen A. 1994. "Privatization and Telecommunications: The Case of Venezuela." In Bjorn Wellenius and Peter A. Stern, eds., *Implementing Reforms in the Telecommunications Sector: Lessons from Experience*. Washington, D.C.: World Bank.

Pliszkiewicz, M. 1992. "Privatisation et droit social en Pologne." *Revue Internationale de Droit Economique* 3: 431–40.

Popova, T. 1992. "Laws and Privatization." *Problems of Economic Transition: A Journal of Translations from Russian* 35 (August): 25–40.

Privatisation International. Annual. *Privatisation Yearbook*, London.

Prokopenko, J., ed. 1995. *Management for Privatization: Lessons from Industry and Public Service*. Management Development Series 32. International Labour Organisation, Geneva.

Prosser, Tony. 1990. "Constitutions and Political Economy: The Privatisation of Public Enterprises in France and Great Britain." *Modern Law Review* 53 (May): 304-20.

Quale, Andrew C. 1991. "Papelcol: A Case Study of Privatization in Colombia." Document prepared for the World Bank Legal Department, Washington, D.C., 22 October.

Raftopol, Anthony V. 1993. "Russian Roulette: A Theoretical Analysis of Voucher Privatization in Russia." *Boston University International Law Journal* 11(2): 435–93.

Ramamurti, Ravi, ed. 1996. *Privatizing Monopolies: Lessons from the Telecommunications and Transport Sectors in Latin America*. Baltimore, Md.: Johns Hopkins University Press.

Ramamurti, Ravi, and Raymond Vernon, eds. 1991. *Privatization and Control of State-Owned Enterprises*. EDI Development Studies. Washington, D.C.: World Bank.

Ramanadham, V. V., ed. 1993. *Privatization: A Global Perspective*. London: Routledge.

_____. 1994. *Privatization and After: Monitoring and Regulation*. London: Routledge.

Rapp, Lucien. 1986a. *Les groupes d'entreprises publiques*. Paris: Presses Universitaires de France. Que Sais-je? 2295.

_____. 1986b. *Techniques de privatisation des enterprises publiques*. Paris: Librairies techniques.

_____. 1987a. "Le contexte financier et international des opérations de privatisation." *Revue de Droit des Affaires Internationales* 3: 287–92.

_____. 1987b. "Le secteur public français entre nationalisations et privatisations." *Actualité Juridique, Droit Administratif* (20 May): 303–8.

Rapp, Lucien, and François Vellas. 1992. *Airline Privatisation in Europe*, 2d ed. Paris: Institute of Air Transport.

Raynaud-Contamine, Monique. 1987. "L'application du droit commun aux privatisations." *Actualité Juridique, Droit Administratif* (20 May): 309–313.

Reason Foundation. Annual. *Annual Report on Privatization*. Los Angeles, Calif.

Recio Pinto, Alejandro. 1991. *Privatización en Venezuela: primer caso, Banco Occidental de Descuento*. Caracas, Venezuela: Librerìa Mundial.

Redor, D. 1992. "State Ownership Sector: Lessons of the French Experience." In F. Targetti, ed., *Privatization Process and the Role of the Public Sector in East and West*. Aldershot, England: Dartmouth.

Renzulli, Jeffrey. 1992. "Claims of US Nationals under the Restitution Laws of Czechoslovakia." *Boston College International and Comparative Law Review* 15 (winter): 165–88.

Rhomari, Mostafa. 1989a. "La privatisation des entreprises publiques en Afrique." *Cahiers Africains d'Administration Publique* 32.

_____. 1989b. "Les mesures d'accompagnement de la privatisation en Afrique." *Cahiers Africains d'Administration Publique* 33: 55–67.

Richardson John J., ed. 1990. *Privatisation and Deregulation in Canada and Britain*. Aldershot, England: Dartmouth.

Richer, Laurent, and Alain Viandier. 1991. "L'ouverture minoritaire du capital des entreprises publiques." *Cahier de Droit des Entreprises*.

_____. 1993. "La loi de privatisation Loi 93–923 du 19 juillet 1993." *La Semaine Juridique* 40: 393–99.

Richet, Xavier. 1993. "Privatisation et restructuration des entreprises en Europe de l'Est." *Reflets et Perspectives de la Vie Economique* 32(3–4): 165–68.

Richet, Xavier, and Adam Török. 1993. "La restructuration industrielle et la transition économique en Hongrie." *Reflets et Perspectives de la Vie Economique* 32(3–4): 245–56.

Rider, Christine. 1994. "Privatization in the Transition Economies: A Critique." *Journal of Post Keynesian Economics* 16(4): 589–603.

Rivera, Daniel. 1996. *Private Sector Participation in the Water Supply and Wastewater Sector: Lessons from Six Developing Countries.* Directions in Development Series. Washington, D.C.: World Bank.

Rondinelli, Dennis A., ed. 1994. *Privatization and Economic Reform in Central Europe: The Changing Business Climate.* Westport, Conn.: Quorum Books.

Roth, Gabriel. 1987. *The Private Provision of Public Services in Developing Countries.* New York: Oxford University Press.

Rozenfelds, J. 1993. "Latvia: Legislation and Denationalization of Land." *Law Institute Journal* 67 (May): 358–59.

Ruff, Larry. 1994. "Real Competition." *Electricity Journal* 7(5).

Rutledge, Susan L. 1995. "Selling State Companies to Strategic Investors: Trade Sale Privatizations in Poland, Hungary, the Czech Republic, and the Slovak Republic." CFS Discussion Paper Series 106. World Bank, Washington, D.C.

Sacks, Paul M. 1993. "Privatization in the Czech Republic." *Columbia Journal of World Business* 28(1): 188–95.

Sader, Frank. 1993. "Privatization and Foreign Investment in the Developing World, 1988–1992." Policy Research Working Paper 1202. World Bank, Policy Research Department, Washington, D.C.

_____. 1995. *Privatizing Public Enterprises and Foreign Investment in Developing Countries, 1988–93.* Foreign Investment Advisory Service (FIAS) Occasional Paper. World Bank, Washington, D.C.: International Finance Corporation and the World Bank.

Saghir, Jamal. 1993. "Privatization in Tunisia." CFS Discussion Paper Series 101. World Bank, Washington, D.C.

Saint-Girons, B. 1990. "Aspects constitutionnels de l'évaluation d'entreprises." *Revue Internationale de Droit Economique* 4: 311–17.

_____. 1991. "Le décret du 4 avril 1991 et l'ouverture du capital des entreprises publiques." *Revue Trimestrielle de Droit Commercial* 44: 349–51.

Salaun, F. 1990. "Privatisation et réglementation: le cas de British Gas." *Economies et Sociétés* 4 (January): 53–69.

Salbaing, Christian. 1993. "Les privatisations en Chine." Paper presented to the International Symposium on World Privatizations. Forum International, Nice, December 2–4.

Samson, Ivan. 1993. "La douloureuse intégration allemande." *Reflets et Perspectives de la Vie Economique* 32(3–4): 189–208.

Sandor, L. 1992. "Quelques questions à propos de la privatisation des banques hongroises." *Revue Internationale de Droit Economique* 3: 445–50.

Santini, Jean-Jacques, Jean-Pierre Broclawski, Guy Langueville, and Pierre Uhel. 1986. *Les privatisations à l'étranger: Royaume-Uni, RFA, Italie, Espagne, Japon.* Notes et Etudes Documentaires 4821, Paris: La Documentation Française.

Sarcevic, Petar, ed. 1992. *Privatization in Eastern and Central Europe*. Boston, Mass.: Graham and Trotman.

Sarkozy, Tamas. 1994. *The Right of Privatization in Hungary, 1989–1993*. Translated by Gedeon Dienes. Budapest, Hungary: Akademiai Kiado.

Schjelderup, Guttorm. 1990. "Reforming State Enterprises in Socialist Economies: Guidelines for Leasing Them to Entrepreneurs." Policy Research Working Paper 368. World Bank, Policy Research Department, Washington, D.C.

Schlesser, Jean-Marc. 1992. "Privatisations in France." *International Business Lawyer* 20(6): 295–303.

Schmid, A. Allan. 1992. "Legal Foundations of the Market: Implications for the Formerly Socialist Countries of Eastern Europe and Africa." *Journal of Economic Issues* 26 (September): 707–32.

Schmidt, Klaus-Dieter. 1994. "Treuhandanstalt and Investment Acquisitions: How to Ensure that Contracts are Kept?" Kiel Working Paper 632. Kiel Institute of World Economics, Kiel, Germany.

Schneider, Richard C., Jr. 1993. "Property and Small Scale Privatization in Russia." *St. Mary's Law Journal* (fall): 507–38.

Seth, Rama. 1989. "Distributional Issues in Privatization." *Federal Reserve Bank of N.Y. Quarterly Review* 14(2).

Shafik, Nemat. 1993. "Making a Market: Mass Privatization in the Czech and Slovak Republics." Policy Research Working Paper 1231. World Bank, Policy Research Department, Washington, D.C.

Shaikh, Hafeez, and Maziar Minovi. 1995. "Management Contracts: A Review of International Experience." CFS Discussion Paper Series 108. World Bank, Washington, D.C.

Sharma, Arun Kumar. 1992. "World Model." *LatinFinance* 41 (October): 27–31.

Shibata, Kyohei. 1994. "Airline Privatisation in Eastern Europe and Ex-USSR." *Logistics and Transportation Review* 30(2): 167–88.

Shirley, Mary M. 1994. "Privatization in Latin America: Lessons for Transitional Europe." *World Development* 22(9): 1313–23.

Shirley, Mary, and John Nellis. 1991. *Public Entreprise Reform: The Lessons of Experience*. EDI Development Studies. Washington, D.C.: World Bank.

Shleifer, Andrei, and Robert W. Vishny. 1994. "Politicians and Firms." *Quarterly Journal of Economics* 109(4): 995–1025.

Slupinski, Zbigniew M. 1990. "Polish Privatization Law of 1990." *International Business Lawyer* 18 (November): 456.

Sly and Weigall, National Privatization and Corporatization Division. 1991. *Privatization in Australia*. Melbourne, Australia.

Smith, Peter, and Gregory Staple. 1994. *Telecommunications Sector Reform in Asia: Toward a New Pragmatism*. World Bank Discussion Paper 232. Washington, D.C.

Smith, Stephen C. 1994. "On the Law and Economics of Employee Ownership in Privatization in Developing and Transition Economies." *Annals of Public and Cooperative Economics* 65(3): 437–68.

Smith, Warrick. 1996. "Utility Regulators: Creating Agencies in Reforming and Developing Countries." Paper presented at the International Forum for Utility

Regulation, Expert Group Meeting, London, June 1996. World Bank, Private Sector Development Department, Washington, D.C.

Snoy, Bernard. 1993. "Privatisation et réforme du secteur financier en Europe Centrale et Orientale." *Revue Internationale de Droit Economique* 2: 257–66.

Sonko, Karamo N. M. 1994. "A Tale of Two Enterprises: Swaziland's Lessons for Privatization." *World Development* 22(7): 1083–96.

Spulber, Nicolas, and Asghar Sabbaghi. 1994. *Economics of Water Resources: From Regulation to Privatization.* Boston, Mass.: Kluwer Academic.

Stanbury, W. T. 1985. "Crown Corporations, Mixed Enterprises and Privatization: A Bibliography." In Thomas E. Kierans and W. T. Stanbury, eds., *Papers on Privatization.* Montreal, Canada: Institute for Research on Public Policy.

Steindorff, Ernst. 1993. "Carl Zeiss: réunification et privatisation." *Revue Internationale de Droit Economique* 2: 105–10.

Stigler, G. 1971. "The Theory of Economic Regulation." *Bell Journal of Economics and Management Science* 2: 3–21.

St. Giles, Mark, and Sally Buxton. 1995. "Investment Funds and Privatization." In Ira W. Lieberman and John Nellis, eds., *Russia: Creating Private Enterprises and Efficient Markets.* World Bank Studies of Economies in Transformation Paper 15. Washington, D.C.

Suzuki, Hiroaki. 1992. "Lessons Learned from the Guinea Privatization Program: Critical Analysis of the Divestiture Program of Public Enterprises." World Bank, Africa Technical Department, Washington, D.C.

Svejnar, Jan, and Miroslav Singer. 1994. "Using Vouchers to Privatize an Economy: The Czech and Slovak Case." *Economics of Transition* 2(1): 43–69.

Sykes, A., and C. Robinson. 1987. *Current Choices: Good Ways and Bad to Privatise Electricity.* London: Centre for Policy Studies.

Syu, Agnes. 1995. *From Economic Miracle to Privatization Success: Initial Stages of the Privatization Process in Two SOEs on Taiwan.* Lanham, Md.: University Press of America.

Takano, Yoshiro. 1992. *Nippon Telegraph and Telephone Privatization Study: Experience of Japan and Lessons for Developing Countries.* World Bank Discussion Paper 179. Washington, D.C.

Tankoano, A. 1990. "La privatisation des entreprises publiques nigériennes." *Revue Congolaise de Droit* 7–8: 118–40.

Tantin, G. 1987. "Problèmes spécifiques aux salariés posés par les lois de privatisation." *Droit et Pratique du Commerce International* 13(4): 603–34.

Taylor, Robert, and Eloy Vidal. 1994. "Fast Turnaround for Venezuela's Telephones." *FPD Note* 2. World Bank, Office of the Vice President for Finance and Private Sector Development, Washington, D.C.

Tenenbaum, Bernard. 1996. "Regulation: What the Prime Minister Needs to Know." *Electricity Journal* (March): 28–36.

Tenenbaum, Bernard, Reinier Lock, and James V. Barker. 1992. "Electricity Privatization: Structural, Competitive and Regulatory Options." *Energy Policy* 20(12): 1134–60.

Tesche, Jean, and Sahar Tohamy. 1994. "A Note on Economic Liberalization and Privatization in Hungary and Egypt." *Comparative Economic Studies* 36(2): 51–72.

Thepaut, J. 1992. "Hongrie: le régime des concessions de service public." *Banque Française du Commerce Extérieur, Actualités* 268 (December 1991–January 1992): 23–24.

Thiry, Bernard. 1994. "L'entreprise publique dans l'Union Européenne." *Annals of Public and Cooperative Economics* 65(3): 413–36.

Thomas, B. J. 1994. "The Privatization of United Kingdom Seaports." *Maritime Policy and Management* 21(2): 135–48.

Thomas, Scott. 1993. "The Politics and Economics of Privatization in Central and Eastern Europe." *Columbia Journal of World Business* 28(1): 168–79.

Thorne, Alfredo. 1993. "Eastern Europe's Experience with Banking Reform: Is There a Role for Banks in the Transition?" Policy Research Working Paper 1235. World Bank, Policy Research Department, Washington, D.C.

Thynne, Ian, ed. 1995. *Corporatization, Divestment and the Public-Private Mix: Selected Country Studies.* Hong Kong: Forward Printing Co., for the Asian Journal of Public Administration, in collaboration with the International Association of Schools and Institutes of Administration.

Train, Kenneth E. 1991. *Optimal Regulation: The Economic Theory of Natural Monopoly.* Cambridge, Mass.: MIT Press.

Tyson, W. J. 1995. "Bus Deregulation: The Planning Dilemma." *Transport Reviews* 15(4): 307–1.

Ulissi, Roberto. 1994. "Privatization in Italy: The Legal and Institutional Framework."

UNCTAD (United Nations Conference on Trade and Development). 1993a. *Accounting, Valuation and Privatization.* New York: United Nations, Program on Transnational Corporations.

———. 1993b. *Trade and Development Report 1993.* New York: United Nations.

———. 1995. *Comparative Experiences with Privatization: Policy Insights and Lessons Learned.* New York: United Nations.

United Nations, Department for Development Support and Management Services. 1993. *Methods and Practice of Privatization.* New York: United Nations.

United Nations, Economic Commission for Europe. 1992. *Legal Aspects of Privatization in Industry.* New York: United Nations.

Upper, Jack L., and George B. Baldwin, eds. 1995. *Public Enterprises: Restructuring and Privatization.* Washington D.C.: International Law Institute.

Valbonesi, Paola. 1995. "Privatising by Auction in the Eastern European Transition Countries: The Czechoslovak Experience." *MOCT-MOST: Economic Policy in Transitional Economies* 5(1): 101–31.

Valentiny, Pal. 1991. "Hungarian Privatization in International Perspective." *Public Enterprise* 11(2–3): 141–50.

Van Brabant, Jozef M. 1991. "Property Rights Reform, Macroeconomic Performance, and Welfare." In Hans Blommestein and Michael Marrese, eds., *Transformation of Planned Economies: Property Rights Reform and Macroeconomic Stability.* Paris: OECD.

Varin, Christian. 1993. "République Fédérative Tchèque et Slovaque: le contexte économique d'une déchirure." *Reflets et Perspectives de la Vie Economique* 32(3–4): 223–44.

Veljanovski, Cento. 1993. *The Future of Industry Regulation in the UK: A Report by an Independent Inquiry.* London: European Policy Forum for British and European Market Studies.

Veljanovski, Cento, ed. 1991. *Regulators and the Market: An Assessment of the Growth of Regulation in the UK.* London: Institute of Economic Affairs.

Vickers, John S., and George K. Yarrow. 1985. *Privatization and the Natural Monopolies.* London: Public Policy Centre.

_____. *Privatization: An Economic Analysis.* Cambridge, Mass.: MIT Press.

Villar Rojas, Francisco. 1993. *Privatización de servicios públicos: la experiencia española a la luz del modelo británico.* Madrid: Editorial Tecnos.

Vincent, Anne. 1995. "Enterprises et holdings publics fédéraux: Restructurations et privatisations, 1992–1995." *Courrier Hebdomadaire du CRISP* 1488–89. Brussels: Centre de recherche et d'information socio-politiques.

Vittas, Dimitri. 1996. "Designing Mandatory Pension Schemes: Some Lessons from Argentina, Chile, Malaysia, and Singapore." *FPD Note* 72. World Bank, Office of the Vice President for Finance and Private Sector Development, Washington, D.C.

Voisin, Colette. 1995. "La privatisation, une question 'd'incitations': propriété, réglementation et information." *Revue d'Economie Politique* 105 (May–June): 481–514.

Voljc, Marko, and Joost Draaisma. 1993. "Privatization and Economic Stabilization in Mexico." *Columbia Journal of World Business* 28(1): 122–33.

Vukmir, Branko. 1991. "Privatization in Croatia." *Public Enterprise* 11(2–3): 163–74.

Vuylsteke, Charles. 1988. *Techniques of Privatization of State-Owned Enterprises.* Vol. 1, *Methods and Implementation.* World Bank Technical Paper 88. Washington, D.C.

Weisman, Lorenzo. 1987. "Objectifs et contraintes de l'introduction des actions d'une entreprise en cours de privatisation sur un marché étranger." *Revue de Droit des Affaires Internationales* 3: 293–94.

Welfens, Paul J., and Piotr Jasinski. 1994. *Privatization and Foreign Direct Investment in Transforming Economies.* Aldershot, England: Dartmouth.

Wellenius, Bjorn, and Peter A. Stern, eds. 1994. *Implementing Reforms in the Telecommunications Sector: Lessons from Experience.* Washington, D.C.: World Bank.

Wells, Louis T., and Eric S. Gleason. 1995. "Is Foreign Infrastructure Investment Still Risky?" *Harvard Business Review* 73 (September–October): 44–53.

White, Peter. 1994. "Public Transport: Privatization and Investment." *Transport Policy* 1(3): 184–94.

_____. 1995. "Deregulation of Local Bus Services in Great Britain: An Introductory Review." *Transport Reviews* 15(2): 185–209.

White, Peter, and Stephen Tough. 1995. "Alternative Tendering Systems and Deregulation in Britain." *Journal of Transport Economics and Policy* 29(3): 275–89.

Williams, Christopher. 1993. "New Rules for a New World: Privatization of the Czech Cement Industry." *Columbia Journal of World Business* 28(1): 62–69.

Williams, Evan, and Stephen Franks. 1992. "Legal Aspects of Divesture: The New Zealand Experience." Document prepared by Chapman Tripp Sheffield Young (New Zealand) for the World Bank Legal Department.

Willig, Robert D. 1994. "Public versus Regulated Private Enterprise." In Michael Bruno and Boris Pleskovic, eds., *Proceedings of the World Bank Annual Conference on Development Economics 1993*. Washington, D.C.: World Bank.

Wilson, Ernest J. 1991. "The Third Phase of the Polish Revolution: Property Rights." *Public Enterprise* 11(2–3): 119–32.

Wilson, Gavin. 1993. "The Privatization of Swarzedz Furniture Company: Lessons from Poland's First Underwritten Public Offering." *Columbia Journal of World Business* 28(1): 18–35.

World Bank. 1993. *Argentina's Privatization Program: Experience, Issues, and Lessons.* Washington, D.C.

_____. 1994a. "Privatization and Environmental Assessment: Issues and Approaches." Environmental Assessment Sourcebook Update 6 (March). World Bank, Washington, D.C.

_____. 1994b. "World Bank Assistance to Privatization in Developing Countries." Operations Evaluation Report 13272. World Bank, Operations Evaluation Department, Washington, D.C.

_____. 1994c. *World Development Report 1994: Infrastructure for Development*. New York: Oxford University Press.

_____. 1995a. *World Development Report 1995: Workers in an Integrating World*. New York: Oxford University Press.

_____. 1995b. *Bureaucrats in Business: The Economics and Politics of Government Ownership*. New York: Oxford University Press.

_____. 1996a. *Getting Connected: Private Participation in Infrastructure in the Middle East and North Africa*. Washington, D.C.

_____. 1996b. *World Development Report 1996: From Plan to Market*. New York: Oxford University Press.

World Bank and CEUPP (Central European University Privatization Project). 1994. "Eastern European Experience with Small-Scale Privatization." CFS Discussion Paper Series 104. Washington, D.C.

World Equity and IFC. 1993. *Privatization in Emerging Markets*. London: IFR Publishing.

Yarrow, George. 1986. "Privatization in Theory and Practice." *Economic Policy* 2 (April): 324–77.

Young, David S. 1991. "The Role of Business Valuation in the Privatization of Eastern Europe." *Public Enterprise* 11(2–3): 201–8.

Young, Ralph A. 1991. "Privatisation in Africa." *Review of African Political Economy* 51 (July): 50–62.

Geographic
Classification of References

DEVELOPING COUNTRIES

General

Adam, Cavendish, and Mistry 1992
Ambrose, Hennemeyer, and Chapon 1990
Augenblick and Custer 1990
Bouin and Michalet 1991
Cook and Kirkpatrick 1988
Kikeri, Nellis, and Shirley 1992
Nankani 1988
Roth 1987
Sader 1993

Sader 1995
Shirley and Nellis 1991
Smith 1996
Vuylsteke 1988
World Bank 1994a
World Bank 1995b
World Bank 1996a
World Bank 1996b
World Equity and IFC 1993

Africa

General

Ahene and Katz 1992
Akuete and others 1992
Drum 1993
Grosh and Mukandala 1994
Guerraoui and Richet 1995
Kerf and Smith 1996
Mwangi 1986

Nellis 1986
Rhomari 1989a
Rhomari 1989b
Schmid 1992
Smith 1994
Young 1991

Algeria

Bouzidi 1993

Guerraoui and Richet 1995

Egypt

Tesche and Tohamy 1994

Ghana

Danso 1992

Guinea

Rivera 1996

Suzuki 1992

369

Morocco	Guerraoui and Richet 1995
Niger	Tankoano 1990
Senegal	Caverivière 1990
Swaziland	Sonko 1994
Togo	Ayassor 1990

Tunisia

Guerraoui and Richet 1995	Saghir 1993

Latin America and the Caribbean

General

Baer 1994	Glade 1991
Baer and Birch 1994	Holden and Rajapatirana 1995
Baer and Conroy 1993	Idelovitch and Ringskog 1995
Baer and Conroy 1994	LatinFinance (yearly supplement)
Berenson 1991	Lieberman 1994
Castillo 1995	Ramamurti 1996
Covarrubias and Maia 1994	Shirley 1994
Flouret 1994	Smith 1994

Argentina

Alexander and Corti 1993	Levy and Spiller 1993
Baer and Birch 1994	Maciel 1992
Covarrubias and Maia 1994	Mooney and Griffith 1993
De Kessler 1993	Muller 1994
Gerchunoff 1992	Ramanadham 1994
Gerchunoff and Canovas 1995	Ramamurti 1996
Herrera 1993	Rivera 1996
Hill and Abdala 1993	Vittas 1996
Idelovitch and Ringskog 1995	World Bank 1993

Bolivia	Mallon 1994

Brazil

Baer and Birch 1994	Pinheiro and Giambiagi 1994
Baer and Conroy 1994	

Chile

Baer and Birch 1994	Bitran and Serra 1994
Baer and Conroy 1994	Castillo 1995

Covarrubias and Maia 1994
Galal 1994
Galal and Shirley 1994
Galal and others 1994
Hachette and Lüders 1993
Levy and Spiller 1993

Lüders 1993
Ramamurti 1996
Rivera 1996
Sharma 1992
Vittas 1996

Colombia

Baer and Conroy 1994
Covarrubias and Maia 1994

Quale 1991
Rivera 1996

Costa Rica

Covarrubias and Maia 1994

Cuba

Haines 1995

Guyana

Prokopenko 1995

Ramanadham 1994

Jamaica

Covarrubias and Maia 1994
Levy and Spiller 1993

Prokopenko 1995
Ramamurti 1996

Mexico

Baer and Birch 1994
Baer and Conroy 1994
Barnes 1992
Castillo 1995
Galal and Shirley 1994

Galal and others 1994
Lopez-de-Silanes 1996
Ramamurti 1996
Rivera 1996
Voljc and Draaisma 1993

Peru

Conradt 1993

Covarrubias and Maia 1994

Venezuela

Gizang and Sabater 1994
Pisciotta 1994
Ramamurti 1996

Recio Pinto 1991
Taylor and Vidal 1994

Asia

General

Chen 1994
Gouri 1991

Smith and Staple 1994

Bangladesh

Bhaskar and Khan 1995

China

Bolton 1995
Huchet 1993
Liufang 1995

Milor 1994
Salbaing 1993

Indonesia

Chen 1994

Korea, Republic of

Kim, Kim, and Boyer 1994

Malaysia

Chen 1994
Galal and Shirley 1994
Galal and others 1994
Hensley and White 1993

Jomo 1995
Malaysia 1991
Parker 1994a
Vittas 1996

Mongolia

Denizer and Gelb 1993

Milor 1994

Pakistan

Looney 1994

Ramanadham 1994

Philippines

Chen 1994
Levy and Spiller 1993

Milor 1994

Singapore

Vittas 1996

Sri Lanka

Prokopenko 1995

Ramanadham 1994

Taiwan (China)

Da Silva Cornell 1993

Syu 1995

Thailand

Chen 1994

Central and Eastern Europe and the Former Soviet Union

General

Acs and Fitzroy 1994
Andreff 1992
Andreff 1993a
Andreff 1993b
Arbess and Varanese 1993

Blommestein and Marrese 1991
Bohm and Kreacic 1991
Borish, Long, and Noël 1995
Borish and Noël 1996
Boycko, Shleifer, and Vishny 1994

Buck, Thompson, and Wright 1991
Clavel and Sloan 1991
Csaba 1994
Dallago, Ajani, and Grancelli 1992
Demougin and Sinn 1994
EBRD and CEEPN 1993
English 1991
Estrin, Gelb, and Singh 1995
Ewing, Lee, and Leeds 1993
Feinberg and Meurs 1994
Frydman and Rapaczynski 1994
Gelpern 1993
Goldenman 1993
Goldenman 1994
Gray 1993a
Gray 1993b
Gray and Hanson 1993
Gray and Jarosz 1993
Guerraoui and Richet 1995
Hyclak and King 1994
Im, Jalali, and Saghir 1993
Jackson and Bilsen 1994
Kiss 1994
Lee and Nellis 1991
Lieberman 1994
Lieberman and others 1995
Milor 1994
Newbery 1994

Nuti 1991
OECD 1993
OECD 1995a
OECD 1995b
Popova 1992
Ramanadham 1994
Richet 1993
Rider 1994
Rondinelli 1994
Rutledge 1995
Sarcevic 1992
Schjelderup 1990
Schmid 1992
Shibata 1994
Shirley 1994
Smith 1994
Snoy 1993
Thomas 1993
Thorne 1993
United Nations 1992
Van Brabant 1991
Vuylsteke 1988
Welfens and Jasinski 1994
World Bank 1996b
World Bank and CEUPP 1994
World Equity and IFC 1993
Young 1991

Bulgaria

Due and Schmidt 1995
Jackson and Bilsen 1994

Mintchev 1993

Czechoslovakia, Czech Republic, and Slovak Republic

Anderson 1994
Appel 1995
Borish and Noël 1996
Bouin 1994
Czech Ministry 1993
Dlouhy and Mladek 1994
Earle and others 1994
Egerer 1995
Estrin, Gelb, and Singh 1995
Fogel 1994
Glick and Richter 1991
Goldstein and Horakova 1993
Jackson and Bilsen 1994
Marcincin and Wijnbergen 1995

OECD 1993
OECD 1995a
OECD 1995b
Parker 1994a
Pechota 1991
Prokopenko 1995
Renzulli 1992
Rutledge 1995
Sacks 1993
Shafik 1993
Svejnar and Singer 1994
Valbonesi 1995
Varin 1993
Williams 1993

Hungary

Borish and Noël 1996
Crane 1991
Earle and others 1994
Estrin, Gelb, and Singh 1995
Gabor 1991
Guerraoui and Richet 1995
Gueullette 1992
Hanson 1992
Inzelt 1994
Jackson and Bilsen 1994

Laki 1995
OECD 1993
OECD 1995a
Richet and Török 1993
Rutledge 1995
Sandor 1992
Sarkozy 1994
Tesche and Tohamy 1994
Thepaut 1992
Valentiny 1991

Kazakstan

OECD 1995b

Latvia

Rozenfelds 1993

Lithuania

OECD 1995b

Poland

Albrecht and Thum 1994
Blaszczyk and Dabrowski 1993
Borish and Noël 1996
Earle and others 1994
Estrin, Gelb, and Singh 1995
Greenspan-Bell and Kolaja 1993
Harder and Taylor 1993
Jackson and Bilsen 1994
Jedrzejczak 1991
Johnson, Kotchen, and Loveman
Krawczyk and Lopez-Lopez 1993
Lissowska 1993

Michalski 1991
Milor 1994
Nuti 1991
OECD 1993
OECD 1995a
OECD 1995b
Pliszkiewicz 1992
Rivera 1996
Rutledge 1995
Slupinski 1990
Wilson 1991
Wilson 1993

Romania

Earle and Sapatoru 1994
Jackson and Bilsen 1994

Lhomel 1993

Russian Federation

Barberis and others 1995
Bim 1994
Bogdanowicz-Bindert and Ryan 1993
Bornstein 1994
Boycko, Shleifer, and Vishny 1995
Buck, Filatotchev, and Wright 1994
Crosnier 1992
Dimitriyev and Petkoski 1994
Giemulla 1995
Hedley 1992
Intriligator 1994

Johnson and Kroll 1991
Joskow, Schmalensee, and
    Tsukanova 1994
Lieberman 1993b
Lieberman and Nellis 1995
McFaul 1995
McFaul and Perlmutter 1995
Milor 1994
Nelson and Kuzes 1994
OECD 1995a
OECD 1995b

Petkoski 1994
Petkoski and Yamnova 1994

Raftopol 1993
Schneider 1993

Slovenia

Ellerman, Korze, and Simoneti 1991
OECD 1995a

Prokopenko 1995

Ukraine

IFC 1993
Milor 1994

Prokopenko 1995

Yugoslavia

Drouet 1992

Vukmir 1991

INDUSTRIAL COUNTRIES

General

Baily and Pack 1995
Bizaguet 1988a
Button and Weyman-Jones 1994
Chadwick 1859
European Conference of Ministers
    of Transport 1993
European Conference of Ministers
    of Transport 1995a
European Conference of Ministers
    of Transport 1995b

Guerraoui and Richet 1995
Kramer and others 1993
Loyrette and d'Ormesson 1987
McConville and Sheldrake 1995
Neven, Nuttall, and Seabright 1993
Rapp and Vellas 1992
Thiry 1994
United Nations 1992

Australia

Martin 1995

Sly and Weigall 1991

Belgium

Brion and Moreau 1995
Bouchard 1991

Nuchelmans 1992
Vincent 1995

Canada

Bouchard 1991
Garant 1990
Prokopenko 1995

Richardson 1990
Stanbury 1985

Denmark

Katznelson 1990

France

Andreff 1992
Andreff 1993b
Baudeu 1987

Bizaguet 1988b
Bouchard 1991
Boutard-Labarde 1987

Brousolle 1993
Cameron 1961
Cartelier 1992
Conseil d'Etat 1985
Conseil d'Etat 1989
Cour des Comptes 1990
Debène 1991
Delahaye 1987a
Delahaye 1987b
De Sarrau 1987
Durupty 1988
Durupty 1993
Guerraoui and Richet 1995
Heald 1995
Israël 1986

Lee and Bartos 1987
Loyrette and d'Ormesson 1987
Marcilhacy and Dangeard 1987
Martinand 1994
Moreau 1987
Prosser 1990
Rapp 1986a
Rapp 1986b
Rapp 1987b
Raynaud-Contamine 1987
Redor 1992
Richer and Viandier 1991
Richer and Viandier 1993
Saint-Girons 1991
Schlesser 1992

Germany

Balasubramanyam 1994
Dodds and Wächter 1993
Elling 1992
Jones Day 1991
Konig 1988
Laurin 1993

McKenna & Co. 1992
OECD 1995a
Samson 1993
Santini and others 1986
Steindorff 1993

Israel

Gurkov 1994

Italy

Gioscia 1993

Santini and others 1986

Japan

d'Ormesson 1987
Fukui 1992
Oniki and others 1994

Santini and others 1986
Takano 1992

New Zealand

Cavana 1995
Donaldson 1994
Duncan and Bollard 1992

Franks 1993
Galal and Shirley 1994
Williams and Franks 1992

Norway

Covarrubias and Maia 1994

Spain

Baer and Birch 1994
Dehesa 1993

Santini and others 1986
Villar Rojas 1993

Sweden

Prokopenko 1995

Turkey

Kjellström 1990

United Kingdom

Armstrong, Cowan, and Vickers 1994
Baily and Pack 1995
Baird 1995
Beesley and Littlechild 1989
Bennett and Cirell 1992
Bishop, Kay, and Mayer 1994
Bishop, Kay, and Mayer 1995
Buck, Thompson, and Wright 1991
Covarrubias and Maia 1994
Dnes 1991
Dnes 1993
Foreman-Peck and Millward 1994
Foster 1992
Galal and Shirley 1994
Galal and others 1994
Heald 1991
Helm 1994
Howles and Harvey 1993
Hunt and Lynk 1995
Kay, Mayer, and Thompson 1986
Levy and Spiller 1993
Lipworth 1993

Liu 1995
Magliveras 1991
Marcilhacy and Dangeard 1987
McConville and Sheldrake 1995
Millward and Singleton 1995
Ogden 1994
Parker 1994b
Parker 1994b
Prosser 1990
Ramanadham 1994
Richardson 1990
Salaun 1990
Santini and others 1986
Thomas 1994
Tyson 1995
Veljanovski 1991
Veljanovski 1993
Villar Rojas 1993
White 1994
White 1995
White and Tough 1995

United States

Baily and Pack 1995
Bhattacharyya, Parker, and
  Raffiee 1994
Chandler and Feuille 1994
Covarrubias and Maia 1994

Cramton 1995
Kodrzycki 1994
Lopez-de-Silanes, Shleifer, and
  Vishny 1995
Noll and Owen 1994

Specialized Journals

The following reports or magazines focus specifically on privatization:

Carnegie Council Privatization Project, published by the Carnegie Council on Ethics and International Affairs (170 East 64th St., New York, N.Y. 10021)

International Privatization Update, published monthly by Financial Market Research, Inc. (P.O. Box 33, Castleton-on-Hudson, N.Y. 12033)

Michigan Privatization Report, published quarterly by Mackinac Center for Public Policy (119 Ashman Street, P.O. Box 568, Midland, Mich. 48640)

Privatisation International, published monthly by Privatisation International Ltd. (Suite 510, Butlers Wharf Business Centre, 45 Crulew Street, London, England SE1 2ND)

Privatization Watch, published monthly by the Reason Foundation (3415 S. Sepulveda Blvd., Suite 400, Los Angeles, Calif. 90034)

Public Works Financing and *Public Works Financing International*, published monthly (154 Harrison Ave., Westfield. N.J. 07090).

Some yearbooks and other annual publications provide an update of the state of privatization around the world or in specific regions of the world:

Privatization in Latin America, Miami, Fla., supplement to *LatinFinance*

Annual Report on Privatization, Reason Foundation, Los Angeles, Calif.

Privatisation Yearbook, Privatisation International Ltd., London

A number of journals have published special issues focusing on privatization:

Columbia Journal of World Business 29(1), focus issue on privatization, spring 1993

Droit et Pratique du Commerce International 13(3), special on privatization, 1987

Euromoney, February 1996, special issue on privatization

Hastings International and Comparative Law Review 14(4), "Privatizations: Trends and Developments of the Early 1990s," 1994

International Financial Law Review, September 1992, special supplement on privatization

International Financial Law Review, April 1994, "Privatization: A World Privatization Guide"

Public Enterprise 11(2–3), thematic issue on privatization in reforming socialist economies, 1991

Quarterly Review of Economics and Finance 33 and 34, "Latin America: Privatization, Property Rights, and Deregulation," 1993 and 1994, respectively

Reflets et Perspectives de la Vie Economique 32(3–4), "Privatisation et restructuration des entreprises en Europe de l'Est," 1993

Revue de Droit des Affaires Internationales 3, 1987

Revue économique 47(6), "Les privatisations : Un état des lieux," 1996

Revue Internationale de Droit Economique 3, 1992

Internet Resources

Privatization information is available through a broad variety of sites on the Internet. These sites may change frequently and new ones are added constantly. Some sites are updated regularly, others not. The information below is provided for illustrative purposes only to help the reader start an Internet search.[*] It is in no way an exhaustive listing of available information. A more direct way to search for privatization material that should yield additional and more up-to-date information is to use Internet search engines.

The table below highlights some of the existing country-specific privatization sites. Depending on the country, a site may include the address and contact numbers of the privatization agency, office, or ministry; details on the minister or head of the agency; the text or reference of the privatization legislation; a description of the program; profiles of companies to be privatized; ongoing tenders, and so on.

Embassies and consulates, in particular in the United States, may have Internet sites with useful information on the country's privatization program. See, for example, in addition to the examples given in table A.1, the February 1996 issue of the newsletter of the consulate of Mexico in New York City
<http:/quicklink.com/mexico/prensa/notefeb.htm>

Additional country-specific sites may be found in a variety of ways, including links to national government servers through *<http://www.eff.org/govt.html>* and to Russian and East European sites through *<http://www.pitt.edu/~cjp>*, for example.

An increasing number of on-line sites and newsgroups provide information on privatization. Registration is required to gain access to several of these sites. Sites equipped with search engines allow the user to track the available information. Search engines may be sensitive to spelling differences. Where British rather than American spelling is used, the search should be for privatisation (with an 's').

Privatization Middle East & North Africa is issued on-line every Monday *<http:/www.pmena.com>*. The Privatization Monitor is a Mexican Web site with many links to other privatization sites worldwide *<http://www.trace-sc.com/private.htm>*.

---

*The author wishes to thank Omer Karasapan for his contribution to this overview of Internet resources on privatization.

Table A.1 Country-Specific Privatization Sites on Internet

Country	Internet site
Brazilian privatization program (information from CLC, the Brazilian stock exchange's clearing system)	<http://www.clc.com.br>
Bulgarian Privatization Agency	<http://www.privatization.bg> (see also <http://www.bulgaria.com/embassy/wdc/privatization>)
Croatian Privatization Ministry	<http://vrh1.vlada.hr/ministarstva/privathr.htm>
Estonian Privatization Agency	<http://www.eea.ee>
Hungarian Privatization Agency (APV RT)	<http://www.meh.hu/apv>
Israeli privatization program (Ministry of Finance)	<http://www.mof.gov.il/mof3.html>
Lithuanian State Privatization Agency	<http://www.nerisena.lt/komerc/turt> (see also <http://www.ltembassyus.org/private.html>)
Macedonian Privatization Agency	<http://www.soros.org.mk/mk/privat/en> <http://www.wonet.com.pl/privatization>
Romanian Development Agency	<http://www.rda.ro> (see also <http://www.embassy.org/romania/economic/economic.html)
Turkish privatization program (information provided by the Ministry of Foreign Affairs)	<http://inter.mfa.gov.tr/grupc/private.htm> (see also <http://turkey.org/private.html>)
Uganda, Privatization Unit of the Ministry of Finance & Economic Development	<http://uganda.privatization.org>
Zambian Privatization Agency	<http://www.zamnet.zm/zamnet/zambus/zpa> (see also <http://mbendi.co.za/orgs/cbfy.htm>)

Privatization information is also available through many sites that are not specifically dedicated to this subject matter. The "Business Monitor Online" provides information on international trade and investment, including privatization. The information available is provided by lawyers, accountants, banks, consultants, government bodies, and so on <http://www.businessmonitor.co.uk>. TradePort, a California-based site, gives access to economic and business information on many countries <http://www.tradeport.org/ts/countries>.

Several private organizations or foundations promoting privatization worldwide have home pages listing their activities and publications. This is the case, for example, of the Adam Smith Institute in London <http://www.cyberpoint.co.uk/asi>, the Cato Institute in Washington, D.C., or the Center for International Private Enterprise also in Washington, D.C. <http://www.cipe.org>.

Multilateral and regional organizations also maintain sites that contain information about privatization. The World Bank's Web site is at *<http://www.worldbank.org>*. The International Finance Corporation at *<http://www.ifc.org>*. The Multilateral Investment Guarantee Agency (MIGA) of the World Bank Group provides information on privatization programs and investment opportunities through IPA*net*, its "on-line global investment marketplace" *<http://www.ipanet.com>*. The Asian Development Bank may be reached at *<http://www.asiandevbank.org>*, the Inter-American Development Bank at *<http://www.iadb.org>*, the European Union at *<http://europa.eu.int>*, the OECD at *<http://www.oecd.org>*, the UN Industrial Development Organization at *<http://www.unido.org>*, the International Telecommunication Union at *<http://info.itu.ch>*, and so on. Many bilateral aid agencies with privatization programs are also on-line, as is the case with USAID (*<http://www.info.usaid.gov>*). Searches on privatization (or privatisation) will often yield projects supported by such agencies, publications, seminars, conferences, and so on.

This is only the tip of the iceberg. The Internet will offer many more sources of information on privatization to those patient enough to surf.

Subject Index

Property rights **34–35, 46–53**, 56–59, 88,
  89–95, 108, 112, 128, 134–135, 159,
  161, 163, 164, 243, 248–249, 285, 291–
  293, 339. *See also* Intellectual property
Public administration 22, 24–26, 93–94,
  101, 108–109, 154, 163, 171–172, 199,
  263, 268, **273–274**, 278, 280–281, 285,
  287, 291, 295–296
Public assets (sale) **92–94**, 95, 172
Public domain **92–94, 340**
Public enterprise
  breakup 19, 23, 55, 67, 95, **105–106**,
    107, 109, **212–215**, 216–221, 223,
    224, 226, 250–251, 287
  creation **33–37**, 57, 91–92, 128, 245–
    246
  definition 340
  exclusion as buyer. *See* Restrictions
  legal status **26–28**, 38, 60, 66, 89, 90,
    93, 95, 97, **101–105**, 108–109, 114,
    123, 125, 250, 291
  legislation 37, 91–92, 94, 95, 100, 109,
    140, 246, 291
  management 58, 94, 96, 97, 100, 103,
    106, 109, 120, 137, 143, 153–154, 164,
    167–169, 175–176, 259
  privatizable 24–26, 115–118, 131, 180
  size 28, 135, 146
  See also Constitution, Corporate gov-
    ernance, Corporatization, Divesti-
    ture, Nationalization, Perfor-
    mance, Privatization, Restructur-
    ing, Valuation
Public finance legislation 53, 92, **107–
  108**, 139–142, 150
Public flotation 17, 29–30, 58–59, 60–61,
  68–70, 86, 101, 119–120, 122–124, 126,
  136, 167, 178–179, 191, **193**, 218, 226,
  228, 233, 234, 236, 241, 250–252, **255–
  256**, 267, 340
Public interest 21, 24, 52, 55, 91, 236, 248,
  265, 268, 278, 280, 294
Public offering. *See* Public flotation
Public procurement 36, 54, 97, 108
Public relations **30–31**, 180, 194, 296
Public service 10, **24–26**, 35, 45, 93, 205,
  224, 226, 231, 242, 248, 253, 257, 258,
  261–266, 274, 286, 289, 291
  See also Electricity, Gas, Transport,
    Telecommunications, Water
Publicity 31, 34, 118, 124, 126, 200, 277,
  281, 283

Railways 3, 4–5, 6, 12, 77, 93, 100, 125,
  127, 166, 204, **206–207**, 212–214, **225–
  227**, 229, 237, **245**, 248–249, 252, 261–
  262, 274
Ratification 45, 94, 113, 118, 150, 157, 168
Referendum 151, 247, 253
Regulation
  impact of 269–272
  of competition 53–56
  of infrastructure sectors 9, 213–215,
    258–283, 289–290, 293–294
  of privatization funds 124, 183, **186–
    188**, 189–190
  privatization of **280–281**, 286, 290,
    298–299
  self **281–282**, 284
Regulatory bodies **271–282**
  advisory 274, 277, 290
  appeal **279–280**
  autonomy 240, 269, 273, **275–277**,
    282, 290
  decisions 218, 221, 223, 241, 261–269,
    272, 279
  establishment 240, 241, 273–277, 285
  multisectoral **278–279**, 285
  powers 240, 273, **274–275**, 278, 279,
    286
Reputation 57, 200, 269, 270, 282, 284, 290
Restitution 2, **48–50**, 128, 340
Restrictions
  on buyer selection **127–129**
  on privatization 35–36, 43, 46–48, 92,
    93, **94–95**, 103, 115, 121, 127–132,
    144, 146, 243, **246–249**, 297.
  on public-sector participation 27, 92,
    116, **127–128**, 144
  on share transfers. *See* Transferability
  See also Constitution, Discrimination
    Foreign investment, Golden share,
    Investors
Restructuring of enterprises 23, 53, 67,
  71–72, 78, 80, **95–107**, 162, **164**, 168–
  169, 189, 212–242, **250–251**, 288. *See
  also* Liquidation
Risk
  for governments **11–12**, 137–138
  for investors **11–12**, 20–21, **22**, 34, 52,
    61, 80–82, 88, 114, 138–140, 185, 189,
    193, **268–271**, 277
Roads 35, 93, 166, **208**, 214, 225, 249
Role of the State 19, 24–25, 45, 53, **289–
  291**
Rule of law **33–34**, 291, 294

Geographic Index

Index of Enterprises, Agencies and other Organizations